THE
PEOPLE
EXCELLENCE
STAR

ENDORSEMENTS

There is little doubt, reading through various publications, that a key challenge of business, large and small, is to rethink what and how we do things in the people leadership space. It also seems through conversations with clients that "thought leadership" is important, but that "action leadership" is even more crucial given how our timelines for business performance and health have become a lot shorter. Theo manages to bridge the gap between thinking about how we lead people to what we can practically do. In this book, Theo provides both useful thinking frameworks, but also some practical guidelines on what to DO as we navigate the future.

Dr Anton Verwey – Executive Strategy and Innovation, inavit iQ (Pty) Ltd

In any organisation, people excellence is a critical strategic agenda item. The challenges pertaining to people excellence are complex and formidable, more especially now given the global pandemic. This book is a must read if you wish to know how to be a star at people excellence. This book will guide you to "stress test" your current star rating or creditworthiness of your people excellence, and enable you to progress your endeavours to significantly and continuously improve your current status.

Solidly grounded in the most recent research, vast experience, leading practice, and deep thought leadership, this book provides a compelling, comprehensive and integrated people excellence road-map which is powerful, progressive, ongoing, infused and virtuous. I recommend this read with great enthusiasm, especially now.

Dr Shirley Zinn, Chair and Non-Executive Director on multiple Boards

Being a star in people excellence is arguably the only sustainable competitive advantage that any organisation can have. *The People Excellence Star: A Strategic Organisational Stress Test* provides an outstanding guide for executives and organisational development practitioners and consultants to achieve people excellence. The book is packed with practical ideas for simple implementation. The text is easy to read and use, yet still grounded in substantiated theory and research, making the book an indispensable reference work to achieve organisational excellence.

Prof Mias de Klerk, Professor: Leadership and Organisational Behaviour, Director: Centre for Responsible Leadership Studies (Africa), University of Stellenbosch Business School

Whilst a financial balance sheet reveals the financial health of an organisation, Theo superbly identifies the criteria for creating a healthy and productive people balance sheet in an invigorating organisational climate to maximise an organisation's people assets and to limit its people liabilities.

Dr Andre Parker: Business Scientist and Strategic Thought Leader

First published in 2021.

ISBN: 978-1-86922-909-2 (Printed)
eISBN: 978-1-86922-910-8 (PDF ebook)

Published by KR Publishing
P O Box 3954
Randburg
2125
Republic of South Africa

Tel: (011) 706-6009
Fax: (011) 706-1127
E-mail: orders@knowres.co.za
Website: www.kr.co.za

Typesetting, layout and design: Cia Joubert, cia@knowres.co.za
Cover design: Marlene De Lorme, marlene@knowres.co.za
Editing and Proofreading: Jennifer Renton, jenniferrenton@live.co.za
Project management: Cia Joubert, cia@knowres.co.za

THE PEOPLE EXCELLENCE STAR

A Strategic Organisational Stress Test

Theo H. Veldsman

kr
publishing

2021

ACKNOWLEDGEMENTS

The People Excellence Star. A Strategic Organisational Stress Test is the outcome of the encouragement, support, and enablement of many, directly and indirectly:

- My dearest family, of whom my wife, Annie, stands first and foremost in the queue. Baie, baie dankie vir alles, Meisie. Also, to our most supportive children – Talita and Lawrence; Dieter and Zani. Yes, and our little people with whom we have been blessed to date, our grandchildren – Arianna and Lawrence – for the amazing, fresh ways of looking at the world which you have opened our eyes to.

- Lumka Gumede, our house manager, for the uncountable cups of coffee, and keeping my study a pleasure to work in.

- Wilhelm Crous, Managing Director of Knowres, for the unbounded faith in taking on the risk again of another as-yet unproven book.

- Cia Joubert and her technical team for producing a book of excellent quality, making its use only but an enriching experience.

- Esthea Conradie for her excellent research support, sometimes at very short notice, to which she always responded with lightning speed.

- My clients over many years in the area of People Excellence, from whom I have learnt a lot and have gained deep, great wisdom.

- My esteemed colleagues with whom I have had the pleasure to collaborate in this area.

- The reviewers of my book for the time taken to review my book, and the wise counsel given.

  Praise to God, our Heavenly Father, in Jesus Christ, for all His undeserving grace and blessing, particularly during these uncertain and trying times.

SHORT TABLE OF CONTENTS

EXTENDED TABLE OF CONTENTS

ABOUT THE AUTHOR

Theo is regarded as a thought leader in South Africa and beyond with respect to people management and the psychology of work. Over many years he has demonstrated his ongoing ability to pro-actively identify emerging people and leadership needs and arrive at fit-for-purpose, innovative solutions that are simultaneously theoretically and practically sound. He has a proven ability to move seamlessly between theory and practice, and vice versa.

He holds a PhD Industrial Psychology. He is a registered Industrial Psychologist and Research Psychologist and accredited HRM Practioner. He prefers to call himself a Work Psychologist.

Theo has extensive academic and consulting experience gained over the past 35 years in strategy formulation and implementation; strategic organisational change; organisational (re)design; team building; leadership/management and strategic people/talent management. He consults with many leading local and overseas organisations, in the roles of advisor, expert and coach/mentor at the senior management and executive levels. Over his career he has straddled the academic and practice worlds seamlessly. He refers to himself as a pracademic.

He is the author of nearly 220 technical/consulting reports/articles covering the above-mentioned areas, of which about 45 are accredited articles. He has authored three books; co-edited seven books; and has contributed 17 book chapters.

Up to the end of 2016, when he retired, he has been a Professor and Head of the Department of Industrial Psychology and People Management, Faculty of Management, University of Johannesburg. Since the beginning of 2017 he has been a Visiting Professor at the same Department. He is Extra-ordinary Professor at the University of Stellenbosch Business School.

He has led the profession of Psychology and Industrial Psychology nationally as president on several occasions. He has been awarded Fellow status by the Society of Industrial and Organisational Psychology of South Africa (SIOPSA), and was the 2012 recipient of a Life-Long Achievement Award from the South African Board for People Practices (SABPP). In 2016 the Department of Industrial Psychology and People Management presented him with a Life Long Achievement Award.

He is available on LinkedIn and writes a regular Blog at theohveldsman.com. He can be reached at theoveld@mweb.co.za.

Theo co-edited *Leadership: Perspectives from the Frontline*, and authored *Designing Fit-for-Purpose Organisations: A comprehensive, integrated route map, Future-Fit Leaders: A diary to your leadership journey,* and *Into the People Effectiveness Arena. Navigating between Chaos and Order,* all published by KR Publishing.

CHAPTER 1

THE IMPERATIVE OF PEOPLE EXCELLENCE

"Success is to make others dance." (Ben Carson)

"Today, the only thing that makes capital dance is talent." (Jonas Ridderstrale & Kjell Nordström)

"The secret of joy in work is contained in one word—excellence. To know how to do something well is to enjoy it." (Pearl S. Buck)

In our current, global Knowledge Society, 85% and upwards of an organisation's assets are intangible (e.g., reputation, brand, patent rights, organisational capabilities, intelligence, and know-how) rather than tangible (e.g., facilities, technology, finance, and products/services).[1] In the order of 70% of these intangible assets are resident in people's knowledge, expertise, skills and experience.[2] Through their creativity, ingenuity and innovation, people are the primary generators, disseminators and users of knowledge – the fuel of the Knowledge Society.

Given the imperative for disruptive (even destructive) innovation to stay ahead of the game in the Knowledge Society, the 21st century organisation will be an ideas/imagination business.[3] In such organisations, accepted traditions and ruling conventions are challenged; the new is conceived and made real; boundaries are shifted and redefined; unknown/unexplored territories are opened up; the improbable and impossible are made attainable; and future-probing experimentation, testing, innovation, learning, and teaching occur incessantly.

All of the above is driven by the creative thinking power of people with their core capabilities of openness to, and the generation of new ideas, ingenuity, creativity, and imagination.[4] We are moving to the 'create' not 'compete' economy, with the former providing the only enduring source of competitiveness.[5][6] Hence, people have moved centre stage in the continued viable performance and success of organisations, in the present and future. They are, and will become even more so, the only true value unlockers and wealth creators in the emerging new order, because only people can be imaginative, innovative and creative.[7] When organisations select the top 20% of the most talented candidates for a work role, they frequently realise a 10% increase in productivity, a 25% decrease in unscheduled absences, a 20% increase in sales, a 30% increase in profitability, and a 10% decrease in resignations.[8]

The central role of people becomes even more crucial within the emerging "compelling, memorable experience-based" economy.[9] This economy revolves around the ongoing, real time creation and retention of inimitable, memorable customer and employee experiences in order to gain and maintain a competitive edge. This economy is furthermore permeated by the pressure for organisations to be responsible, social citizens with a strategic focus on sustainability.[10][11] Against this backdrop, the experience-based Client and People Value Propositions of organisations have to be re-imagined and re-invented in real time, all the time, in previously unimaginable, sustainable ways.[12] Only people can make this happen.

If people are central to the continued viability of organisational performance and success in the present and the future, knowing the state of their People Excellence is critical for every organisation. If there is on top of this criticality a global war for top talent, then 'critical' as imperative turns into *mission*-critical. It becomes the stark choice between merely surviving because of a shortage of talent. Or thriving because of an abundance of having the right talent in the organisation at all times, making a real difference as value unlockers and wealth creators. People have thus become the strategic leverage (or value) for the continued, future viability of organisations.[13][14]

Yet within the emerging new order, the war for talent has taken on a qualitatively different tone. Firstly, the war has shifted from merely attracting the best people to ensuring that they are fully engaged, continuously grow, and are committed to stay. Secondly, that the attracted 'can do' people truly want and ought to make a real difference-making, purpose-directed contribution that serves the greater good. The 'hard' talent war of 'can do' attraction has become even harder by turning into a 'soft' talent war of want, ought to, and purpose. It is about crafting and maintaining a (hyper-) personalised, meaningful experience of thriving, and hence personal fulfilment, for people in the organisation. In turn, ensuring a continuously viable organisation in the emerging new order.[15][16] A highly individualised people experience of and at work has become the fulcrum to, and leverage for, People Excellence.

Organisations that pursue effective people experience practices reap the following positive outcomes:[17]

- Organisational: 2.2x more likely to exceed their financial goals; and 2.4x more likely to delight customers;
- Innovation: 3.7x more likely to adapt well to change; and 4.3x more likely to innovate effectively; and
- People: 5.1x more likely to create a sense of belonging; 5.2x more likely to be a great place to work; and 5.1x more likely to engage and retain people.

In search of People Excellence, the purpose of this chapter is to set the scene regarding the People Excellence journey you are embarking on. To this end, the following themes are elucidated: defining People Excellence; People Excellence as imperative; the need for an integrated strategic stress test of People Excellence; and an introduction to *The People Excellence Star. A Strategic Organisational Stress Test.*

DEFINING PEOPLE EXCELLENCE

People Excellence can be defined as consistently achieving exceedingly well with the people of the organisation. When there is People Excellence, organisations are unlocking real, differentiating value and continuously creating worthy, lasting wealth with its people to the amazed delight of all of the organisation's stakeholders. In the process, the organisation is great at making its people thrive. Its people are the best they can, and want to be. Hence, they are experiencing genuine, deep personal fulfilment. They are flourishing.[18][19] In these organisations people are ends in and of themselves, and not treated as means to ends.[20]

The 'all stakeholder' view alluded to in the above description of People Excellence is consistent with the growing view of the organisation as a good social citizen, serving the common good of humanity in a sustainable manner: leaving the world a better a place for upcoming generations who will also be able to satisfy their needs.[21] The organisation is endeavouring to be the best in *and* for the world.[22] This demands that organisations be purpose-driven.[23] In turn, this gives their people the opportunity to find meaning in their work by being purpose-driven in and of themselves. Organisations that operate with a clear and driving sense of purpose, beyond the goal of just making money, outperformed the S&P 500 by a factor of 14 between 1998 and 2013.[24] Purpose-driven organisations make more money; have more engaged employees; have more loyal customers; and are better at innovation and transformational change.[25]

Put metaphorically, People Excellence signifies an organisation being THE shining star with respect to its people. It is seen and used independently as THE people standard. The organisation has institutionalised the circular, value-unlocking/wealth creating, core value chain, depicted in Figure 1.1 in the form of a People Excellence Triangle. As can be seen in this figure, People Excellence sits at the confluence of Thriving People; Delighted Stakeholders as Beneficiaries; and a Viable Organisation. In turn, People Excellence results in an outstanding level of People Effectiveness in the organisation. The former is thus the strategic means to the latter as an outcome, recursively feeding back on the former in a continuous virtuous cycle.

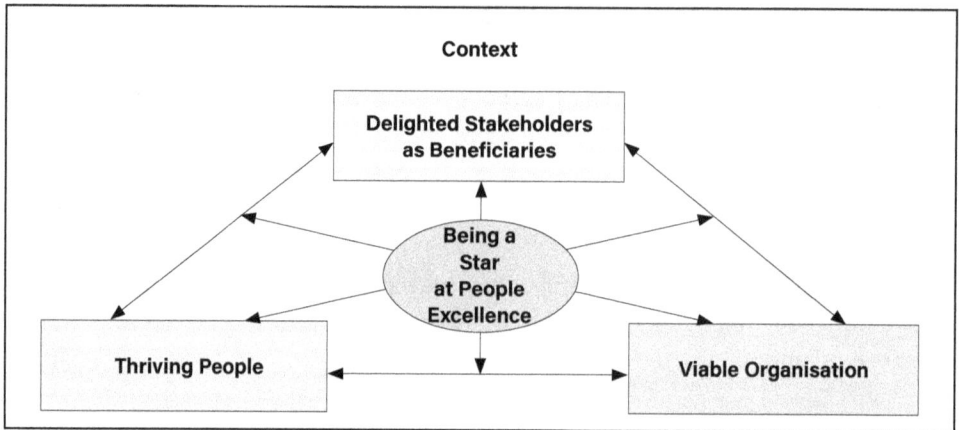

Figure 1.1: The People Excellence Triangle

PEOPLE EXCELLENCE AS IMPERATIVE

If the centrality of people in an experience-based Knowledge Society is accepted as imperative in ensuring the ongoing viability of the organisation, then People Excellence needs to become a regular Board and Executive strategic agenda item for ongoing, in-depth, vigorous dialogue, and discussion.[26] Beyond the confines of the Board and Executive, People Excellence must also permeate the everyday organisational narrative regarding ongoing strategic direction and guidance.

People Excellence therefore must not, and cannot, be side-lined to the People (or HR) Function as a lesser, 'nice-to-hear' matter, only requiring ad hoc attention in a transactional, cost-efficiency manner. Or, only become a priority when a people crisis upends the organisation, such as industrial action, a pressing shortage of key talent, rising customer dissatisfaction, or a pandemic.[27] The ongoing People Excellence dialogue must trigger strategically directed interventions initiated from wherever in the organisation. People Excellence must be continually and radically re-imagined and re-invented to shift competitive boundaries in the 'create', experience-based economy through creatively engaged people.

Given people's mission-criticality in future viable organisational performance and success, if mergers/acquisitions are chosen as the strategic means to grow an organisation, it would be essential to conduct a comprehensive due diligence of the People Excellence of the organisation(s) concerned. Only in this way can one arrive at an accurate estimate of the true value to place on the targeted organisation, because people are accepted as central to the true value to be placed on the assessed organisation(s). For various other reasons, investors, regulators and society also have a growing keen interest in the state of People Excellence of organisations.[28]

THE NEED FOR AN INTEGRATED STRATEGIC STRESS TEST OF PEOPLE EXCELLENCE

If the imperative of thriving people is accepted as necessary for future viable organisational performance and success, as well as delighted stakeholders, how can one assess the overall 'Creditworthiness' of an organisation's People Excellence? What is needed is an integrated Strategic Stress Test of People Excellence. If People Excellence means being THE shining star with respect to the people of the organisation, it is proposed that such a Stress Test be called the 'People Excellence Star.'

Metaphorically, a star is the bearer of light in a threatening and unknown dark. It provides a fixed point to plot one's direction. In this way, it assists one to reach one's destination despite distractions and the dark unknown. Like a star is used for navigational purposes, the aim of the People Excellence Star is to serve as a navigational means to provide a steady compass setting for guiding, assessing, transforming, and maintaining an organisation's People Excellence.[29] A stark contrast to a shining Star is a Black Hole organisation: an organisation that is inhuman and inhumane, which exploits and destroys its people.

The Star as strategic stress test of the organisation's People Creditworthiness provides the baseline diagnostic assessment for the crafting of the organisation's Strategic People Interventions, given the strengths and weaknesses of the organisation's People Excellence as unveiled by the test. This is superseded by monitoring and tracking the People Excellence journey of the organisation. The power of the People Excellence Star is that it provides a map of the territory called 'People', which frames systemic, dynamic, strategic people thinking in an organisation. Given the above discussion, it should be patently clear that the People Excellence Star must be owned by the whole leadership community of the organisation.

AN INTRODUCTION TO *THE PEOPLE EXCELLENCE STAR. A STRATEGIC ORGANISATIONAL STRESS TEST*

Purpose

The purpose of *The People Excellence Star. A Strategic Organisational Stress Test* is to propose and elucidate the People Excellence Star as a strategic creditworthiness stress test of how well an organisation is doing with respect to its people. Seen from an integrated, strategic vantage point, my book aims to answer the question: What are the difference-making, leading organisational conditions that enable thriving people who truly are unlocking real, amazing value, in this way creating worthy, lasting wealth – consistently and continuously – in turn, bringing about a viable organisation for all of its delighted stakeholders?

Consequently, depending on the outcome of the Strategic Stress Test, what people interventions must be crafted and rolled out to strategically enhance and strengthen the People Excellence – and in turn the People Effectiveness – of the organisation?

Unique value-adds

The People Excellence Star. A Strategic Organisational Stress Test endeavours to deliver three, unique value-adds.

An integrated, balanced, strategic perspective

Although People Excellence has received attention in both the theoretical literature and in practice for many years, the approach to and assessment of it have frequently been at a tactical-operational level, are typically fragmented, and are siloed into stand-alone Excellence Domains/Elements. These are frequently punted individually as THE silver bullet to ensure People Excellence. Fads and fashions also play their enticing and seducing roles on the side.

People Excellence is furthermore is often framed one-sidedly from the organisation's perspective, ignoring the perspective of people who are active contributors to, and beneficiaries of, People Excellence. This frequently results in people becoming only the means to People Effectiveness as the end.

In the to-be-discussed exposition of the People Excellence Star, equal weight will thus be given to the simultaneous synchronicity of the organisational and people perspectives. This is why People Excellence was described above as attaining the simultaneous synchronicity of thriving people, aimed at delighting stakeholders AND a viable organisation (refer Figure 1.1).

The use of the word 'integrated' refers thus concurrently, *firstly,* to the integration from a strategic vantage point of the fragmented Excellence Domains in the literature. And, *secondly,* through integration, achieving the simultaneous, balanced synchronicity of organisational and People Excellence perspectives.

A practice perspective, solidly grounded in thought leadership, research evidence, and leading practices

The focus of the People Excellence Star is firmly on the practice of People Excellence in organisations. This book is about assisting in making People Excellence happen at the coal face of the daily functioning of organisations. It also provides insights into possible strategic people interventions which can form the basis for crafting the Strategic People Intent of the organisation, given the uncovered People Excellence gap.

Yet this practice perspective is not pulled out of thin air. It draws extensively on the best thought leadership; the latest research; and cutting-edge practices regarding People Excellence. Hence the Star rests on sound, robust, and tested foundations.

Relevance to the new World of Work

The new World of Work, to be called the emerging new order, forms the explicit frame of reference for the construction and content of the People Excellence Star. This order is discussed extensively in Chapter 3, and then progressively expanded on in later chapters. In Chapter 3, themes such as the underlying, basic dynamics of the emerging new order; the major Forces of Change shaping the emerging new order such as the growth of the VICCAS world; exponentially accelerating technological innovation as manifested in the Fourth Industrial Revolution; and the profile of the worker of the future, are discussed in depth.

The subsequent discussions in later chapters regarding the different Excellence Domains/Elements making up the People Excellence Star have a direct and immediate relevance to the emerging new order faced by organisations, in the present and future, within which they have to realise People Excellence.

Themes addressed

The story line of *The People Excellence Star. A Strategic Organisational Stress Test* proceeds as follows:

- **Chapter 1** provides an orientation to the need for, and the nature of, the journey we are embarking on to strategically test the creditworthiness of an organisation's People Excellence.
- **Chapter 2** explicates the proposed People Excellence Star as integrated Strategic Stress Test with its respective Excellence Domains and Elements.
- **Chapter 3** addresses the People Excellence Context with its emerging People Excellence Requirements.
- **Chapters 4 to 8** deal respectively with the five People Excellence domains that make up the People Excellence Star: 1 – Identity; 2 – Capacity: 3 – Delivery; 4 – Outcomes; and 5 – Relationships.
- **Chapter 9** provides an integrated picture of People Excellence in terms of the complete People Excellence Star by telling the story of People Excellence as synergistic fusion energising the organisation.

- **Chapter 10** elucidates – through a complexity view of People Excellence – the journey towards People Excellence which genuinely unleashes overall, synergistic fusion in the organisation.

Target Audience

The first target audience of *The People Excellence Star. A Strategic Organisational Stress Test*, is executive organisational leadership who are accountable and responsible to their Board for the People Excellence of their organisation. What is the state of their organisation's People Excellence, and what needs to/will be addressed to bring about People Excellence in their organisation if it is to have thriving people as a catalyst to a viable organisation?

The second target audience is the Organisational/People Effectiveness or Organisational Development Unit of an organisation, which carries the responsibility as people experts to enhance the People Excellence of their organisation through competitive people effectiveness. This embraces engendering and maintaining the organisational conditions under which people can do/are doing the right things right in an outstanding manner, in order to make/keep their organisation a viable entity, and in the process thrive.[30] In this way, *The People Excellence Star. A Strategic Organisational Stress Test* can be seen as providing a comprehensive work agenda – a scope of work – of what such a Unit should cover.

Thirdly, Strategic People Effectiveness/Organisational Development Consultants as a third target audience can use *The People Excellence Star. A Strategic Organisational Stress Test* as a source guide when assisting organisations to enhance their People Excellence. In particular, this book is for consultants who work at the strategic, organisation-wide level with the top leadership of an organisation, with the aim of enhancing the People Excellence of the total organisation. This may require a multi-disciplinary consulting team that is able to work in-depth across all the People Excellence Domains (see Chapter 2).

Finally, the fourth target audience, *The People Excellence Star. A Strategic Organisational Stress Test* can be used at the post-graduate level in a Masters (including a MBA) or Doctoral programme in Strategic People (or HR) Leadership/ Management in a module covering either Organisational/People Effectiveness/ Excellence and/or Organisational Development.

How to use this book

The People Excellence Star. A Strategic Organisational Stress Test provides a comprehensive map of the territory called 'People Excellence'. This map can be used to:

- understand the topology of the territory, called 'Desirable People Excellence', as explicated through the People Excellence Star;

- assess one's own organisation's 'As Is' People Excellence against its desired 'To Be' People Excellence; and

- determine the gap between the organisation's desired 'To Be' and 'As Is' People Excellence to identify possible Strategic People Excellence interventions, which will form the basis of crafting the Strategic People Intent with strategic initiatives of the organisation.

In light of the above, *The People Excellence Star. A Strategic Organisational Stress Test* is accompanied by an online work book in which 'As Is' state assessments of the reader's own organisation against the desired 'To Be' state of People Excellence can be done, and possible interventions conceived/identified. The work book can be downloaded at https://kr.co.za/the-people-excellence-star-workbook/ and the password is WORKBOOK.

Wherever the above icon appears in *The People Excellence Star. A Strategic Organisational Stress Test,* the work book can be perused at the appropriate section, and you as the reader can conduct a 'To Be'/'As Is' Reflective People Excellence Assessment to identify possible strategic interventions with respect to that Domain/Element of People Excellence. The work book follows exactly the same structure as this book.

Conventions followed

Two types of endnotes appear at the end of each chapter of *The People Excellence Star. A Strategic Organisational Stress Test*, which are indicated by consecutive numbers in the text:

i.   *Reference Endnotes*: References are referred to by numbers in normal font in the text, for example.[1][2] The references are provided in abbreviated form in the endnotes given after the chapters. Full references are listed in the References Section at the end of the book. The centrality of an Excellence topic – its relative importance over time in the field of People Excellence – is often reflected in the number and dates of references provided for the topic concerned.

I have tried to be as comprehensive as possible in my referencing to give due recognition. Where I have not given such recognition, I offer my sincere apologies. It is unintentional. Given my extended number of years in the field, certain thinking has become part of my intellectual DNA. However, I do acknowledge that omissions do not release me of my personal and intellectual debt to the parties concerned.

ii. *Explanatory Endnotes:* These notes are indicated in the text by numbers in bold, italics, for example.[(1)(2)] These endnotes either extend a point made in the text; provide additional or different views on the point elucidated in the text; or explicate the theoretical source of a position taken.

All the figures and tables in the book have been constructed by me, except if otherwise indicated.

SUMMARY

The purpose of this chapter was to put forward the case that people are the only true value unlockers and wealth creators in the emerging compelling, memorable, experience-based economy. They are central to ongoing viable organisational performance and success. People Excellence is about thriving people truly unlocking real, amazing value and creating worthy, lasting wealth – consistently and continuously – in this way ensuring a viable organisation for delighted stakeholders. Strategically knowing the state of the organisation's People Excellence – the People Creditworthiness of the organisation – hence becomes a mission-critical imperative for each and every organisation, including its Board, Leadership, and stakeholders.

There is a pressing need for an integrated strategic People Excellence Stress Test that can be used by organisations to gauge their People Excellence and take appropriate strategic actions to enhance it. The purpose of *The People Excellence Star. A Strategic Organisational Stress Test* is to address this need by proposing and elucidating the People Excellence Star as an integrated test of how well an organisation is doing with its people: its People Creditworthiness.

Using the new world of work as a frame of reference, it is endeavoured in *The People Excellence Star. A Strategic Organisational Stress Test* to present in a strategic, yet practical way, an integrated means to assess the People Creditworthiness of an organisation, paying equal attention to the people and organisational perspectives. In addition, the intention is to provide insight into possible strategic People Excellence interventions, which can form the basis of crafting the Strategic People Intent of the organisation. All of the aforementioned are firmly rooted in best thought leadership, latest research, and cutting-edge practices. In this way, it is endeavoured to make integration, balance, robustness, and relevance the unique value-adds of the *People Excellence Star: A strategic organisational Stress Test*.

Chapter 2 sets out to elucidate the proposed People Excellence Star as an integrated Strategic Stress Test of People Excellence with its respective Excellence Domains and associated Excellence Elements.

THE DOMAINS AND DYNAMICS OF THE PEOPLE EXCELLENCE STAR

"Success is the ability to hitch your wagon to a star while keeping your feet on the ground." (Anonymous)

"When you have had a taste of excellence, you cannot go back to mediocrity." (Maximillian Degenerez)

"One that desires to excel, should endeavour it in those things that are in themselves excellent." (Epictetus)

"Excellence is doing ordinary things extraordinarily well." (John Gardner)

In Chapter 1, I outlined the pressing need for an integrated Strategic People Excellence Stress Test that organisations can use to gauge their People Excellence, before taking appropriate strategic action to enhance their People Creditworthiness. The imperative need for such a test has been triggered by people moving centre stage as the only true value unlockers and wealth creators in the continued future success of organisations, triggered by ongoing, relentless, disruptive innovation in the experience-based Knowledge Society. In the final instance, People Excellence is about thriving people truly unlocking real, amazing value, in this way creating worthy, lasting wealth for delighted stakeholders – consistently and continuously – and ensuring a viable organisation.

The purpose of this chapter is to describe at a high level the proposed People Excellence Star – with its respective Excellence Domains and Elements – as an integrated Strategic Stress Test of the People Creditworthiness of an organisation. The Excellence Domains with their respective Elements were drawn from several sources:

- The extensive People Excellence literature by thought leaders over many years, such as Arnold Bakker, Michael Beer, Wayne Cascio, Jim Collins, Jac Fritz-Enz, Arie de Geus, Ed Lawler, Mark Huselid, Wiliam Joyce, Christo Nel, Nitin Noria, Jerry Porras, Jeffrey Pfeffer and Dave Ulrich.

- The latest research on topics related to People Excellence such as strategy; strategic talent management; organisational design, culture and climate; high performance/commitment work systems; work engagement; as well as positive psychology addressing flourishing, thriving and fulfilled people, and their well-being.

- The regular Global Best Companies To Work For, Most Admired Companies, Human Capital, and CEO surveys, and reporting by leading consulting institutions.
- My own research and publications over many years in the area of People Management/Excellence.
- My consulting assignments for over 35 years, particularly in the areas of People Strategic Intent and People Excellence.

It must be noted here that although the primary focus of the People Excellence Star is aimed at practice, the way in which it was composed implies an underlying theoretical perspective of People Excellence. It is not my purpose in *The People Excellence. A Strategic Organisational Stress Test* to argue and critically weigh up the theoretical views drawn on implicitly, given my book's practice focus. As a pracademic, my intention is to map a praxeology of People Excellence: the 'science' of the practice of People Excellence.

However, the more important underpinning theoretical views and insights informing the People Excellence Star are given in explanatory endnotes, indicated by endnote numbers in bold italics in the text. The reader can be assured that the practice-aimed, People Excellence Star rests on a theoretically robust and informed foundation, including the latest research related to People Excellence. Of course, the conception of the proposed People Excellence Star is of my own doing, based on these theoretical inputs.

Furthermore, the proposed People Excellence Star is prescriptive in espousing theory-based and research-supported leading practices. Hence, the Star is not merely descriptive but also normative in its intention to serve as a reference point in making People Excellence, and in turn People Effectiveness, a reality in an organisation.

This chapter unfolds as follows: firstly, the overall People Excellence Star is presented; secondly, the respective Excellence Domains, with their associated Excellence Elements making up the Star, are discussed; thirdly, People Excellence as the outcome of the overall synergistic fusion between the Excellence Domains and their constituent Elements is explicated; and lastly, the stress testing of People Excellence in terms of levels, stakeholders, views and methods is discussed.

THE PROPOSED PEOPLE EXCELLENCE STAR

Figure 2.1 depicts graphically the proposed People Excellence Star as an integrated People Excellence Stress Test with its respective Excellence Domains and Elements.[1]

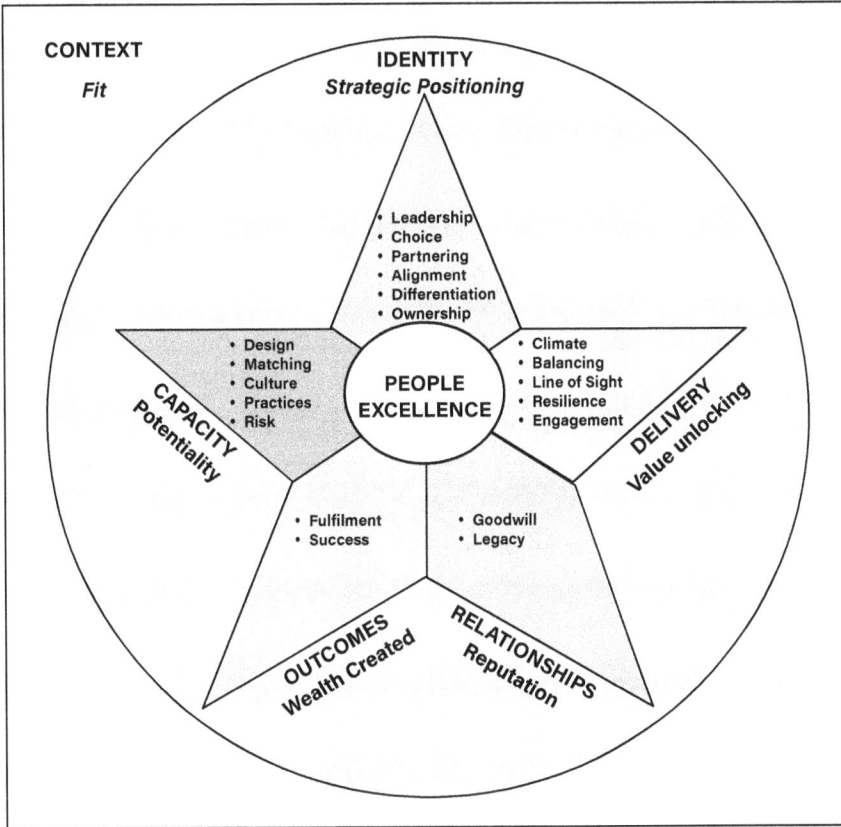

Figure 2.1: The People Excellence Star

As per Figure 2.1, it is important to note, *firstly*, that the People Excellence Star is embedded in a context. The context represents the strategically demarcated operating arena of the organisation in which it endeavours and aspires to compete.[2] Ultimately, People Excellence is achieved when a good fit exists. There is overall synergy between the operating arena of the organisation (its external context) and the content awarded to the Excellence Domains/Elements by the organisation (its internal context) relative to its people.[3] I.e., there is a good Context-Organisation-People fit.

Secondly, according to Figure 2.1 the proposed People Excellence Star is made up of five interdependent, reciprocally influencing Excellence Domains: Identity, Capacity, Delivery, Outcomes, and Relationships. In terms of Figure 2.1, the respective strategic thrusts (or themes) of the different Domains are: Identity = Strategic Positioning; Capacity = Potentiality; Delivery = Value Unlocking; Outcomes = Wealth Created; and Relationships = Reputation. The order in which the Domains are discussed below is reflective of the approximate progressive People Excellence journey that needs to be followed in the organisation. It also forms the unfolding structure for the subsequent chapters.

In terms of Figure 2.1, *thirdly*, each Excellence Domain of the People Excellence Star is composed of a number of Excellence Elements, which are also interdependent and reciprocally influencing, making up at a detailed level the integrated Strategic Stress Test of an organisation's People Creditworthiness. The 20 Excellence Elements are covered in the form of Excellence Questions in subsequent chapters.

The choice of the proposed Excellence Domains/Elements follows the Pareto Principle: which 20% of the possible Domains/Elements will make an 80% difference in terms of the organisation's People Excellence? These Domains/Elements have been distilled from the sources listed in the introduction to this chapter.

THE MAKE-UP OF THE PEOPLE EXCELLENCE STAR

In this section a high level overview is given of the Excellence Domains with their respective Excellence Elements making up the proposed People Excellence Star (refer Figure 2.1).

Excellence Domain 1: Identity

This Excellence Domain entails the designated strategic role that people are expected to play relative to the Identity of the organisation: Who and what are we? What do we stand for and aspire to? The Identity of the organisation encompasses its Purpose, Vision, Strategic Intent, Core Values and Legacy.[4] The overarching Excellence Question with regard to this Excellence Domain is: Has the appropriate strategic positioning of people with respect to the organisation's future viability relative to its Identity, been explicitly and deliberately chosen, and is it being put into practice in the organisation through the right strategic actions?

Six Excellence Elements make up this Domain:

- *Leadership:* The organisation is led in a people-centric way.
- *Choice:* An upfront, clear, deliberate Strategic People Choice has been made regarding the strategic role that people must play in the viability of the organisation.
- *Partnering:* The People Professionals of the organisation are true strategic partners whose contributions to the success of the organisation are eagerly sought out and highly cherished.
- *Alignment:* The organisation's Identity and Critical People Imperatives are strategically aligned to create ongoing, strategic synergy.

- *Differentiation:* An inimitable, distinct and coherent Strategic People Choice – made up of the organisation's strategic configuration of the World of Work for itself, its People Charter, its Desired People Profile and its People Value Proposition – is in place.
- *Ownership:* The people of the organisation have taken committed ownership of the organisation's strategic positiong regarding its people.

Excellence Domain 2: Capacity

This Excellence Domain is about the 'people readiness' of the organisation for its intended strategic journey into the future in realising its Identity. The overarching Excellence Question relative to this Excellence Domain is: Has the organisation created the necessary people potentiality (or made the necessary people investment) to achieve what it sets out to achieve as captured in the organisation's Identity?

Five Excellence Elements make up this Domain:

- *Design:* The organisation has a fit-for-purpose organisational design.
- *Matching:* The Core Organisational and People Capacities are matched within the progressively unfolding strategic horizon of the organisation.
- *Culture:* The organisation is 'glued' together by a distinct, strong but flexible Organisational Culture.
- *Practices:* The organisation is using High Commitment/High Involvement People Practices that have been translated into a corresponding people management tool set.
- *Risk:* The organisation has a risk mitigation strategy and plan in place to deal proactively with its people risks in accordance with its risk appetite.

Excellence Domain 3: Delivery

This Excellence Domain entails the actual vs. desired value being unlocked by the organisation's people, given its people potentiality (or investment). The overarching Excellence Question regarding this Excellence Domain is: What value is being unlocked by the organisation's people, and concurrently the active presence/absence of enablers (and on the downside, the barriers) to high, real time, people engagement and performance in the organisation?

Five Excellence Elements make up this Domain:

- *Climate:* The organisation is infused by an invigorating Organisational Climate.

- *Balancing:* At all levels – individual, team, organisational – the right dynamic balance exists between work demands and required resources, attained through awarded/exercised autonomy.
- *Line of Sight:* A clear line of sight exists in the organisation between Effort – Performance – Valued Recognition/Rewards.
- *Resilience:* People deal with the stresses, trauma, and strains engendered by the continuous radical and fundamental changes facing the organisation with confident resilience. They are change-fit.
- *Engagement:* People are highly engaged in their work and organisation.

Excellence Domain 4: Outcomes

This Excellence Domain encompasses the actual contribution of people to the organisation's performance and success relative to its Identity, currently and going into the future. The overarching Excellence Question about this Excellence Domain is: What wealth has been created by the organisation's people for its stakeholders?

Two Excellence Elements make up this Domain:

- *Fulfilment:* People believe and experience that the organisation is delivering on its People Brand Promise as expressed in its People Value Proposition.
- *Success:* The organisation has deep insight – based on real time, in time intelligence – into the contribution of its people towards its success and continued viability.

Excellence Domain 5: Relationships

This Excellence Domain refers to the social capital being nurtured and grown with stakeholders by the organisation and its people, and what lasting, worthy legacy it is leaving behind. The overarching Excellence Question regarding this Excellence Domain is: What reputation does the organisation have amongst its key stakeholders within its operating arena in terms of the difference it is making?

Two Excellence Elements make up this Domain:

- *Goodwill:* The organisation has a high level of goodwill in the bank with its stakeholders.
- *Legacy:* The organisation is building a worthy, lasting legacy for upcoming generations.

PEOPLE EXCELLENCE AS THE OVERALL OUTCOME OF SYNERGISTIC FUSION WITHIN THE PEOPLE EXCELLENCE STAR

The picture of People Excellence Star given in Figure 2.1 is static. But, People Excellence is a verb, not a noun. Analogous to the continuous nuclear fusion of hydrogen and helium at the core of a star through the combination of atomic nuclei which generates and releases ongoing energy, creating light[5], People Excellence is the outcome of the overall, continuous, powerful, virtuous fusion between all of the above Excellence Domains with their constituent Elements. Everything affects everything else in an ongoing energising/de-energising way.

The People Excellence Domains with their commensurate Elements act together in positive, rhythmic and synergistic concert, in this way capacitating the organisation to achieve exceedingly well with its people. Domains and Elements configure into a dynamic pattern that is expressive of an upward, virtuous cycle of increasing People Excellence. The organisation is a 'shining star' with respect to people. Of course, a downward, vicious cycle of decreasing People Excellence is also possible in an organisation. This type of organisation is a 'Black Hole' when it comes to people.

The interdependent and reciprocally influencing relationships between the Excellence Domains – through their commensurate Excellence Elements – cannot be overstressed. Earlier discussed Domains build on latter discussed Domains – and vice versa – in a reciprocal, synergistic and integral way to form and function as an integrated whole in a systemic, organic, and emergent way like a star. The degree of overall organisational integration was found to be a significant differentiator between high- and low-performing organisations.[6] The to-be-explicated, operating laws governing the ongoing synergistic fusion of the People Excellence Star as an integrated whole are: fit, congruence, re-enforcement, multiplication, and wisdom, as well as systemic, organic and dynamic Both/And fusion.[7] This dynamic perspective on the People Excellence Star resonates with the underlying foundational view of the organisation as a living, emergent, self-organising, social ecosystem.[8] This view derives from a complexity world view.[9]

At the end of each chapter – in the progressively unfolding discussion of the People Excellence Star – the overall, ongoing, powerful, virtuous synergistic fusion between the discussed Excellence Domains and their constituent Excellence Elements will be elucidated through storytelling regarding the desired People Creditworthiness with respect to the respective Domain with its Elements. A progressive picture will thus be built across the Domains, chapter-by-chapter, such that a comprehensive, integrated People Excellence story will be told in Chapter 9 of the overall synergistic fusion within the total People Excellence Star.

The progressively unfolding story will build a People Excellence Value Chain from Chapters 4 to 8. In this way, the static picture of the People Excellence Star given in Figure 2.1 will be metamorphosed into an overall integrated, dynamic picture that in the final instance is reflective of a dynamic, organic, systemic and synergistic whole. However, this very same picture will be challenged in Chapter 10 from a complexity view of reality in order to arrive at what is believed to be a genuine picture of the overall synergistic fusion to be established within the People Excellence Star if the organisation is to attain true, lasting People Excellence. Figure 2.2 depicts this progressively unfolding story of People Excellence told in building a praxeology of People Excellence. The unfolding story also reflects an evolution to higher levels of complexity in how to view People Excellence.

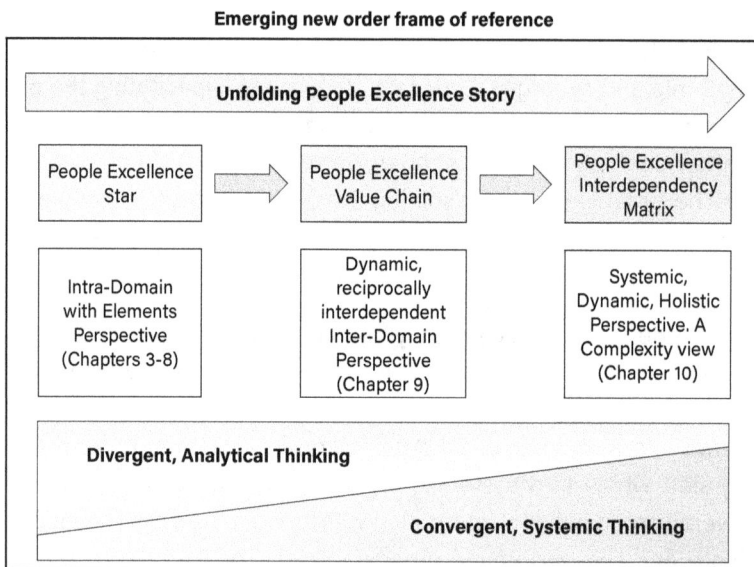

Emerging new order frame of reference

Unfolding People Excellence Story

People Excellence Star	People Excellence Value Chain	People Excellence Interdependency Matrix
Intra-Domain with Elements Perspective (Chapters 3-8)	Dynamic, reciprocally interdependent Inter-Domain Perspective (Chapter 9)	Systemic, Dynamic, Holistic Perspective. A Complexity view (Chapter 10)

Divergent, Analytical Thinking

Convergent, Systemic Thinking

Figure 2.2: Progressively unfolding story of People Excellence

If the story of People Excellence is going to be progressively told, what is storytelling all about? At their core, organisations are dialogical networks that are constituted, nurtured, and maintained by organisational members. Organisations are woven and held together by the stories being told and retold many times in the organisation.[10] In this case, the story to be told is regarding an organisation's People Excellence. Genuine stories and storytelling create shared dialogical spaces where people can participate jointly through conversation around the topic at hand.

Stories and storytelling represent and convey complex, multi-faceted realities like People Excellence to listeners in a simple, interesting, stimulating and effortless way in order to make sense; give meaning; and ascribe purpose to the reality being engaged with. Stories inspire, stimulate, and make things understandable, believable, and memorable. At its most basic level, as a conversation storytelling weaves together what is being said, listened to, and responded to between people into a tangible, rich, shared tapestry of meaning. Without stories well told, organisations become de-energised and void of meaning.

Stories provide organisational members with the necessary shared language and vocabulary to engage meaningfully and with understanding with the reality they face and interact with, such as People Excellence. Having created a shared understanding through storytelling, participants can intervene insightfully.

STRESS TESTING PEOPLE EXCELLENCE IN THE ORGANISATION: LEVELS, STAKEHOLDERS, VIEWS AND METHODS

The stress testing of an organisation's People Creditworthiness must consider four stress testing variables: levels, stakeholders, views and methods. Each is discussed in turn.

Levels

Four reciprocally interdependent levels of stress testing People Excellence can be distinguished:[11]

- Macro level: The organisation as a whole.
- Meso level: Organisational units.
- Micro level: Teams.
- Micro level: Individuals.

The focus of *The People Excellence Star. A Strategic Organisational Stress Test* is on the macro level – i.e., the organisation as a whole – using a strategic vantage point. Naturally, People Excellence at this level can/needs to be deconstructed to the other levels, depending on the aim of the stress test to determine the granular People Creditworthiness of the organisation. What is the status of Excellence at the lower levels of the organisation? Where is it outstanding and where is it poor? In turn, how does it manifest itself in a summated form at the organisational level? What are the interdependencies of the People Excellence's Domains and Elements at the different levels? And how similar or different are the variables affecting People Excellence at the different levels?[12]

Stakeholders

Stress testing the People Creditworthiness of an organisation, whatever level is being used, can be done by soliciting the views of one or more stakeholders, such as the Board, leadership, organisational members in general, customers, suppliers, shareholders, and/or community.[13] Regardless of the stakeholder(s) chosen, a representative sample must be drawn for the selected stakeholder grouping. A multi-stakeholder approach is highly recommended to arrive at a robust, triangulated picture of the 'true' People Excellence of an organisation. This is in contrast to the parochial, one-sided, siloed view of a single stakeholder.

Views

Top-down and/or bottom-up views of People Excellence can be established in an organisation. Hence, the connection can be determined between the leadership's intentions and actions with respect to People Excellence in the organisation (top down), and organisational members' interpretation and experience of such thinking and actions (bottom up).[14]

Vast differences may exist between the leadership's talking and walking of People Excellence in their organisation, and/or organisational members' interpretation and experience of the what, how and why of the leadership's intentions and actions regarding People Excellence.[15] A complicating, mediating variable is the high likelihood that the degree of similarity between various parties may vary by organisational level.

Methods

Various methods can be used to conduct the stress testing: interviews, focus groups, and/or questionnaires. The choice of a method must be carefully weighed up in light of each method's strengths and weaknesses in terms of reliability and validity, as well as its breadth and depth. I.e., the richness of the data collected. A multi-method approach, applied differentially across levels, stakeholders and views, would be most powerful.

In summary, the most powerful Stress Test of People Excellence in an organisation uses multi-level, multi-stakeholder, top-down/bottom-up views, and a multi-methods approach, to arrive at a triangulated, true determination of an organisation's People Creditworthiness.

SUMMARY

The purpose of this chapter was to elucidate the proposed People Excellence Star. The Star represents an integrated, strategic oprganisational People Excellence Stress Test to direct, guide, intervene into, and track the People Creditworthiness of an organisation. The results of the Stress Test can be used as input into the crafting of the organisation's Strategic People Intent, with its corresponding strategic initiatives related to the People Excellence gaps to be closed.

The People Excellence Star is composed of five interdependent, reciprocally influencing Excellence Domains: Identity, Capacity, Delivery, Outcomes, and Relationships. The Excellence Domains are made up of 20 Excellence Elements in total. The respective Excellence Domains and Elements were discussed briefly as a prelude to a detailed discussion in the forthcoming chapters. Thereafter, People Excellence as the outcome of the overall synergistic fusion amongst the Excellence Domains with their constituent Elements was explicated. The progressively unfolding story told of People Excellence will move from an Intra-Domain perspective, through an Inter-Domain Perspective, to a Systemic Whole perspective.

The chapter concluded by listing the stress testing variables to consider when determining the People Creditworthiness of the organisation: levels, stakeholders, views, and methods. It was argued that the most powerful Stress Test of People Excellence in an organisation is a multi-level level, multi-stakeholder, top-down/ bottom-up view, in conjunction with a multi-method approach, in order to arrive at a true determination of an organisation's People Excellence.

Next, the People Excellence Context and respective Excellence Domains with their commensurate Excellence Elements are discussed. First, the People Excellence Context is discussed in the following chapter; followed in Chapters 4 to 8 by the Excellence Domains: Identity through Capacity, Delivery, Outcomes to Relationships.

PEOPLE EXCELLENCE STAR

CONTEXT: FIT

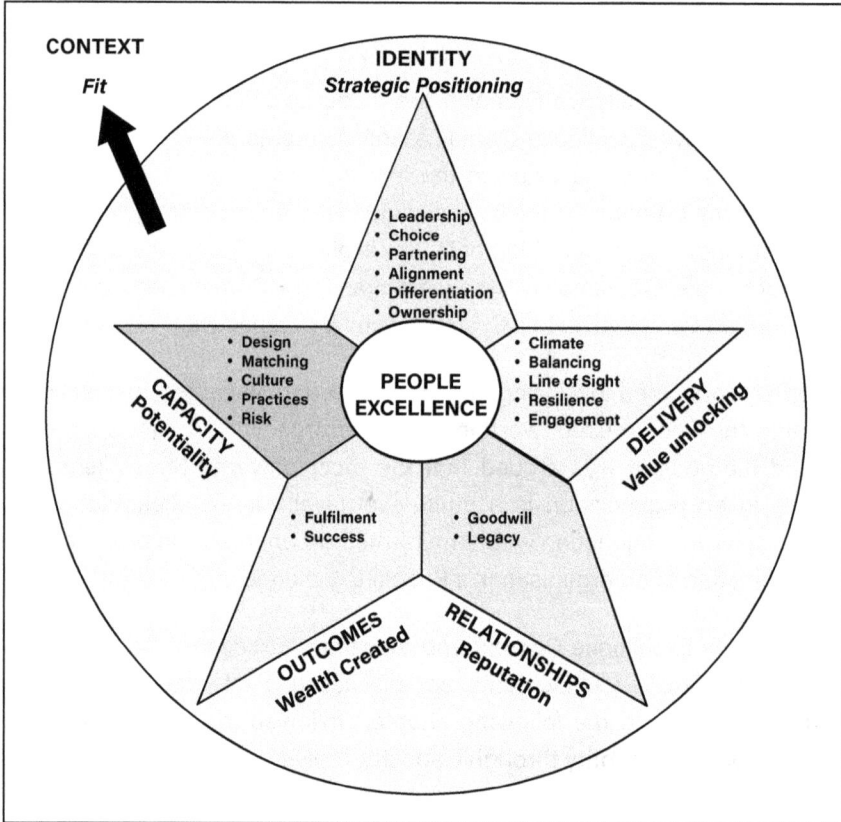

CHAPTER 3

THE PEOPLE EXCELLENCE CONTEXT: FIT

"Chaos is found in the greatest abundance wherever order is sought. Chaos always defeats order because it is better organised." (Terry Pratcher)

"If the rhythm of the drumbeat changes, the dance steps must adjust." (Kenyan proverb)

"If you're not confused, you don't know what's going on." (Anonymous)

All organisations are embedded in a chosen context. Within this context the organisation chooses a strategically demarcated operating arena in which it endeavours to compete viably. The context and the organisation with its people form an inseparable, seamless, holographic and dynamic whole – one cannot be understood without the other. Organisations and their contexts reciprocally co-evolve and unfold. Engaging with the inseparable organisation-context relationship requires, *firstly,* deciding what strategic contextual posture and attitude to adopt in engaging with the context; *secondly,* building an in-depth understanding of the context with its accompanying challenges, demands and requirements, now and into the future; and, *thirdly,* determining what is necessary to attain a good fit between the organisation and its context.[1]

All of the above apply to People Excellence equally: the context imposes certain people challenges, demands and requirements on the organisation, now and into the future. People Excellence is achieved when a good *fit* exists. I.e., there is overall synergy between the operating arena of the organisation (its external context) and the content awarded to the Excellence Domains and Elements by the organisation (=its internal context), relative to its people.[2] The external operating arena dictates and sets People Excellence Requirements for the organisation.

In turn, the externally imposed People Excellence Requirements must be translated into a People Excellence Specification. This acts as a reference point according to which the internal organisational context must be set up to attain People Excellence as manifested in thriving people, delighted stakeholders, and a viable organisation (cf. Figure 1.1). The form this translation takes is framed by the to-be-discussed-below, strategic contextual posture and engagement attitude adopted by the organisation. Ultimately, People Excellence is the synergistic outcome of the interaction between how People Excellence is conceived, institutionalised, and lived in the organisation, and the context in which the organisation has chosen to operate strategically, and aspires to compete viably over its strategic time horizon.[3]

Without a deep understanding of the People Excellence Requirements set by the organisation's context, People Excellence cannot be properly thought through, institutionalised, and lived in the organisation. As a departure point on the journey to People Excellence, a thorough understanding of the organisation's context hence must be built substantively and qualitatively over the organisation's strategic time horizon, and then translated into a future-referenced People Excellence Specification. This Specification provides the fountainhead for a contextual-goodness-of-fit People Vision for the organisation.

As a departure point in Chapter 1, it was stated that the broad context in which people have become mission-critical as the only true future value unlockers and wealth creators – enabling viable organisational performance and success – is the emerging innovative, 'compelling, memorable experience-based' economy, embedded in the Knowledge Society. Against this backdrop, the purpose of this chapter is to explore in greater depth, although still at a high level, the emerging new order in the context which gives rise to certain People Excellence Requirements being imposed on organisations in general. In turn, these People Excellence Requirements have to be translated into a future-fit People Excellence Specification set for the organisation's People Excellence Domains and Elements, and by implication its people.

The following topics are addressed in this chapter: the choice of a Strategic Contextual Posture and Engagement Attitude; the underlying basic dynamics of the emerging new order; the substantive major Forces of Change shaping this order; the Qualities infusing the Forces of Change; and finally, a suggested generic, high level People Excellence Specification – the source of a contextually-fit, People Vision for the organisation – as necessitated by the emerging new order.

CHOICE OF A STRATEGIC CONTEXTUAL POSTURE AND ENGAGEMENT ATTITUDE

The leadership of an organisation has to choose a strategic contextual posture and engagement attitude as a vantage point to the Context.[4] In choosing a vantage point, leadership can adopt different Contextual Attitudes in engaging with the Context. Contextual Engagement Attitudes are made up of two dimensions in terms of which leadership can engage contextually, i.e.:

- degree of contextual change: Recreate/Transform vs. Maintain/Enhance; and
- time orientation: Present-directed vs. Future-directed.

The options tied to each dimension give four possible Contextual Engagement Attitudes, framing leadership's engagement with the Context. These options are depicted in Figure 3.1.

CONTEXT

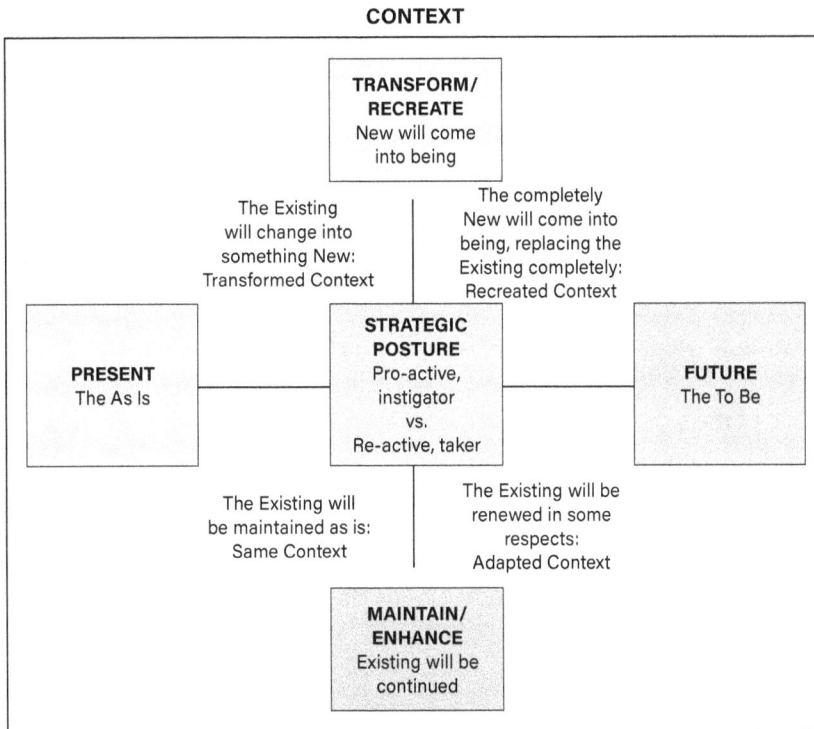

Figure 3.1: Strategic Contextual Postures and Engagement Attitudes

The choice of a specific Contextual Attitude is a function of the Strategic Contextual Posture adopted by an organisation's leadership: a Reactive taker of change vs. a Proactive instigator of change regarding the context (given in the middle block of Figure 3.1). In the first instance, the organisation is a follower of events in the context, and merely adapts to contextual shifts, i.e., Maintain/Enhance. This is mostly Present-directed with an extrapolation into the Future. In the latter case, the organisation takes the lead as a source of the contextual changes and shifts, i.e., Transform/Recreate. This is mostly Future-directed, even in dealing with the Present. The choice of a Contextual Engagement Attitude, with its accompanying Strategic Contextual Posture, frames how leadership would perceive, interpret, and act upon the contextual challenges, demands and requirements faced by the organisation.

Genuine strategic People Excellence assumes that the organisation's leadership has chosen a Strategic Contextual Engagement Attitude that is predominantly a Transform/Recreate Frame from a Future perspective, leveraged from a Strategic Contextual Posture of being a Proactive instigator of change. This Strategic Contextual Posture and Engagement Attitude appear to be the most appropriate vantage point from which to view the emerging new order to craft a contextual-fit, People Excellence Specification.

You can now do a Reflective Assessment: Strategic Contextual Posture and Engagement Attitude (Work Sheet 1 in the Work Book), if you wish to do so.

THE UNDERLYING, BASIC DYNAMICS OF THE EMERGING NEW ORDER

A fundamental, radical transformation is occurring in the underlying basic dynamics of the world as we know it presently. This transformation represents an emerging new order that is reshaping the current world in its totality and essential nature. The very fabric of the current world is being rewoven into a fundamentally new, dynamic tapestry.

Figure 3.2 depicts the basic, underlying dynamics of the emerging new order, using the words 'Order' and 'Chaos' as acronyms.

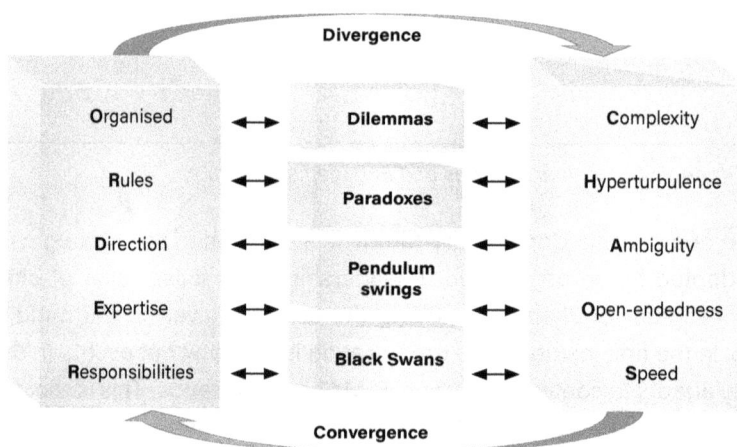

	Divergence	
Organised	↔ Dilemmas ↔	Complexity
Rules	↔ Paradoxes ↔	Hyperturbulence
Direction	↔ Pendulum swings ↔	Ambiguity
Expertise	↔ Black Swans ↔	Open-endedness
Responsibilities	↔	Speed
	Convergence	

Figure 3.2: The constant oscillation between Order and Chaos in the emerging, new order

According to Figure 3.2, this dynamic is one of continuous, rapidly accelerating oscillations, and progressively widening gap of the unfolding, future Divergence and Convergence between Order (e.g., **O**rganised) and Chaos (e.g., **C**omplexity), with the resultant challenges faced by organisations regarding to this oscillation (e.g., Dilemmas). We are living in the Chaordic Age, which necessitates a chaordic response and intense dialogue by organisations regarding their Purpose relative to the context in which they wish to operate.[5]

Organisations are facing a higher frequency of Dilemmas (e.g., Do we compete and/or co-operate?); Paradoxes (e.g., Do we focus on the present *and* the future simultaneously? Do we need to be proactive *and* reactive? Do we use Simplicity *and* Complexity as vantage points?)[6]; Pendulum swings (e.g., When do our strengths invert to become weaknesses – the Icarus Paradox?)[7]; and Black Swans (e.g., How do we become crisis-proof and able to bounce back effectively when a crisis like Covid-19 hits us?).[8] All of the above occur against the backdrop of the accelerating oscillation between Order and Chaos through a progressively widening Divergence and Convergence.

The world is transforming into Complicated Contexts of Unknown Knowns to Complex Contexts of Unknown Unknowns, and even Chaotic Contexts of Unknowables. It is shifting from the Domain of Best Practice through the Domain of Experts, to the Domains of Emergence and Rapid Response, towards Confusion.[9] This is the Age of Continuous Discontinuities. All in all, organisations are facing, and increasingly will face, a higher frequency of more far-ranging and intricate wicked challenges, issues and problems, making the world a riskier place to operate in.[10]

The above described underlying basic dynamics of the emerging new order sets at least the following People Excellence Requirements: agility, resilience, flexibility, responsiveness, self-reliance, and the ability to make sense of and give meaning to dualities, polarities and confusion. People have to be high on the psychosocial capitals of optimism, hope, perseverance, and courage.

MAJOR FORCES OF CHANGE SHAPING THE EMERGING NEW ORDER

The above discussed basic underlying dynamics of the emerging new order are infused by at least five major reciprocally interacting, snowballing Forces of Change, which have significant implications for organisations going into the future.[11] These Forces are graphically illustrated in Figure 3.3.

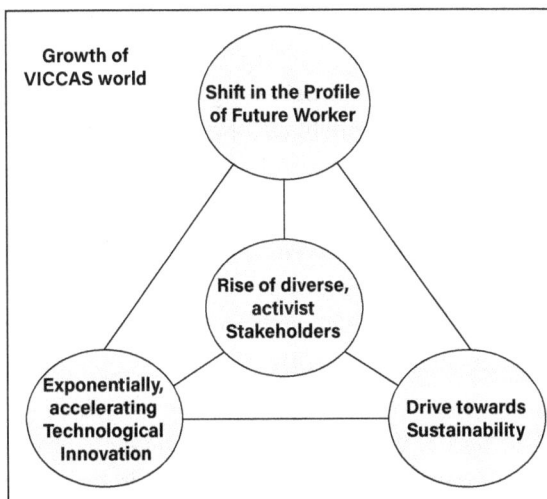

Figure 3.3: Forces of Change shaping the emerging, new order

Each of the five Forces of Change, depicted in Figure 3.3, are discussed next.

Growth of the VICCAS World

Qualitatively, the overall context can be characterised as the VICCAS (an extension of VUCA) world of increasing **V**ariety, **I**nterdependency, **C**omplexity, **C**hange, **A**mbiguity, and **S**eamlessness (i.e., boundaryless).[12] Everything and everyone are immersed in, and infused by, this world. Various degrees and permutations of these features exist over different contexts that change over time. Organisations continually have to sense, assess, and monitor VICCAS in their operating arenas, requiring high agility.[13]

The *Force of Change: Growth of the VICCAS World* sets at least the following People Excellence Requirements: having a global mindset; having the ability to work across boundaries; interconnecting, collaborating and networking constantly; being risk-seeking and -tolerant; continuously re-inventing oneself and one's ways of doing things; as well as ongoing experimenting and learning.[14]

Exponentially accelerating Technological Innovation

Exponentially accelerating technological innovation can be encapsulated in the term 'Fourth Industrial Revolution', characterised by the acronym, DIVAS:[15]

- *Digitisation*: making everything and anything computer readable and processable anywhere (e.g., digital records of everything such as voice and facial recognition; biometrics; block chain; cybercurrency).

- *Interconnectivity*: everyone/everything talking to everyone/everything (e.g., the worldwide web; social media; smart phones; the Internet of Things; cloud computing; virtual collaboration platforms like Skype and Zoom; the merging of disciplines like info-tech, bio-tech and nano-tech into one).

- *Virtualisation*: being present and delivering in cyberspace on an ongoing basis anything, anywhere, anytime, anyhow, for anyone, seamlessly merging physical and virtual reality into one, i.e., the "phygital" reality[16] (e.g., augmented reality; streaming of entertainment; virtual equipment as a parallel, digital equivalent of their physical counterparts).

- *Automation*: performing a process or practice, and taking decisions and actions, through technological means with no/minimal human mediation (e.g., robotics, 3D printing, Artificial Intelligence (AI)).

- *Smart*: generating data from everything/anyone, affecting machine learning through feedback, and/or turning data into intelligence through decision-making algorithms to take focused, automated, real time, in time, decision-making, and predictive decisions and actions (e.g., AI, machine learning, decision-making algorithms, cloud).

Table 3.1 gives examples of DIVAS ways of working with the overall, expected benefits.[17][18]

Table 3.1: Examples of DIVAS ways of working with the overall, expected benefits

---

Doing the work

❑ Complementary humans-machines working together, supplementing each other with knowledge, expertise and skills. Division of work: humans defining problems/desired outcomes; machines helping find, but mainly producing solutions; and humans verifying the acceptability of the delivered solutions in satisfying needs.

❑ Algorithmatised (=automated) routine tasks – building 'routine smartness' in operations, enabling workers to focus on higher level, more meaningful tasks (='algocratic orchestration').

❑ Digitised virtualisation (=augmented reality) of end-to-end work processes with associated data/intelligence in real time, allowing real time doing, monitoring, tracking, and intervention, being spacetime location free.

❑ More reliably deliver, control, predict, monitor, and track processes than humans, also removing the need for detailed governance as an oversight process.

❑ Real time, in time, flexible product/service innovation and continuous improvement at an ever accelerating speed within shortened innovation cycles.

❑ Converting expert judgement and knowledge work done by professionals into decision-making algorithms, either automated or appli-fied for use by para-professionals.

Enabling the work

❑ Intelligence-informed, faster, real time communication, problem-solving and decision-making. Also real time validated, predictive, 'what if', proactive decision-making.

❑ Intelligently automate planning, co-ordination, scheduling and interactions: who is to meet, when, where and why (='algocratic orchestration').

❑ Real time, in time, intelligence-rich work setting, enabling and empowering people to act in a smart way.

❑ Appli-fied, self-help and connectivity on a smartphone.

❑ Appli-fied interactions: social media.

❑ Just-in-time, real time training and development as and when needed.

Organising the work

❑ Fluid, autonomous, self-organising by role incumbents and teams as demanded by changing customer and work requirements.

❑ Virtualised, distributed (or shared) leadership.

❑ Power shift from those with authority to those with expertise and relationships.

❑ Real time, agile, self-designing networking, replacing hierarchy with fewer organisational levels – flatter organisation.

Working together

❏ More equalised, participative relationships, both vertically (i.e., hierarchically) and horizontally (i.e., laterally).

❏ Wide, boundaryless, cross-functional and multi-disciplinary collaboration in all directions – inside and outside of the organisation – virtually enabled and working in real time together all the time, unconstrained by spacetime boundaries.

Interacting with stakeholders

❏ Boundaryless, real time stakeholder involvement.

❏ Personalised customisation, based on 360 degree customer insights in real time, all the time.

❏ Real time, in time stakeholder intelligence with respect to, for example, clients, suppliers, regulators and communities.

❏ Provision of real time intelligence to clients to make them increasingly 'smart' in using products/services.

❏ Crowdsourcing – internally and externally – of ideas, opportunities, product/service enhancements, resources, funding.

OVERALL EXPECTED BENEFITS

Faster; better; different; new; cheaper; lower risks; fewer errors; greater predictability; and ongoing, re-imagined and re-invented stakeholder experiences.

The speed of exponentially accelerating technological innovation has created a significant gap between the current capabilities of people and the rapidly evolving/re-invented requirements of their work roles. The people with the needed capabilities may not even exist in the market. Organisations will thus have to develop their own people in-house. In many instances head hunting will be a 'no-go', or have a low probability of success.[19] A number of trends, explicated below, underscore these points.

A 2016 McKinsey report predicts that 800 million workers could be displaced in 42 countries, or a third of the global workforce, because of the Fourth Industrial Revolution. It is estimated that between 10% to 49% of all jobs globally have a high likelihood of disappearing over the next 10 years plus.[20][21] Further, it is estimated that 60% of all occupations have 30% of tasks that can be automated.[22][23] The 'human' share of labour hours will decline from 71% to 58% by 2022 for today's known tasks. At the same time, newly emerging tasks will create new work for people.[24]

The World Economic Forum estimates that 42% of the skills required from the global workforce will change between 2018 and 2022. By 2022, no less than 54% of all employees will require significant reskilling and upskilling.[25] In January 2020, the

World Economic Forum warned that the world is facing a reskilling emergency. It estimated that more than one billion people would have to be reskilled by 2030.[26]

The *Force of Change: Exponentially accelerating Technological Innovation* sets at the least the following People Excellence Requirements:

(i)   The challenge of virtuous, optimised people-technology integration in order to ensure human dignity and well-being; stewardship (=care for the assets entrusted to the organisation); and sustainability (=leaving the world a better place for upcoming generations).[27]

(ii) A reconfigured portfolio of people capabilities, weighted differently for the worker of the future. 'Soft' capabilities will grow in demand, while 'hard' capabilities like professional/technical competencies will be accepted as givens. The higher level soft capabilities which are likely to be in demand will be capabilities such as critical thinking, inquisitiveness, imagination, innovative thinking/acting, creativity, systemic/holistic thinking, paradigm/mindset questioning, complex problem-solving, collaboration/teaming, inclusivity, empathy, learning, resilience, agility, people management skills, and a service orientation.[28]

(iii) The rapid (re)building of existing and new people capabilities needed by the 4th Industrial Revolution.

(vi) The intensification of the war for talent, moving beyond merely attracting the desired people to a far greater emphasis on engaging, growing, and retaining attracted people.

(iv) Participative, people-centric leadership.

Shift in the Profile of the Future Worker

Triggered by the above Forces of the VICCAS world and accelerating Technological Innovation, the further expanding growth in the escalating dominance of Intangible Assets relative to Tangible Assets, increasing to more than the currently estimated 85% alluded to in Chapter 1. Concurrently, people's share of about 70% plus of Intangible Assets will become even greater because of the the growing need for people's creativity, innovation, (soft) expertise, knowledge, skills, and experience. Going into the future, people will become even more critical value unlockers of the potential contained in the assets of their organisations, by means of which sustainable wealth is to be created for more discerning, demanding customers.

Given the increasingly critical role of people, careful attention must be paid to the profile of the worker of the future – given in Table 3.2 – who organisations will approach with the intention of attracting, performing, growing and retaining.[29]

Table 3.2: High level profile of the worker of the future

HIGH LEVEL PROFILE OF THE WORKER OF THE FUTURE
• Growing proportion of independents/freelancers (=nomad or gig workers) with certain specialist knowledge, expertise and experience, contracting individually with organisations to deliver/contribute to their products/services within definitive timeframes. Increasingly, even full time employees will have the same mindset, values and attitudes of independents/freelancers. The shift will be from 'employees' to 'associates', 'partners' and 'collaborators'. • Much more diverse in terms of make-up, however profiled, for example in terms of generations (up to at least four, in some cases even five, generations in the work setting), gender, ethnicity, nationalities, and values. The expectation is for all-embracing inclusivity. This diversity moderates the intensity, combination, and weighting of all of the below features. • More demanding in terms of what they expect from organisations: reputable, high profile organisations with credible, purpose-driven, influenceable leadership; and work settings that are challenging, stimulating, meaningful, purposeful, collaborative, team-based, and offer ongoing learning and development opportunities. Employment will be taken up at people's own behest at a time and place decided by them, built around their needs and aspirations relative to where they are in their self-navigated careers. • Seeking out work settings that will allow them to actualise their potential and apply their knowledge, skills, and experience fully and in innovative ways to remain employable. • Expectation to work in an information/intelligence rich setting, preferably self-generated, and being highly technology enabled. • Desire to be judged by what they can contribute and the results they (can) produce, and not by the hours they spend at work and/or the number of activities they perform within a given period of work time. • To be enabled and empowered as leaders in their own right, in their own spaces. • Greater demand for optimal work/life integration because the boundaries between life and work have dissipated completely because of virtual connectivity, giving them the capability to work anywhere, anytime, anyhow, with anyone, on anything. • The question, "What is in it for me?", will feature much more strongly on their personal radar screens, with the person putting him/herself at the centre of his/her self-crafted and navigated, individualised work role, career and World of Work. More frequent job, organisational and career changes. • Engagement and identification with an organisation will occur on terms and objectives set by the individual within shorter time frames of commitment to any given cause, issue and/or organisation.

- Care for the total well-being of a person, fuelled by the desire to be engaged as total beings in terms of their hearts, minds, souls and spirits, and addressing all their basic needs.

- Much more inner-directed, assertive, calculative, independent, mobile, and more aggressively seeking meaning and purpose (='Why, and to what end am I doing this?') regarding the work and organisations they engage with.

The *Force of Change: Escalating Dominance of Intangible Assets*, with in particular the growing, critical importance of people, sets at least the following People Excellence Requirements: (i) creating distinct, compelling, fulfilling, memorable employee experiences; (ii) which address the whole person – body, mind, soul and spirit; and (iii) satisfy the complete range of a person's basic needs (to be discussed later); (iv) being led by people-centric, shared, purpose-driven leadership; and (v) the opportunity and autonomy given for self-leadership. All of these must be viewed within the context of different employment and work relationships between organisations and their people, fuelled by especially the first two Forces of Change, namely the growth in the VICCAS world, and the exponentially accelerating DIVAS Technological Innovation.

Drive towards Sustainability

The growing adoption, sometimes enforced, by organisations, of the core purpose of sustainability through stewardship: leaving the world a better place for current and upcoming generations, concurrently caring for the assets entrusted and used by an organisation on behalf of, and for, the common good. I.e., organisations serving humanity and not only themselves in a self-centred and -promoting manner.[30]

From an organisational (or institutional) vantage point, sustainability can be expressed in five interdependent Ps (an extension of the triple bottom line of profit-people-planet)[31]:

- *Productivity* – the effective and efficient use of resources.
- *Prosperity* – wealth creation by all, fairly and equitably distributed to all.
- *People* – engendering the well-being of, and care for, people such that they become 'better' and more fulfilled.
- *Peace* – promoting harmony and co-operation between and within stakeholders (i.e., shareowners, employees, suppliers, clients, communities, and society at large) by building healthy, constructive interactions.
- *Planet* – restoring and ensuring the ecological well-being of the universe and the environmental footprint of the organisation.

Sustainability regarding the above 5 Ps can be described in terms of four actions: (i) *recover* what has been destroyed/lost; (ii) *renew* what exists; (iii) *restore* the existing to the necessary level/state; and (iv) *retain* the existing at the desired level/state.[32]

The *Force of Change: Growing Sustainability Drive* sets at least the People Excellence Requirement of purpose-driven, values-based people who are directed and guided by the core value orientation of sustainability through stewardship. Their orientation is: "We can make the world a better place for all, now and in the future". They are people who are high on the psychosocial capitals of optimism, hope, perseverance and courage.

The rise of diverse, activist Stakeholders

Within the centre of the triangle of the above three forces of change, immersed in the VICCAS world, the organisation is enmeshed in an ever-extending, increasingly diverse range of activist stakeholders with shifting interests, demands and expectations, most frequently in conflict, demanding trade-offs. They group around issues, generations and/or interests. At a minimum, activist stakeholders demand socially responsible organisations that are publicly accountable to society.

Stakeholders' increasingly strident voices are significantly amplified by social media, enabling their rapid mobilisation, nationally and globally. Concurrently, there is growing frequency of the (deliberate, targeted) spread of misinformation, fake news, and post-truths.[33]

The *Force of Change: Diverse, Demanding Stakeholders* sets at least the following People Excellence Requirements: (i) people having an embeddedness perspective – the organisation and its context form an inseparable, seamless, holographic, dynamic whole, an ecosystem; (ii) adopting an outside-in, service vantage point – stakeholders with their interests, demands, expectations and needs are the depature point[34]; and (iii) engaging with stakeholders in terms of an inside-in vantage point from a firmly entrenced, visible and clearly articulated Identity position (=who and what I am, stand for and aspire to), serving as a secure reference point in the VICCAS world described above.

QUALITIES INFUSING THE MAJOR FORCES OF CHANGE

Infusing the above Forces of Change affecting the World of Work, and recursively feeding back into them, is the *'Maths' of the emerging new order*: Intelligently respond twice as fast, deliver twice as much, at twice the speed, at half the cost, within half the accepted product/service life span, and doing all of the aforesaid on a continuous, sustainable basis: everywhere, anytime, anyone, anyhow, anything.[35] This 'Maths' functions according to the following *Competitive Equation*: The continuous delivery of innovative, customised, high quality products/services, simultaneously bringing costs down and getting products/services more quickly to markets, from conception to commercialisation.[36]

The above discussed Maths and Competitive Equation invoke the consequential, merciless *imperative of relentless, ongoing, disruptive (even destructive) innovation* as THE critical strategic, renewal success factor for organisations aspiring to remain future-ready and -fit.[37][38] Not merely to survive, but to thrive going into the future. This implies a fierce entre- and intrapreneurial spirit pervading organisations if they wish to remain viable.[39][40] In turn, the relentless, ongoing disruptive innovation requires *continuous, deep relearning, learning, and unlearning by all.*[41]

The *Qualities infusing the Forces of Change* set at least the following People Requirements: people who think critically; are inquisitive; have strong, vivid imaginations; demonstrate innovative and creative thinking/acting; are agile, resilient, flexible, responsive, self-reliant, and self-directed; and have a passion for continuous learning.[42]

HIGH LEVEL PEOPLE EXCELLENCE SPECIFICATION FOR THE EMERGING NEW ORDER

In Chapter 1, People Excellence was described in general as achieving exceedingly well with the people of the organisation: thriving people truly unlocking real, amazing value which creates worthy, lasting wealth for all of its delighted stakeholders, consistently and continuously, in this way ensuring a high likelihood of a viable organisation. People Excellence means an organisation is THE shining star with respect to its people.

In this chapter, it was argued that People Excellence is ultimately achieved when a good fit exists externally between the organisation's context in terms of its People Requirements, and the content awarded by the organisation internally to the Excellence Domains with their respective Elements. This poses the question: Given a certain context, what must the overarching People Excellence Specification for the organisation look like in terms of the content to be awarded to the Excellence Domains with their respective Elements?

The context considered must be strategically conceived from the future-into-the-present: Given the organisation's strategic horizon, e.g., 5 to 10 years out, what will the future context be like, and what must the future-referenced People Excellence Specification be like to enable the organisation to actualise its desired, future state?

The People Excellence Specification, befitting the future-referenced context, provides a departure point for what People Excellence as a desired, internal end-state in the final instance, must look like for the organisation concerned.

The People Excellence Specification is the operationalisation of People Excellence when an organisation is achieving exceedingly well with its people – its 'People Excellence Vision' so to speak – whilst befitting the People Requirements of the organisation's context. This is the concretisation of the above description of People Excellence in general relative to the People Requirements of the organisation's context: Our people are unlocking real, amazing value and creating worthy, lasting wealth, consistently and continuously, to the delight of all stakeholders of the organisation. This is an 'outside-in', 'business by design' approach to the generation of a People Excellence Specification.[43] Figure 3.4 gives a graphic summary of the above discussion.

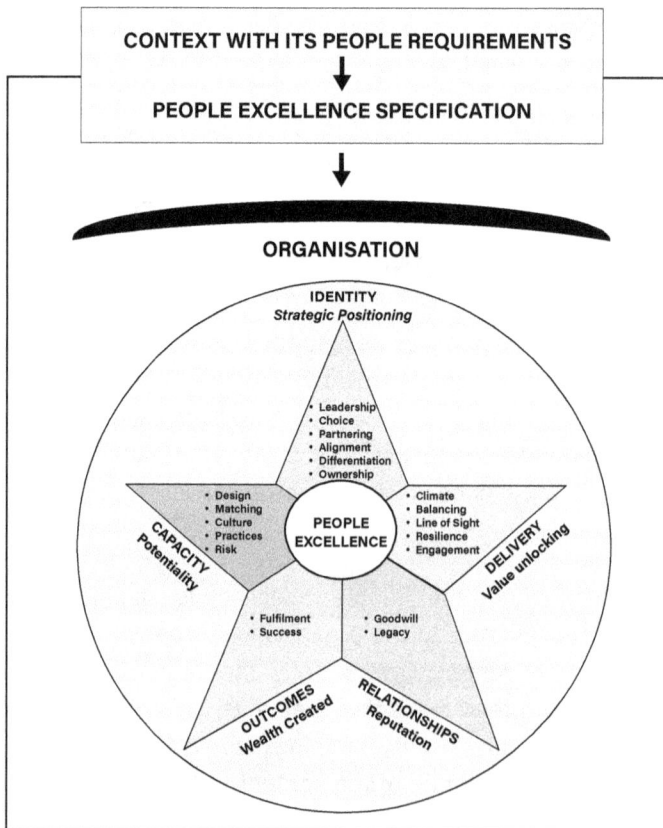

Figure 3.3: Translating the People Requirements of the organisation's Context into a People Excellence Specification for the organisation's People Excellence Star

The People Requirements of the emerging new order were identified in the above discussion of the underlying basic dynamics of the emerging new order; the substantive, major Forces of Change shaping this order; and the Qualities infusing the Forces of Change. Figure 3.5 provides a summarised view of the future-expected People Requirements of this order.

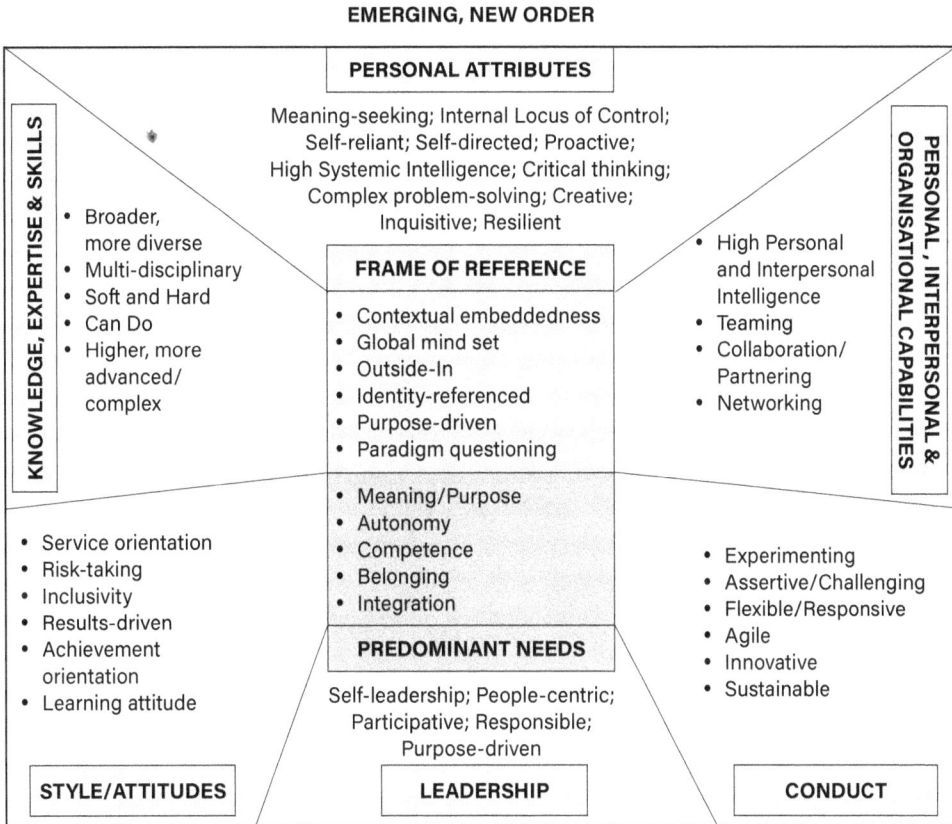

EMERGING, NEW ORDER

PERSONAL ATTRIBUTES

Meaning-seeking; Internal Locus of Control;
Self-reliant; Self-directed; Proactive;
High Systemic Intelligence; Critical thinking;
Complex problem-solving; Creative;
Inquisitive; Resilient

KNOWLEDGE, EXPERTISE & SKILLS

- Broader, more diverse
- Multi-disciplinary
- Soft and Hard
- Can Do
- Higher, more advanced/ complex

FRAME OF REFERENCE

- Contextual embeddedness
- Global mind set
- Outside-In
- Identity-referenced
- Purpose-driven
- Paradigm questioning

PERSONAL, INTERPERSONAL & ORGANISATIONAL CAPABILITIES

- High Personal and Interpersonal Intelligence
- Teaming
- Collaboration/ Partnering
- Networking

- Meaning/Purpose
- Autonomy
- Competence
- Belonging
- Integration

- Service orientation
- Risk-taking
- Inclusivity
- Results-driven
- Achievement orientation
- Learning attitude

- Experimenting
- Assertive/Challenging
- Flexible/Responsive
- Agile
- Innovative
- Sustainable

PREDOMINANT NEEDS

Self-leadership; People-centric;
Participative; Responsible;
Purpose-driven

STYLE/ATTITUDES   **LEADERSHIP**   **CONDUCT**

Figure 3.4: Overall view of future-expected People Requirements

It is proposed that the above-described emerging new order faced by organisations, at present and going into the future, with its consequential People Requirements as per Figure 34, necessitates the following general People Excellence Specification. This Specification serves as a normative reference point to People Excellence as a future-directed, desired end-state in the organisation. However, it is to be customised to match the Identity of the organisation concerned (to be discussed under Excellence Domain 1: Identity) relative to its chosen operating arena:

> *Highly enabled, empowered and resilient people, who strongly identify with and feel valued by the organisation, and are productively and innovatively engaging collaboratively through personally purposeful and meaningful ways, to viably and sustainably create inimitable, delightful experiences for stakeholders.*

Explanations of some of the key terms included in the above People Excellence Specification are required:

- *Enabled:* People have the wherewithal to do the work in terms of their personal capabilities and resources.
- *Empowered:* People have the freedom to act (=the autonomy) in their areas of accountability/responsibility relative to stakeholders.
- *Agile:* The nimbleness to move at speed in a flexible, responsive way matched to the rate of change.
- *Innovatively:* Ongoing, zero-based, renewal and re-invention.
- *Collaboratively:* Working with other parties in networking, partnering ways, both inside and outside the organisation.
- *Viably:* The assured, continued existence of the organisation.
- *Sustainably:* Serving the common good by leaving the world a better place for upcoming generations.

The People Excellence Specification spells out how people in the organisation must act to thrive in the emerging new order as described above, in this way contributing to making the organisation successful and viable in the present and future. The necessary conditions – as informed by the People Excellence Dimensions and Elements – must now be set up within an organisation for its people to be able to act in this way. The synergistic fusion sought is a good Context-Organisation-People fit.

An aside thought to entertain seriously, is that the People Excellence Specification can be turned into the Vision of the People Function of the organisation if the Function is to act as the organisation's people custodians (see Excellence Question 3: Partnering).

The above People Excellence Specification as desired end state – a proposed version of the organisation's People Excellence Vision, derived from the People Requirements posed by the emerging new order – will be used in subsequent chapters as the normative reference point in giving content to the People Excellence Domains with their Elements.

You can now do a Reflective Assessment: People Excellence Specification (Work Sheet 2 in the Work Book) if you wish to do so.

PEOPLE EXCELLENCE STAR

IDENTITY: STRATEGIC POSITIONING

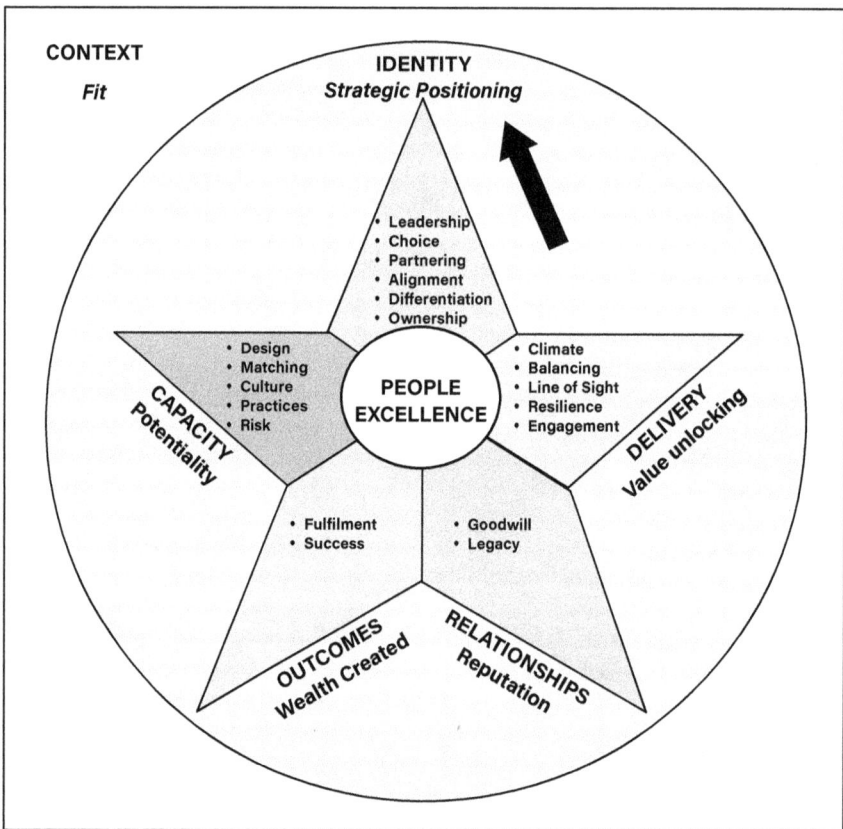

CONTEXT

Fit

IDENTITY
Strategic Positioning

- Leadership
- Choice
- Partnering
- Alignment
- Differentiation
- Ownership

- Design
- Matching
- Culture
- Practices
- Risk

CAPACITY
Potentiality

PEOPLE
EXCELLENCE

- Climate
- Balancing
- Line of Sight
- Resilience
- Engagement

DELIVERY
Value unlocking

- Fulfilment
- Success

- Goodwill
- Legacy

OUTCOMES
Wealth Created

RELATIONSHIPS
Reputation

CHAPTER 4

PEOPLE EXCELLENCE DOMAIN 1 – IDENTITY: STRATEGIC POSITIONING

"Excellence is to do a common thing in an uncommon way." (Booker T. Washington)

"If you deliver excellence right now, that gives you the best shot at the best future you've got coming." (Robert Forster)

"Pursue excellence and success will follow." (Rancho)

Within the parameters set by a contextually derived, People Excellence Specification, the Departure Point and Foundation for People Excellence is to be found in the *Excellence Domain 1: Identity*, with its thrust of *Strategic Positioning*. This Excellence Domain sets the direction for, forms the anchor to, and leverages, all of the other Excellence Domains. It deals with the overarching Excellence Question: Has the strategic contribution of people in the viable, future success of the organisation been explicitly deliberated, chosen, and implemented? This Domain sets the true north for People Excellence in the organisation within its operating arena, as reflected in its placement in the People Excellence Star (see on the opposite page).

As also illustrated in the People Excellence Star on the opposite page, Excellence Dimension 1: Identity is made up of six interdependent Excellence Elements: *Leadership, Choice, Partnering, Alignment, Differentiation,* and *Ownership.* Each Element is discussed in turn, in the order listed. The chapter concludes by telling the integrated People Excellence story of the synergistic fusion to be generated by this Domain.

However, before discussing the different Excellence Elements making up this Domain, the concept of 'Organisational Identity' must first be explicated. It is posited that the departure point of, and foundation for, People Excellence in the organisation is a clearly defined, distinct and strongly entrenched Organisational Identity.[1] Identity plays this role because it encompasses the 'Why' of the organisation which links it to society, in particular through its Purpose (see below). Organisational Identity represents the fulcrum of the spiritual capital of the organisation.[2] It manifests what kind of socially responsible citizen the organisation aspires to be. Organisational Identity finds its concrete expression in its espoused and experienced Organisational Image and Reputation amongst its stakeholders (discussed further under Excellence Dimension 5: Relationships).

It has been found that high performing organisations are twice as likely as their peers to be more effective at defining an inspirational Organisational Purpose that highly engages their people.[3] Organisations with a strong sense of Purpose show higher customer satisfaction; an increase in productivity and profitability; and lower staff turnover.[4]

Organisational Identity (*we*, *us* and *them*) relates to the understanding amongst stakeholders of who and what the organisation is; what it stands for and does; where it belongs; and what it aspires to: *How do we see ourselves? How are we seen? How do we wish to be seen?*[5] The most widely accepted defining features of Organisational Identity find their expression in the organisation's core, distinctive, differentiating, and enduring attributes.[6] In the emerging new order with its hyper-turbulence and hyper-fluidity, Organisational Identity – in particular, Purpose (see below) – provides a fixed reference point and secure anchor for an organisation, also with respect to People Excellence.[7] Hence, its mission-critical strategic importance. The People Excellence Specification gives an external, and Organisational Identity an internal, reference point to the organisation regarding People Excellence within its operating arena.

The constituent, reciprocally interdependent elements of Organisational Identity are depicted in Figure 4.1.[8][9] In a clearly defined, distinct, and strongly entrenched Organisational Identity, all the elements depicted in Figure 4.1 are congruent and holographically referenced (=one element reflects, and in turn is reflective of, all of the other elements).[10]

IDENTITY

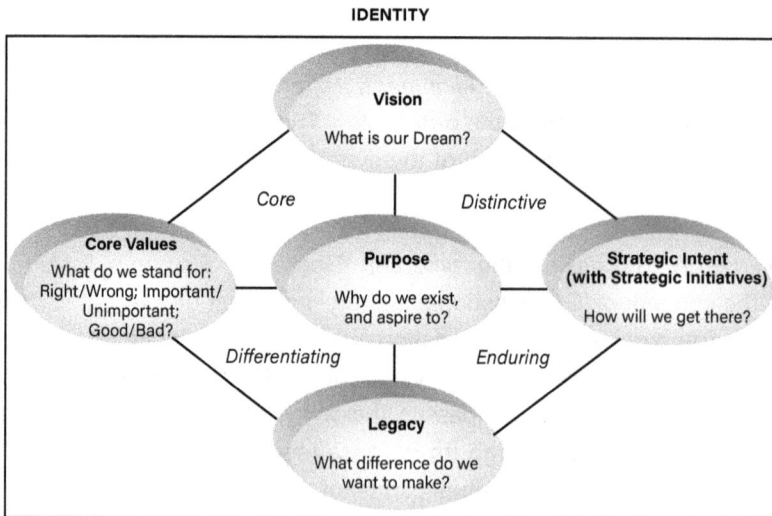

Figure 4.1: Constituent elements of Organisational Identity

Exercising the right choices regarding the Organisational Identity directly affects its continued viability.[11] Organisational Identity sets the parameters for the desired

People Excellence within the organisation as a socially responsible citizen, relative to its operating arena. Growing flourishing, thriving and fulfilled people – i.e., People Excellence – will capacitate the organisation to be viable.

In the unfolding discussion of People Excellence going forward, it will be assumed that the organisation has adopted an appropriate Identity. In the final instance, such an Identity will be one that gives the organisation credibility and legitimacy in the eyes of its stakeholders. When in the discussion an element of Identity is referred to, e.g., Strategic Intent, the total Identity of the organisation will be assumed by implication, given the holographic nature of Organisational Identity.

Next, the respective Excellence Elements making up this Excellence Domain, starting with Leadership, will be discussed.

PEOPLE EXCELLENCE
QUESTION 1: LEADERSHIP

Is the right leadership manifested in the organisation?

Excellent leadership is probably the most important (or significant) differentiator between more or less successful organisations.[12] Such leadership takes an organisation from good to great[13], and from Low to High Commitment/High Involvement/High Performance.[14] As the saying goes: People join organisations; they stay because of the leadership.[15] Excellent leadership can make anything between a 15% and 40% difference in an organisation's performance, depending on the context in which the leadership is demonstrated.[16][17]

The People Excellence Specification sets the overarching parameters for the type of leadership necessary to make People Excellence a reality in the organisation. This is leadership for whom it is natural to set up and maintain organisational conditions under which people can be, and are, highly enabled, empowered and energised, i.e., people-centric leadership.[18] People-centric leadership satisfies the basic psychological needs of followers (to be discussed under Excellence Question 2: Choice), making them thrive and feel fulfilled through being highly engaged. Leadership able to do this is seen – in a reciprocal manner – even more positively by followers.[19]

The quality of answers given to the subsequent People Excellence questions making up this Excellence Domain is a direct function of putting the right leadership in place from the word 'Go', because leadership must create the conditions for People Excellence. Even more so, Leader Excellence is the golden thread running through the entire People Excellence Star in its entirety. It permeates the total Star into its very core.

In determining the right leadership to bring People Excellence about in the organisation, four excellence themes will be discussed regarding Leadership Excellence, assuming people-centric leadership as a departure point: Shared leadership; choosing the appropriate Leadership Stance; a productive and healthy Leadership Process; and the right Leadership Qualities.

Shared leadership[20]

The emerging new order elucidated in Chapter 3 has resulted, inter alia, in the growing need for organisations to move:

- *from* THE leader – the sole, supposedly all-knowing and all-powerful individual at the top of the organisation exercising leadership at his/her (sole) discretion;
- *to* SHARED (or distributed) leadership – concurrent, interdependent leadership at all organisational levels and functions – to effectively deal with the more demanding, constantly changing, and radically different context, both internally and externally to the organisation.

Amongst other things, shared leadership implies viewing the collective of leaders in an organisation as a potential community of practice – a Leadership Community. 'Potential', because a community of practice – in this case a Leadership Community – has to be deliberately thought through, set up, and maintained. Viewing the collective of leaders in an organisation as a Leadership Community goes beyond seeing the organisational hierarchy and function as the typical way of getting things done in the organisation. However, a Leadership Community does not replace, but rather complements, the hierarchy and function by addressing *organisation-wide* challenges, issues and problems – in this case, People Excellence – spanning across hierarchy and function in order to jointly address the wicked challenges, demands and requirements of the emerging new order.

The shift from individual to shared leadership implies that People Excellence becomes a *collective* leadership agenda item for the organisation as a whole. The Leadership Community must collectively bring about People Excellence across the total organisation. It is a shared accountability and responsibility. In the ensuing discussion, People Excellence will be explicated from a shared leadership vantage point. For brevity's sake, only the term 'leadership' will be used in further discussions, but implying 'shared' leadership throughout.

Choice of an appropriate Leadership Stance[21]

As a Vantage Point, the leadership of an organisation has to deliberately and explicitly choose a point of view regarding what leadership will be about in their organisation, and how they live it. This Vantage Point must fit the organisation in terms of the type of leadership it needs, in the present and into the future. Leadership's chosen Vantage Point finds its concrete expression in a Leadership Stance: 'What is our definition of leadership which befits our organisation?' A Leadership Stance can be equated to the Purpose of leadership.[22]

Three Basic Leadership Stances can be distinguished, which are graphically depicted in Figure 4.2:[23]

- 'How' leadership: *Transactional* leadership – operational execution.
- 'Whereto' leadership: *Transformational* leadership – the envisioning and realisation of a shared dream, guided by a set of core values as guiding principles.
- 'Why' leadership: *Transcendental* leadership – providing Purpose and Meaning by leaving a worthy, lasting Legacy behind.[24]

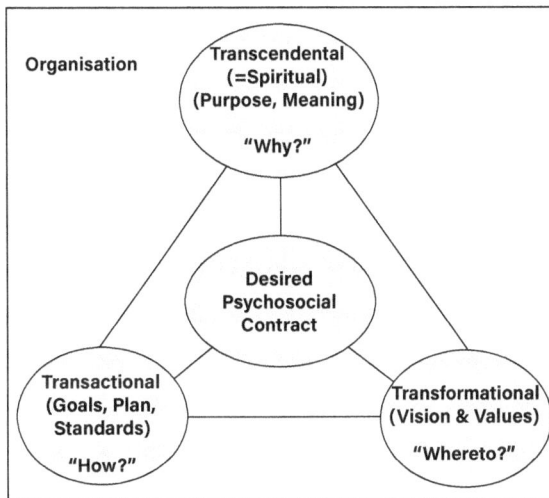

Figure 4.2: Basic Leadership Stances

Note: The concept 'Psychosocial Contract' will be discussed under the next Excellence Question

The leadership of the organisation has to craft a Leadership Stance which will be the most suitable mix of the three Basic Leadership Stances – more or less Transactional, Transformational and Transcendental – which have a goodness-of-fit with their organisation. The chosen Stance will set up the Vantage Point from which leadership will fulfil their roles in their organisation.

The specific differential weighting of the three Basic Leadership Stances to arrive at the appropriate mix for an organisation is a function of at least the following factors:

- The organisation's contextual and stakeholders' features.
- Organisational Identity.

- Where the organisation is in its life cycle, e.g., start-up or dynamic growth.
- The psychosocial contract that leadership wishes to establish with its stakeholders.

A chosen Leadership Stance also has to be weighted differently depending on the organisational level implicated. Leadership at the lower organisational levels typically have a heavier weighting of a Transactional Stance, whereas at the higher organisational levels, there is a heavier weighting of a Transcendental Stance. All three basic Stances, however, always have to be present in a chosen, overall Stance.

The chosen Leadership Stance must be translated and operationalised into a Leadership Charter (or Philosophy). The Charter contains the 'Commandments' of what is acceptable leadership in the organisation: 'With respect to leadership, this is what we stand for, believe in, aspire to, and act like.' I.e., the Charter specifies in concrete terms the organisation's beliefs, values, norms, attitudes, and conduct regarding leadership. The Charter must be lived every day by the leadership of the organisation.

Historically there have been shifts in the relative mix of the three Basic Leadership Stances, as shown in Figure 4.3. These shifts can be attributed to changes in the demands imposed by the Leadership Context. At present, the features and dynamics of the emerging new order have resulted in a higher weighting of Transformational and Transcendental Leadership Stances, especially a principled (=value-based) Transcendental Leadership Stance as 'Why' leadership.[25] A Transformation/ Transcendental Leadership Stance will be used as the normative reference point for People Excellence in the discussion going forward.

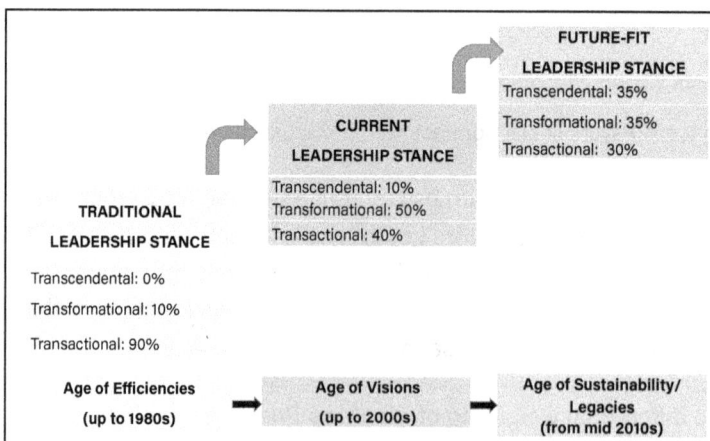

Figure 4.3: Historical shift in the relative mix of the three Basic Leadership Stances

A productive and healthy Leadership Process

From the chosen Leadership Stance as Vantage Point, leadership leads through a Leadership Process. The Leadership Process must be performed in a *productive* – it gets results, and *healthy* way – it is people-centric, making people flourish and thrive. Through a productive and healthy Leadership Process – i.e., building and maintaining high interpersonal value and capital – leadership will transform mere stakeholders (including people) into dedicated followers. I.e., engaged parties who are passionate about the desired future pursued by the organisation, as expressed in its Identity. Given the right Leadership Stance, a productive and healthy Leadership Process provides a solid dynamic platform from which to leverage People Excellence.

Through a productive and healthy Leadership Process, leadership co-conceives and co-actualises a shared, desired future with the people of the organisation who have been turned into inspired, committed, passionate, and engaged followers. Leaders who proactively take charge of their organisation's future by pursuing a shared, chosen, desired future will be architects of the future with the organisation's people, and not victims of the future.

The portfolio of seven critical actions that make up the Leadership Process – to be performed in concurrent, juggling ways, individually and severally, by leadership – are depicted in Figure 4.4.[26] This process must embrace the integrated wholeness of the person to be led – body, mind, soul and spirit – if it is to be genuinely people-centric.[27]

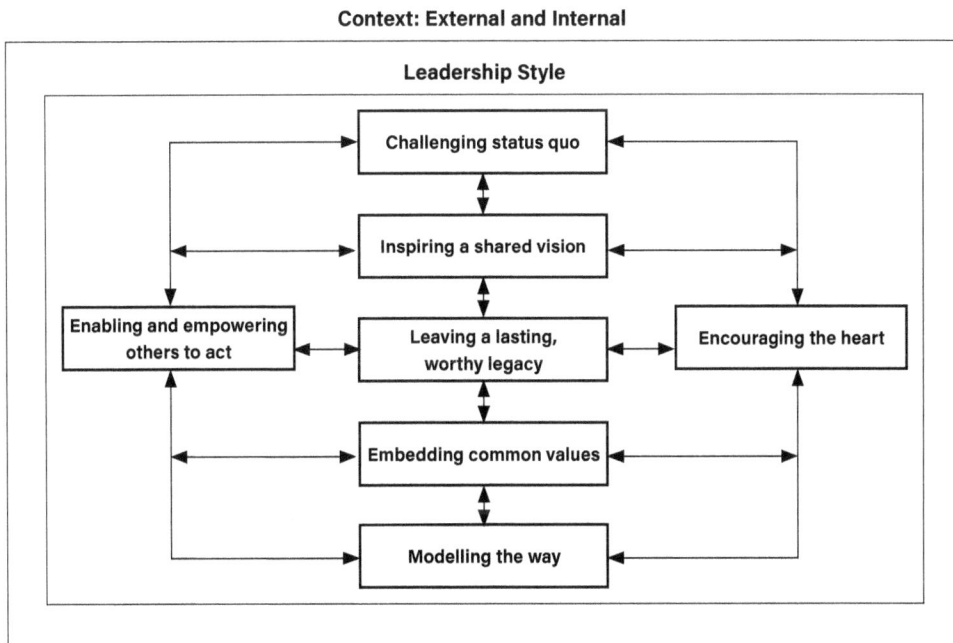

Figure 4.4: The Leadership Process embedded in a selected Leadership Style

The Leadership Process depicted in Figure 4.4 is executed through a chosen Leadership Style befitting the context and followers, premised on leadership having the required abilities for the context. The range of possible Styles is shown in Figure 4.5.[28]

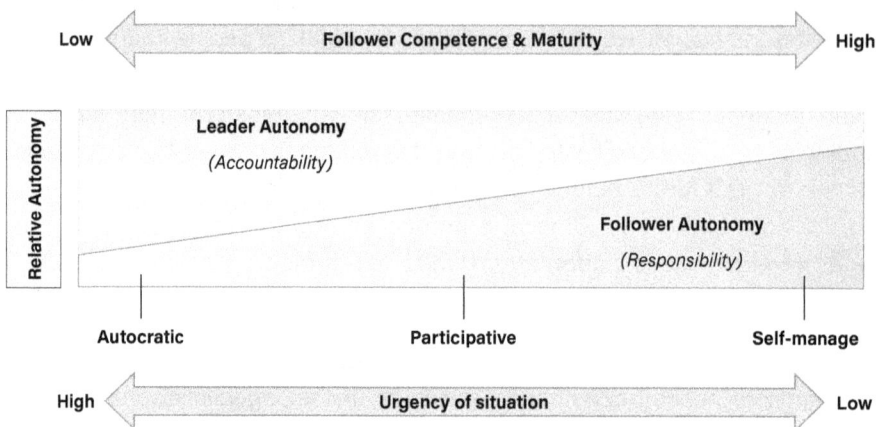

Figure 4.5: Leadership Styles

According to Figure 4.5, three Leadership Styles are possible:

- *Autocratic:* Leadership makes the decision and instructs those responsible to do the work – Tell, and also possibly Sell.

- *Participative:* Leadership asks for input from the responsible parties, considers their input, makes the decision, and instructs them (=consultative). Or, all the accountable and responsible parties jointly debate the intended action and make the decision together (=co-determine).

- *Self-manage*: The responsible party (or parties) consults upwards with leadership as the accountable party, makes the decision and informs leadership accordingly. Or, the responsible party (parties) takes the decision independently, and merely informs leadership.

In the emerging new order with its chaordic dynamic (see Chapter 3), People Excellence requires at least a Participative Leadership Style regarding the leadership's own area of accountability, and Self-management for followers' areas of accountability. This gives followers the autonomy to be agile and take speedy decisions and actions in the hyper-turbulent and hyper-fluid world they face. (This style provides the pre-condition for Excellence Question 13: Balancing that addresses the autonomy awarded to people.) The Participative Style allows leadership to draw on the expertise, skills, and experience of followers, which is essential in the emerging new order.

Necessary Leadership Qualities

A productive and healthy Leadership Process, executed through the right Leadership Style – and leveraged from the right Leadership Stance – is infused by at least the following Leadership Qualities[29], expressive of servant leadership[30]:

- *Legitimacy:* Leadership is given the 'licence' to lead.
- *Inspiration:* Bringing dedication and passion to the vision pursued by the organisation.
- *Humility:* Leading through a stewardship attitude.[31]
- *Integrity:* Acting consistently with honesty from inner convictions.
- *Ethical:* Being good, doing good, and ensuring good.
- *Authenticity:* Being truly genuine, sincere, and caring in dealing with others.

The **affirmative answer** to the People Excellence Question 1: Leadership, is: *Whilst applying a shared, predominantly Transformational/Transcendental Leadership Stance – and visibly demonstrating the Leadership Qualities of legitimacy, inspiration, humility, integrity, ethical, and authenticity – leadership enables and empowers the organisation's people through a productive, healthy Leadership Process to actualise a desired, inspiring future for the organisation for all.*

You can now do a Reflective Assessment: Leadership (Work Sheet 3 in the Work Book), Leadership, if you wish to do so.

PEOPLE EXCELLENCE QUESTION 2: CHOICE

Has a clear, deliberate Strategic People Choice been made – entrenched in the commensurate Psychosocial Contract – by the organisation, and do all 'people' thinking and actions in the organisation resonate with this Choice and Contract?

Every organisation makes a Strategic Choice – implicitly/by default or explicitly/deliberately – regarding the strategic role people must play in the success and viability of the organisation, now and into the future. Making a clear, deliberate Strategic People Choice presumes that the organisation has a clearly defined, distinct, differentiating, and strongly entrenched Organisational Identity.

Having adopted the appropriate Organisational Identity – which is core, distinctive, differentiating, and enduring – the Strategic People Choice Question can be split into two Excellence sub-themes: (i) making the right, explicit, deliberate *Strategic People Choice*; and (ii) setting up a *Psychosocial Contract*, commensurate with this Choice.

The right, deliberate Strategic People Choice

At least three basic Strategic People Choices can be distinguished:[32]

- *Choice 1:* People as a *cost* to the organisation.
- *Choice 2:* People as an *asset* (or even the most important asset) of the organisation.
- *Choice 3:* People as the *value unlockers and wealth creators* of the organisation.

Each choice has an underlying view of how people are seen by the organisation, and how they must be led and managed. Additionally, the people view is framed by a fixed or growth mindset. A *fixed mindset* centres around the belief that the abilities of people are innate, given, and cannot really be developed much, if at all, over time. A *growth mindset* is based on the belief that people's abilities are malleable, and can be significantly developed and expanded. A chosen people view, framed by a certain mindset, sets up the parameters for how later Excellence Elements will be conceived and set up.[33]

The respective Strategic People Choices entail the following:

- **Choice 1 – People as a cost to the organisation**

  In Choice 1, people are seen as an unavoidable cost to be minimised 'at all costs' by the organisation. They are merely hired hands. Employees are to be utilised – even exploited – to the one-sided, maximised benefit of the organisation with minimal people training – and yes, definitely no development – and well-being expenditure. The organisation has a short-term employment relationship with people – the shorter the better! – until they have been utilised to the fullest by the organisation for its sole benefit.

  Within a fixed mindset, people are viewed in this Choice as merely seeking the satisfaction of their physiological, existence needs. They are at most replicable cogs in a machine (=organisation), who can be substituted randomly and at will. Under this choice, people management is purely legalistic because it aims to at most satisfy the minimum acceptable level of labour law compliance in order not to land up in the labour court.

- **Choice 2 – People as an asset, or even the most important asset, of the organisation**[34]

  In terms of Choice 2, people as a resource must be acquired, utilised, traded, accounted for, and cared for like any other asset owned by the organisation. As the organisation's most important asset, however, people must receive more attention and better treatment than the other assets. People are not a cost to, but an investment made by the organisation. Within a growth mindset, people are viewed in this Choice as sophisticated brains (=the asset), seeking the satisfaction of higher order needs like competence, and maybe actualisation.

People management under this choice is about the investment in the right people in the right numbers at the right time in the right place. People are able to perform maximally as a well-cared-for resource. The emphasis of people management is on a best–in–class human resources value chain to look after this valuable asset well. Simultaneously, aggressively growing the human capital of the organisation in tandem with the other assets of the organisation. Under this choice, the growth mindset is one-sidedly controlled by leadership at their discretion: to invest or not? Organisational members have little say in the investment.[35]

- **Choice 3 – People as the value unlockers and wealth creators of the organisation**

  Choice 3 entails that *all* the people employed by the organisation are seen as genuine partners, taking co-responsibility for the longer term success of the organisation. As the only true value unlockers and wealth creators in the organisation, people are given a real stake in the organisation and share the wealth created by them in significant ways. For people to be full-blown value unlockers and wealth creators, conditions in the organisation must allow people to flourish because work is experienced as meaningful and purpose-aligned. Hence, they thrive. People are put first in all the organisation's thinking, decisions, and actions.

  In this Choice, people are seen as complex, multi-dimensional, holistic beings – depicted in the form of a cube in Figure 4.6 – composed of:

  - a *Personal Identity;*
  - progressively stacked, interdependent *Dimensions of Being/Becoming of* increasing Dimension maturity and well-being; through abilities (or competencies) (=developed potential) (or competencies); to wisdom (=the experience of how and when to use abilities); and
  - a set of six *Basic Needs.* The needs are arranged concentrically in three squares: (i) *meaning (or purpose)* and *actualisation* (inner square); (ii) *competence* and *autonomy* (middle square); and (iii) *belonging (or relatedness)* and *security* (including existence) (outer square). All of the needs are active for a person all of the time in various weightings, relative to the person's wants, circumstances and life history.[36][37]

PERSONAL IDENTITY

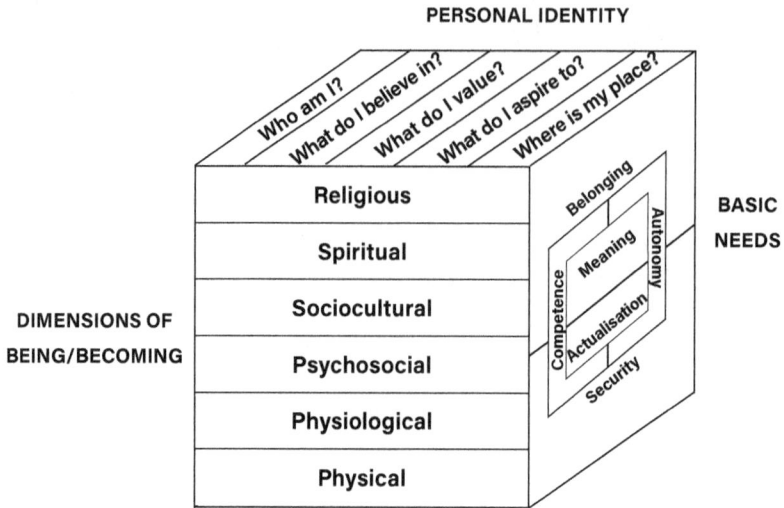

Figure 4.6: People as complex, multi-dimensional, holistic beings

To the extent that: (i) a person's Basic Needs are satisfied across her/his Dimensions of Being/Becoming, growing in maturity and well-being; (ii) within an enabling and empowering organisational setting; (iii) in turn allowing her/him to develop a distinct, integrated, authentic Personal Identity; (iv) a person will flourish, and hence thrive, because he/she will be highly engaged in his/her quest to be the best he/she can be, wants to be, and aspires to be.[38] This people view is fully embedded in a growth mindset, with the individuals' development of their potential being under a high level of personal discretion. This is in contrast to Choice 2: People as an asset, where this discretion is largely under the control of leadership: We will manage your career.

People management under this choice will focus on engendering high levels of people commitment and engagement within a high involvement/high performance work setting. It is not only about the right people in the right numbers at the right time in the right place who are able to perform, as in the case of Strategic People Choice 2. It is, additionally, and even more importantly, about people being willing to perform, wanting to perform, and being allowed to perform, and finding purpose and meaning through their performance and contribution across all their Dimensions of Being/ Becoming, in the process shaping and crystalising their Personal Identity (refer to Figure 4.6). Organisationally, it is about architecting productive and fulfilling employee experiences, befitting people as complex, multi-dimensional, holistic beings.

Under Choice 3 everyone in the organisation is seen and treated as talent, not just successors or high potential people. Hence the 'solid citizens' (not the 'dead wood') of the organisation, who consistently meet their performance requirements but have realised their potential fully or do not wish to take on greater responsibility, are also seen and treated as talent. Consequently, all of the people employed by the organisation – regardless of their talent status – are regarded as value-adding and wealth-creating members of the organisation. This implies that everyone has a role to play in the success and continued viability of the organisation.

Table 4.1 provides a summary of the above discussed three Strategic People Choices.

Table 4.1: Strategic People Choices

OPTION 1: COST	OPTION 2: (MOST IM-PORTANT) ASSET	OPTION 3: VALUE UNLOCKERS AND WEALTH CREATORS
• People viewed as an unavoidable input cost • Numbers are all that count • Invest as little as possible in people • Short term employment relationship with people – the shorter the better • People are viewed as merely seeking the satisfaction of their physiological existence needs • A fixed mindset • People management focuses on minimum legalistic compliance	• People viewed as the most important asset • People as an asset can be acquired, utilised, and traded • As assets, people must be cared and accounted for • People are viewed as embodied, sophisticated brains, seeking the satisfaction of some higher order needs, in particular competence and actualisation • A growth mindset under leadership discretion • People management focuses on a best-in-class human resources value chain, aggressively growing the human capital of the organisation in tandem with the other assets of the organisation	• People are central to, and co-responsible for, organisational success • Take care of the organisation's people, and organisational outcomes will take care of themselves • Leading people is a key expectation and role of leadership • People are seen as complex, multi-dimensional, holistic beings • A growth mindset under individual, personal discretion • People management focuses on engendering high levels of people commitment and engagement within an enabling and empowering work setting

In the emerging new order, with the growing view that the organisation must be a good social citizen serving the common good, and the imperative of disruptive innovation (outlined in Chapters 1 and 3) placing people centre stage[39], Choice 3 is the only real choice in pursuing People Excellence in a sustainable manner. As alluded to above, this Choice is all about creating enabling and empowering conditions that will engender the high commitment and complete engagement of the bodies, minds, hearts, souls, and spirits of all of the organisation's people at all times. In this way, a shared, desired future is identified and actualised for the organisation, putting it viably ahead of the game. This Choice implies being a genuinely people-centric organisation.

Every answer to the still-to-be-discussed, People Excellence Questions must be aligned to the organisation's chosen Strategic People Choice. Choice 3 will therefore be assumed in all of the discussions of the subsequent Excellence Questions, viewed against the backdrop of the emerging new order.

However, it is critical to not only make a Strategic People Choice, but to ask whether leadership actually walks the talk in terms of living out their Choice in their thinking, decisions and actions. Choice 3 must permeate the organisation into its very being and becoming.

Commensurate Psychosocial Contract

The basic, 'under-the-water' relationship between the organisation and its people is grounded in a Psychosocial Contract.[40][41] The formal Employment Contract depicts the 'above-the-water' formalised, organisation-people relationship. In terms of their basic relationship, a Psychosocial Contract entails the two-way expectations of the reciprocal obligations that the organisation and its people have of each other regarding their respective demands and inducements.[42]

From the organisation's side, these expectations are related to performance (=demands) and recognition/rewards (=inducements). From the people's side, these expectations are with respect to opportunities (=inducements) and needs/values/meaning (=demands). Demands and Inducements can be physical, physiological, psychosocial, and socio-cultural. Trust forms the very foundation of the contract. Trust within the Psychosocial Contract refers to the meeting of reciprocal obligations as promised – consistently and predictably – over time, under all circumstances.[43]

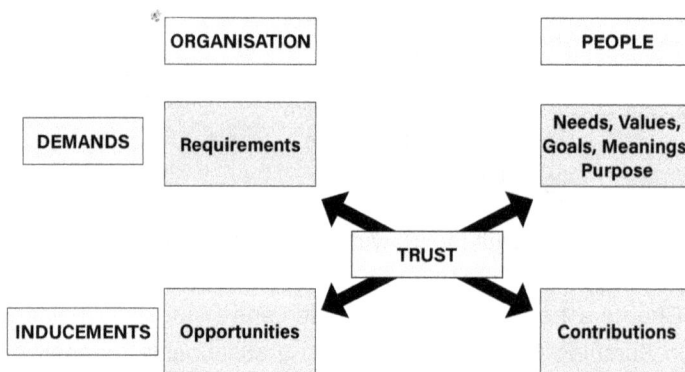

Figure 4.7: Psychosocial Contract as a reciprocal, two-way relationship between the organisation and its people

The different parties to the Contract may have different perceptions of what it entails, and over time the extent to which reciprocal obligations are met.[44] A psychosocial contract between parties also has a life cycle, from creation, through maturity, to termination.[45] A breach of the psychosocial contract, and hence the trust on which it rests, typically results in lower engagement, performance, organisational citizen behaviour, job satisfaction, organisational commitment, physical/psychological well-being, and higher turnover intentions. The reverse is true if the contract is fullfilled.[46]

The emerging new order has fundamentally transformed the basic Psychosocial Contract between working persons and employing organisations, also affecting the role of leadership. Some of the more important shifts are set out in Table 4.2.[47]

Table 4.2: Old vs. New Psychosocial Contracts

Old Psychosocial Contract	New Psychosocial Contract
Employer offers – Predictability; Certainty; Stability; Conformity, Commitment	**Working person offers** - Creativity; Ingenuity; Up to date expertise/skills; Risk-taking; Adaptability; Tolerance for risk, change, unpredictability; Self-management; Accountability
Employ offers (= career promise) – Employment security; Prescribed training and development; Linear career progression with greater status/rewards/benefits; Care when in trouble	**Employing organisation offers (= work experience promise)** Challenging, meaningful work; High work autonomy; Life long learning; Career opportunities; (High) performance-based rewards; Care for well-being; Tenure for as long as the organisation needs the person's skills and expertise; Social citizenship
Employee Expects – Lifelong employment; Assured tenure-linked pay; Steady, vertical promotion, typically in organisational silos	**Working person expects** – Fulfilling work experiences; Ample learning opportunities to ensure ongoing employability; Need satisfaction; Autonomy; Cutting edge technology; Flexibility
Employer expects in return – Organisational needs take priority over personal needs	**Employing organisation expects in return** – Self-reliance: Resilience; Use of expertise/skills; Agility; Change-fitness
General mode of working – Rigid structure and positions/jobs; Set work patterns; Standardised, formalised, routinised; Certainty	**General mode of working** – Safe and healthy setting; Fluid designs, work roles, and work patterns; Individualised; Disruptive innovation; Experimentation; Ongoing learning
Values – Organisation-centric: Loyalty; Conformity; Obedience; Paternalism	**Values** – Person-centric; Meaning/Purpose; Independence; Commitment; Life-work balance/integration; Individualised; Respect and dignity

Psychosocial contracts can be characterised in terms of being Transaction-based (Imposed or Negotiated) vs. Relationship-based (Purpose-fulfilment or Value-added); and Power-driven (Extrinsic or Intrinsic) vs. Needs-driven (Tit-for-tat or Co-creation). Based on these dimensions, four types of Psychosocial Contracts can be distinguished, as depicted in Figure 4.8.[48]

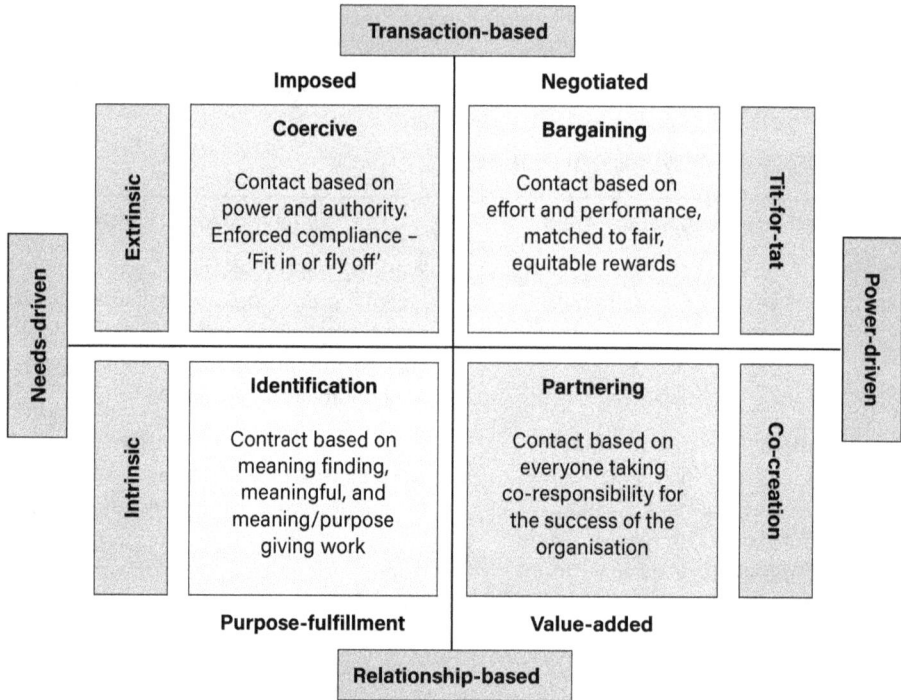

Figure 4.8: Types of Psychosocial Contracts

What must also be considered is that *prospective* organisational members have anticipatory Psychosocial Contracts. These people have pre-employment expectations regarding what they desire the Psychosocial Contract to be, which may vary by generations.[49] Organisations thus have to proactively build a good understanding of the anticipatory contracts held by the types of people it wants to attract and retain. Only in this way can they ensure a good fit between the actual Psychosocial Contract in their organisation, and the anticipatory Contracts of prospective organisational members.

The chosen Strategic People Choice by an organisation requires the deliberate setting up of a commensurate, reinforcing Psychosocial Contract between the organisation and its people. Strategic People Choice 3: Value-unlocking and wealth-creating people being central to a viable organisation in the emerging new order, implies that the organisation must have a commensurate Psychosocial Contract with its people, allowing the organisation to engage them fully as value unlockers and wealth creators. The chosen Contract must also be aligned to the adopted Leadership Stance, in this instance a pre-dominantly Transcendental ('Why')/Transformational ('Whereto') Stance (see Excellence Question 1: Leadership).

It is suggested that the commensurate Psychosocial Contract for Strategic People Choice 3 has to be a predominant mix of two types of contract (refer to Figure 4.8), which can be described as a High Commitment/High Involvement Contract.[50][51][52]

> **Partnering** (Co-sharing/Value-added): a contract in which everyone in the organisation, from the top to the bottom, takes co-responsibility for the organisation's success; intertwined with a contact of **Identification** (Purpose-fulfilment/Intrinsic): a contract revolving around personally internalised, purposeful, meaning-giving work, grounded in the organisation's Identity.

(The other two contracts – Coercive and Bargaining – are also always present, but to a far lesser extent. They are, in any event, 're-coloured' by the dominance of the Partnering/Identification Contract.)

It is submitted that a Partnering/Identification Contract is the only one that will make the organisation great at creating the conditions under which its people will thrive. It appears to be the only contract that will allow people to be the best they can, and want to, be. They will flourish because they are thriving, and therefore experience genuine, deep, authentic fulfilment.

Table 4.3 provides an overview of the typical Organisational (as represented by its leadership) and Organisational Members' expectations of each other informing a High Commitment/High Involvement Contract.[53]

Table 4.3: A High Commitment/High Involvement Contract – Typical Leadership and Organisational Members' Expectations of each other

LEADERSHIP EXPECTATIONS	ORGANISATIONAL MEMBERS' EXPECTATIONS
Dedication to the organisation's Identity in its full ambit	Role modelling the Organisational Identity
Personal leadership: Self-reliant and -directed	People-centric leadership
Collaboration and team work	Autonomy with matching responsibility and authority
High engagement and performance	Participative leadership

LEADERSHIP EXPECTATIONS	ORGANISATIONAL MEMBERS' EXPECTATIONS
Agility	Stability
Honest sharing	Transparency and openness
Organisational interests above personal interests	Work-Life integration/balance
Openness to feedback	Opportunity to speak truth to power
Talking and walking are the same	Talking and walking are the same
Vibrant organisational citizenship	Inclusivity, egalitarianism
Ongoing learning and teaching	Flexibility and responsiveness
Performance meets agreed-upon rewards	Fair, equitable sharing of rewards by all

Having made a clear, deliberate Strategic People Choice: People are central to the organisation's success, supported by a commensurate High Commitment/ High Involvement Psychosocial Contract, and leveraged by a Transformational/ Transcendental Leadership Stance, an organisation next must consistently 'walk the talk' by ensuring alignment of the total People Territory (i.e., its People Strategic Intent, policies, value-chain, practices, decisions, and actions) with its Choice and Contract. Often, organisations are schizophrenic in that their talking and walking regarding their people are not the same. It is as if the organisation is living in two realities, and the twain shall never meet.

The **affirmative answer** to the People Excellence Question 2: Choice, is: *The Strategic People Choice of people as value unlockers and wealth creators is central to the success of the organisation, with a reinforcing commensurate High Commitment/ High Involvement Psychosocial Contract of Partnering/Identification. The talking and walking of this Choice and Contract is manifested daily in an uncompromising and consistent manner in the organisation in all its people thinking and actions.*

You can now do a Reflective Assessment: Choice (Work Sheet 4 in the Work Book), if you wish to do so.

PEOPLE EXCELLENCE
QUESTION 3: PARTNERING

Do the expected role and contributions of People Professionals within the organisation match the organisation's Strategic People Choice?

The strategic positioning of People Professionals, and hence their role and contribution within the organisation, is a direct function of the organisation's Strategic People Choice: *Choice 1* – People as a cost; *Choice 2* – People as an (or the most important) asset; or *Choice 3* – People as value unlockers and wealth creators. The expected role and contributions of the organisation's People Professionals must match the Choice made.

As was discussed under Excellence Question 2: Choice in the emerging new order in which people are moving centre stage, Strategic People Choice 3 is the only real Choice in pursuing People Excellence in a sustainable, viable manner. This Choice implies that People Professionals must fulfil the role of Strategic Organisational Partners. From a strategic organisational perspective, they must partner synergistically with the organisation's leadership in order to take shared responsibility to bring about and maintain the enabling and empowering organisational conditions under which the organisation's people can, want to, and do contribute fully to the organisation's ongoing success, and the realisation of its Envisioned Legacy relative to its Purpose.[54][55] This necessitates a strong People Function presence and voice at the Board and Executive levels of the organisation.

People Professionals are the crucial catalysts in bringing about People Excellence, as manifested in thriving people who flourish and consequently experience fulfilment in the organisation. However, at all times the organisation's people are led by the leadership of the organisation. They are not 'owned' by the People Function. That is why the organisation's leadership must take full accountability as a leadership community for the organisation's People Excellence.[56]

In fulfilling the overarching role as Credible Activists, People Professionals as Strategic Organisational Partners must act as the people custodians of the organisation. As leaders in their own right, they must reflect the adopted Leadership Stance of their organisation[57] (see Excellence Question 1: Leadership). People Professionals must also have a discernible people point of view as true People Experts in the organisation, and be acknowledged as such (see Pillar 2 below).[58]

Assuming Strategic People Choice 3, the People Professionals' action space reflective of this Choice is depicted in Figure 4.9.[59]

WORLD OF PEOPLE PROFESSIONALS

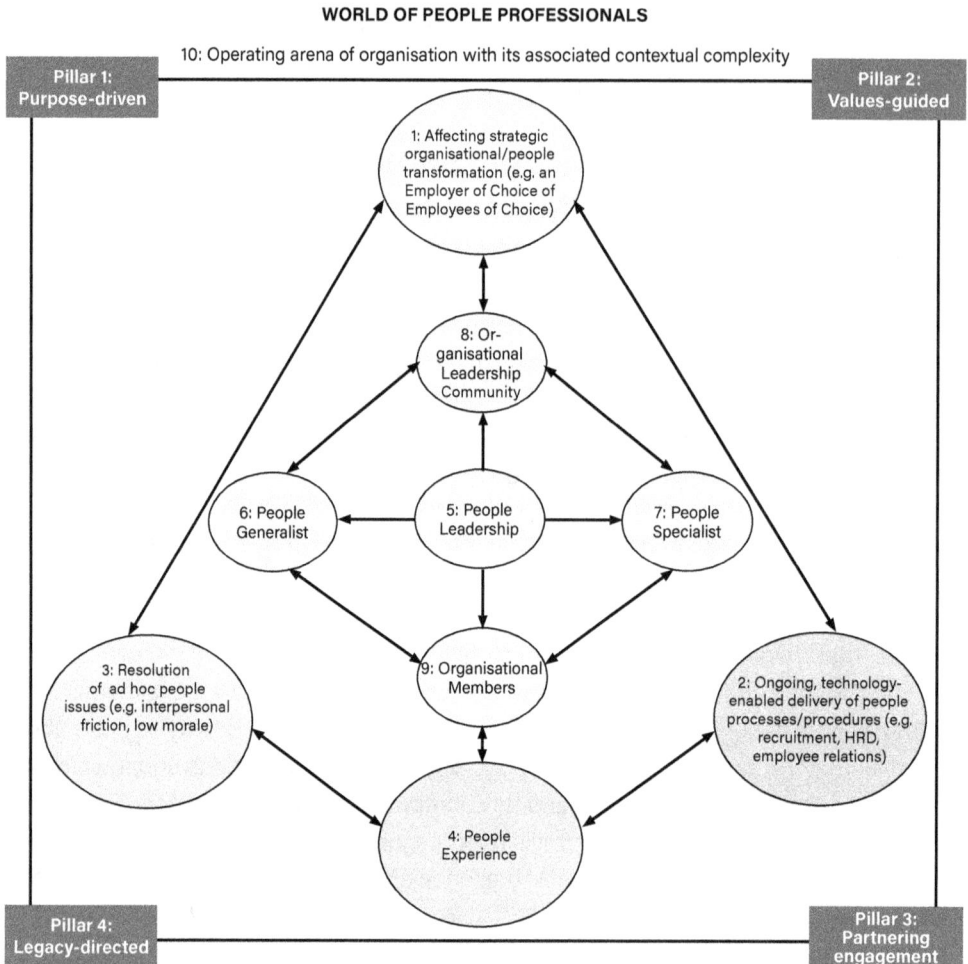

Figure 4.9: People Professionals' action space within the organisation

As per Figure 4.9, the building blocks of the People Professional's Strategic Partnering World are the below:

(i) The four *Pillars* on which this world rests, analogous to the three legs of an oil rig:

- *Pillar 1: Purpose-driven.* People Professionals must have a clear raison d'etre. As explicated in the discussion up to this point, this is Organisational/People Effectiveness, manifested in People Excellence.

- *Pillar 2: Value-guided.* People Professionals must be the stewards of the People and Ethics[60] of the organisation. They must be guided by an explicit People (or Work) Charter – a set of fundamental beliefs about people and the rights they have in the work place – that is expressive of this stewardship. These are the immutable, not-to-be broken, inalienable people beliefs/rights about the World of Work people Professionals must be willing to stand up and be counted for in their dealings with organisations, leaders/managers, individuals, clients, and fellow People Professionals. Such a Charter will be explicated under Excellence Question 5: Differentiation.

- *Pillar 3: Partnering engagement.* Under Strategic People Choice 3, People Professionals must shift their engagement mode from being a conventional Technical Specialist to a true Strategic Organisational Partner. These shifts are given in Table 4.4.[61]

Table 4.4: Shifts in the engagement mode of People Professionals

From a Technical Specialist...	**...to a Strategic Organisational Partner**
• Intra-Organisation: Closed system perspective	• Organisation-in-context: Eco-systems perspective
• Inside-Out mindset	• Outside-In mindset
• Present-centric	• Future-centric
• Functional specialist	• Organisational practitioner
• Product-centric, transactional contributions	• Client-centric, transformational contributions
• Technical solutions	• Organisational solutions
• Risk avoidance, reactive	• Risk-seeking, proactive
• Activity, cost focus	• Output, value focus
• Management Practices	• People experiences
• Processes	• Relationships
• Numbers and rules	• Ethics and values

- *Pillar 4: Legacy-directed.* People Professionals must passionately pursue the quest of leaving the world a better place for upcoming generations. This quest is made up of at least five interdependent legacy elements:

  - *A High Performance Organisation:* being highly productive and wise in utilising the resources at its disposal.

  - *A High Wealth Organisation:* creating and distributing significant wealth for *all* of its stakeholders (i.e., shareholders, employees, suppliers, clients, communities and society at large).

  - *A High Authentic Organisation:* nurturing and caring for *all* of its people, such that they become 'better' and more 'fulfilled'.

  - *A High Responsibility Organisation:* acting as a reliable steward of the societal assets entrusted to it, using them in a sustainable manner whilst unlocking value and creating wealth.

     –   *A High Co-opetition Organisation:* constructive and healthy stakeholder partnering, seeking win-win relationships.

Without the right pillars, the world of People Professionals will be irrelevant to the operating arena of the organisation, as it will be unable to support the other building blocks making up the People Professionals world in a value-adding way.

(ii)   The expected four-faceted *scope of practice* of the People Professionals (Circles 1-4), e.g., affecting strategic organisation/people transformation and the ongoing, technology-enabled delivery of people processes/procedures). Although always present on the radar screen of the People Professional, the different facets may be weighted strategically differently at different times.

(iii) Expressed in terms of three *role types* (Circles 5-7), e.g., People Generalists.

(iv) Regarding primarily internal *stakeholders* (Circles 8 and 9), e.g., organisational leadership community.

(v)   Associated with the emerging new order infusing the *operating arena of the organisation with the associated contextual complexity* of the organisation (Circle 10), within which all the aforementioned are embedded and unfold.

The **affirmative answer** to the People Excellence Question 3: Partnering, is: *The People Professionals of the organisation are true strategic organisational partners in their roles as People Experts, acting as Credible Activists, whose value-adding and innovative contributions are eagerly sought out and truly cherished in attaining viable organisational success, because they co-enable and co-ensure a high likelihood that the people of the organisation will thrive as boundary-busting value unlockers and wealth creators through productive and satisfying experiences.*

You can now do a Reflective Assessment: Partnering (Work Sheet 5 in the Work Book), if you wish to do so.

PEOPLE EXCELLENCE
QUESTION 4: ALIGNMENT

People-wise, is the organisation strategically aligned to its Identity?

People Excellence requires that the organisation creates continuous strategic synergy. Strategic synergy is a function of an organisation having an explicit, focused People Strategic Intent that is fully aligned with, and supports, the organisation's Identity, in particular its Strategic Intent. Examples of such organisational Strategic Intents are

Product/Service Innovation, Operational Efficiency, and Customer Centricity[62], each of which imposes different People Excellence requirements. Organisations with an explicit, formal people strategy perform 35% better than their peers.[63]

The Key People Imperatives – forming the foundational core of the People Strategic Intent and setting its basic strategic parameters – must thus be strategically aligned to the organisation's Identity. The Key People Imperatives can also be seen as the Strategic People Thinking Framework for the organisation. This strategic alignment is the first, foundational step in establishing an inimitable, distinct, and coherent Strategic People Position for the organisation (see Excellence Question 5: Differentiation).

Five Key People Imperatives, with their corresponding Organisational Identity elements, can be distinguished as shown in Table 4.5.[64][65]

Table 4.5: Key People Imperatives with their alignment to the organisation's Identity

ORGANISATIONAL IDENTITY	KEY PEOPLE IMPERATIVE	ALIGNMENT BETWEEN THE ORGANISATIONAL IDENTITY AND KEY PEOPLE IMPERATIVES
Purpose **('Why')**	**People Capabilities** **('Can do')**	The basic people abilities – both hard (i.e., skills, knowledge, expertise) and soft (i.e., personal attributes, attitudes, values, conduct) – required by the organisation to deliver on its *Purpose* (=*the business of the business*).
Vision **('Whereto')**	**People Energy** **('Will do')**	The required people's motivational power to realise the organisation's *Vision* (=the *dream* of the organisation).
Core Values **('How')[66]**	**People Legitimacy** **('Should do')**	The 'rightfulness' and 'legitimacy' regarding what the organisation stands for, how it conducts its business, and how it lives its espoused values (=the *core values or ideology of the organisation*) that people must meet: the people's necessary normative mindset.

ORGANISATIONAL IDENTITY	KEY PEOPLE IMPERATIVE	ALIGNMENT BETWEEN THE ORGANISATIONAL IDENTITY AND KEY PEOPLE IMPERATIVES
Strategic Intent ('What')	People Autonomy ('Allowed to do')	The accountability, authority, and freedom people will be given to act relative to the organisation's *Strategic Intent, Initiatives and Goals* (=*organisational aspirations*), which they have to pursue on a daily basis.
Legacy ('Wherefore')	People Fulfilment ('Want to do')	The need fulfilment that people could aspire to, wish for, experience, and will receive in the organisation as a consequence of their conduct, effort and performance, in accordance with the *organisational outcomes* achieved and the *legacy* being left behind.

The People Imperatives given in Table 4.5 can be converted into a full Organisational Effectiveness (OE) (=Organisational viability/success) Equation, expressive of the tight strategic alignment to be created and maintained between the Organisation Identity and Key People Imperatives, creating strategic alignment synergy.[67][68]

Organisational Effectiveness = f(People Capabilities/Organisational Purpose x People Energy/Organisational Vision x People Legitimacy/Organisational Core Values x People Autonomy/Strategic Intent x People Fulfillment/Legacy)

Important to note with respect to the above equation is the *multiplicative relationships* between its constituent elements: an increase/decrease in the value of an element will significantly enhance/detract from the overall Organisational Effectiveness of an organisation. A value of zero for one or more element will reduce the Organisational Effectiveness to nought.

This equation unequivocally demonstrates the intimate and synergistic relationship and interdependency amongst and between the People Strategic Intent, expressed in the strategic requirements set by the Key People Imperatives, and the Identity of the organisation. Essentially, the above equation covers the goodness of fit between the People (P) and Organisation (O), resulting in a certain level of Organisational Effectiveness within a given context (C): OE=P-O-C.

As an aside. Paradoxically, if an organisation has adopted the wrong Organisational Identity relative to its operating arena, a good fit between the Key People Imperatives to create strategic synergy with the wrong Organisational Identity will just get the organisation deeper into trouble, because the organisation will be succeeding well with its people, but with respect to the wrong things!

The **affirmative answer** to the People Excellence Question 4: Alignment, is: *A high alignment exists between Organisational Identity and the Key People Imperatives through the dynamic optimisation of the multiplicative relationship between all of the Identity and Imperative constituent pairs, resulting in a strong strategic synergy manifested in high Organisational Effectiveness.*

You can now do a Reflective Assessment: Alignment (Work Sheet 6 in the Work Book), if you wish to do so.

PEOPLE EXCELLENCE QUESTION 5: DIFFERENTIATION

Does the organisation have an inimitable, distinct, and coherent Strategic People Position?

Within the strategic parameters set by the Organisational Identity – Key People Imperatives Alignment, the next requirement for People Excellence in the organisation is to adopt an inimitable, distinct and coherent Strategic People Position. This Position will provide the necessary strategic, organisational foundation to People Excellence, and its resultant people competitive edge.

This Position can be visualised in the form of a Strategic People Position Triangle, made up of the organisation's People Charter, Desired People Profile, and People Value Proposition. This Triangle pivots centrally around how the organisation wishes to strategically configure the World of Work for itself. Figure 4.10 depicts this 'inverted' Strategic People Position Triangle. Why 'inverted'? The 'Inverted' Triangle demonstrates graphically that the People Charter forms the normative foundation of the other two components of the Triangle.

Context-derived, People Excellence Specification

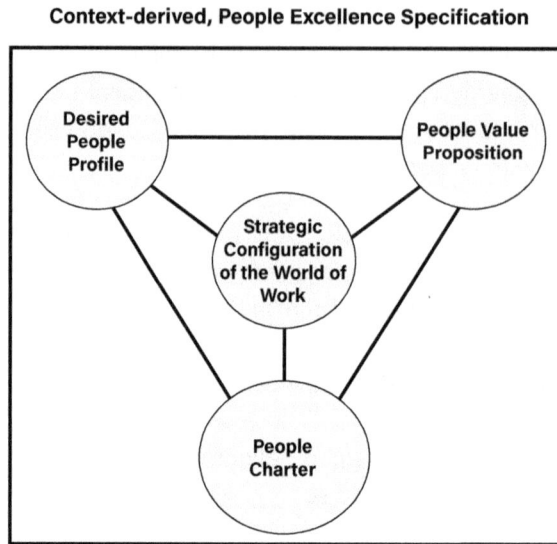

Figure 4.10: Strategic People Position Triangle

The content awarded to the components of the Strategic People Position Triangle must be derived from, aligned to, and give concrete expression to:

- the organisation's Strategic People Choice 3: People as value unlockers and wealth creators, with its commensurate Psychosocial Contract of High Commitment/High Involvement;
- the strategic configuration of the organisation's World of Work; and
- the process of complying with the People Excellence Specification, derived from the emerging new order.

Each component of the Strategic People Position Triangle is discussed next, in the order of the strategic configuration of the organisation's World of Work, People Charter, Desired People Profile, and People Value Proposition.[69]

Strategic configuration of the organisation's World of Work

As a departure point to its Strategic People Choice with regard to its People Charter, Desired People Profile, and People Value Proposition, the organisation has to make a deliberate, explicit choice – from a people perspective – of how it endeavours to strategically configure the World of Work for itself as an organisation. Put slightly differently, it is the organisation's strategic conceptualisation of what the DNA of everyday work delivery will look like in the organisation.

If a humane World of Work is to be configured, the organisation's World of Work must take into consideration the requirements set by people as complex, multi-dimensional, holistic beings in terms of their Dimensions of Being/Becoming, Basic Needs, and Personal Identity (see Figure 4.6). For example, if work is configured to be 'Remote, dispersed and online', how will such work be given a 'human face' in terms of belonging with respect to the other Excellence Elements? In turn, this strategic configured World of Work for the organisation will set as a departure point the strategic parameters for formulating the organisation's People Charter, Desired People Profile, and People Value Proposition.[70]

Figure 4.11 depicts some of the more critical dimensions the organisation must consider in strategically configuring the World of Work for itself relative to humane work requirements.[71] The configuration choices are not 'Either-Or' but 'And/Both', with the relative weighting of options. For example, the relative weighting of personalised *and* standardised work conditions; or remote, dispersed, online locations *and* physical, centralised, on locations. The pattern of choices must be reciprocally supportive and intelligible to form a coherent World of Work within the organisation.

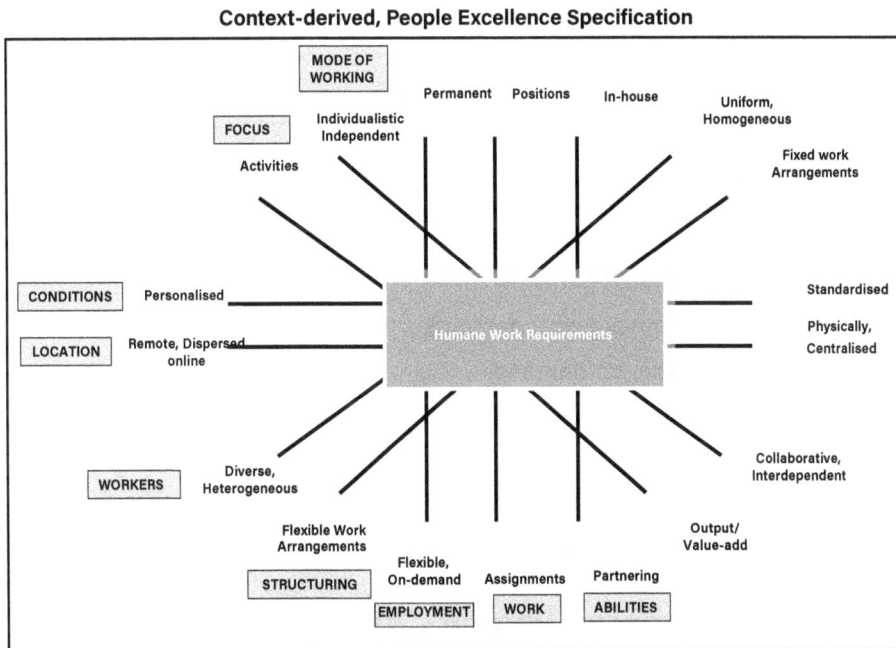

Figure 4.11: Critical variables in strategically configuring the World of Work of the organisation

According to Figure 4.11, by way of an example, an organisation can choose to configure its World of Work strategically as follows (the percentages reflect the relative weighting of a choice):

- *Mode of Working*: Individualistic, Independent (25%) and Collaborative, Interdependent (75%)

- *Focus:* Activities (20%) and Output/Value-add (80%)
- *Conditions:* Standardised (40%) and Personalised (60%)
- *Location:* Remote, dispersed, online (90%) and Physical, centralised, on location (10%) (=hybrid working)
- *Workers:* Uniform, Homogeneous (0%) and Diverse, Heterogeneous (100%)
- *Structuring:* Flexible (85%) and Fixed (15%) work arrangements
- *Employment:* Flexible, on-demand (40%) and Permanent (60%)
- *Abilities:* Partnering (50%) and In-house (50%)

Due consideration must be given to how the strategic, configured World of Work must be operationalised in a humane manner into, for example, People Practices (see Excellence Question 10: Practices), such that people can flourish, thrive and feel fulfilled.

The emerging new order as explicated in Chapter 3 points to the following typical unfolding configuration of the World of Work:[72]

- *Mode of Working:* Collaborative, Interdependent
- *Focus:* Output/Value-add
- *Conditions:* Personalised
- *Location:* Remote, dispersed, online [73]
- *Workers:* Diverse, Heterogeneous
- *Structuring:* Flexible work arrangements
- *Employment:* Flexible, on-demand
- *Abilities:* Partnering

Within the strategic parameters set by the organisation's strategic configuring of its World of Work, the coherent formulation of an inimitable, distinct People Charter, Desired People Profile, and People Value Proposition can now proceed.

Clear, explicit, shared People Charter

The first component of the inimitable, distinct and coherent Strategic People Position Triangle is a clear, explicit, shared People Charter (Philosophy, Manifesto or Compact). The People Charter sets normative people guidelines for the other two elements of the Strategic People Position Triangle. It must also fit the People Excellence Specification set by the emerging new order (refer to Chapter 3). It further relates to the Key People Imperative: People Legitimacy ('Should do') (see Table 4.5).

The People Charter encompasses the organisation's fundamental beliefs about its people, and the rights they can lay claim to in the World of Work. The People Charter not only gives concrete expression to the Strategic People Choice made by an organisation, but also operationalises in tangible, practical detail the nature of the desired Psychosocial Contract between the organisation and its people. This is similar to Organisational Identity which provides a fixed reference point and secure anchor to the organisation. In the emerging new order, the People Charter plays a similar normative (or values-referenced) foundational role regarding the desired organisation-people relationship.[74] It characterises what decent (or good) work in the organisation should look like if people are to flourish, thrive, and be fulfilled. It also acts as one of the pillars – Pillar 2 – to the action world of People Professionals explicated under Excellence Question 3: Partnering (see Figure 4.9). The People and Leadership Charters (refer Excellence Question 1: Leadership) must be congruent.

Metaphorically, the People Charter is comprised of the 'Ten Commandments' that direct and guide the day-to-day, people-organisation interactions. Typical 'commandments' contained in a People Charter are given in Table 4.6. Examples of the translation of these commandments into actual People Practices are also given.[75][76] Of necessity, the chosen People Practices (Excellence Question 10: Practices) must be aligned to the Charter.

Table 4.6: People Charter

COMMANDMENTS	TRANSLATION INTO PEOPLE PRACTICES: EXAMPLES
With respect to working persons and the World of Work, we believe and value the following: • regard each person as unique in his/her make-up, beliefs, needs and aspirations; • treat every person under all circumstances with equal respect and dignity; • accept people as responsible, trustworthy adults; • deal with everyone in a fair, transparent, truthful and equitable manner; • treat others as we wish to be treated; • create ongoing development opportunities for people to realise their full potential;	Examples of corresponding People Practices include: • ensuring job security through employability; • providing challenging, meaningful and decent work; • offering individualised work arrangements; • aligning work demands and resources, allowing high work autonomy (a high degree of independent decision-making in a person's area of accountability/responsibility); • providing ongoing, intense training and development of all persons across their careers;

COMMANDMENTS	TRANSLATION INTO PEOPLE PRACTICES: EXAMPLES
• empower (i.e., the freedom to act) and enable (i.e., the wherewithal needed to perform) people to make contributions commensurate with their knowledge, expertise, skills, and experience; • allow everyone the opportunity to pursue his/her own interests equally without detriment to any other person(s) and to mutual benefit; • keep people at all times fully informed, actively listen to them, and involve them in and allow them to influence decisions that affect them; • create a work setting in which persons can act morally, truthfully and with integrity within a climate of trust; • provide a safe, healthy, secure and attractive work setting to ensure personal and collective well-being; • give due recognition for effort and performance, and recognise/reward people equitably and fairly, relative to organisational results; • create an enriching work experience which gives people a sense of meaningful and satisfying accomplishment, of personal growth and learning, of worth, as well as of belonging and community; • nurture a sense of social responsibility and good citizenship within and beyond organisational boundaries; and • maintain Work-Life balance and integration.	• empowering people to use their knowledge, skills, and experience to the fullest extent; • teaming and team work; • ensuring an information-rich organisation with equal access by all to all information; • guaranteeing participative decision-making; • creating inclusive, shared leadership; • building an ethical organisation which is directed and guided in all its decisions and actions by a set of core values according to which it acts at all times; • designing a diverse, inclusive organisation which builds on the strengths of everyone; • providing work that is fairly and equitably rewarded; and • ensuring the non-intrusion of work demands and requests into the private lives of employees, e.g., no after-hour, week-end or vacation e-mails, SMSes and WhatsApps.

The People Charter needs to be co-created, co-owned, and co-lived by everyone in the organisation. It serves as the final court of appeal for an aggrieved party if there has been a breach of some kind in the organisation-people relationship. A way of validating the People Charter is to independently create the intended, desired people experience to be generated by the organisation, then 'back translate' this experience into the commandments making up the People Charter to see whether the Charter as a normative foundation will engender the desired experience. The intended, desired people experience also must be 'forward translated' into the People Value Proposition (see below), Organisational Design (Excellence Question 7: Design) and People Practices (Excellence Question 10: Practices) to ensure that they will be aligned to, and in support of, the intended, desired people experience.[77]

Desired People Profile

The Desired People Profile – the second component of the Strategic People Position Triangle – refers to the organisation having a clear picture of the ideal type(s) of person it wants to employ, now and going into the future, aligned to the organisation's Identity. Put differently: 'What will it take to succeed and thrive in our organisation as a person?' The Desired People Profile gives a comprehensive, integrated picture of the ideal person the organisation strategically endeavours to attract, engage, and retain.

This person will capacitate the organisation with a high likelihood of navigating successfully towards its chosen, desired future through its Strategic Intent within its operating arena with its specific People Requirements, and correspondingly derived People Excellence Specification.[78] The Desired People Profile is generic, and has to be turned into work role-related, people specifications when the organisational design is architected (see Excellence Question 7: Design). The Desired People Profile relates to the Key People imperative: People Capabilities ('Can do') (see Table 4.5).

Figure 4.12 gives the dimensions of a comprehensive, Desired People Profile.[79] Although the Profile must be organisation-specific, the view of future-expected People Requirements and the Specification of the emerging new order can serve as a handy starting point (see in particular Figure 3.4).

Context-derived, People Excellence Specification

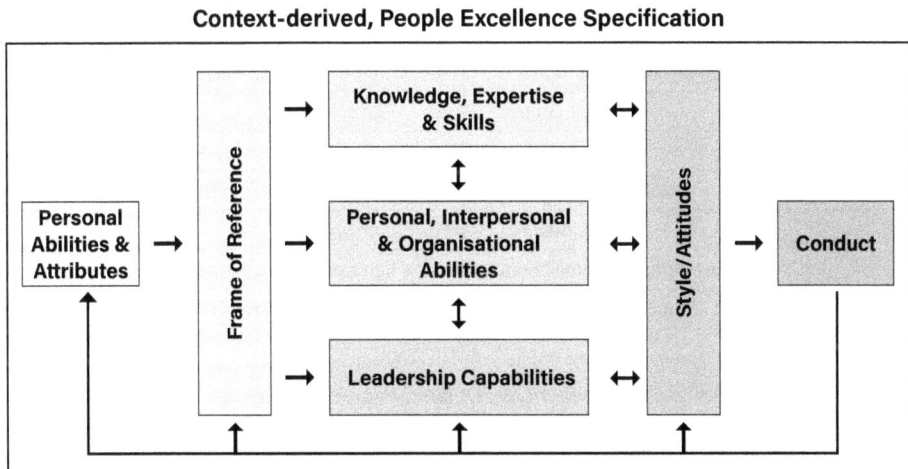

Figure 4.12: Dimensions of a comprehensive, Desired People Profile

With reference to the People Excellence Specification derived from the emerging new order, a useful way of arriving at a Desired People Profile is to follow an outside-in profiling process by *firstly,* profiling the Expected, Desired People Conduct if People Excellence is to become a reality in the organisation. *Secondly,* using this Conduct to populate – in reverse order, from right to left in Figure 4.12 – the other profile dimensions.

Figure 4.13 depicts a portfolio of possible behaviours which can be used to generate a profile of Expected People Conduct.[80] The range of possible behaviours given in Figure 4.13 is categorised according to the Expected People Conduct typically associated with Predictable, Routinised vs. Agile, Creative People Conduct.

PREDICTED, ROUTINISED PEOPLE CONDUCT	AGILE, CREATIVE PEOPLE CONDUCT
Low organisational identification	High organisational identification
Infrequent, innovative/creative behaviour	Frequent innovative/creative behaviour
Individualistic behaviour	Cooperative, interdependent behaviour
Repetitive, predictable behaviour	Flexible, responsive behaviour
Short term focus	Medium/Long term focus
Dependent, externally referenced behaviour	Independent, internally referenced, behaviour
Low concern for quality	High concern for high quality
Low risk orientation	High risk orientation
Concern for activities	Concern for results
Little accountability/responsibility	High accountability/responsibility
Inflexible to change	Flexible to change
Low task orientation	High task orientation
Passive involvement	Active involvement
Focus on efficiency (= Doing things right)	Focus on effectiveness (= Doing right things)
Single, simple decisions/actions	Complex, diverse decisions/actions
Low self control	High self control
Low initiative	High initiative
Weak self-leadership	Strong self-leadership
Individualism	Team work
Low tolerance for mistakes	High tolerance for mistakes
Single, loop learning	Double, loop learning

Figure 4.13: Dimensions of a comprehensive, Desired People Profile

The Expected, Desired People Conduct, aligned to the People Excellence Specification of the emerging new order, and the Strategic People Choice 3: People as value unlockers and wealth creators with its commensurate High Commitment/High Involvement Psychosocial Contract, is the behavioural portfolio of Agile, Creative People Conduct (the right column of Figure 4.13). Using the Expected, Desired People Conduct as a reference point, the other dimensions of the Desired People Profile (refer to Figure 4.12) can now be generated. Once populated, an inverted Profile validation process can be followed: work from the left in Figure 4.12 across the other profile dimensions to the right to confirm whether they will result in the Expected, Desired People Conduct.

Compelling People Value Proposition

Once the Desired People Profile has been generated for the organisation, meeting the People Excellence Specification of the emerging new order, a matching People Value Proposition (PVP) (or 'Employee Value Proposition') must be crafted.[81] The PVP forms the third component of the Strategic People Position Triangle. A PVP deals with the compelling reasons why the desired persons the organisation wishes to employ will join, engage, and stay with the organisation. From a prospective employee's perceptive, a PVP answers the key question: 'Will I flourish if I join the organisation? And because I flourish, will I thrive as a total person, and hence feel fulfilled?'[82]

Financially, 42% of high performing organisations are more likely to have an explicit, formalised PVP than lower performing organisations.[83] Organisations with strong PVPs are 10% less likely to have challenges with the attraction and retention of critical people, and voluntary turnover is 17% lower. These organisations are also almost three times more likely to have high employee engagement.[84] A compelling PVP is one of the top five drivers of employee engagement.[85]

In the experience-based Knowledge Society, with its imperative of disruptive innovation and continuous learning, a PVP endeavours to coherently and transparently convey to prospective/current employees the organisational conditions that will engender people's full immersion of body, mind, heart and spirit in the organisation's work, enabling them to flourish as complex, holistic human beings. They will flourish in terms of Personal Identity, Being/Becoming Dimensions, and Basic Needs (refer to Figure 4.6). And because they are flourishing, they are thriving – they are involved, energetic, passionate and growing.[86]

The PVP has to be translated into the People Brand (or Employee Brand) of the organisation.[87] For a People Brand to be a powerful, competitive differentiator, it must be valuable, rare, and difficult to imitate. The Brand promises that people joining, engaging with, and staying at the organisation will have a certain employee experience. The organisation will truly provide conditions under which people can thrive. It must thus come across as authentic, transparent, and honest. The PVP, and consequential

People Brand, must pervade the total organisation into its very being.[88] It must become part of the very DNA of the organisation. The People Professionals must lead the People Branding Process as one of their critical, strategic partnering contributions.[89]

The challenge to organisations in the emerging new order is how to balance the tension – especially across multiple stakeholders – between on the *one hand* a forward-looking People Brand able to attract different types of people who are matched to where the organisation is going strategically in the future. AND, *on the other hand,* its Brand in the present for its current people. It is a case of juggling multiple Organisational Identities in the present whilst considering the future.[90] (See further in this regard Figure 5.2, Excellence Question 8: Matching.)

The elements of a full-blown, well thought through and holistic PVP, represented by the acronym CCARRLO, are given in Figure 4.14.[91] The bubbles in Figure 4.14 – linked to the respective PVP elements – depict the content that organisations in pursuit of People Excellence would typically give to the respective PVP elements. These elements must be used to build a powerful, compelling People Brand. It must be able to attract, engage and retain the desired people – bodies, minds, hearts and spirit – through the promise that they will flourish, and hence thrive. The PVP elements may also be weighted in terms of their relative importance within the overall PVP.

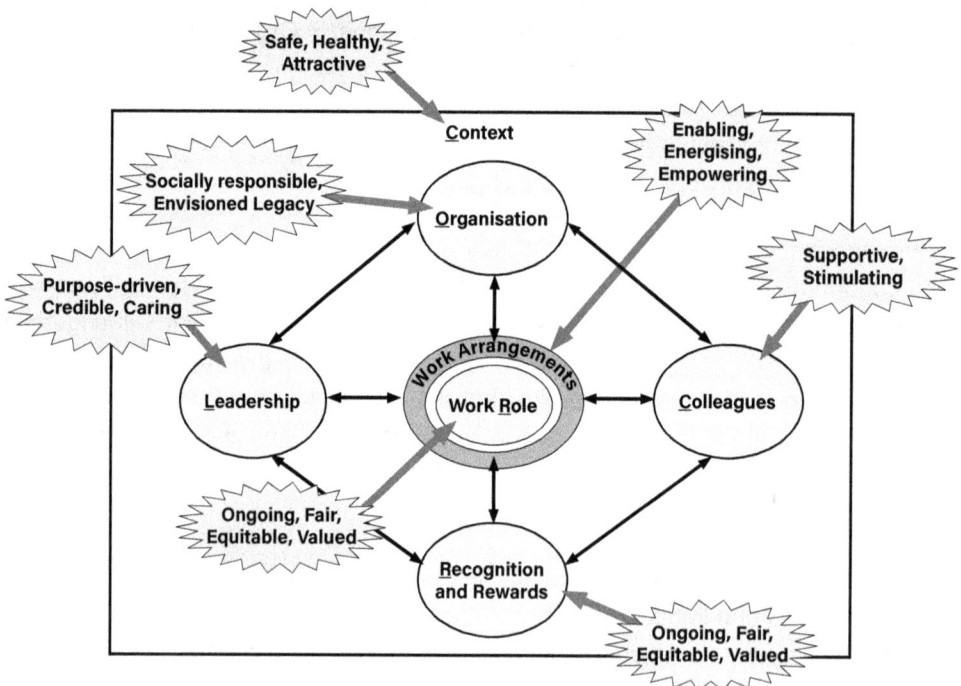

Figure 4.14: A full blown, well thought through, compelling People Value Proposition: CCARRLO[92][93]

The PVP given in Figure 4.14 depicts an overall, generic PVP for the organisation in its totality. An even more sophisticated approach to a PVP is segmenting the organisation's desired employees by the centrality they award to work in their lives. I.e., the importance and value they place on work.[94] And, then to craft employee-segment specific PVPs.[95] Figure 4.15 provides the work centrality dimensions according to which employees can be segmented.

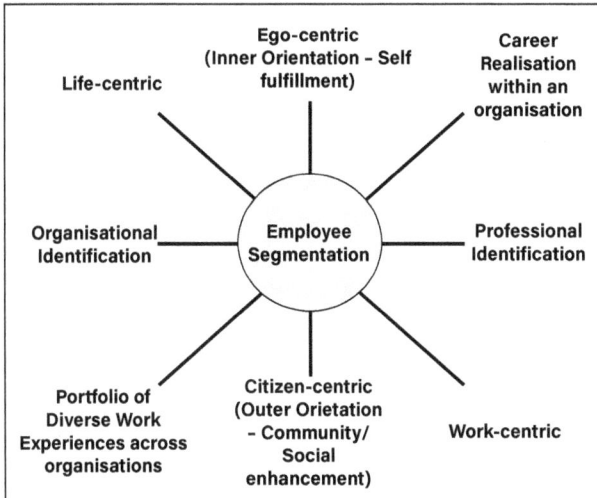

Figure 4.15: Employee segment dimensions

Based on the employee segment dimensions given in Figure 4.15, Table 4.7 provides five basic types of employee segments. To make segments 'real' and easy to grasp, Personas can be created as archetypical examples of real persons representing the respective segments. Inversely, Personas can also be created first, and then segment-specific PVPs formulated. Segment-specific PVPs must be formulated based on the work centrality needs of the different segments to craft really powerful, differentiating People Brands by segments. A person may move across different segments over his/her work life cycle.

Table 4.7: Basic types of employee segments

EMPLOYEE SEGMENT	WHAT	WHERE	HOW	WHY
Career-driven *Work is equal to Life*	Organisational Identification	Work-centric	Career realisation	Ego-centric
Work-Life Integration *Equal balance between Work and Life*	Organisational Identification	Life/Work-centric	Career realisation	Citizen-centric

EMPLOYEE SEGMENT	WHAT	WHERE	HOW	WHY
World Citizen *Working anywhere to gain different cultural experiences*	Professional Identification	Work-centric	Experience Portfolio	Citizen-centric
Mobile *Working anywhere to gain professional experience*	Professional Identification	Work-centric	Experience Portfolio	Ego-centric
Transition *Between jobs, organisations, and/or careers*	Professional Identification	Life-centric	Experience Portfolio	Ego-centric

The **affirmative answer** to the People Excellence Question 5: Differentiation, is: *an inimitable, distinct, and coherent Strategic People Position, framed by a strategically configured World of Work – the Strategic People Triangle made up of People Charter, Desired People Profile, and People Value Proposition – expressive of the Strategic People Choice of people as value unlockers and wealth creators, and a High Commitment/ High Involvement Psychosocial Contract of Partnering/Identification, compliant with the set People Excellence Specification of the emerging new order.*

You can now do a Reflective Assessment: Differentiation (Work Sheet 7 in the Work Book), if you wish to do so.

PEOPLE EXCELLENCE
QUESTION 6: OWNERSHIP

Have the organisation's people taken a personalised, committed ownership of the organisation's Identity, its Strategic People Choice, and its differentiating People Position?

People Excellence necessitates that all people in the organisation, regardless of status and level, take ownership of who and what the organisation is; what it stands for; where it is going; what it wants to achieve; and what lasting difference it wants to make, organisationally and people-wise.[96] In short, people understand and own (=identify with) their organisation's Organisational Identity, including its translation into the organisation's chosen Strategic People Choice and crafted Strategic People Position, as well as the subsequent roll-out of People Excellence into the successive Excellence Domains and Elements. They feel they belong in the organisation – this is where they want to be, and where they want to make a contribution. They have a sense of being connected to the organisation at a deep level because they can identify with what it stands for.[97][98]

Strong, shared ownership of a robust, distinct Organisational Identity across all of the organisation's people moulds the organisation into a vibrant, cohesive action community.[99] Ownership – 'The preferred place where I want to be' – forms the basis from which to grow a high affective-normative commitment – 'I belong here' – to the organisation's Identity.[100] Taking up ownership of the organisation's Identity in an affective-normative committed way presumes a Partnering/Identification Psychosocial Contract (see Excellence Question 2: Choice).

A high affective-normative, committed ownership of the organisation's Identity by organisational members is all-embracing: physically (=being present in person); cognitively (=a deep understanding); emotionally (=a good feeling about); and morally (=it is ethically and legitimately right to be here). Organisational members as whole persons are thus fully and totally attached to, and immersed in, the organisation's Identity.[101]

Committed ownership hence is a verb, not a noun; it is dynamic, not static. It is not a given. It has to be grown and nurtured, but can also erode. Committed ownership cannot be commanded top-down, but has to be earned by leadership through the legitimacy awarded by the people of the organisation to leadership to lead them. It grows, and is shared, from the bottom-up. Through the legitimacy awarded, people become passionate, dedicated followers of leadership, and genuine followership emerges. Leadership has been given a 'licence' by people to lead them.

But more than merely owning and being committed to the organisation's Identity at a subjective distance by internalising the Organisational Identity personally, *each* person in the organisation has externalised the organisation's Identity by translating it fully into his/her specific work setting and role. They then enact it in a committed way according to the promise contained in the Organisational Identity, expressed in its Organisational Image and Reputation. Everyone in the organisation must make her/his ownership of its Identity real though their commitment to localise and customise it into their daily work spaces and roles. There cannot be a remote Identity from on-high, conveyed at a 'distance' by the CEO in his/her annual/quarterly road shows, with which one can only subjectively identify. An Identity must be externalised into a personalised, localised work space, and be aligned to the espoused Organisational Identity.[102]

However, committed ownership is not a once-off, located, single event with regard to the Excellence Domain: Identity and its Excellence Elements. It is an ongoing, snowballing process that grounds and sets up the conditions for all of the other subsequent Excellence Domains, especially engagement. Leadership must engender, nurture, and grow committed ownership all the time for People Excellence to be present in all that the organisation stands for, is, and aspires to. Committed ownership is also a clear sign that people are flourishing, and hence thriving, in the organisation, in this way contributing to keep the organisation a viable entity. Without a high level of committed ownership, the continued viability of the organisation is at risk.

In the emerging new order of hyper-fluidity and hyper-turbulence, a personalised, internally owned, and work place externalised, located Identity by every organisational member provides a secure anchor and fixed reference point. This Identity gives meaning to the shared purpose and envisioned legacy pursued by the organisation. Consequently, every person in the organisation – from the CEO to the messenger – is enabled and empowered to become a strategic contributor by concretely living out the organisation's Identity in a personally embraced way in their accountable work space. Being personally owned, the organisation's Identity becomes – individually and collectively – important, valued, pursued, meaningful, and purposeful.

However, the challenge in the emerging new order is how to nurture the minimum accepted levels of committed ownership in and across the organisation's people, given the gig-economy which has a growing proportion of independents/freelancers forming part of organisation's employees. There is also an effect on committed ownership caused by the increasing organisational mobility of people, who are staying for shorter periods of time with an organisation.[103] A highly virtual working mode also negatively affects the engendering, nurturing, and growth of committed ownership.

It has been found that affective-normative commitment is positively related to engagement, performance, citizenship, well-being, and health. It also is a good predictor of withdrawal and retention.[104] For example, it was found that organisations with highly committed people outperformed organisations with less committed people by between 47% and 200% in 2002 and 2010, respectively.[105] A sense of workplace belonging also led to an estimated 56% increase in job performance; a 50% reduction in turnover risk; and a 75% decrease in employee sick days.[106]

The **affirmative answer** to the People Excellence Question 6: Ownership, is: *Everyone is a committed owner of the organisation's Identity, as well as of its Strategic People Choice and Position, as personally internalised and externalised into his/her accountable work space and role.*

You can now do a Reflective Assessment: Ownership (Work Sheet 8 in the Work Book), if you wish to do so.

SYNERGISTIC FUSION WITHIN PEOPLE EXCELLENCE DOMAIN 1: IDENTITY

Strategic Positioning synergy regarding the Excellence Domain: Identity can be described as follows: Identity encompasses putting the right leadership in place as a departure point to engender and grow People Excellence, before making the appopriate choice regarding the strategic, value-adding role people must play in the organisation's performance and success, and consequently its continued future viability. Accordingly, the right roles must be awarded to People Professionals in the organisation, given the selected strategic people choice. Next, strategic alignment between the organisation's Identity and Key People Imperatives must be ensured to generate strategic synergy, followed by generating an inimitable, distinct and coherent Strategic People Position. This must be framed by a strategic configuration of the World of Work in and for the organisation, made up of a clear, explicit and shared People Charter; a Desired People Profile; and a compelling People Value Proposition. Lastly, building and nurturing committed ownership – internalised and externalised – amongst all organisational members to all of the above.

Figure 4.16 depicts the above Excellence synergy in the form of the first building block towards a complete People Excellence Value Chain, highlighted by the coloured circle. Important to note is the reciprocal interdependencies and dynamic, organic coherence between all the Excellence elements making up the Excellence Dimension. This occurs time-wise in a linear progression from Leadership, through Choice, Partnering, Alignment, and Differentiation to Ownership when the Excellence Elements are put in place.

Once the Elements are in place, the reciprocal interdependencies between the Elements settle over time in a non-linear fashion into either an upward spiralling virtuous cycle – a strengthening and refinement of Strategic Positioning, or into a downward spiralling, vicious cycle – the erosion of the Strategic Positioning of People Excellence. Each cycle has a knock-on effect on the subsequent Excellence Domains. The essence of synergistic fusion in this Domain therefore lies in *Congruence*. Congruence entails the consistent, harmonious 'hanging together' at the same time of all of the Excellence Elements making up this Excellence Domain.

Also important to note in the figure are the extended lines for Leadership (=directing and shaping) and Ownership (=buy-in and support), illustrating their onward influence on the other, still-to-be-discussed, Excellence Domain. As stated in the introduction to this chapter, this Excellence Domain forms the Departure Point of, and Foundation for, People Excellence, and the still-to-be-discussed Excellence Domains.

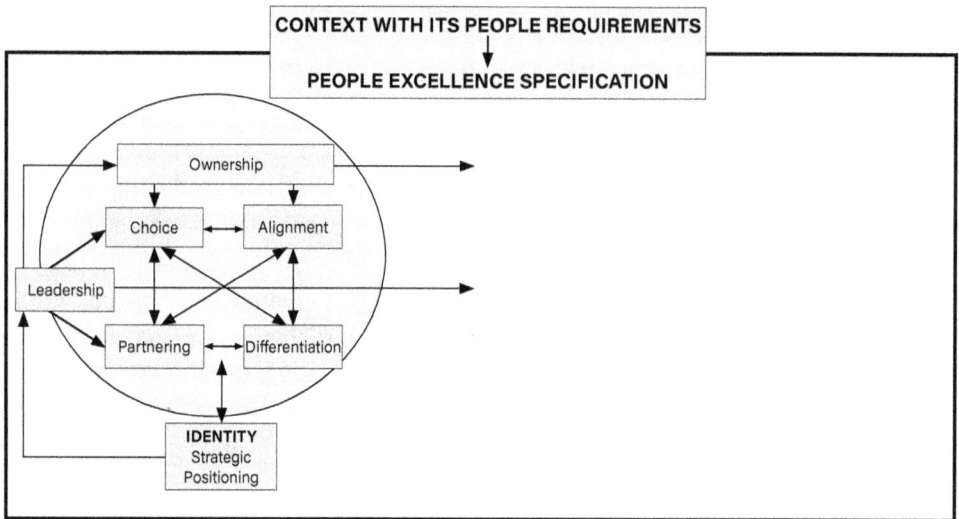

Figure 4.16: Synergistic fusion of Congruence within Excellence Dimension 1: Identity

The desired synergistic fusion to be generated by the People Excellence Domain 1: Identity, as explicated above in terms of leading thinking, research, and practices with regard to its six Excellence Elements: Leadership, Choice, Partnering, Alignment, Differentiation, and Ownership – as referenced against the People Excellence Specification of the emerging new order – is given in the shaded box below.

PEOPLE EXCELLENCE SPECIFICATION

Highly enabled, empowered and resilient people, who strongly identify with and feel valued by the organisation, and are productively and innovatively engaging collaboratively through personally purposeful and meaningful ways, to viably and sustainably create inimitable, delightful experiences for stakeholders.

PEOPLE EXCELLENCE DIMENSION 1: IDENTITY
Strategic Positioning

Whilst applying a shared, predominantly Transformational/Transcendental Leadership Stance – and visibly demonstrating the Leadership Qualities of legitimacy, inspiration, humility, integrity, ethical, and authenticity – the leadership of our organisation enables and empowers our people through a productive, healthy Leadership Process to actualise a shared, desired future for our organisation for all.

Our people are seen as the only true value unlockers and wealth creators in our organisation, and are central to its continued viablility (our Strategic People Choice). As true partners, our people take co-responsibility for our organisation's success, and strongly identify with who and what we are as an organisation, including what we stand for and aspire to (our Psychosocial Contract). We talk and walk this People Choice with its commensurate Contract in all of our daily people thinking and actions in an uncompromising and consistent manner.

In their capacity as People Experts, the People Professionals of our organisation act as true strategic organisational partners by being Credible Activists. Their value-adding and innovative contributions are eagerly sought out and truly cherishing in attaining continued organisational success and viability. They co-enable and co-ensure a high likelihood that our people will thrive as boundary-busting value unlockers and wealth creators through the productive and satisfying experiences they have.

In our organisation a high alignment exists between our Organisational Identity and the Key People Imperatives. This alignment is attained through the dynamic optimisation of the multiplicative relationship between all of the Identity and Imperative constituent pairs. This results in a strong strategic synergy manifested in high Organisational Effectiveness.

All of our people actions are directed and guided at all times by our inimitable, distinct, and coherent Strategic People Position, which is framed by a strategic configuration of the World of Work for our organisation. This Position is made up of the triangle of our People Charter, our Desired People Profile, and our all-pervasive, compelling People Value Proposition – translated into our People Brand Promise – expressive of our Strategic People Choice that sees our people as value unlockers and wealth creators, and our High Commitment/ High Involvement Psychosocial Contract (based on Partnering/Identification). Our Strategic People Choice is re-affirmed on an ongoing basis by our people's beliefs about, and actual experience of, our organisation.

Everyone in our organisation, regardless of level or status, is the committed owner of our Organisation Identity, as well as our Strategic People Choice and Position, as personally internalised and externalised into their accountable work space and role.

You can now do a Summative Reflective Assessment: Synergistic fusion – Congruence of Excellence Dimension 1: Identity (Work Sheet 9 in the Work Book), if you wish to do so.

PEOPLE EXCELLENCE STAR

CAPACITY: POTENTIALITY

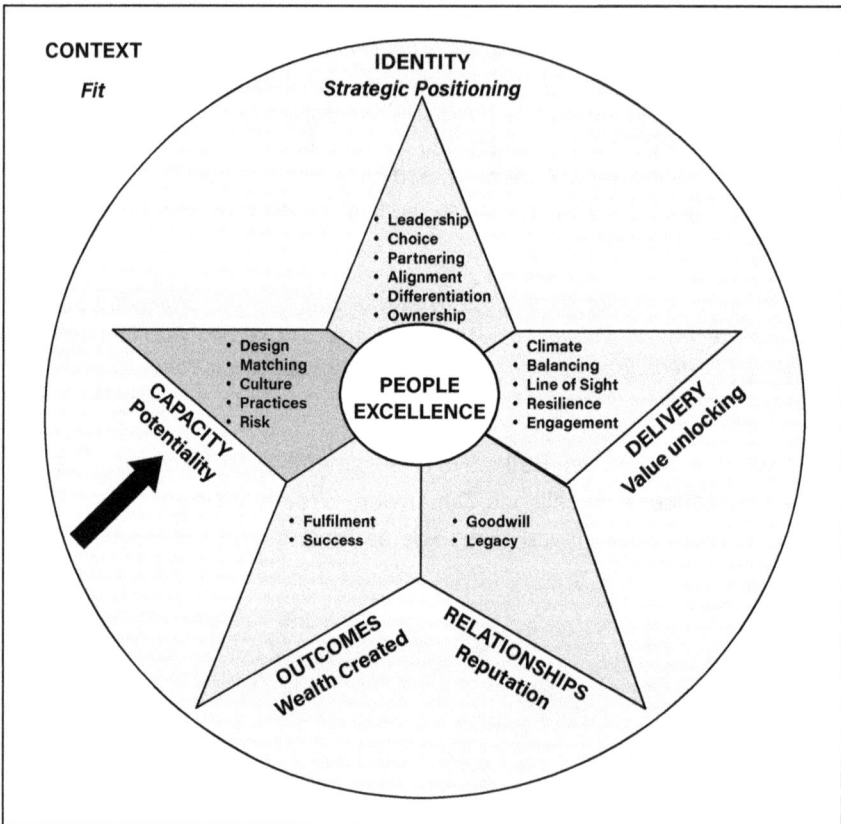

CHAPTER 5

PEOPLE EXCELLENCE DOMAIN 2 – CAPACITY: POTENTIALITY

"Excellence is never an accident. It is always the result of high intention,
sincere effort, and intelligent execution; it represents the wise choice of many
alternatives – choice, not chance, determines your destiny." (Aristotle)

"Excellence is the unlimited ability to improve the quality of what you have to offer." (Rick Pitino)

"Great companies are defined by Purpose, Process and People."
(Sumantra Goshal & Christopher Bartlett)

The Excellence Domain 1: Identity has been stress-tested: Has the strategic positioning of people in the future success and viability of the organisation been explicitly deliberated, chosen, and rolled out? Put slightly differently, has the right strategic foundation regarding people been laid by adopting the right strategic thinking framework with respect to flourishing and thriving people? Metaphorically, are we in the right place with our people for what we are setting out to achieve?

At this point, we know our organisation's people creditworthiness in this Excellence Domain (=Leadership, Choice, Partnering, Alignment, Differentiation, and Ownership), we understand what our strengths and weaknesses are, and we have pointers towards the strategic interventions needed to close the excellence gap. As noted, this Excellence Domain creates the strategic parameters for setting up the subsequent Domains.

Next, the *People Excellence Domain 2: Capacity* must be stress-tested. The thrust of this Excellence Domain is *Potentiality*. It deals with the overarching Excellence Question of whether the organisation has put in place the necessary conditions to engender, nurture, grow, and maintain People Excellence in the organisation within the strategic parameters set by the Excellence Domain 1: Identity. These conditions create the potential space for the organisation's people to flourish and thrive; delight stakeholders; and contribute to making and keeping the organisation viable.

The created capacity is mere potentiality which must be realised in Excellence Domain 3: Delivery by the organisation's people in terms of value unlocking. Thus the key question regarding Excellence Domain 2: Delivery under discussion here is: Has the organisation made the required, upfront people investment to create the potentiality for it to be a viable organisation through attaining an unassailable competitive edge with its people?[1] The Excellence Domain 3: Capacity is informed by an iron cast principle – one gets what one invests in and for. From another angle, this Excellence Domain is about the 'people readiness' of the organisation for its unfolding, strategic journey into the future to successfully realise its Identity within Excellence Domain 3: Delivery. No Capacity, no Delivery.

As illustrated in the People Excellence Star on the opposite page, Excellence Domain 2: Capacity encompasses the five Excellence Elements of *Design, Matching, Culture, Practices, and Risk.* Each is discussed in turn, in the order listed. The chapter concludes by weaving the integrated People Excellence story of the synergistic fusion to be generated within this Domain.

PEOPLE EXCELLENCE QUESTION 7: DESIGN

Does the organisation have a fit-for-purpose organisational design, architected around meaningful work?[2][3]

Organisational design (or architecture) (OD) refers to the Operating Model of the organisation. It entails the 'logic' deployed by the organisation to establish, unlock and deliver ongoing value for its stakeholders. It pertains to *how* the required work of the organisation must be allocated, done, and governed, i.e., its delivery logic. The design of the organisation provides the designated boundaries of accountability, responsibility, and authority regarding the work to be done within and by the organisation. A fit-for-purpose design must ensure that the right things get done in the right places at the right times by the right people, teams, and units, governed by the necessary checks and balances.

The following excellence themes are explicated regarding Design: The Levels and Dimensions of a complete design; the critical indicators of a fit-for-purpose design; a fit-for-purpose design for the emerging new order; a people-centric design; and the benefits of a fit-for-purpose design.

The Levels and Dimensions of a complete design

A fit-for-purpose organisational design will cover, comprehensively, holistically and congruently, the design in its full ambit, by:[4][5]

- *Levels:* Aligned Strategic (=Total Organisational Design), Tactical (=Organisational Unit Design), and Operational (=Daily mode of working in terms of Work Teams and Work Roles); and
- *Dimensions:* Horizontal (=Dividing Work Processes into Work Units), Vertical (=Requisite Complexity Levels of Work) and Lateral (=Integrating Mechanisms and Governance Model).

The architected design must remain strategically in force for the same period for which the Organisational Identity – in particular its Strategic Intent – will be in place.

A distinction must also be drawn between the organisational design as *intended* (=the desired design); *espoused* (=the verbalised design as communicated); and *enacted* (=the design as it actually operates on a daily basis). Ideally speaking, all three designs must be the same. However, in practice there are frequently significant differences between them. The assessment of the fitness-of-purpose of the organisational design must occur on the enacted design which is the real, active design, reflecting the actual delivery logic of the organisation which solicits certain people conduct – desirable and undesirable – in the organisation.

The critical indicators of a fit-for-purpose Design

The more important critical indicators of a fit-for-purpose design are:

- it ensures a best fit between the organisation and the context in which it operates;
- it translates the organisation's Identity – expressed inter alia in its Strategic Intent, initiatives and goals – into clearly demarcated work units, day-to-day work flows, and modes of working, as well as its requisite Levels of Work and well-defined work roles with a clear delineation of responsibilities, accountabilities and authority (=sound governance);[6]
- it is aligned to the Desired People Profile, and engenders the Expected Desired People Conduct (see Excellence Question 5: Differentiation);
- it builds, enhances and protects the organisation's in-depth core capabilities, organisation- and people-wise (see Excellence Question 8: Matching), putting the organisation on a hard-to-beat strategic trajectory of viability;
- it ensures the virtuous (i.e., value-referenced), optimal integration of people and technology;[7][8][9][10]
- it mobilises the organisation in a focused manner to meet market/customer needs in a responsive, value-adding manner, in this way creating great (=inimitable) customer experiences;
- it moulds the organisation's Identity, leadership, people, culture, resources and performance into a coherent, synergetic whole;
- it directs and shapes organisational and people conduct and performance in the desired direction;[11] and
- it enables high customer and employee retention.

A fit-for-purpose Design for the emerging new order

The shift towards a fit-for-purpose organisational design in the emerging new order is moving from a mechanistic to an organic organisational design. Table 5.1 provides an overview of this shift.[12]

Table 5.1: Shift from a Mechanistic to an Organic Organisational Design

FROM MECHANISTIC...	...TO ORGANIC
Function-driven	Purpose-driven
Closed boundaries	Open boundaries
Parts	Systemic whole
Sameness (=Cloning)	Inclusive diversity
Stability	Growth/Change
Top down, hierarchal control	Front line empowerment
Centralised	Distributed
Authority/Power	Relationships/Expertise
Departmentalised	Networking
Jobs	Teams/Roles
Tasks	Assignments

The shift seen in Table 5.1 is demonstrated in the move from a Command-and-Control Organisational Shape (=mechanistic design) – the 'pyramid' – to a High Networking/ High Engagement/High Responsibility Organisational Shape (=organic design) – the 'spider web'[13][14] – more befitting the emerging new order. The organisation is seen more as a people-centric, action community built around strong, deep relationships; providing mutual support; and engendering physical, mental, and spiritual well-being[15] This move is depicted in Figure 5.1.[16][17][18]

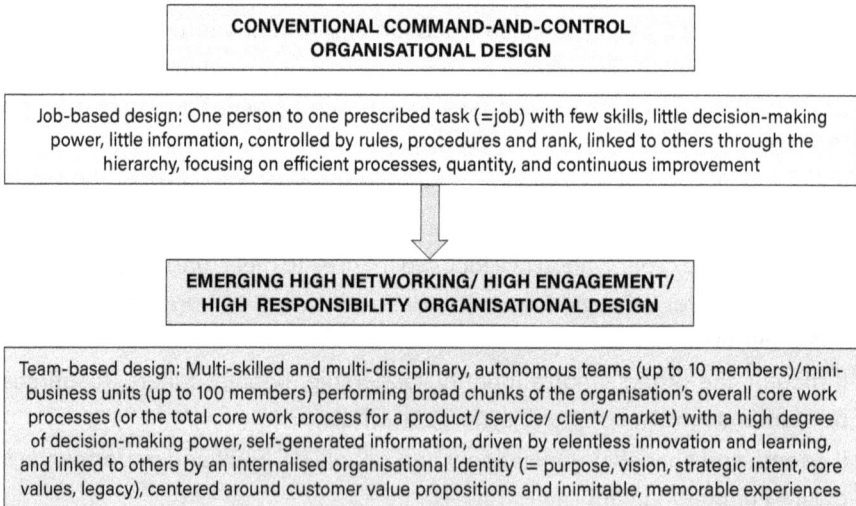

CONVENTIONAL COMMAND-AND-CONTROL ORGANISATIONAL DESIGN

Job-based design: One person to one prescribed task (=job) with few skills, little decision-making power, little information, controlled by rules, procedures and rank, linked to others through the hierarchy, focusing on efficient processes, quantity, and continuous improvement

⬇

EMERGING HIGH NETWORKING/ HIGH ENGAGEMENT/ HIGH RESPONSIBILITY ORGANISATIONAL DESIGN

Team-based design: Multi-skilled and multi-disciplinary, autonomous teams (up to 10 members)/mini-business units (up to 100 members) performing broad chunks of the organisation's overall core work processes (or the total core work process for a product/ service/ client/ market) with a high degree of decision-making power, self-generated information, driven by relentless innovation and learning, and linked to others by an internalised organisational Identity (= purpose, vision, strategic intent, core values, legacy), centered around customer value propositions and inimitable, memorable experiences

---

Figure 5.1: Move from a Command-and-Control Organisational Shape to a High Network/High Engagement/High Responsibility Organisational Shape

Within the emerging new order, the High Network/High Engagement/High Responsibility Organisational Shape has to be architected around ambidexterity.[19][20] This entails finding the real-time, dynamic, optimal balance between:

- stability: the discipline of ensuring continuity and certainty through time (*transactional-exploitative order*); and

- ongoing re-invention, re-configuration, and self-designing: stretching to deal with continual, fast (radical) change triggered by the imperative of disruptive innovation (*transformative-explorative chaos*).

The organisation is therefore in a state of dynamic stability.[21] It has been found that organisations that are stable *and* fast simultanuously are three times more likely to be high performing than those that are fast but concurrently lack stability.[22]

A people-centric Design: Meaningful work

In the final instance, a fit-for-purpose organisational design – enabling People Excellence – must ultimately be people-centric.*[23]* Highly people-centric organisations are three times more likely to have a growth rate of 10% or more than low people-centric organisations.[24] Meaningful work has been found to be the most important People Excellence indicator of a people-centric design as it allows people to thrive and flourish.[25][*26*] Meaningful work relates to the Work Role element of the CCARRLO PVP discussed under Excellence Question 5: Differentiation (see Figure 4.15). Meaningful work implies a direct line of sight to the organisation's Purpose as contained in its Identity. It has been found that higher Meaningfulness is enabled by more Organic Organisational Designs, as given in Table 5.1.[27]

Meaningfulness pertains to the degree to which people experience their work – and its resultant outcome – as being of real, lasting significance and worth to them: (i) by becoming more of oneself through one's work; (ii) by allowing one to express one's true self; (iii) by bonding with others in a deep way; and (iv) by making a true difference through the value one's work delivers to stakeholders.

As worthy work, meaningfulness pertains to: (i) *doing well*: work that is good in itself; (ii) *doing with*: authentic work relationships with others; (iii) *doing good*: work that is of benefit to others[28]; and (iv) *doing beyond:* work that serves the greater good.[29] In turn, meaningfulness nurtures greater personal authenticity[30] and high work engagement.[31] In the final instance, however, meaningfulness is in the eye of the beholder, i.e., the person doing the work. Does a person experience the work as meaningful or not, regardless of whether the intention was to architect meaningful work?

Benefits of a fit-for-purpose Design

The way the organisation is designed – its fitness-for-purpose – has a profound effect on its capacity to perform effectively.[32] This includes not only the organisation's ability to live and actualise its Identity successfully, but also to:

- create inimitable, memorable experiences for customers and employees;
- faciliate optimal resource deployment and utilisation;

- enable an efficient mode of working;
- engender an optimal flow of people energy;
- solicit the expected, desired people conduct;
- trigger the correct level of engagement by people; and
- nuture a healthy Organisational Culture, climate and dynamics.

In turn, this affects the overall performance of the organisation, and ultimately its continued viability. An organisation can indeed compete by its design.[33] In a study by Bain of companies in eight industries across 21 countries, it was found that organisations with top quartile Operating Models – i.e., clear, robust, fit-for-purpose designs – had a five-year compound average revenue growth that was 120 basis points higher than those in the bottom quartile, together with operating margins that were 260 basis points higher.[34] McKinsey has found that organisations that excelled at design, grew their revenues and shareholder returns at nearly twice the rate of their industry peers. Yet, only 10% of respondents stated that their organisation had realised its design's full potential.[35]

The **affirmative answer** to the People Excellence Question 7: Design, is: *the organisation has a fit-for-purpose design – architected around meaningful work for everyone – ensuring that the right things get done in the right places at the right times by the right persons, teams, and units, governed by the necessary checks and balances.*

You can now do a Reflective Assessment: Design (Work Sheet 10 in the Work Book), if you wish to do so.

PEOPLE EXCELLENCE QUESTION 8: MATCHING

Are the Core Organisational and People Capacities matched within the progressively unfolding strategic horizon of the organisation?

The adopted Organisational Design specifies the functional requirements of the Core Organisational and People Capabilities required by the Operating Model as the delivery logic of the organisation.[36] The Core Capabilities enable the organisation to gain a sustainable competitive edge in its chosen markets, and thus sustain its viability. Capabilities can be substantive, e.g., a technology, process, resource, key product/service, strategic customer and/or key talent. Or, be qualitative, such as agility, ambidexterity, responsiveness and innovativeness.

Core Organisational and People Capabilities must be dynamically matched at all times in real time within the progressively unfolding strategic horizon of the organisation. This matching will ensure that the required overall capacity to deliver has been 'installed' and is available timeously in the organisation.[37] The dynamic matching must ensure a good organisation-person match. At an individual level, an organisation-person match affects people's job satisfaction and intention to leave. The better the fit, the higher people's job satisfaction and the weaker their intention to leave.[38] At an organisational level, a medium improvement in the organisation-person fit (also including an Organisational Culture fit) is associated with a 15% improvement in Return-on-Investment (ROI) per employee.[39] Executive leadership plays a crucial role in ensuring the matching of Core Organisational and People Capabilities, and in realising the competitive advantage locked up in this matching.[40]

Two Excellence themes will now be discussed with respect to Matching: the Strategic People Capabilities Demand and Supply Equation; and Strategic Talent Mix.

The Strategic People Capabilities Demand and Supply Equation

Framed by the organisation's Identity, Core Organisational Capabilities refer to the critical/unique abilities, uniquely combined in a hard-to-imitate manner, that are required and leveraged to give the organisation a distinct, competitive edge.[41][42] The delivery of the Core Organisational Capabilities – the people demand side of the organisation – has to be directly mirrored by the available, matched People Capabilities – the people supply side of the organisation – in terms of the desired people profile(s).[43]

The people capability (read 'human capital') of an organisation is related to its performance: an increase in the necessary human capital by one standard deviation increases organisational performance by 0.21 of a standard deviation. This relationship is even stronger by a factor of 71% when the human capital is organisation-specific rather than general. I.e., matching the organisation's people capability to its unique Strategic Intent has an even greater effect on its performance.[44]

The Core Organisational and People Capabilities match is a concrete operationalisation of Excellence Question 4: Alignment, forming part of Excellence Domain 1: Identity, which entails:

- a high alignment between the complementary pairs of Organisational Identity elements and the Key People Imperatives; and
- the realisation of the desired Organisational Effectiveness through optimising the multiplicative relationship between all of the constituent pairs of the Organisational Effectiveness Equation.

Taking this strategic alignment further, Figure 5.2 depicts the dynamic process of matching Core Organisational and People Capabilities within the unfolding, strategic time horizon of the organisation.[45]

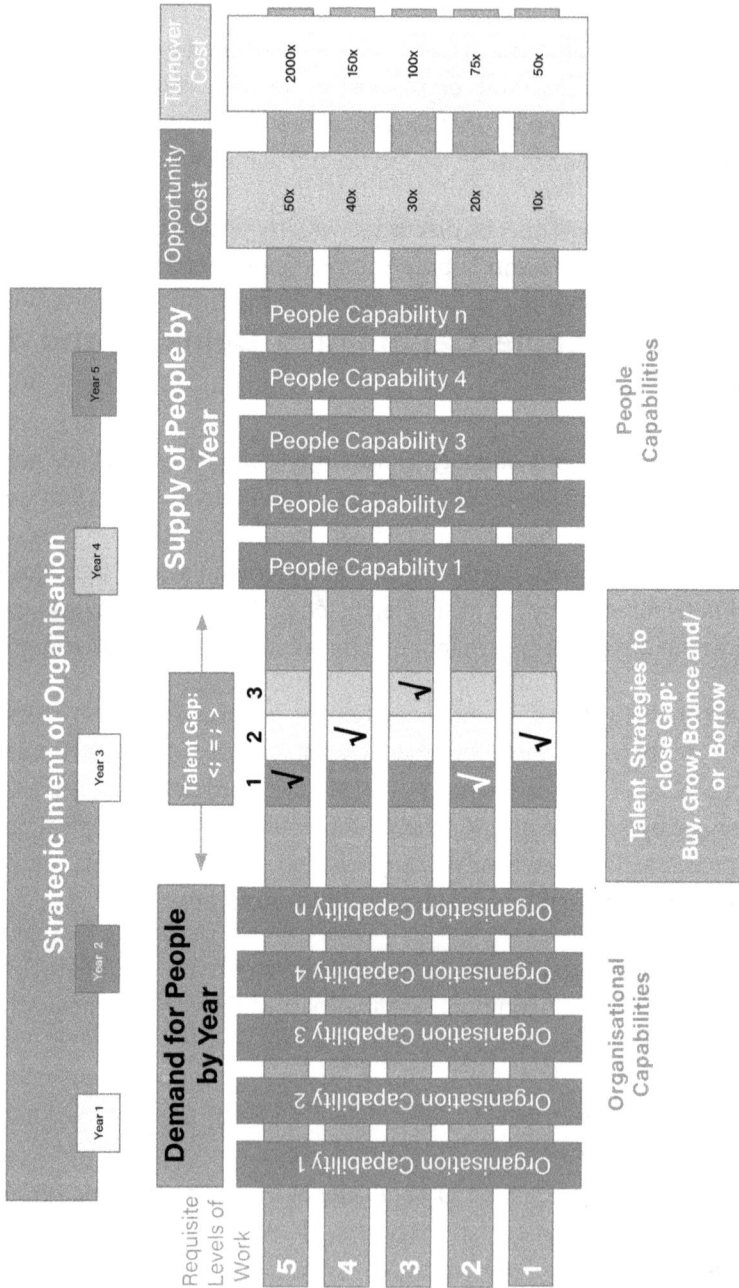

Figure 5.2: Dynamically matching Core Organisational and People Capabilities – befitting the organisation's Strategic Intent – over its unfolding, strategic time horizon

According to Figure 5.2:

- the *Demand for and Supply of People Capabilities* must be matched dynamically over the unfolding, strategic time horizon of the organisation – in this case, five years – by its five requisite Levels of Work (LOWs) and Core Organisational and People Capabilities 1 to n. Ideally speaking, two minutes before a person is required, she/he is available; [46]

- there is an *opportunity cost* of not filling a Work Role. The expected value that would be lost if a Role is not filled when needed – the opportunity cost – is given down the right-hand side of Figure 5.2. E.g., 50x Total Cost to Company (TCC) at LOW5 per Role; 40x Total Cost to Company at LOW4 per Role; and so on[47];

- the *turnover cost* of a person resigning, going down the right-hand side of Figure 5.2. E.g., is, for example, 200x TCC at LOW5 per person; 150x Total Cost to Company at LOW4 per person; and so on[48];

- In the middle of Figure 5.2, the *People Gap* is depicted as Demand>Supply (Column 1); Supply>Demand (Column 2); and Demand=Supply (Column 3); and

- the mix of appropriate *Talent Strategies* to close the Gap must be selected: Grow, Buy, Bounce (=Outsource) and/or Borrow (=Insource). The People Strategies must focus in particular on strategically pivotal (or mission-critical) Roles/Positions, now and going into the future, giving the organisation an unassailable competitive edge[49] *and thus keeping it viable.* The emerging new order is demanding new people capabilities that are not freely available, or do not even exist, which will force organisations to place a heavy emphasis on growing their own talent (see Chapter 3).[50][51][52]

Strategic Talent Mix

Relative to its Strategic Intent and its Desired People Profile at the organisational level (see Figure 4.13), a talent-driven organisation covers in terms of its talent: (i) both the present and the future; as well as (ii) how its talent must look the same and may/will look different at the end of its strategic planning period (Year 5 in Figure 5.2).[53] An explicit, deliberate strategic talent mix (or portfolio), as shown in Figure 5.3, has to be crafted in terms of the relative weighting given to the different categories of the organisation's overall talent profile, as set by the organisation's Strategic Intent:

- Category 1: the same talent profile here-and-now – maintaining the *status quo* talent profile (Maintenance/Present).
- Category 2: the same talent profile needed in the future – an *extrapolation* of the existing talent profile (Maintenance/Future).
- Category 3: adding additional abilities to the current talent profile going into the future – an *enriched* talent profile (Renewal/Present).
- Category 4: a completely different talent profile in the future, but not being in the organisation at present: an *anticipated new talent* profile (Renewal/Future).

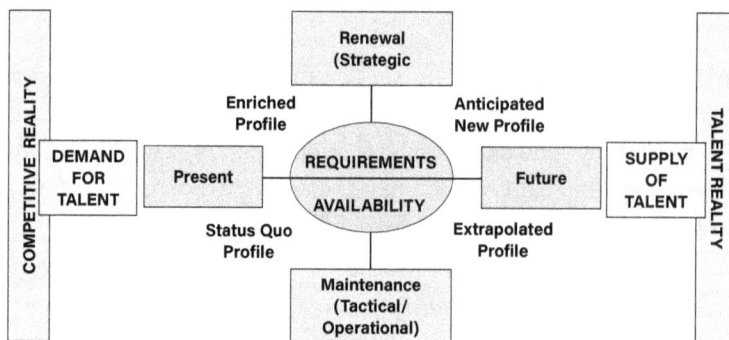

Figure 5.3: Strategic Talent Positioning

Hypothetically, if an organisation estimates that it will need 2,000 people at the end of its strategic planning cycle of Year 5, it will have to distribute them percentage-wise across the four strategic talent mix categories given in Figure 5.3 – using the comprehensive talent profile shown in Figure 4.13 – to describe the talent needed in each category. This means that talent-driven organisations have clarity regarding their strategic talent mix over their progressively unfolding strategic horizons. It can readily be accepted that the emerging new order will impose a heavier weighting of Categories 3 and 4.

With respect to Category 4: Anticipated New Profile (see Figure 5.3), an organisation must ensure that its current PVP will be able to attract new talent, or the PVP must be recrafted. As discussed before, an organisation may need to balance the tension across multiple stakeholders between, on the *one hand,* a forward-looking People Brand, able to attract different types of people who are matched to where the organisation is going in the future, AND, *on the other hand,* its Brand in the present, attracting similar people.

Getting the dynamic matching of the People Demand and Supply sides right means, People Excellence-wise, having at any given time the right people in the right numbers at the right time in the right place, who are able, willing, allowed, and want to perform, leveraged by a personalised sense of purpose and meaning.[54][55] This match finds its People Excellence expression in strong strategic people (or talent) pipelines with respect to the organisation's different Talent Pools, e.g., Succession, High Potential, Solid Citizens, New Entrants, and Alumni, which are closely aligned to the organisation's Identity, especially its Strategic Intent.[56] Talent pools can also be demarcated in terms of the types of talent to be attracted and retained: permanent, contacted, freelancers, gig, and temporary.

The People Value Chain – attract-perform-grow-retain – provides the platform and leverage for establishing organisational routines to build the strategic people pipeline and the respective Talent Pools making up the pipeline.[57] A timespace free, gig work relationship, strategic configuration of the world of work by the organisation would allow for a much wider choice of talent, sourced globally (see Excellence Question 5: Differentiation).

The **affirmative answer** to the People Excellence Question 8, Matching, is: *a dynamic match exists at any given time between the Core Organisational and People Capacities of the organisation, as synchronised relative to its progressively unfolding strategic horizon.*

You can now do a Reflective Assessment: Matching (Work Sheet 11 in the Work Book), if you wish to do so.

PEOPLE EXCELLENCE QUESTION 9: CULTURE

Is the organisation 'glued' together by a distinct, strong but flexible Organisational Culture?

Organisational Culture refers to the distinct, shared ways of seeing, interpreting, and acting upon the world which is deeply institutionalised in the organisation. It is the 'glue' holding the organisation together. Given the emerging new order permeated by the VICCAS world, it is argued in some quarters that Organisational Culture is the new 'structure' holding the organisation together.[58][59] Organisational Culture is made up of the collection of conscious/unconscious shared assumptions, beliefs, values and norms, which are translated and enacted upon in distinct ways of thinking, deciding, doing, and valuing persons and things in the organisation on a daily basis.[60]

Organisational Culture frames, mobilises, directs, guides, and focuses people energy in a shared way in the organisation as it endeavours to realise its strategic aspirations. It enables people to 'see' things but also 'blinds' them to others. It has been found that the leadership of an organisation and its Organisational Culture correspond highly – up to 70% – such that Organisational Culture and leadership are seen in some quarters as two sides of the same coin.[61] In addition to a Leadership-Organisational Culture fit people-wise, achieving a high People-Organisational Culture fit is critical to direct and guide People Excellence on an ongoing, institutionalised, daily basis in the organisation.[62] Such a fit is associated with greater commitment, higher engagement, better performance, more innovation, more learning, higher job satisfaction, less people stress and strain, better well-being, and greater retention.[63]

Organisational Culture enables the appropriate and successful conception, crafting, roll out, and execution of the organisation's Identity, including its Strategic Intent, affecting its performance and long term viability.[64] As has been said, "Culture eats Strategy for breakfast" (ascribed to Peter Drucker). Thus a Strategic Intent of Product/ Service Innovation, and a Strategic People Choice of people as value unlockers and wealth creators, necessitates a corresponding highly enabling, empowering, innovation-engendering, and achievement-driven Organisational Culture, giving the organisation a difficult-to-imitate distinctiveness.[65][66] A high Strategic Intent-Organisational Culture alignment strengthens the Strategic Intent-People Strategy relationship, and the consistent roll out of the latter.[67] In turn, Organisational Culture must also be congruent with the architected design of the organisation in order to reinforce and support the design.[68] Within the emerging new order, the High Network/High Engagement/High Responsibility Organisational Shape is architected around ambidexterity, creating the conditions for innovation. Organisational Culture furthermore sets the conditions under which the espoused People Practices (see Excellence Question 10: Practices) of the organisation truly become the accepted, institutionalised, every day ways of doing things in the organisation.[69] Recursively, the People Practices reinforce and support the Organisational Culture.

A strong, distinct Organisational Culture can improve organisational performance by 20% to 30% compared to a weak, unremarkable culture.[70][71] A strong Organisational Culture furthermore brings about organisational alignment, cohesion, consistency, predictability, and highly motivated (=engaged) and loyal (=committed) organisational members. It channels and shapes people's attitudes, conduct, and energy in the right direction.[72]

Although strong (i.e., highly coherent), an Organisational Culture must, however, concurrently be flexible (or malleable) to adapt 'easily' in tandem with the organisation's Identity changes, continuous disruptive innovation, and/or contextual challenges, demands and requirement shifts. If an Organisational Culture is strong but rigid, it will imprison an organisation in a culture that over time may incapacitate it to innovate and change with the times.[73]

The functions, layers, hard- and software of Organisational Culture, ideal Organisational Culture, and Organisational Culture types are discussed next.

Functions of Organisational Culture

Organisational Culture provides the organisation and its members with answers to the following questions in a collective, integrative way[74]:

- *Stakeholders*: Who are our stakeholders? What are their interests and needs? How do we satisfy these interests and needs in a fair and equitable way?

- *Purpose:* Who are we? What do we aspire to? What drives us, and why?

- *World View*: What is our explanation, understanding, and prediction of the make-up of the world, how it works/should work, and how we must relate to and interact with it?

- *Ideology*: What value do we place on persons, things, events, and outcomes? What is right/wrong, important/unimportant, beautiful/ugly, true/false? An ethical Organisational Culture has been shown to be an important determinant of employee engagement.[75] The Organisational Culture of productive and financially successful organisations – framed by a growth mindset – contains the norms of collaboration, innovation, and integrity/ethical behaviour. These norms foster greater trust and commitment amongst organisational members.[76]

- *Mode of Working:* What is our style of relating to people, things, events, and outcomes, also in terms of the use of power? How do we interact and behave, both internally and externally?

The first two functions – stakeholders and purpose – enable the organisation to externally adapt. I.e., ensure a good organisation-context fit. The last three functions – world view, ideology, and mode of working – enable internal organisational relationship integration. I.e., member involvement and consistency.[77] The relationship between Organisational Culture (=external adaptation and internal integration) and affective commitment (=committed ownership) is mediated by organisational members' perceived sense of Psychosocial Contract fulfilment. A high sense of fulfilment results in a positive experience of a supportive/caring Organisational Culture, in turn strengthening the affective commitment of organisational members.[78]

Layers of Organisational Culture

Organisational Culture manifests itself through four interdependent layers, depicted in Figure 5.4. A deeper layer changes and shapes a shallower layer, which has to be congruent with a deeper layer.[79] All of these layers will be affected by the operating arena of the organisation, in particular differences in national cultures across the arena which will demand a certain level of cultural intelligence to negotiate.[80]

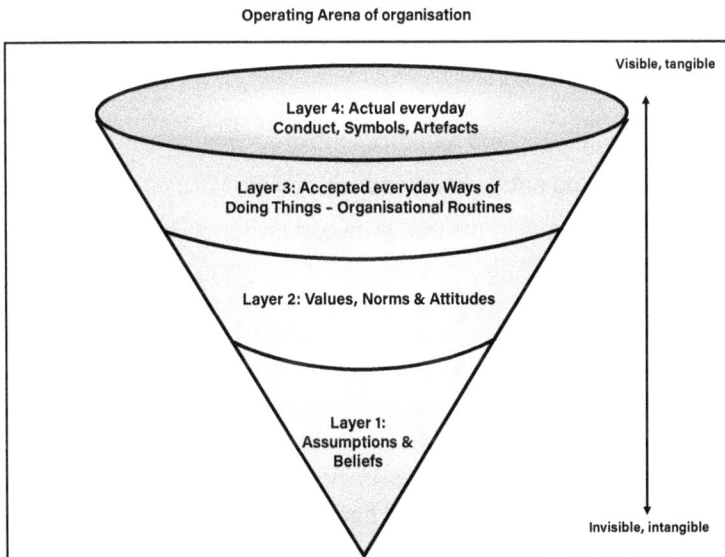

Operating Arena of organisation

Visible, tangible

Layer 4: Actual everyday Conduct, Symbols, Artefacts

Layer 3: Accepted everyday Ways of Doing Things - Organisational Routines

Layer 2: Values, Norms & Attitudes

Layer 1: Assumptions & Beliefs

Invisible, intangible

Figure 5.4: Layers of Organisational Culture

Hard- and Software of Organisational Culture

A chosen Organisational Culture must be translated into, and find their matched manifestation in, the hard- and software of the organisation[81], illustrated in Figure 5.5. The elements of the hard- and software that must mutually support and reinforce each other are placed in proximity of each other in Figure 5.5.[82] The approximate Layers of Organisational Culture (refer to Figure 5.4) they represent are also indicated.[83]

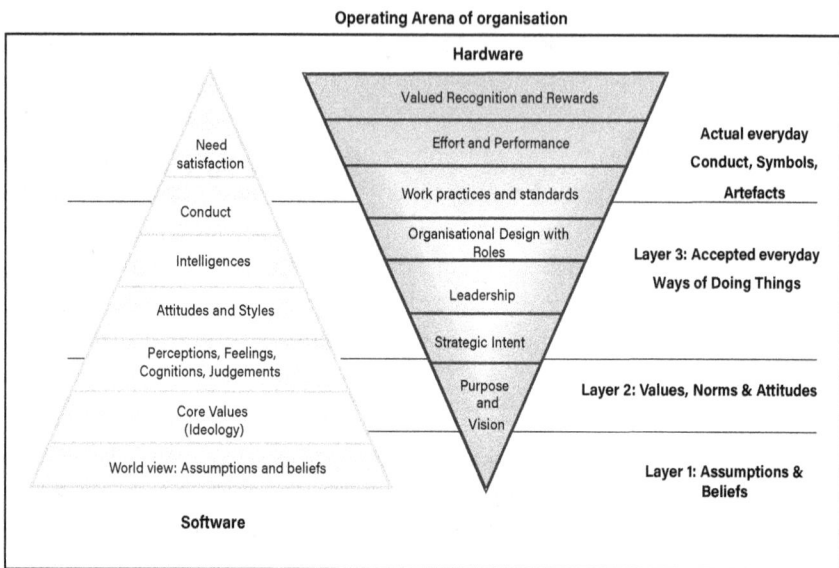

Operating Arena of organisation

Hardware

Valued Recognition and Rewards

Effort and Performance

Actual everyday
Conduct, Symbols,
Artefacts

Need satisfaction

Work practices and standards

Conduct

Organisational Design with Roles

Intelligences

Layer 3: Accepted everyday
Ways of Doing Things

Leadership

Attitudes and Styles

Strategic Intent

Perceptions, Feelings, Cognitions, Judgements

Purpose and Vision

Layer 2: Values, Norms & Attitudes

Core Values (Ideology)

World view: Assumptions and beliefs

Layer 1: Assumptions & Beliefs

Software

Figure 5.5: Hard- and software of Organisational Culture

Ideal Organisational Culture

The ideal Organisational Culture[84]:

- is aligned to, strengthens, and reinforces the organisation's and people's Identities;
- has been internalised and is identified with by all;
- is explicit and conscious in the integrative, daily functioning of the organisation;
- is strong, but simultaneously dynamically flexible to respond rapidly to changes in the operating arena of the organisation;
- is caring and supportive of organisational members; and
- promotes and embraces diversity, in all of its various manifestations, in an all-inclusive way – persons, disciplines, functions, beliefs, views and histories. It allows each organisational member to be a person in his/her own right in the organisation. A person can be true to her/himself. It nutures psychological safety for all. An inclusive culture thus counters the cloning of organisational members and groupthink.[85]

Types of Organisational Culture

Organisational Culture can be characterised according to two dimensions, resulting in four types of Organisational Culture.[86] These dimensions are:

- Performance vs. Relationship Orientation; and
- Control vs. Commitment Orientation.

The four Organisational Culture types that can be constructed from these two dimensions are:

- Achievement (Performance/Commitment);
- Caring (Commitment/Relationship);
- Power (Relationship/Control); and
- Role (Control/Performance).

Figure 5.6 provides detail descriptions of the four Organisational Culture types, as infused by underlying core qualities, e.g., an Internal vs. External Focus. These are pure types. Usually an organisation has a dominant culture type with elements of the other types being present to a lesser degree at the same time.[87] As depicted in Figure 5.6, the culture type dominant in the organisation must fit its Identity. Naturally, all of the aforementioned – i.e., the functions, layers and hard- and software of Organisational Culture – are manifested differently in each of the culture types.

The emerging 'compelling, memorable, experience-based' economy, with the imperative of ongoing, relentless disruptive innovation and necessity of continuous deep learning/teaching, points strongly towards an Achievement/Caring Organisational Culture[88], providing a high sense of belonging. Organisations that establish a belonging/inclusive culture are twice as likely to meet/exceed their financial targets; three times more likely to be high performing; six times more likely to be innovative and agile; and eight times more likely to achieve better organisational outcomes.[89] This culture is infused by innovation[90], life-long learning[91], and the reinforcement of an ambidextrous organisational design. It must also be aligned to the derived People Excellence Specification for the emerging new order.[92]

An explicitly adopted, well developed, and fully institutionalised – a 'mature' Organisational Culture type - would fulfil all of the functions explicated above for culture; would be congruent across the respective cultural layers; would be well entrenched in both the hard- and software of the Organisational Culture, which would also be congruent; and would meet the features of the ideal Organisational Culture.

The **affirmative answer** to the People Excellence Question 9: Culture, is: *the organisation is glued together by a distinct, strong but flexible Achievement/Caring*

Organisational Culture – aligned to its Identity – which is seamlessly translated into the organisation's hard- and software, enabling and empowering people to achieve outstandingly in mutually supportive ways.

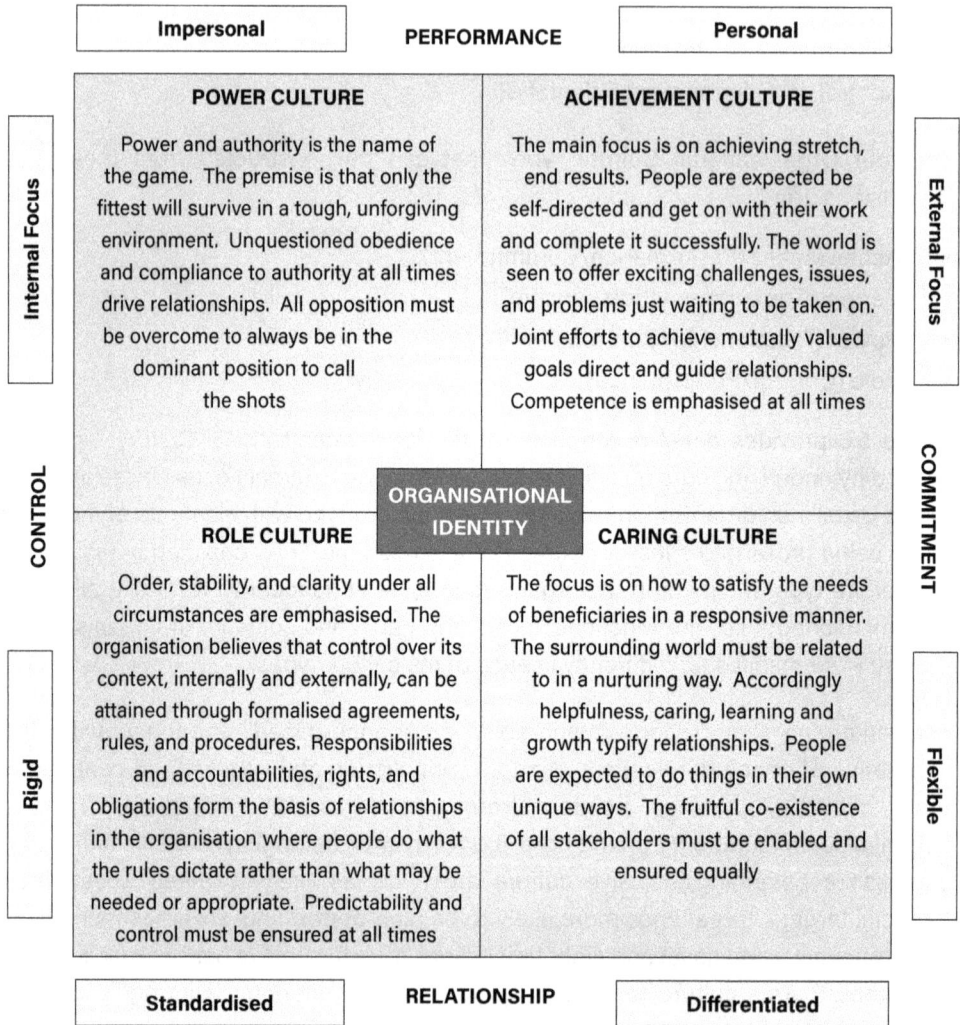

	Impersonal	PERFORMANCE	Personal	
Internal Focus	**POWER CULTURE** Power and authority is the name of the game. The premise is that only the fittest will survive in a tough, unforgiving environment. Unquestioned obedience and compliance to authority at all times drive relationships. All opposition must be overcome to always be in the dominant position to call the shots		**ACHIEVEMENT CULTURE** The main focus is on achieving stretch, end results. People are expected be self-directed and get on with their work and complete it successfully. The world is seen to offer exciting challenges, issues, and problems just waiting to be taken on. Joint efforts to achieve mutually valued goals direct and guide relationships. Competence is emphasised at all times	**External Focus**
CONTROL	**ROLE CULTURE** Order, stability, and clarity under all circumstances are emphasised. The organisation believes that control over its context, internally and externally, can be attained through formalised agreements, rules, and procedures. Responsibilities and accountabilities, rights, and obligations form the basis of relationships in the organisation where people do what the rules dictate rather than what may be needed or appropriate. Predictability and control must be ensured at all times	ORGANISATIONAL IDENTITY	**CARING CULTURE** The focus is on how to satisfy the needs of beneficiaries in a responsive manner. The surrounding world must be related to in a nurturing way. Accordingly helpfulness, caring, learning and growth typify relationships. People are expected to do things in their own unique ways. The fruitful co-existence of all stakeholders must be enabled and ensured equally	**COMMITMENT**
Rigid				**Flexible**
	Standardised	RELATIONSHIP	Differentiated	

Figure 5.6: Organisational culture types

You can now do a Reflective Assessment: Culture (Work Sheet 12 in the Work Book), if you wish to do so.

PEOPLE EXCELLENCE
QUESTION 10: PRACTICES

Has the organisation crafted a coherent, aligned set of High Commitment/High Involvement People Practices, and effectively translated them into a commensurate people management tool set for daily use?

The organisation must put in place the appropriate People Practices (=People Policies)[93] that will solicit the Expected, Desired People Conduct to be manifested by its people (see Excellence Question 5: Differentiation).[94] The Practices must match the people the organisation wishes to attract, engage, grow and retain. All of these aim to create the conditions for the organisation's people to be highly engaged on a daily basis, in this way bringing about People Excellence. Metaphorically, this is where the 'rubber is hitting the road' as far as leading people on an everyday basis in the organisation is concerned.

The purpose of People Practices is to provide strategic leverage to the organisation by directing and shaping the conduct of organisational members towards the Expected Desired People Conduct; build Core Organisational and People Capabilities; and create favourable conditions for outstanding organisational performance and success with people.[95] Concurrently Practices must create favourable conditions with the accompanying resources, under which people will be engaged, flourish, and hence thrive, because they feel safe, valued, cared for, and supported.[96] In this way, the continued viability of the organisation will be enabled, people-wise. That is why People Practices relate primarily to the Key People imperative: People Energy ('Will do') (see Table 4.5).

The following themes are discussed below: A coherent, strategically aligned bundle of Practices; Low vs. High Commitment/High Involvement Practices; the committed ownership of Practices; and the effects of Practices.

A coherent, strategically aligned bundle of People Practices[97]

No single People Practice (=the proverbial silver bullet) will ensure the Expected, Desired People Conduct. A coherent, synergistic and mutually reinforcing bundle of Practices must be crafted[98], covering the entire people value chain across the whole organisation at all levels. The crucial guiding question when crafting a bundle of Practices is: Will this bundle create and maintain the favourable conditions and resources through which people would be able to demonstrate the Expected Desired Conduct, allowing them to flourish and hence thrive, concurrently allowing the organisation to perform excellently people-wise? Thriving here entails the manifestation of high work performance; high engagement; high work enjoyment and satisfaction; high well-being; making innovative, valuable contributions; demonstrating constructive organisational citizenship; and high retention. In turn, this will ensure a viable organisation in terms of organisational performance and success.[99]

The right bundle of Practices can have this effect because it provides the condition for an invigorating Organisational Climate to come about, engendering positive outcomes to emerge (see Excellence Question 12: Climate). Recursively, these positive outcomes invoke even more favourable perceptions of the People Practices in force.[100] And so, the virtuous cycle continues unabatedly.

The bundle of People Practices crafted must be organisation-specific[101] and fit the Strategic Positioning of People Excellence in the organisation, incorporating its Organisational Identity.[102] However, People Practices bundles may vary across Strategic Intents.[103] E.g., High Commitment/High Involvement People Practices (see below) appear to be more suited to, and give higher returns for, a Differentiation (=innovation-driven) Strategic Intent. This is in contrast to a Cost Strategic Intent which requires Low Commitment/Low Involvement Practices.[104] High Commitment/High Involvement People Practices must also match the People Excellence Specification of the emerging new order (refer to Chapter 3).

A People Practices bundle must furthermore operationalise into the everyday ways of doing things regarding the people in the organisation: (i) the Strategic People Choice of the organisation with its commensurate Psychosocial Contract; and (ii) its Strategic People Position (=the Strategic People Choice Triangle of People Charter, Desired People Profile, and People Value Proposition relative to how the organisation has strategically configured its World of Work). In general, People Practices relate to the Work Arrangements element of the CCARRLO PVP discussed under Excellence Question 5: Differentiation (see Figure 4.15). In the case of employee segment-specific PVPs, segment-aligned bundles of People Practices have to be crafted befitting different personas.[105] Within a bundle, individual choice regarding specific options with respect to a Practice may be offered. This allows for the crafting of a highly personalised people experience.

A People Practices bundle must also match the operating arena of the organisation by taking into account cultural, institutional and regulatory differences across contexts within its arena. In the case of a multinational organisation, the cultural context of the organisation's operating arena may make some Practices more or less suitable.[106][107]

A bundle of People Practices must be aligned to the chosen, fit-for-purpose organisational design of the organisation by reinforcing and supporting its operating model. Low Commitment/Low Involvement People Practices befit a Command-and-Control Organisation, whereas High Commitment/High Involvement People Practices befit a High Networking/High Engagement/High Responsibility Organisation (see Table 5.1 and Figure 5.1). The same applies to a strong/flexible High Achievement/High Caring Organisational Culture and Climate. All of the above impose the strategic requirement of Agile, Creative People Conduct as the Expected, Desired Conduct to attain People Excellence.

A coherent, synergistic, mutually reinforcing bundle of People Practices furthermore must cover the total people value chain of *Attract-Perform-Grow-Retain*. The bundle of Practices must aim to have a balanced mix to *Enable* (=capacitate), *Energise* (=motivate) and *Empower* (=act autonomously) people to do their work in the organisation.[108][109]

In turn, the crafted bundle has to be translated into the appropriate people management tool set (=people processes, procedures and systems) to be used by everyone in the organisation on a daily basis. In this respect, leadership plays a critical mediating role in the effectiveness of People Practices in the organisation. E.g., Transformational leadership strengthens the positive effect of High Commitment/High Involvement Practices in the organisation.[110] Yet the positive effect of Transformational leadership on organisational identification, engagement, and turnover intentions is mediated by the presence of High Commitment/High Involvement Practices in the organisation.[111]

Therefore, the earlier statement that: 'People join organisations; they stay because of leadership' (see Excellence Question 1: Leadership) must be qualified to read: 'People join organisations, but stay to the extent that leadership's talking is translated into daily, concretely experienced, High Commitment/High Involvement Practices and Tools.'

Low vs. High Commitment/High Involvement People Practices

Table 5.2 gives examples of some of the more important High Commitment/High Involvement People Practices (given on the right-hand side of the table) – premised on Strategic People Choice 3: People as value unlockers and wealth creators, and a commensurate High Commitment/High Involvement (=Partnering/Identification) Psychosocial Contract – soliciting Agile, Creative People Conduct. In contrast, the traditional Low Commitment/Low Involvement People Practices (the left-hand side of the table) are typically premised on Strategic People Choice 1: People as costs, with the commensurate Coercive/Bargaining contracts, soliciting Predictable, Routinised

People Conduct.[(112)(113)] The Practices are categorised by the actions making up the people value chain: Attract-Perform-Grow-Retain, and the aim of a specific Practice – Enable, Energise, or Empower.

Table 5.2: Low Commitment/Low Involvement vs. High Commitment/High Involvement People Practices

PEOPLE VALUE CHAIN	LOW COMMITMENT/LOW INVOLVEMENT PRACTICES	HIGH COMMITMENT/HIGH INVOLVEMENT PRACTICES	AIM OF PRACTICE
Attract	Employees/Contractors	Organisational members/associates	Energise
	Employment insecurity	Employability	Energise
	Homogenous employees ('More of the Same')	Inclusive, diverse organisational members/associates	Energise
	Standardised treatment	Personalised treatment	Energise
	Physical status differentiation, e.g., executive office suites, private parking spots, executive dining lounges, business/first class travel	No status differentiation: egalitarian treatment of all. Only differentiation because of organisational requirements, like business/first class travel for longer than a certain number of travelling hours	Energise
	One-way Person/Job match: Knowledge, Skills, Experience (KSE) only	Two-way, integrated, holistic Person/Total Organisation (e.g., Identity, culture) match	Enable
	Detailed, formalised people management standard operating procedures	High level people management principles, applied using own discretion	Empower
	Fixed working hours	Flexible working hours	Empower
	Physical work location	Online, virtual or hybrid work location	Empower
Perform	Some employees are talent (=gifted)	All organisational members, present and past, are talent (=gifted)	Enable
	Laid-down Duties/Tasks/Jobs	Self-designing Assignments/Roles/Teams	Empower
	Supervisor-set work schedules	Self-set work schedules	Empower
	Prescribed 'best way' of doing work	Continuous improvement and innovation	Empower
	Narrow specialisation	Multi-skilling and multi-tasking	Enable
	Restricted interaction with beneficiaries of organisation	Unrestricted interaction with beneficiaries of organisation on an as-needs basis	Empower

PEOPLE VALUE CHAIN	LOW COMMITMENT/LOW INVOLVEMENT PRACTICES	HIGH COMMITMENT/HIGH INVOLVEMENT PRACTICES	AIM OF PRACTICE
	Immediate work setting involvement	Organisation-wide setting involvement	Empower
	Hierarchical reporting lines and communication	All round communication: everyone talking to everyone	Empower
	Closed meetings and closed-door policy	Open meetings and open-door policy	Empower
	Information scarce: given when asked for; or on need-to-know basis	Information rich; self-generated	Empower
	Centralised problem-solving and decision-making (=low autonomy) removed from front line (=tight control)	Localised problem-solving and decision-making (=high autonomy) where action must be taken. Tight-loose governance: Tight on organisation's Identity; Loose on autonomy to act in own space	Empower
	Win-lose problem-solving and conflict resolution	Win-win problem-solving and conflict resolution	Empower
	Fixed budgets, set annually	Flexible budgets, adjusted in real time	Empower
	Supervisor-led, infrequent performance feedback, focusing on activities and performance deficiencies	360 degree, continuous performance feedback, focusing on outcomes/impact and performance enhancement	Energise
	Set (extrinsic), fixed recognition and rewards	Extrinsic/intrinsic, flexible, skills/performance-based recognition and rewards	Energise
	Business is for business only	Social citizenship: serving the common good; community involvement/support	Energise
Grow	Infrequent/no job rotation	Regular job rotation	Enable
	Scheduled, classroom training and development	Real time, in time, just-in-time, blended, lifelong learning	Enable
	Narrow, specialist skills range	Broad, generalist skills range	Enable
	Career management	Career navigation	Enable
	Industrial relations	Employee relations	Enable
	Mediated support	Self-help	Energise
	Welfare as related to work only	Well-being of total person	Enable

PEOPLE VALUE CHAIN	LOW COMMITMENT/LOW INVOLVEMENT PRACTICES	HIGH COMMITMENT/HIGH INVOLVEMENT PRACTICES	AIM OF PRACTICE
Retain	Standardised, dour work space	(Personalised) attractive, stimulating work space	Energise
	Work central to life	Work-Life Balance/Integration	Enable
	Fixed vacations	Variable vacations and sabbaticals	Energise
	Self-interest	Citizenship	Energise

An important consideration with respect to the People Practices given in Table 5.2 is the extent to which they can be DIVAS-itised á lá the Fourth Industrial Revolution: digitised, interconnected, virtualised, automated, appli-fied, intelligentised, and self-helpified. However, a serious caveat must be noted. One must resist the temptation to lead with the latest 4th IR technology in which it replaces the human touch and face. Instead, one must lead with the type of human and humane World of Work one wants to configure strategically (see Excellence Question 5: Differentiation), supported by the right People Practices. It cannot be technology for the sake of technology, but technology as an enabling means to enhance the people experince.[114] Humane Practices must be insitutionalised that respect people's dignity, and engender their well-being.[115]

The committed ownership of People Practices

In crafting and rolling out a People Practices bundle, it is critically important to build committed ownership amongst organisational members to the Expected, Desired People Conduct – translated into a reinforcing crafted bundle of People Practices for the organisation – to obtain people's buy-in. (This is a direct continuation and reinforcement of Excellence Question 6: Ownership.) Committed ownership (=organisational identification) increases the positive perception of People Practices, leading to organisational citizen behaviour and a lower intention to quit.[116]

Organisational members must understand and fully interpret the why, what, and how of the implicit 'messages' that Practices convey to them in terms of Expected, Desired Conduct in the same way as intended by leadership: 'The Practices are there to Enable-Energise-Empower for you to flourish, and hence thrive.' If there is a significant disparity, the Practices will contribute negatively to the perceptions of organisational members and their actual experiences of thriving, or not. The Practices will be misconstrued, resulting in different effects than intended. Or, will be resisted and/or rejected.[117]

The effects of People Practices

Organisations with good People Practices are on average 105% more profitable than their peers.[118] People (=HRM) Practices have a strong, positive correlation with financial performance, market performance (strongest) and operational performance.[119] High Commitment/High Involvement People Practices have a significant relationship with organisational returns, which – when compared to Low Commitment/high Involvement – can typically be in the order of 30% to 50%.[120]

A one standard deviation increase in the presence of an effective High Commitment/High Involvement Work System and its closer alignment with the organisation's Strategic Intent (=competitive strategy) is associated with a $42,000 (in 1990s value) per employee increase in the organisation's market value. Additionally, one standard deviation indice changes in a more effective High Commitment/High Involvement Work System with closer strategic alignment are associated with respectively 21% and 23% increases in shareholder value.[121]

The **affirmative answer** to the People Excellence Question 10: Practices, is: a *coherent, strategically aligned bundle of High Commitment/High Involvement People Practices is in place, soliciting and supporting Agile, Creative Conduct, converted into a powerful people management tool set, enabling, energising, and empowering people to be the very best they can and want to be, and hence thrive.*

You can now do a Reflective Assessment: Practices (Work Sheet 13 in the Work Book), if you wish to do so.

PEOPLE EXCELLENCE QUESTION 11: RISK

Does the organisation have a People Risk Mitigation strategy and plan, addressing its people risks proactively?

A hyper-turbulent and hyper-fluid world, because of the imperative of disruptive innovation, necessitates taking risks, which are frequently significant. As discussed in Chapter 1, the ruling conventions of doing things must be challenged; the new must be explored and discovered; accepted boundaries must be broken down; unknown/unexplored territories must be opened up; the improbable and impossible must be made achievable; and ongoing future-probing experimentation and testing must occur in real time. Intra- and entrepreneurial thinking and doing must become a way of life.[122]

As has been discussed before, against the backdrop of the accelerating oscillation between Order and Chaos through rapidly successive Divergence and Convergence – outlined in Chapter 3 – the world is transforming into Complicated Contexts of Unknown Knowns to Complex Contexts of Unknown Unknowns, and even Chaotic Contexts of Unknowables. The shift is to the Domains of Emergence, Rapid Response, and Confusion.[123]

Ongoing risk assessment and mitigation by the organisation has thus become mission-critical in ensuring and securing a sustainable future for the organisation. The risk assessment and mitigation process allows the organisation to systematically and proactively consider the actions to be taken if and when probable adverse events occur that may detrimentally affect the organisation's performance, and its continued existence. Its viability may be significantly compromised, even be unrecoverable. Risk assessment and mitigation have a direct bearing on organisational resilience (to be discussed under Excellence Question 16: Resilience).

Without any doubt, people risk management is an inherent part of sound corporate governance, and hence also People Excellence.[124] Risk management forms a central theme of the South African King III report on corporate governance, deserving of ongoing Board attention.[125] With respect to people risk mitigation, People Excellence pertains to proactively protecting people as a critical investment of the organisation. They are a key ingredient of the organisation's set of 'crown jewels' in a world in which people have become central to outstanding organisational performance and success. It has been asserted that people risks are probably the biggest source of organisational risk in the emerging new order.[126] People risk management provides the organisation with a proactive and reactive response capability regarding unanticipated, adverse people events.

Typically People Excellence requires the ongoing, thorough, proactive, and integrated assessment of high probability/high impact people risks that may affect the organisation detrimentally, in the present and future. In essence, the people risk revolves around the disruption or a break down in not having, at any given time, the right people in a right number at the right time in the right place, who are able, willing, allowed, and want to perform, leveraged from a personalised sense of purpose and meaning. Examples of specific people risks are toxic leadership; strategic talent unavailability/loss; HIV/Aids; industrial relations disruptions; discriminatory and sexual harassment law suits; safety and health risks; and sub-optimal people-technology integration.[127][128]

The risk assessment must be converted into a risk mitigation strategy and plan that covers the ways and means of reducing people risks to acceptable levels in accordance with the organisation's risk appetite. Such risk reduction can occur through the minimisation, transfer, or elimination of the identified, high probability/high impact people risks. Organisations should also map 'best' responses to unexpected events in accordance with the organisation's risk appetite.

The **affirmative answer** to the People Excellence Question 11: Risk, is: *the organisation has a formalised, comprehensive, up-to-date, People Risk Mitigation Strategy and Plan that address the organisation's people risks proactively in accordance with its risk appetite.*

You can now do a Reflective Assessment: Risk (Work Sheet 14 in the Work Book), if you wish to do so.

SYNERGISTIC FUSION WITHIN PEOPLE EXCELLENCE DOMAIN 2: CAPACITY

Potentiality synergy with regard to the Excellence Domain: Capacity can be described as follows: Capacity entails having a fit-for-purpose organisational design, architected around meaningful work for everyone; dynamically matching the Core Organisational and People Capabilities required by the organisation within its progressively, unfolding strategic horizon; knitting the organisation together through a distinct, strong but flexible Organisational Culture; crafting a bundle of High Commitment/ High Involvement People Practices, soliciting and supporting the Expected Desired People Conduct, and effectively translating them into a commensurate people management tool set for daily use in the organisation; and having a people risk mitigation strategy and plan in place, addressing the organisation's people risks proactively in accordance with its risk appetite.

Figure 5.7 depicts the above Excellence synergy graphically in the form of the second building block towards a complete People Excellence Value Chain, highlighted in the coloured circle. Again, it is important to note the reciprocal independencies and dynamic, organic relationship between all of the Excellence Elements making up this Excellence Domain. *Firstly,* the progressive, sequential, linear alignment order of the five Excellence Elements: Design, through Matching, Culture, Practices, to Risk (i.e., the order of the discussion above). *Secondly,* the reinforcing foundation that Culture provides to the four other Excellence Elements, hence its placement in Figure 5.7 behind the other four Elements' blocks. *Thirdly,* the operational translation of Design and Culture into Practices, which must reinforce Matching.

Like the previous Excellence Domain, all of the reciprocal interdependencies form either an upward spiralling virtuous cycle or a downward spiralling vicious cycle of People Excellence conditions over time. The essence of the synergistic fusion in this Domain lies in *Reinforcement.* Reinforcement encompasses a later Element supporting and strengthening an earlier Element.

In Figure 5.7, the extended lines for Leadership and Ownership indicate their onward influence on the still-to-be-discussed Excellence Dimensions. The direct connection between Leadership and Culture also illustrates their close, co-variant relationship. This implies that Culture is an important leverage that leadership can use to reinforce the content awarded to the other four Excellence Elements in this Excellence Domain.

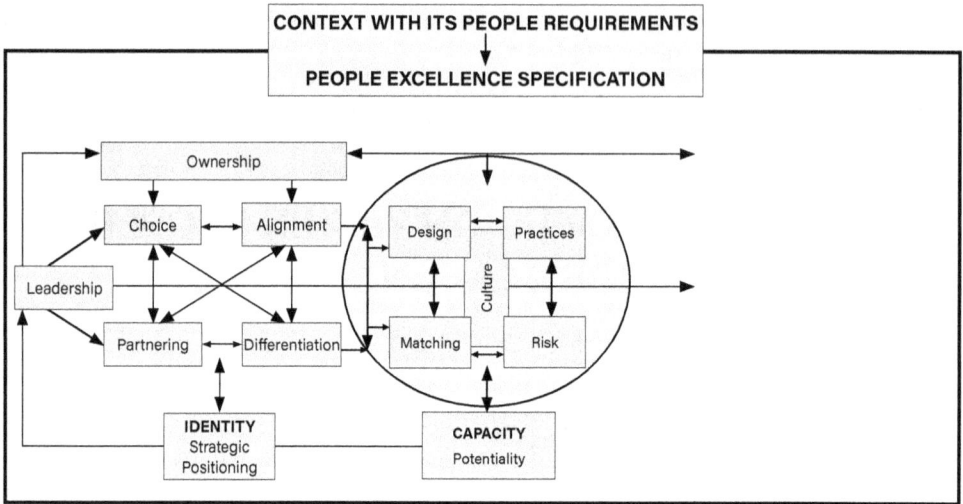

Figure 5.7: Synergy fusion of Reinforcement within the Excellence Dimension 2: Capacity

The desired synergy to be generated by the People Excellence Domain 2: Capacity, as set out above in terms of leading thinking and practice with regard to the five Excellence Elements: Design, Matching, Culture, Practices, and Risk – as referenced against the People Excellence Specification of the emerging, new order – is given in the shaded box below.

PEOPLE EXCELLENCE SPECIFICATION

Highly enabled, empowered and resilient people, who strongly identify with and feel valued by the organisation, and are productively and innovatively engaging collaboratively through personally purposeful and meaningful ways, to viably and sustainably create inimitable, delightful experiences for stakeholders.

People Excellence Domain 2: Capacity Potentiality

Our organisation has a fit-for-purpose design that ensures the right things get done in the right places at the right times by the right people, teams, and units, governed by the necessary checks and balances. Our design is architected around meaningful work: our people experience their work – and its resultant outcome – as being of real, lasting significance that is worthwhile to them and our stakeholders. Because we have moved from a Command-and-Control Organisational Shape to a High Network/High Engagement/ High Responsibility Organisational Shape, our design enables and empowers everyone to

---

contribute to creating inimitable, memorable experiences for our customers/clients and people, who for this very reason choose to stay with us. We are indeed competing with our organisational design through the amazing value we unlock and the abundance of wealth we create – consistently and predictably – in innovative ways.

In our organisation a dynamic match exists at any given time between our strategically required Core Organisational and People Capacities, which are closely synchronised within our progressively unfolding strategic horizon. We have a clear understanding of the strategic talent mix we require going into the future in terms of the different categories of our overall talent profile as imposed by our organisation's Strategic Intent. At all times we have the right people in the right numbers at the right time in the right place, who are able, willing, allowed, and want to perform, all driven by a personalised sense of purpose and meaning. All in all, we have a strong strategic talent pipeline for our organisation in terms of our different Talent Pools.

Our organisation is glued together by a distinct, strong, but flexible Achievement/Caring Organisational Culture – our shared ways of seeing, interpreting, and acting upon the world; the personality of our organisation – aligned to our Organisational Identity. Our Culture has been translated in an aligned way into our organisation's hard- and software. Our Culture enables and empowers our people to perform outstandingly in mutually supportive ways. Though strong, our Culture is flexible enough to adapt 'easily' in response to Organisation's Identity changes, ongoing disruptive innovation, and/or contextual challenges, demands and requirement shifts.

We have crafted a coherent, strategically aligned bundle of High Commitment/High Involvement People Practices, and are able to solicit and support Agile, Creative People Conduct because they enable, energise, and empower our people. This bundle has been converted into a powerful people management tool set that enables, energises, and empowers our people to be the very best they can and want to be, and hence thrive.

We are prepared – proactively and reactively – for the people risks our organisation may have to deal with at any time. In this way, we have enhanced our organisation's capacity to deal excellently with unexpected, adverse people events. Through learning from such events, we become even better prepared to address future people risks more effectively.

You can now do a Summative Reflective Assessment: Synergistic fusion – Reinforcement of Excellence Dimension 2: Capacity (Work Sheet 15 in the Work Book), if you wish to do so.

PEOPLE EXCELLENCE STAR

DELIVERY: VALUE UNLOCKING

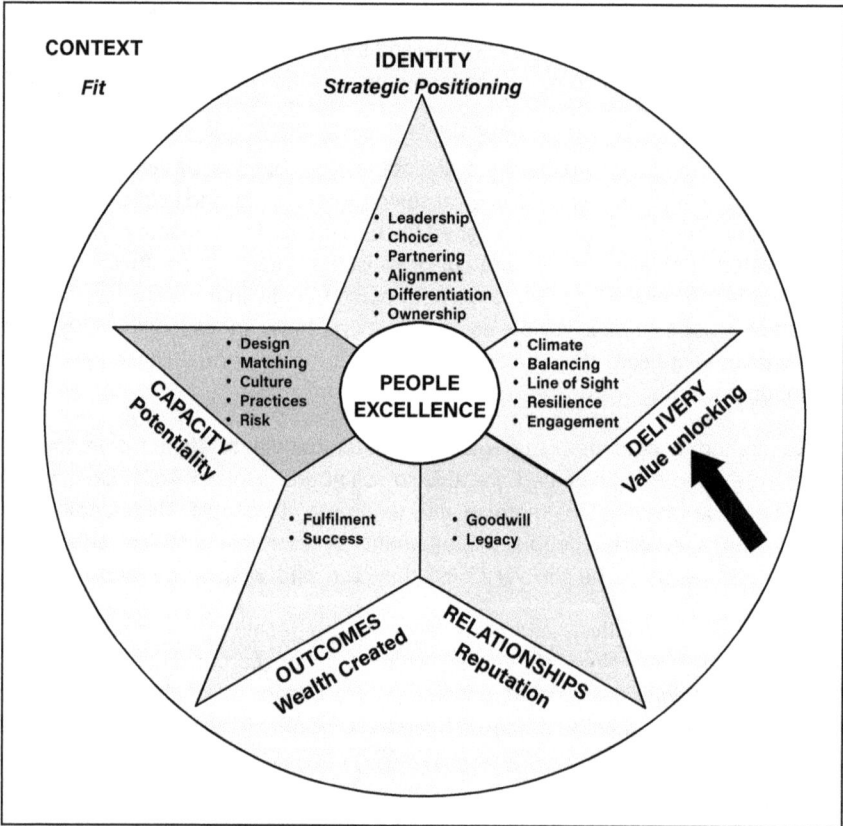

CHAPTER 6

PEOPLE EXCELLENCE DOMAIN 3 – DELIVERY: VALUE UNLOCKING

"If you deliver excellence right now, that gives you the best shot at the best future you've got coming." (Robert Forster)

"If you don't do it with excellence, don't do it at all! Because if it's not excellent, it won't be profitable or fun." (Robert Townsend)

The Excellence Domains 1: Identity – Strategic Positioning and 2: Capacity – Potentiality have been stress-tested. At this point, we know our organisation's People Creditworthiness and possible interventions regarding *firstly*, the strategic positioning of our people in the sustainable, future success of our organisation, and *secondly*, whether the necessary people potentiality (or investment) has been made to set up the required People Excellence conditions for thriving people, outstanding organisational performance and success, making the organisation viable going into the future.

Next, the *People Excellence Domain 3: Delivery* has to be stress-tested. This Excellence Domain deals with *actual* people performance: *Value Unlocking*, and therefore the immediate enablers – and on the downside, the immediate constraints (or barriers) – to real time individual, team, organisational unit, and overall organisational performance. The Domain relates to the excellence of the organisation and its people 'in action', so to speak. People and organisations of excellence seek to add value at all times in all they do.[1]

The Strategic People choices made in Excellence Domain 1: Identity set the strategic parameters for putting in place the necessary conditions for the organisation's people to flourish and thrive; delight stakeholders; and contribute to making and keeping the organisation viable in Excellence Domain 2: Capacity. The mere potentiality contained in the created capacity has to be realised in Excellence Domain 3: Delivery. Hence, the created potential capacity of Domain 2 either enables or constrains actual delivery in Domain 3.

As illustrated in the People Excellence Star on the opposite page, the Excellence Domain 3: Delivery encompasses the five *Excellence Elements* of Climate, Balance, Line of Sight, Resilience, and Engagement. Each is discussed in turn in the order listed.

PEOPLE EXCELLENCE QUESTION 12: CLIMATE

Is the organisation infused by an invigorating Organisational Climate?

Organisational Culture has been described as the institutionalised glue holding the organisation together daily in a distinct, shared way, i.e., its personality (see Excellence Question 9: Culture). It is the ingrained, shared ways of seeing, interpreting, and doing things in the organisation. Organisational Climate, meanwhile, refers to the ongoing, varying mood (or vibe) permeating the organisation, often as a consequence of its Organisational Culture. It is the way things are experienced by people in the organisation.[2] Organisational Culture is thus more fixed and durable, whilst Organisational Climate is more variable and temporary. Similar to Organisational Culture, leadership plays a key role in engendering the Organisational Climate that exists in the organisation.[3]

Organisational Climate and its dimensions, Organisational Climate types, and the ideal Organisational Climate and its outcomes, are discussed next.

Defining Organisational Climate

Organisational climate is the 'touchable atmosphere' and style with which people work together in the organisation – the 'spirit and mood' imbuing the organisation. It is the 'smell and feel of the place.' The atmosphere can be comfortable, bearable, or uncomfortable, unbearable. Analogous to weather conditions that can be sunny, fine, rainy, or cold, Organisational Climate is either performance-enhancing and caring, or performance-destructing and toxic.

Organisational Climate arises out of the joint sense and meanings that organisational members as a collective award to their individual, daily experiences within and of the organisation and fellow organisational members. This results in certain commonly shared perceptions, thoughts, judgements, and feelings about the ruling mood pervading the organisation. The ruling mood is co-constructed by organisational members from their shared daily experiences-of, attributions-made-to, sense-made-of, and meanings-awarded-to organisational aspects, such as organisational goals, policies and standards, practices, work structures and processes, authority and accountability, relationships, leadership, recognition/rewards, organisational events, and achievements.[4] In particular, the People Practices in force with their translation into a people management tool set applied daily in the organisation.[5]

These aspects – e.g., goals, standards, and practices – are collectively perceived, seen, judged, and felt to be tough or comfortable; encouraging or discouraging; freeing-up or constraining; caring or demeaning. Though experienced individually at first, the more a mood is shared as a collective, pervasive experience throughout the whole organisation, the more it turns into its Organisational Climate. Thus, the origin of Organisational Climate lies in individual experiences. In turn, the climate infects individuals' experiences of the organisation, affecting their conduct. Organisational members may be exposed to the same climate but may vary in how they feel about it.[6] The stronger the climate, the more organisational members will agree on a common experience of said climate.[7]

Dimensions of Organisational Climate

An organisational climate can be profiled in terms of contrasting climate poles on various dimensions of the *specific* mood infusing the organisation in response to the experiences-of, attributions-made-to, sense-made-of, and meaning-awarded.[8] Figure 6.1 depicts these elements, in the process profiling contrasting Invigorating vs. Suffocating Climates.[9]

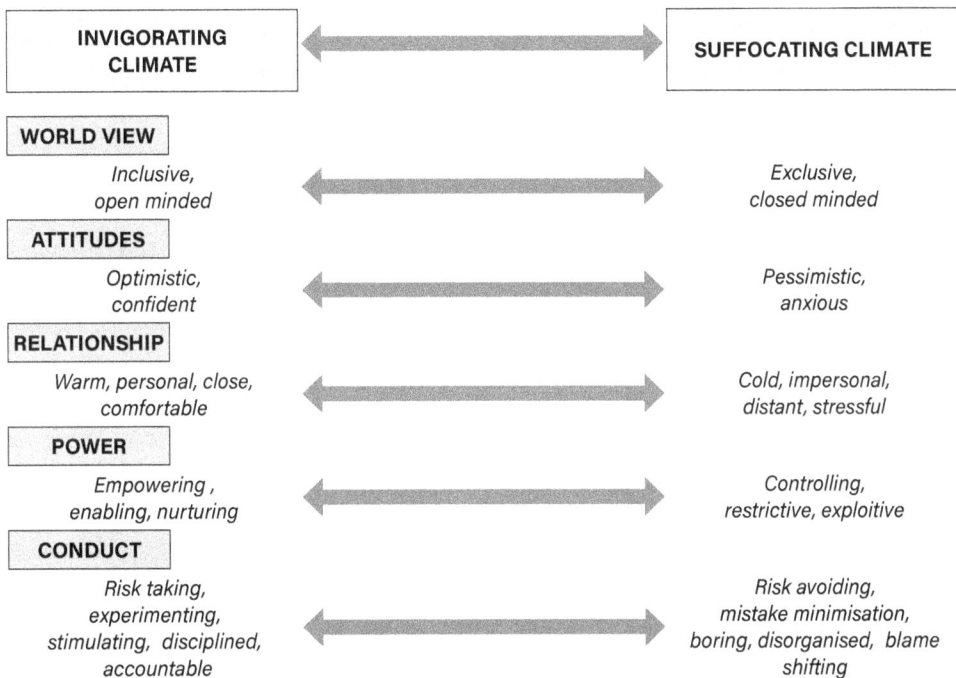

INVIGORATING CLIMATE		SUFFOCATING CLIMATE
WORLD VIEW		
Inclusive, open minded		Exclusive, closed minded
ATTITUDES		
Optimistic, confident		Pessimistic, anxious
RELATIONSHIP		
Warm, personal, close, comfortable		Cold, impersonal, distant, stressful
POWER		
Empowering, enabling, nurturing		Controlling, restrictive, exploitive
CONDUCT		
Risk taking, experimenting, stimulating, disciplined, accountable		Risk avoiding, mistake minimisation, boring, disorganised, blame shifting

Figure 6.1: Invigorating vs Suffocating Climates

The People Excellence Specification of the emerging new order demands an invigorating Organisational Climate. Such a climate needs to be in support of the Strategic People Choice 3: People as value unlockers and wealth creators, with its commensurate High Commitment/High Involvement Psychosocial Contract of Partnering/Identification. An invigorating climate also makes the ambidextrous, High Networking/High Engagement/High Responsibility Organisation, set up around meaningful work, a reality. It creates the enabling conditions under which people can be engaged and manifest agile, creative, and innovative behaviour.

Organisational Climate types

A distinction can be drawn between: (i) a general (or generic) Organisational Climate; and (ii) a climate for something. I.e., an organisational facet-specific climate such as a climate for innovation, diversity, service, safety or ethics in the organisation. This often arises out of the Identity of the organisation (in particular its Strategic Intent). Because organisational facet-specific climates represent climates for particular aspects of the organisation, many of these facet-specific climates may be present in an organisation at any given point in time.[10][11] As discussed here, the focus of People Excellence is on the overall Organisational Climate which may be supported by facet-specific climates, like a climate for innovation, client-centricity, and/or inclusivity.

Table 6.1 gives examples of general Invigorating – *Pioneering and Stewardship* – and Suffocating – *Heritage, Greed, Clan* and *Doomsday* – Climates based on the dimensions with their contrasting poles making up an Organisational Climate, as given in Figure 6.1.[12]

Table 6.1: Invigorating vs. Suffocating Organisational Climates

CLIMATE TYPE	CORE THEME	ELEMENTS	ORGANISATIONAL NARRATIVE	DESIRED OUTCOME
INVIGORATING: PIONEERING	Bountiful opportunities	Inclusive, open minded (*world view*). Optimistic, confident (*attitude*); Warm, personal, close (*relationship*); Empowering, enabling, nurturing (*power*); 'Calculated' risk-taking, experimenting, stimulating, chaotic (*action*)	"We fervently believe in what we do as we move into the unknown, unexplored." "We will conquer the world against all odds." "Eventually the world will see our point of view and/or be convinced of what we do."	Future-directed achievement based on innovative, relationship-driven, need satisfaction.
INVIGORATING: STEWARDSHIP	Entrusted caring	Inclusive, open minded (*world view*); Optimistic, confident (*attitude*); Equitable, objective, warm, personal, close (*relationship*); Empowering, enabling (*power*); Risk-taking, experimenting, disciplined, accountable (*action*)	"We have been entrusted to care for and grow the assets entrusted to us, sustainably." "We have to act at all times in an ethical, fair, equitable and transparent way." "In all of our actions we remain ultimately responsible and accountable to all of our stakeholders."	Sustainable and ethically guided value, unlocking and wealth creation in a fair and balanced manner for all stakeholders concerned.

CLIMATE TYPE	CORE THEME	ELEMENTS	ORGANISATIONAL NARRATIVE	DESIRED OUTCOME
SUFFOCATING: HERITAGE	God's gift to mankind	Exclusive, closed minded (*world view*); Optimistic, confident (*attitude*); "Imperious" cold, impersonal, distant (*relationship*); Controlling, disabling (*power*); Risk avoidance, mistake minimisation (*action*).	"Preserve what we have." "The past is to be revered for all that is, in all its goodness." "Our past success will certainly ensure future success." "Extend and endorse what we have been and presently are into the future." "What we have and do represent the ultimate good and fixed point of reference." "The future is but merely an extension of our glorious past."	Maintain and entrench the revered status quo as crystallised from our glorious past for the benefit of others, but solely on our terms.
SUFFOCATING: CLAN	Privileged entitlement	Exclusive, closed minded (*world view*); Optimistic, confident (*attitude*); Cold, impersonal, distant, controlling, restrictive (*relationship*); Risk avoidance, mistake minimisation (*action*)	"You are either with us or against us." "Divide, conquer and rule." "Within our group there are rulers and servants, an inner and outer circle." "There is only one way of seeing the world: ours." "We say what gets done and how." "Sure, try new things, but only on our terms."	Achievement regardless of costs and sacrifices to others to the benefit of a small, privileged, entitled inner group.
SUFFOCATING: GREED	Runaway profiteering	Exclusive, closed minded (*world view*); Optimistic, confident (*attitude*); Cold, impersonal, distant (*relationship*); Controlling, restrictive (*power*); Risk-taking, mistake minimisation, blame shifting (*action*)	"Money makes the world go round." "Live for today as if there is no tomorrow: Instant gratification." "Profit is the be-and-end-all." "The more the money/ profit, the better."	Making money for selfish, self-serving gains and reckless consumption, regardless of the cost to, and consequences for, whosoever.
SUFFOCATING: DOOMSDAY	Apocalypse now	Exclusive, closed minded (*world view*); Pessimistic, anxious (*attitude*); Warm, personal, close (*relationship*); Controlling, disabling (*power*); 'Abdicated' risk avoidance, mistake minimisation (*action*)	"The world and/or our organisation is coming to an end, let's huddle together and await the inevitable." "Let's openly share our fears, anxieties, frustrations, and talk about the good old days when we had unbounded hopes, dreams and ideals."	Making people comfortable with the inevitable, imminent collapse of the organisation, assisting them to have quality time for the period that remains.

CLIMATE TYPE	CORE THEME	ELEMENTS	ORGANISATIONAL NARRATIVE	DESIRED OUTCOME
			"There is a (slight) chance of an (unknown) possible saviour." OR, "Our expected (anonymous) saviour is coming from an unknown place but his/her estimated time of arrival is undisclosed. Then our newly created, glorious world will replace the present, doomed world out there that is coming to a sure end."	Or, preparing people to be ready for the new millennium that will dawn once the eagerly awaited saviour arrives.

Ideal organisational climate

An ideal Organisational Climate nurtures and affirms the dignity and worth of individuals. It creates a psychologically safe space (=I can be who I am, want to be, and aspire to be without any come-backs); provides meaningfulness (=My work is worthwhile and of value); and makes a person psychologically available (=I am present, prepared, and willing to take the risks associated with engaging and contributing fully).[13] Concurrently, the ideal Organisational Climate engenders empowering, meaningful work experiences, resulting in positive views of leadership and strong followership. In this way, the physiological, psychosocial, and spiritual (not to be equated to religious) well-being of leadership and followers are grown, engendered, and sustained. They are flourishing, and hence thriving.[14]

An ideal climate nurtures a "virtuosa" organisation[15] which can be characterised as having:

- a high 'stock' of psychosocial capital amongst organisational members – high levels of self-efficacy, optimism, hope, perseverance, courage, and resilience[16]; and

- a strong virtue-ality, modelled by the organisation's leadership, manifested in a high presence of humaneness, truthfulness, open-mindedness, justice, creativity, curiosity, and prudence.[17] The qualities of outstanding leadership listed under Excellence Question 1: Leadership also nurture this modelling: legitimacy, inspiration, humility, integrity, ethical, and authenticity.

Jointly, a high stock of psychosocial capital and virtue-ality nourishes an increasingly Invigorating Organisational Climate though a virtuous, upward cycle, setting even more favourable conditions for higher committed ownership – the stay intention of organisational members – and, hence levels of engagement – the energy levels of organisational members.[18] Leadership is also seen more positively. And vice versa in the case of a vicious, downward cycle.

Outcomes of Organisational Climate

An Organisational Climate is to a large extent THE externalisation of people's actual, internal experience of the organisation, because the mood (or vibe) of the organisation infects like a pandemic all of its people over time into their very being and becoming.[19] The climate affects people's level of trust in the likely fulfilment of the Psychosocial Contract; their (affective) commitment; and hence organisational identification, engagement, goal achievement, creativity, innovation, job satisfaction, corporate citizenship behaviour, morale, stress, psychological safety, well-being, absenteeism, and retention. All of these in turn affect customer satisfaction, as well as organisational learning and performance.[20] A good person-climate fit[21], as well as empowering leadership[22], are in most cases preconditions for these positive effects to occur.

The **affirmative answer** to the People Excellence Question 12: Climate, is: *the presence of an Invigorating Organisational Climate nurturing a high stock of psychosocial capital and virtue-ality in the organisation, recursively engendering an even more Invigorating Climate."*

You can now do a Reflective Assessment: Climate (Work Sheet 16 in the Work Book), if you wish to do so.

PEOPLE EXCELLENCE
QUESTION 13: BALANCING

Is the right balance achieved in real time delivery across the organisation between work demands and available resources through the autonomy exercised?

Real time delivery requires maintaining at all times across the whole organisation, the right balance between the work demands imposed and the resources required to meet those demands in order to deliver effectively and efficiently. Finding this balance is an ongoing juggling game, made possible through the autonomy awarded to, and taken up by, the party concerned to affect this balance, whether it is at the individual, team, unit, or organisational level.[23][24][25] The new world of work has introduced different types of autonomy: location, temporal, and work.[26] The first two types were dealt with the strategic configuration of the world of work in and for the organisation (refer Excellence Question 5: Differentiation). Balancing refers to work autonomy, which relates to the Key People Imperative: People Autonomy ('Allowed to do') (see Table 4.5).

Important is the distinction between the autonomy awarded and actually taken up by the party concerned. A party may be awarded high autonomy, but may be unwilling to exercise it due to psychologically unsafe conditions, internally and/or externally. Examples of such internal personal conditions are risk aversion; a lack of confidence; a lack of abilities and experience; and imposed restricting external controls. In short, a lack of personal resources. External contextual conditions include a fear of being sanctioned in the case of failure or mistakes; believing that one is being set up for failure; a lack of recognition/reward for achievements; or leadership who are disempowering and/or disinterested in what one is doing. All in all, the type of empowering Organisational Climate prevalent in the organisation.

Work Demands and Resources Required

Work demands entail the range, variety, and complexity of the tasks to be performed. I.e., the responsibilities allocated (architected through the organisational design) with the accompanying sum total of required energy needed to perform those tasks – physically, physiologically, psychosocially, socio-culturally, and spiritually. *Resources* refer to the available means (or enablers) to get the work done, which can also be physical, physiological, psychosocial, socio-cultural and/or spiritual in nature.

Resources can be[27]:

- extrinsic, e.g., people, technology, finance, time, facilities (any of which can be configured into Core Organisational Capabilities, see Excellence Question 8: Matching), policies/practices, as well as social, leadership and organisational support; and

- intrinsic (=personal or ego), e.g., personal attributes like self-confidence, self-efficacy, knowledge, expertise, and skills; personal, interpersonal and organisational abilities; and the leadership capabilities of the party concerned.

To be most effective, the nature of work demands and available resources must be matched in terms of corresponding types: physical, physiological, psychosocial, socio-cultural, and spiritual. For example, physical demands must be met with physical resources, and so on.[28] After a certain 'tipping point', resources – too many and/or the wrong type – relative to work demands may become 'toxic', like taking too many vitamins. This can also apply to the autonomy awarded (to be discussed below). The key is the right resources at the right time to do the right things (=work demands) with the right autonomy.[29]

Autonomy Awarded/Exercised

Autonomy awarded[30] encompasses the freedom given (or the power/authority to act) to the party concerned to set goals and make decisions in order to take the necessary actions to do the work with the available resources at hand, relative to the work demands.[31] And if necessary, making the necessary adjustments to bring the work demands and available resources into balance. The autonomy awarded and exercised (i.e., taken up) represents the 'action space' given to the party concerned, giving him the opportunity to act with agility, responsiveness, adaptability, and flexibility.[32][33]

In the final instance, the autonomy awarded equates to the empowerment given to people in the organisation. This both presupposes – and recursively realises – an ambidextrous organisational design (see Excellence Question 7: Design).[34] It also presupposes the use of Energise/Empower People Practices (see Table 5.2, Excellence Question 10: Practices), strengthened by participative Transformational/Transcendental Leadership (see Excellence Question 1: Leadership).[35]

At the individual/team level, this balancing act excercised through the taken-up autonomy is called 'job/team crafting'.[36] Crafting entails the degree to which Work Team members/Work Role incumbents – in a self-initiated and -directed way – exercise the right to change the design of their work by shaping, moulding, and redefining it in a (semi-) permanent way. The more individuals believe they have the power to shape their work in order to personalise and individualise it for themselves, the more likely they will find their work meaningful.[37] Team members/Work Role incumbents have two basic motivations for engaging in crafting: to enhance positive aspects of their work, and/or to minimise/eliminate negative aspects of their work.[38]

Attaining balance through awarding the right autonomy resonates directly with people's need for autonomy (see Figure 4.6, Excellence Questions 2: Choice; and 14: Line of Sight).[39] It also gives people a real sense that they own their work space in an accountable way. This deepens their committed ownership (see Excellence Question 6: Ownership) and provides them with psychological safety.[40] In the final instance, crafting through the autonomy exercised improves the person-organisation fit.[41]

Balance/Imbalance

The degree of balance that exists directly sets up the organisational conditions for engagement by people, i.e., their energised willingness to perform:[42]

- The more optimal the balance (=with the right autonomy awarded and the right, available resources, work demands can be met. Or, work demands and/ or resources may have to be changed), the higher people's commitment, engagement, performance, citizenship, satisfaction, and total well-being as a whole person. It also increases the level of psychosocial capital available to people (see Excellence Question 12: Climate). In turn, people make a greater contribution to the continued viability of their organisation, manifested in its competitiveness, profitability, and innovation.

- Inversely, an imbalance between work demands, available resources, and the autonomy awarded (and excercised) will increase the likelihood of disengagement, inadequate performance, poor well-being, high stress levels, burnout, absenteeism, and resignation. An imbalance will be experienced as a breach of the psychosocial contract.[43]

Figure 6.2 illustrates the above discussion.

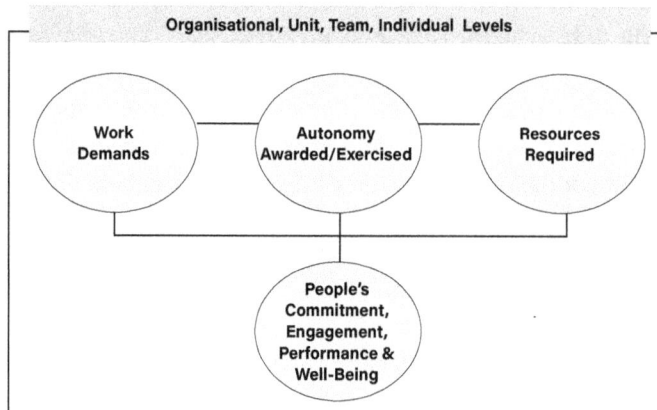

Figure 6.2: Balancing work demands and required resources though the autonomy awarded/exercised

The more the features of the emerging new order – specifically the VICCAS world (outlined in Chapter 3) – infuses the organisation's operating arena, the more the never-ending imperative of the real time, in time, balancing of work demands and required resources. This imperative demands high levels of agility, responsiveness, and flexibility by organisational members. In turn, this necessitates people being awarded and actually exercising high levels of autonomy with respect to the balancing of forever changing work demands and available resources in real time across the organisation.

The **affirmative answer** to the People Excellence Question 13: Balancing, is: *the achievement of an optimal balance between work demands and required resources through the appropriate autonomy being awarded and taken up across the organisation, in order to create the opportunity for high levels of people commitment, engagement, performance, and well-being in the organisation.*

You can now do a Reflective Assessment: Balancing (Work Sheet 17 in the Work Book), if you wish to do so.

PEOPLE EXCELLENCE QUESTION 14: LINE OF SIGHT

Does a clear line of sight exist in the organisation between Effort – Performance – Valued Recognition/Rewards?

People Excellence necessitates a clear line of sight between Effort – Performance – Valued Recognition/Rewards in the organisation.[44] People must believe, and then during delivery actually experience – both individually and collectively – that a certain Effort by them will result in a certain Performance. Consequently, they must believe that there is a high chance that they will receive fair, equitable Recognition/Rewards, which they value as a return on their Performance.[45][46][47] This line of sight relates to the Key People imperative: People Fulfilment ('Want to do') (see Table 4.5).

A clear line of sight will invoke in people a strong sense of flow at work: a state of consciousness in which they will become totally immersed and absorbed in their work, enjoy it without bounds, and be intrinsically motivated by it.[48] The higher the autonomy awarded/exercised by people (see Excellence Question 13: Balancing), the more they can ensure/craft a clear line of sight, which inversely will further strengthen their sense of flow.

A clear line of sight will create a 'pull' effect in the organisation: from Recognition/Rewards back through Performance to Effort. However, this is dependent on whether the Recognition/Rewards on offer by the organisation to its people for the Effort exerted and the Performance attained, are attractive to the individuals concerned. They place a high value on them. Highly valued Recognition/Rewards demand that different types and permutations of them exist in the organisation, attractive to different groups of organisational members as a function of the differentiated segmentations of the organisation's people as contained in the organisation's (segmented) People Value Proposition (see Excellence Question 5: Differentiation).[49]

People thrive when their specific permutation of basic needs – meaning/purpose, actualisation, competence, autonomy, belonging (or relatedness) and security (including existence) – across all of their Dimensions of Being/Becoming, embedded in their Personal Identity (Refer Figure 4.6, Excellence Question 2: Choice), are fulfilled through the valued Recognition/Rewards they receive for their Effort and

Performance.[50] The derived People Excellence Specification for the emerging new order necessitates satisfying especially the needs of meaning/purpose, actualisation, competence, and autonomy.

The types and permutations of Recognition/Rewards – both intrinsic and extrinsic – must not only be aligned to the needs of organisational members, but should also resonate with the organisation's Identity, as translated into an inimitable, distinct, and coherent Strategic People Position for the organisation: its People Charter, Desired People Profile, and People Value Proposition, within its strategic configuration of the World of Work (see Excellence Question 5: Differentiation). Leadership plays a critical role in ensuring this line of sight at all times, in particular the alignment between Organisational Identity, and organisational members' Identities and basic needs.[51]

On the one hand, the direct line of sight of Effort – Performance – Valued Recognition/ Rewards must be embedded in the Organisation Identity-aligned, Strategic People Position of People Excellence.[52] On the other hand, it must be supported and reinforced by an energising Performance Management Process,[53] befitting a High Commitment/High Involvement People Practice (see Table 5.2, Excellence Question 10: Practices. The intention of this Process must be to retain valued people by empowering and enabling them to measurably improve their present and future performance and growth as whole persons. The Performance Management Process hence must be both 'feedforward' and 'feedback' in nature.[54]

As daily, real time, legitimate affirmation of the direct line of sight between Effort – Performance – Valued Recognition/Rewards, an uncompromising differentiation must be made between high, average, and poor performers in the organisation through the Performance Management Process. This differentiation must be based on the comparative Effort exerted, the Performance attained, and consequently the Valued Recognition/Rewards given.

Figure 6.3 provides a graphic summary of the above discussion.

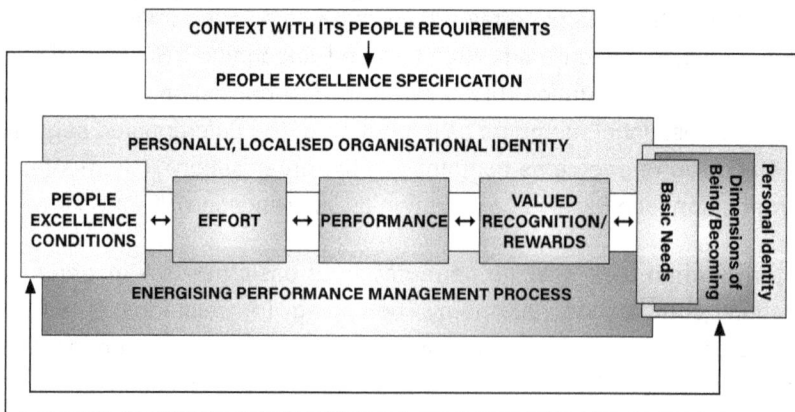

Figure 6.3: A clear line of sight between Effort-Performance-Valued Recognition/Rewards

The **affirmative answer** to the People Excellence Question 14: Line of Sight, is: *a clear link exists between Effort – Performance – Valued Recognition/Rewards in the organisation, taking account of different segmentations of people's needs and wants in the organisation.*

You can now do a Reflective Assessment: Line of Sight (Work Sheet 18 in the Work Book), if you wish to do so.

PEOPLE EXCELLENCE
QUESTION 15: RESILIENCE

Are the people of the organisation change-fit?

The emerging new order is infused by continuous, radical, and fundamental change against the backdrop of the rise of Complicated Contexts of Unknown Knowns to Complex Contexts of Unknown Unknowns, and Chaotic Contexts of Unknowables. The frequency and severity of wicked challenges, issues, and problems – interspersed by Black Swans – are on the increase. As has been stated before, change is the only constant. The emerging new order imposes the imperative of ongoing, relentless, disruptive innovation as THE critical strategic renewal success factor for future-ready and -fit organisations to meet their aspiration to remain viable in the 'creative, compelling, memorable experience-based' economy. Organisations are on a never-ending change journey of re-imagining and re-inventing themselves, requiring change-fit people who are enabled and empowered by effective change navigation and leadership.[55][56] We are in the era of 'always on' transformation.[57]

People Excellence necessitates change-fit people because of the continuous, fundamental, and radical changes in all four of the reciprocally interdependent worlds in which people live. Figure 6.4 depicts the four worlds in which organisational members - as a collaborating action community, tied together by a Psychosocial Contract(s) - are embedded. People co-constitute and co-enact these worlds through ongoing - individual and collective - sense-making, meaning-giving, and purpose-construction.[58]

Context: Emerging new order

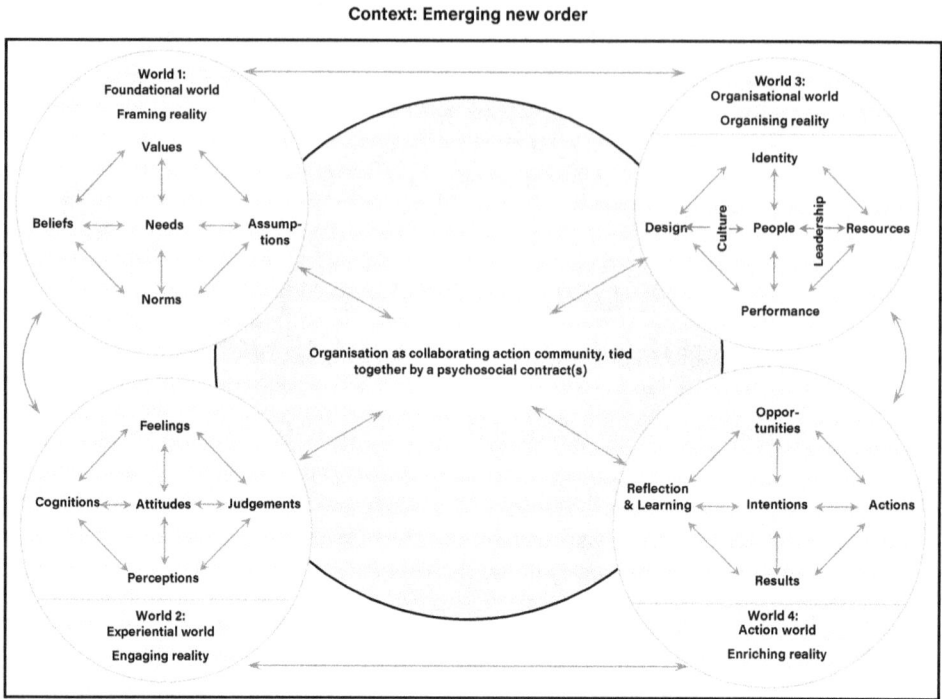

Figure 6.4: The four worlds in which organisational members live

In this instance, People Excellence equates to having people who are at all times change-fit in all four of the worlds depicted in Figure 6.4, relative to the never-ending change journey of their organisation, trigered in World 3. Change-fitness in the emerging new order implies a shift in Worlds 1 and 2 regarding the change navigation mindset and attitude of the people making up the action community. This will establish the right foundation upon which to build and maintain confident resilience as a Core Organisational Capability in Worlds 3 and 4.[59] This foundation provides the organisation and its people with the right set of glasses (World 1) and engagement style (World 2) to navigate change in Worlds 3 and 4.

Each of these worlds will next be explicated from the People Excellence vantage point of change-fit people:

- World 1 – the right change navigation mindset.
- World 2 – the right change navigation attitude.
- Worlds 3 and 4 – confident resilience.

World 1: Right change navigation mindset

According to Figure 6.4, World 1: Foundational World is about framing reality. In this case, it involves the correct framing of change as the reality faced by the organisation and its people. Navigating change – embodied in the journey of the organisation with its people towards actualising a shared, desired, viable future – requires a qualitatively significantly different mindset regarding the change journey under the emerging new order conditions of hyper-fluidity and hyper-turbulence.[60]

Change can no longer be seen as an abnormal, infrequently occurring event with a definitive beginning and end, merely requiring an adaptation to the status quo. Given the departure point of constant, fundamental, and radical change infusing the emerging new order, the required change mindset entails at least the following:

- **The criticality of a clearly defined, distinct, and strongly entrenched Organisational Identity.** As discussed before, Organisational Identity is made up of Purpose, Vision, Strategic Intent, Core Values, and Legacy (see Figure 4.1). Under conditions of hyper-fluidity and hyper-turbulence, Organisational Identity – especially Purpose as Why – acts as the only secure anchor and fixed point of reference. However, the Organisational Identity may need to be constantly re-interpreted and re-operationalised to match continuous contextual shifts. Given these conditions, and matched to Organisational Identity, would be a Transformational ('Whereto')/Transcendental ('Why') Leadership Stance (see Figure 4.2).
- **Change is messy and wicked.** Change navigation is an emerging, iterative, unpredictable, uncertain, unfolding, circular, and organic process of engaging with Unknown Knowns, Unknown Unknowns, and/or Unknowables.
- **A permanent state of unfreezing.** Change navigation is a process of constantly reimagining and reconfiguring aspirations, as well as redefining successive desired states, in real time, all of the time. No fixed journey and final destination exist. Change responsiveness, flexibility, and agility are thus crucial capabilities. At most only dynamic stability can be attained and maintained within the organisation.
- **No holy cows and impossibilities.** Everything – all the conventional ways of seeing, thinking and doing – is on the firing line, up for contention, and has to be questioned from first principles. Even the questions posed have to be questioned. Nothing is holy or given.
- **The low transferability of change success stories.** No generic success change recipe exists. Each journey is unique. It needs its own customised approach and solution every time, even in the same organisation, although Lessons Learnt and general principles can be distilled and applied from one's own and other organisations.

World 2: Right change navigating attitude

Leveraged from World 1's right change navigating mindset befitting the emerging new order, the corresponding right change navigation attitude has to be adopted within World 2: Experiential World (refer to Figure 6.4).[61]

In the emerging new order, one's change navigation attitude cannot be that change can be managed. Either, that it is a band aid to alleviate the 'pains' of change. Or, that it is a linear programme, managed project-like from A to B with pre-set milestones and deadlines, delivered over a pre-defined period of time.

In this order the right change navigation attitude metaphorically is rather that of playing chess. The chess pieces (=the principles and building blocks of a sound change navigation process) have to be applied and played appropriate to the strategic, dynamic unfolding of the game (=the change journey with its evolving, iterative dynamics) and constantly reconceived destination (=sustained viable organisation) relative to the interacting 'To Be', 'As Is' and 'In-Between' change states.

The right change navigating attitude requires a shift in a number of key change principles, given in Table 6.2.

Table 6.2: Required shifts in the Basic Change Navigation Attitude

From a Conventional 'Managed' Attitude…	…To a 'Chess playing' Attitude
• Pushed by problems/issues • From Present-into-Future • Discontinuous event with definitive beginning and end • Single, stand-alone organisational/ change components • Fixed, sequential programmed phases/ steps • People-to-be-changed as passive targets	• Pulled by challenges/opportunities • From Future-into-Present • Continuous, open-ended process • Systemic, organic, interactive patterns of organisational/change components • Thematic waves of re-iterative reconfiguration and future-probing experimentation • People changing by being active participants

Worlds 3 and 4: Confident Resilience

Worlds 1 and 2 must be re-framed to fit the emerging new order in terms of change navigation mindset and attitude. In tandem, the organisation and its people must respond to the ongoing fundamental and radical change within World 3: Organisational World and World 4: Action World (refer Figure 6.4). Within these Worlds, four possible responses can be distinguished: Freeze, Fight, Flee, or Face.

In terms of People Excellence, only the Face response reflects change-fit people. A 'Face' response is the change-fit ability of organisational members to engage – constructively, positively, and maturely – with whatever they are confronted by within the framework of what they want to achieve, collectively and organisationally, over time. They honestly acknowledge and enthusiastically engage with the deep change(s) their organisation is undergoing in the 'In-Between' state, located between the 'As Is' and 'To Be' states. By facing the change in this way, the likelihood is high that they will thrive.

Core to change-fit people and their organisations – able to face the change – is resilience.[62] Resilience enables organisational members to confidently adopt a 'Face' response to changing events, persons, and circumstances.[63] They convey an overall sense of being efficaciously in control of the change they face relative to their intended destiny. They are not a victim of the change rushing upon them.[64] In a complementary way, effective change navigation is inherent to resilience. This highlights the criticality of adopting in Worlds 1 and 2 the right change navigation mindset and attitude, as these provide the right frame of reference for change navigation in Worlds 3 and 4 through building and sustaining resilience.[65]

Ongoing disruptive innovation and real time, iterative experimentation – which simultaneously significantly increases the likelihood of set-backs, mistakes, failures, and crises – demand that people re-invent themselves on an ongoing basis through lifelong learning.[66][67] A mindset shift from 'Know it all' to 'Learn it all' is necessary.[68] All of the above makes the investment in resilience as core capability a top priority. This investment equips people to be change-fit through their confident ability to deal with the emerging new order. They know they will be able to cope with this order, whatever form and shape it takes on.[69] Resilience has thus become mission-critical for all organisations and their people if they want to remain viable in this order.[70]

People with confident resilience do not shy away from, rationalise, scale down, or resist change. For them dealing with change is par for the course. They face up to the change. They know and accept that in successfully addressing the ever-present change needs of their organisation, they are ensuring a viable future for themselves and their organisation. They also understand and accept that at best only dynamic stability, and not permanent stability, can be achieved in their organisation, because change in the emerging new order is innate and continuous. Similar to taking ownership of their organisation's Identity, they take ownership of and translate the ever-present, re-interpreted change need(s), as well as their response to it, into their work roles, daily work, and work settings. The need for change, and the associated actions required to satisfy change needs, are not seen as an executive/senior leadership matter – it is everyone's responsibility.

The following topics are addressed below with respect to resilience: defining resilience with its accompanying dimensions; resilience as an integrated, dynamic process capability; resilience capability levels; as well as the enablers and effects of resilience.[71]

Defining resilience with its accompanying dimensions

Resilience refers to the ability of an organisation and its members to respond proactively and/or reactively to expected and unexpected events and changes – whether constructive or destructive – in its operating arena to better fit in, such that it strengthens and retains its continued viability. In short, it is the ability to bounce back to the necessary/desired state/level of functioning, either proactively by anticipating an event/change, or reacting to an unexpected event/change after it has occurred. The latter response has been the conventional definition of resilience.[72][73] However the emerging new order also demands that organisations build resilence proactively.

Based on this definition of resilience, Figure 6.5 provides a graphic plot on which the resilience capability dimensions of an organisation can be plotted relative to different units of analysis – the individual, team, organisational unit, and the organisation as a whole. This plot enables the organisation to assess its resilience readiness, capability-wise.

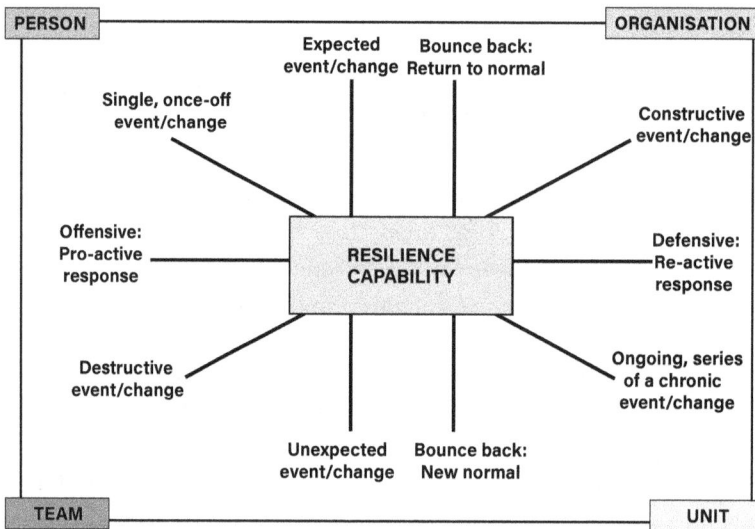

Figure 6.5: Plotting the Resilience Capability of the organisation

Based on Figure 6.5, the following comments are appropriate[74]:

- The *nature of the events/change* to respond to can be: (i) destructive, like a threat, crisis, catastrophe, failure, mistake; or (ii) constructive, such as a new opportunity triggered by, for example, ongoing disruptive innovation, market/competitive forces, customer needs/expectations, and reflective learning.

- The *occurrence of events/changes* can be: (i) exceptional – isolated, once-off, high-intensity, and acute in nature (=a crisis); or (ii) chronic – comparatively lower-intensity but of a high-frequency or high-duration, occurring regularly (i.e., having a rhythm). Examples include the ongoing daily hassles/frustrations of everyday life that could be related to life/work events, major or minor; the disappointment of not winning a major deal; not getting a promotion; or a valuable organisational member resigning.
- The *response to the event/change* can be avoidance/denial, adaptation, re-invention, or re-imagining.
- The *outcome of the bounce back* in response to the event/change could be to succumb; merely survive with a certain level of impairment; or thrive.

Resilience as an integrated, dynamic process capability

Four reciprocally interdependent, process capability stages can be distinguished, which jointly form a resilience meta-capability: [75]

- *Appraise:* the ability to detect and assess – proactively/reactively – critical events/changes that are out of the ordinary within the organisation's operating arena.
- *Respond:* the ability to design and implement appropriate solutions to address the detected event/change to restore the context/organisation/people fit.
- *Recover:* the ability to deal with the impact and consequences (=knock-on effects) of the implemented solution to the detected event/change.
- *Reflect and Learn:* the ability to turn the experiences from the previous stages into information, the information into knowledge, and the knowledge into wisdom (=savvy) in dealing with critical events/changes better and/or differently in the future. I.e., strengthening future resilience. This stage may entail single loop learning (=problem solving); double loop learning (=questioning/reframing mindsets/paradigms), and/or deutero learning (=learning about learning). In the emerging new order, deutero learning has taken a front seat.

The above process capability resilience stages (=the resilience meta-capability) require a complete repertoire of real time, interplaying intelligences – cognitive (e.g., sense-making), emotional (e.g., mindfulness), interpersonal (authenticity, caring), action (e.g., experimentation, improvisation, learning), and contextual (e.g., power bases, collaboration). These should be utilised with respect to all of the organisation's stakeholders, including the building and maintenance of social capital with them (see Excellence Question 19: Goodwill). [76]

Resilience Capability Levels

Organisational resilience is a multi-level capability, made up of four nested layers that are reciprocally interdependent: Persons, Teams, Organisational Units, and the Organisation as a whole, moving from the inner-most layer to the outer-most layer (refer also to Figure 6.5). In terms of the layer (=Persons) to the outer-most layer (=Organisation), resilience must be looked at separately *and* collectively in order to arrive at a complete picture of People Excellence regarding resilience for the organisation and its people.[77] Each layer is discussed below in the above order. Team and Organisational Unit resilience are discussed together because of their similarity.

Personal Resilience

Table 6.3 provides a holistic profile of confident, resilient organisational members.[78]

Table 6.3: Holistic profile of confident, resilient organisational members

SELF	STYLE
• A *well crystallised identity*: The person knows who and what they are as a person. They know what they stand for and aspire to, and how to realise their aspirations. They form an integrated whole. • Anchored in a *higher calling, purpose and meaning*, providing an ultimate 'Why' and 'Whereto' to their thinking, decisions, relationships, and actions. • *The adoption of a set of non-negotiable core values* as a directing and guiding moral compass to their thinking, decisions, relationships, and actions at all times.	• A *'Can Do', 'Make a plan' attitude* in the present, infused by *agility and responsiveness,* allowing them to navigate around, over, or through wicked challenges and problems in an even-tempered manner, in the relentless pursuit of the actualisation of a shared, envisioned legacy. • A sense of *positivity* and *humour* regardless of how adverse the circumstances, pressing the demands, and severe the setbacks faced, are. • *Confident, competent functioning* with deep insight into their *strengths and weaknesses,* with a reaching out to others to complement any areas of weakness. • *Humbleness to learn out of their own mistakes and failures* that they admit honestly and openly to. • *A reflective life style*: the rapid transformation of Experiences into Information; Information into Knowledge; and Knowledge into Wisdom. Inversely, reframing and enriching the former through the latter. • A refusal to nurture a *festering remorse* about what could what have been in the past, but a *letting go of and a moving on.*

• *Authentic relationships* with others. • Timeous *seeking of help* when things go wrong, or when demands and problems are becoming overwhelming. • Ongoing *willingness to learn* from other, more resilient persons.	• *Fearless, courageous, and honest confrontation* of the true reality, regardless of how threatening and powerful it may be. • An *ability to learn faster than the rate of change*, in the process adapting and re-inventing their learning mode to fit the changing circumstances. • Healthy *work-life integration and balance.*
RELATIONSHIPS	**CONTEXT**

Three danger signs of depleting Resilience, which will ultimately lead to poor general well-being, are: *Bad Stress* (=overwhelming work demands relative to available resources); *Burnout,* including change fatigue (=failing, not coping); and *Derailment* (=being rejected by the organisation).[79][80]

Team and Organisational Unit Resilience

Team/Unit resilience relates to the capability of the team/unit to fulfil its mandate – translated into goals – cohesively and inclusively (=remaining together and being dedicated to one another) in spite of events/changes, whether destructive or constructive.[81] The type of team/unit resilience applicable to a specific team/unit is a function of the task interdependency which exists in the team/unit[82]:

• *Pooled* – individual performances are summated to give an overall result.

• *Sequential* – successive building on preceding performances to deliver an overall result.

• *Reciprocal* – concurrent, joint contributions to deliver an overall result.

Given the growing prevalence of virtual team working, an illustration of resilience in this regard is appropriate.[83] Virtual team resilience is the capacity of a virtual team to bounce back from a setback that results in a derailment of virtual team processes. A setback occurs when critical virtual action team processes begin to deteriorate whilst completing tasks. There are four key resources necessary for a virtual team to be resilient:

• *Potency* – the shared collective confidence that team members are effective at accomplishing their tasks.

• *Mental model of teamwork* – team members' shared roadmap of their mode of how to work together effectively.

• *Capacity to improvise* – the team's ability to rapidly improvise/learn something new out of the existing.

- *Psychological safety* – the shared belief that it is safe for members to take interpersonal risks by trying new things; discussing novel ideas; or thinking outside of the box/or even thinking that there is no box at all.

Organisational Resilience

Organisational Resilience refers to the adaptive capability of the organisation to retain, live out, and deliver on its Organisational Identity; one that organisational members can identify strongly with, despite events/changes in its operating arena. Throughout events/changes, the organisation's Identity remains clearly defined, distinct, differentiated, coherent, and strongly entrenched. Simultaneously, the organisation maintains a goodness-of-fit with its context relative to its Identity.

The organisation's clearly defined, distinct, coherent, and strongly entrenched Identity has to be operationalised into specific organisational capabilities, policies, processes, routines, rules, and practices, aimed at building and maintaining resilience.[84] Simultaneously, these organisational components must be sufficiently robust and adaptive to allow the organisation to bounce back to the necessary/desired state/level of organisational functioning. Either proactively by anticipating an event/change; or reactively to an event/change after it has occurred. In short, the organisation remains viable in the present and going into the future, whether it is by returning to the old, or by accommodating the new normal.[85]

Enablers of Resilience

The enablers of resilience embrace the pre-conditions necessary to establish, nurture, and maintain a resilience capability in the organisation across all layers to bring about People Excellence. The preconditions explicated below are linked back to previously discussed People Excellence Elements. As will be seen, most of these Elements are implicated in building and sustaining resilience.

It has also been found that the organisational software is at least, if not more, important than organisational hardware for engendering resilience. The software also ensures that the hardware is adequately mobilised for resilience.[86] People Excellence software elements are highlighted by an asterisk in the below preconditions.

The following preconditions for resilience are essential:

- A clear, robust organisational identity[87] (Excellence Domain 1: Identity)*.
- Transformational/Transcendental leadership[88] (Excellence Question 1: Leadership)*.
- The strategic contribution of People Professionals in providing resilience-building People Practices to the organisation[89] (Excellence Question 3: Partnering).

- Individual organisational commitment and psychological alignment[90] (Excellence Question 6: Commitment)*.

- A networked, team-based organisational design[91], architected around ambidexterity, which optimally balances stability and change[92] with resilience-enabling organisational routines and rules, such as allowing collateral pathways and redundant multiple, alternative courses of action[93] and relentless course correction[94] (Excellence Question 7: Design).

- The right people in the right place at the right time[95] (Excellence Question 8: Matching).

- A flexible, opportunity-driven, innovative Organisational Culture and positive Organisational Climate[96] (Excellence Question 9: Culture and 12: Climate)*.

- The appropriate bundle of People Practices that gives people the opportunity and capacity to bounce back, e.g., flexible work arrangements, development programmes, work-life balance, social support, and well-being programmes[97] (Excellence Question 10: Practices).

- Sound risk management and business continuity planning with good information management[98] (Excellence Question 11: Risk).

- An Organisational Learning Climate, based on a growth mindset[99], engendering experimentation, innovation, risk-taking, challenging, and learning from experiences and errors[100], infused by a high 'stock' of psychosocial capital[101] (Excellence Question 12: Climate)*.

- Enabled and empowered people with strong personal resources with the right mindset and attitude[102] (Excellence Question 13: Balancing)*.

- Strong social networks and high collaboration involving multiple stakeholders[103] (Excellence Question 19: Goodwill)*.

Effects of Resilience

Resilience is positively related to individuals, work, organisations and success in the following ways[104]:

- *Individuals:* organisational commitment, engagement, positivity, less stress, less burn out, organisational citizen behaviour, well-being, career longevity, life satisfaction.

- *Work:* proactive work behaviours, creativity, learning, job performance, job satisfaction.

- *Organisations:* enhanced technological innovation capability, leadership.

- *Success:* organisations high on agility-resilience show a 150% higher return on investment (ROI) and a 500% higher return on equity (ROE).

The **affirmative answer** to the People Excellence Question 15: Resilience is: *the high presence of resilient people with the right change-navigating mindsets and attitudes, who own and embrace with robust, quiet confidence the intended change journey of their organisation as the surest way of securing a viable future for their organisation and themselves.* Posed in the negative: *the absence/low frequency of a high prevalence of Bad Stress, Burnout and Derailment because people are change-fit.*

You can now do a Reflective Assessment: Resilience (Work Sheet 19 in the Work Book), if you wish to do so.

PEOPLE EXCELLENCE QUESTION 16: ENGAGEMENT

How engaged are people in their work?

The awarded/taken up autonomy (Excellence Question 13: Balancing) has created the 'action space' in which an organisation's change-fit people (Excellence Question 15: Resilience) can engage with their designated work – encapsulated in their Work Roles located in the organisational design – in meaningful ways[105] in pursuit of highly valued Recognition/Rewards (Excellence Question 14: Line of Sight). Engagement relates to the Key People imperative: People Energy ('Will do') (see Table 4.5).

The preconditions exist for people to now become and be personally engaged by taking up their work through unlocking real, amazing value and creating worthy, lasting wealth – consistently and continuously – to the continuing, amazed delight of the organisation's beneficiaries. In a sense, engagement is the ultimate climax to, and destination of, the overall People Excellence journey. It is analogous to the final, climaxing movement of a symphony that brings together all of its preceding movements. The status of Excellence Domains 4: Outcomes and 5: Relationships is the outflow of engagement as a consolidation of what came before. Engagement can be seen as a central integrating concept in explaining and understanding individual performance, organisational performance, and competitive advantage.[106]

People are consistently realising high returns on the people investment made by their organisations through the People Excellence preconditions that were set up to engender high engagement, as sketched in the Excellence Domain 2: Capacity.[107][108][109] People are thus performing outstandingly in an upwardly spiralling cycle of increasing value unlocking and wealth creation, in turn enhancing organisational performance and viability all round.[110].

The following topics are discussed below: engagement as a deep, energetic immersion in one's work; 'Beyond Self' engagement; levels of engagement; the profile of a highly engaged organisational member; the engagement equation; and the effects of engagement.

Engagement as a deep, energetic immersion in one's work

High engagement entails the strong identification – and hence the deep, energetic immersion – of people as whole persons with and in their work as contained in their Work Roles. This is above and beyond the 'normal call of duty' – physically, physiologically, psychosocially, socio-culturally, and spiritually – in pursuit of gaining Valued-Recognition/Rewards that can fulfil their basic needs and give expression to their Personal Identity. In short, it is the extra, over-and-above, personal investment – body, mind, soul and spirit – that a person is willing to make in their work to achieve desirable ends, personally and for their team, colleagues, organisational unit, and organisation.[111] People are flourishing in their work, and hence are thriving. Engagement manifests itself differently as a function of the different Work Roles that people occupy in organisations – individual, team, or leadership – as each Role has different push and pull factors.[112]

Whereas committed ownership (see Excellence Question 6: Ownership) relates to an affective attachment to the *organisation per se*, as well as what it stands for, engagement refers to an affective attachment to *one's designated work*. To use a sports metaphor: committed ownership is about getting into a chosen game, and sticking to it. Engagement is about playing the game enthusiastically: body, mind, soul, and spirit.[113]

This is why engagement predicts job performance better than committed ownership (=affective commitment). In turn, committed ownership predicts retention (=withdrawal and turnover) better than engagement. Committed ownership is also more closely related to Organisational Identity (='I belong here') than engagement, which is more closely associated with performance, job satisfaction, innovation, creativity, and well-being (='I want to make a worthy difference').[114] To achieve lasting People Excellence, the organisation's people must concurrently demonstrate high committed ownership and engagement: 'This is where I belong, making a worthy difference.'

'Beyond Self' engagement

People's deep, energetic immersion with and in their work is also manifested in a 'Beyond Self' engagement with their team, colleagues, organisational unit, organisation, and beyond in the form of the 4Cs depicted in Figure 6.6.[115] This 'Beyond Self' engagement strengthens people's sense of belonging and their committed ownership (see Excellence Question 6: Ownership).[116]

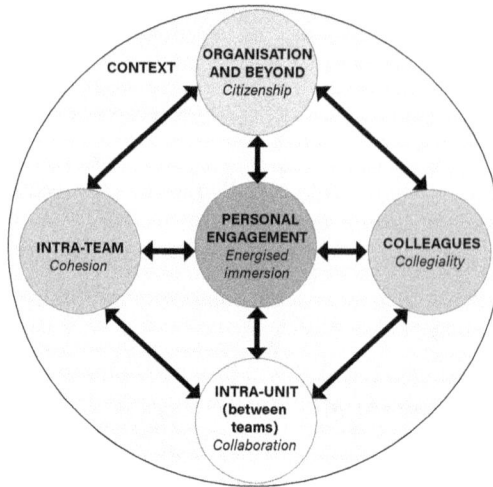

Figure 6.6: Manifestations of 'Beyond Self' Engagement

The manifestations in Figure 6.6 can be called 'knock-on' (or snowballing) engagements, which recursively affect personal engagement and strengthen individual links (=affective commitment) to, and fit with, an organisation. They also increase the sacrifice (read 'cost') of a person leaving the organisation as their embeddedness deepens.[117] Personal engagement affects in-role performance, whereas its respective knock-on manifestations affect extra-role, contextual performance – the performance of the person's team, organisational unit, and organisation overall.[118]

The crux of the present People Excellence question is: does the organisation completely harness and utilise the full capability contained in their people's capabilities (hard and soft), expertise, experience, energy, enthusiasm, creativity, and diversity through the use of the resources put at their disposal, given that the necessary People Excellence pre-conditions have been set up? In addition, through their deep, energetic immersion – driven by ongoing, relentless disruptive innovation and re-invention – are people becoming even more masterful at enhanced value unlocking and wealth creation? Are they afforded the opportunity to learn, unlearn and relearn, and in the process gaining greater wisdom?

Levels of Engagement

Engagement implies that the majority of the organisation's people could be:

- *positively engaged* = going the extra mile; improving, innovating and/or re-inventing the current state; instead of
- *neutrally engaged* = doing the minimum required, demonstrating only satisfysing performance by merely fulfilling minimum work requirements; or

- *negatively engaged* = whether passively (doing nothing by ducking and diving; being absent physically or mentally) or actively disengaged (sabotaging/ undermining the organisation).

The typical engagement distribution coming out of engagement surveys globally is that around 60% to 70% of organisational members are neutrally engaged (=doing the minimum required); around 10% to 15% are positively engaged (=going the extra mile); and about 15% to 20% are negatively disengaged, whether passively or actively.[119] The point is not the exact percentages but the approximate proportions, which show that the majority of people in organisations are just performing the minimum required.

Profile of a highly engaged organisational member

Table 6.4 provides a profile of a highly engaged organisational member.[120][121]

Table 6.4: Profile of a highly engaged organisational member

WORK ENGAGEMENT INDICATORS
Vigour – *Work energy and resilience* (negative: exhaustion)
• At work, a person feels him/herself bursting with energy
• In this work, a person feels strong and resilient
Dedication – *Involvement in work* (negative: cynicism)
• To the person, his/her job is challenging
• The person is enthusiastic about his/her job
• The person takes pride in his/her work
Absorption – *Focused/concentrated on work* (negative: distraction)
• When the person is working, he/she forgets everything else around him/her
• The person is positively and fully engrossed in his/her work
Collaboration – *Working beyond Self* (negative: alienation/withdrawal)
• The person seeks work assistance from others when needed
• The person provides unsolicited help to others at work
• The person goes the unexpected, extra mile with organisational beneficiaries

Engagement Equation

The following "10:6:2" rule applies with regard to the engagement of the organisation's people[122]:

- For every 10% improvement in the engagement of a person, her/his effort level increases by 6%, and decreases the probability of her/him leaving by 9%.
- In turn, every 6% improvement in effort increases a person's performance by 2%.

Effects of Engagement

Engagement is positively related to individuals, work, organisations, and outcomes in the following ways[123]:

- *Individuals:* identification with, and commitment to, the organisation; loyalty; less stress; less absenteeism; an intention to stay (=retention); well-being; basic need satisfaction.
- *Work:* performance, creativity, innovation, productivity, job satisfaction.
- *Organisations:* strategy alignment, strategic implementation, goal clarity, leadership, culture, practices, autonomy, citizenship behaviours.
- *Outcomes:* safety, customer service/satisfaction, organisational performance, financial performance (higher net income and profitability), greater competitiveness.

It is estimated that a negatively engaged person only does two hours of productive work per day, and has a 25% higher chance of leaving. In contrast, a highly engaged person is 30% to 87% more productive, and is 10% less likely to leave.[124] Energised employees are also five times more likely to say they are thriving, and feel less burnt out (60% compared to 81% of de-energised employees).[125]

Organisations with high employee engagement were 202% more profitable than their peers.[126] Organisations with a low overall people engagement lost 2.01% in operating margins, and were 1.38% down in net profit margins over a three year period. Over the same period, high engagement organisations gained 3.74% in operating margins and 2.06% in net profit margins.[127] This implies that the organisation that gets higher engagement by more people at more times in more places can achieve substantively more with exactly the same people.

The **affirmative answer** to the People Excellence Question 16: Engagement, is: *the majority of the organisation's people (> 75%) are highly engaged – demonstrated in high levels of vigour, dedication, absorption, and collaboration – unlocking more value and creating greater wealth than what is normally expected – resulting in delighted stakeholders and an ongoing viable organisation.*

You can now do a Reflective Assessment: Engagement (Work Sheet 20 in the Work Book), if you wish to do so.

SYNERGISTIC FUSION WITHIN PEOPLE EXCELLENCE DOMAIN 3: DELIVERY

Synergistically, *Value Unlocking* regarding the Excellence Domain 3: Delivery embraces permeating the organisation with an invigorating Organisational Climate – a conducive, positive vibe, nurturing a high stock of psychosocial capital and virtue-ality; the achievement in real time delivery across the organisation of an optimal balance between work demands and required resources through the appropriate autonomy being awarded and taken up; establishing a clear line of sight between Effort – Performance – Valued Recognition/Rewards; growing through ongoing learning, change-fit people with the right change navigation mindset and attitude, who demonstrate confident resilience; and highly engaged people, performing outstandingly collaboratively.

Figure 6.7 depicts in the coloured circle the above Excellence synergy graphically in the form of the third building block towards a complete People Excellence Value Chain. Again, it is important to note the reciprocal independencies and dynamic, organic coherence between all of the Excellence elements making up the Excellence Domain. *Firstly,* the progressive, sequential, linear alignment order of the five Excellence Elements: Climate, through Balancing, Line of Sight, Resilience, to Engagement (i.e., the order of the discussion above). *Secondly,* the enabling conditions that Climate provides to the four other Excellence Elements. Hence its placement in Figure 6.9 behind the other four Elements' blocks. *Thirdly,* the leveraging role that Balancing, Line of Sight, and Resilience play with respect to Engagement immersed in an enabling Climate.

Like all of the previous Excellence Domains, over time the reciprocal interdependencies form either an upward spiralling virtuous cycle or a downward spiralling vicious cycle of People Excellence conditions. The essence of the synergistic fusion in the Domain lies in *Multiplication:* Going forward, later Elements strengthen the effects of earlier Elements. And, recursively, the effects of later Elements further strengthen the effects of earlier Elements.

Again, in Figure 6.9, the extended lines for Leadership and Ownership serve to indicate their onward influence on the other two, still-to-be-discussed, Excellence Domains. Also, the direct connection between Leadership and Climate, through to Engagement, illustrating their intimate, co-variant relationship. It also implies that

Climate is a critical enabler that leadership can use to engender Engagement, and then multiply its effect through Balancing, Line of Sight, and Resilience.

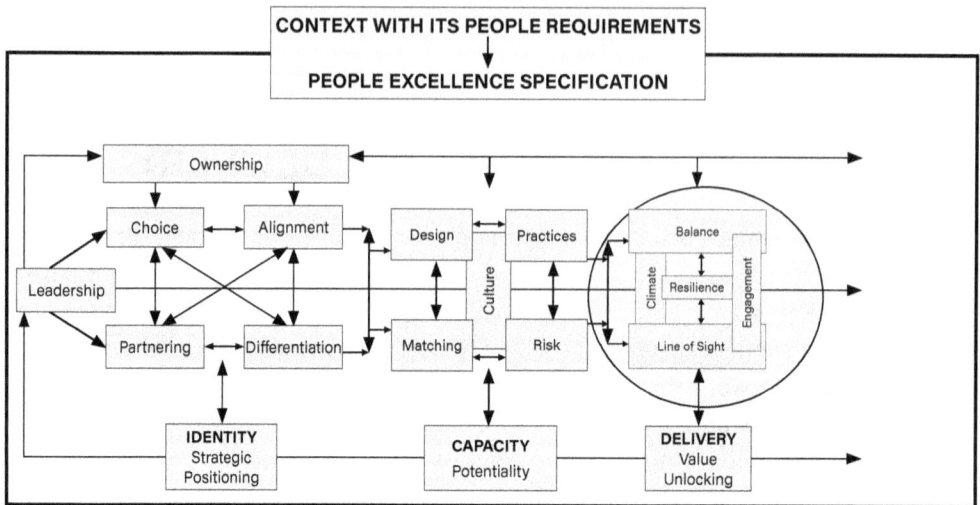

Figure 6.7: Synergistic fusion of Multiplication within the Excellence Dimension 3: Delivery

The desired synergy to be generated by the People Excellence Domain 3: Delivery, as explicated above in terms of leading thinking and practices with regard to the five Excellence Elements: Climate, Balancing, Line of Sight, Resilience, and Engagement – as referenced against the People Excellence Specification of the emerging, new order – is given in the shaded box below.

PEOPLE EXCELLENCE SPECIFICATION

Highly enabled, empowered and resilient people, who strongly identify with and feel valued by the organisation, and are productively and innovatively engaging collaboratively through personally purposeful and meaningful ways, to viably and sustainably create inimitable, delightful experiences for stakeholders.

People Excellence Dimension 3: Delivery

Value Unlocking

At all times, our organisation is infused by an invigorating Organisational Climate – a shared, positive vibe – nurturing a high stock of psychosocial capital, i.e., high levels of experienced efficacy, optimism, hope, perseverance, resilience, and a strong virtue-ality amongst leadership – a high presence of humaneness, courage, open-mindedness, creativity, curiosity and prudence – recursively engendering an even more Invigorating Climate.

Across all organisational levels and areas, our people have the real time, in time, moment-by-moment autonomy to craft an optimal match between their work demands and the resources required to meet these demands. In this way we not only create multiple self-management opportunities for the people of our organisation to experience that they feel that they are personally in control of their work setting at all times, but also engender high people commitment, engagement, performance, and well-being.

A clear link exists between Effort – Performance – Valued Recognition/Rewards in our organisation. We accept that people are unique in what they need and want. Hence different permutations of Recognition/Rewards exist in our organisation. Our people thrive because their specific permutation of basic needs across all of their Being/Becoming Dimensions, and, which are embedded in their Personal Identity, are fulfilled through the valued Recognition/ Rewards they receive for their aligned Effort and Performance.

Our organisation has change-fit people. There is a high presence of resilient people with the right change navigation mindset and attitude, who face with robust, quiet confidence, the intended change journey of our organisation as the surest way of securing a desired future for our organisation and themselves. We regard resilience as a Core Organisational and People Capability. For us, resilience refers to the ability of our organisation and our people to respond proactively and reactively to expected and unexpected events and changes in our operating arena – whether constructive or destructive – in order to better fit in. In this way, we strengthen and retain our continued viability. Our organisation is infused with the minimum prevalence of Bad Stress, Burnout, and Derailment because our people are change-fit.

The vast majority of our people are highly engaged – as demonstrated in high levels of vigour, dedication, absorption, and collaboration – unlocking more value and creating greater wealth than what is normally expected, resulting in an outstanding yield (=return) on the people investment of our organisation.

You can now do a Summative Reflective Assessment: Synergistic fusion – Multiplication of the Excellence Dimension 3: Delivery (Work Sheet 21 in the Work Book), if you wish to do so.

PEOPLE EXCELLENCE STAR

OUTCOMES: WEALTH CREATED

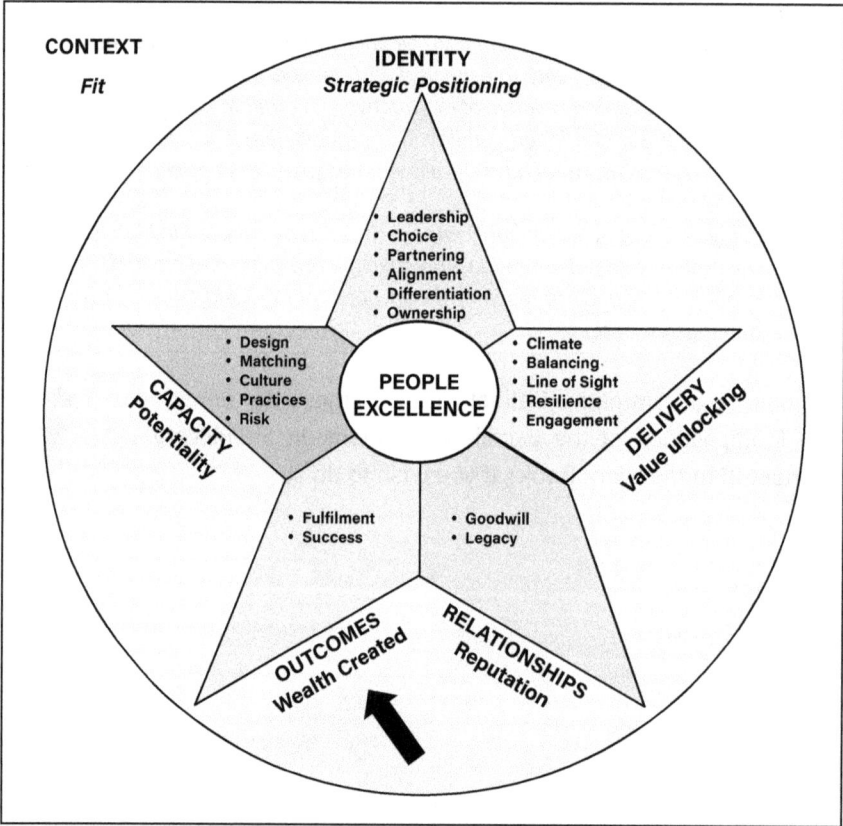

CHAPTER 7

PEOPLE EXCELLENCE DOMAIN 4 – OUTCOMES: WEALTH CREATED

Knowing the cost of everything, but the value of nothing." (Oscar Wilde)

"The will to win, the desire to succeed, the urge to reach your full potential… these are the keys that will unlock the door to personal excellence." (Confucius)

"Perfection is not attainable, but if we chase perfection, we can catch excellence." (Vince Lombardi)

"If you are going to achieve excellence in big things, you develop the habit in little matters. Excellence is not an exception, it is a prevailing attitude." (Colin Powell)

The Excellence Domains 1: Identity – Strategic Positioning;, 2: Capacity – Potentiality; and 3: Delivery – Value Unlocking have been stress-tested. At this point, we know our organisation's People Creditworthiness and possible interventions regarding *firstly*, whether we have chosen the right strategic positioning of our people that will ensure a high likelihood of the sustainable, future success of our organisation; *secondly*, whether we have capacitated our organisation through the necessary investment for excellent people delivery, and hence for continued viable, organisational success; and, *thirdly*, whether our organisation is unlocking outstanding value with our people to the amazed delight of our stakeholders.

Next, the *People Excellence Domain 4: Outcomes* has to be stress-tested. This Excellence Domain deals with the results flowing from people performance: the *Wealth Created*. Although only discussed now, this Dimension, as well as *Excellence Domain 5: Relationships* (to be discussed next), are Dimensions to be tracked and monitored all the time, in real time, providing in-time insight into the effect and impact of the preceding Dimensions – individually and in combination – and taking corrective action. Thus, it may be useful to construct and activate Dimensions 4 and 5 in parallel to Dimensions 2: Capacity and 3: Delivery in order to commence the monitoring and tracking of the latter two Dimensions as they are being rolled out and having an impact. In this way, one will be able to take corrective action from the word 'Go! Dimension 1: Identity does need to be in place first, however.

A further interesting angle to take in enhancing People Excellence in an organisation is to work 'backwards' by using the actual People Excellence achieved in Domains 4: Outcomes and 5: Relationships to provide clues to prioritise People Excellence Questions/interventions in the preceding Excellence Domains: Identity, Capacity and Delivery.

As illustrated in the People Excellence Star on the opposite page, *Excellence Domain 4: Outcomes* encompasses the *Excellence Elements* of *Fulfilment* and *Success.* Each is discussed in turn in the order listed.

PEOPLE EXCELLENCE
QUESTION 17: FULFILMENT

Do the people of the organisation believe and experience in real time that the organisation is truly delivering on its People Brand Promise?

This Excellence Question within the Outcomes Excellence Domain refers to the *people-centric* Outcome resulting from all the preceding Excellence Domains. The *organisational* Outcome, also within this Domain, is addressed by Excellence Question 18: Success (to be discussed next).

People Excellence Question 17: Fulfilment encompasses the degree to which the people of the organisation believe and experience in real time that their organisation is truly meeting its People Brand Promise as contained in its People Value Proposition (PVP).[1] The Fulfilment relates to the Key People imperative: People Fulfilment ('Want to do') (see Table 4.5).

People Excellence requires that the overwhelming majority of the organisation's people believe and experience full delivery on the People Brand Promise to them as whole persons. A backward-looking, affirmative answer can be given to the PVP question: 'Will I flourish if I join the organisation? And because I flourish, will I therefore will thrive, and hence will I feel fulfilled as a whole person?'

From Flourishing through Thriving to Fulfilment

To be truly significant, organisational members' belief in, and experience of, flourishing through thriving to fulfilment and back, must be all embracing, and cover the whole person in all of his/her integrated, systemic, and organic complexity: Needs-Being/ Becoming Dimensions-Personal Identity. People must believe and experience that they are the best they can be, want to be, and aspire to be, now and going into the future.[2] This discussion is graphically illustrated in Figure 7.1 in terms of people as complex, multi-dimensional, holistic beings.

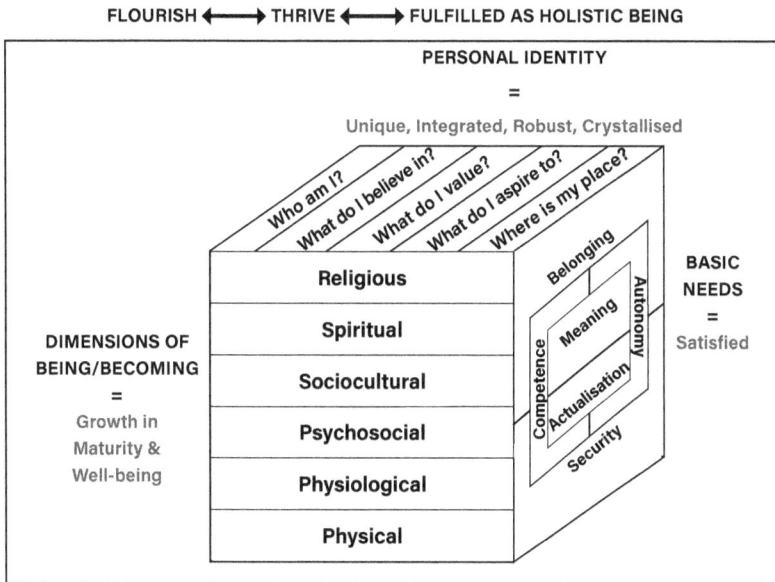

Figure 7.1: Flourishing, Thriving, and being Fulfilled as a whole Person

The People Brand Promise Journey

The experiential delivery of the People Brand Promise is not a single, once-off event. It is an unfolding, iterative journey of ongoing, successive states of experiential delivery on the Promise, as expressed in the Brand across the total organisational landscape covering all of the People Excellence Domains. The Brand is a dynamic verb, not a static noun. The People Brand promise thus embraces both content and process simultaneously.[3] This journey is depicted in Figure 7.2.[4]

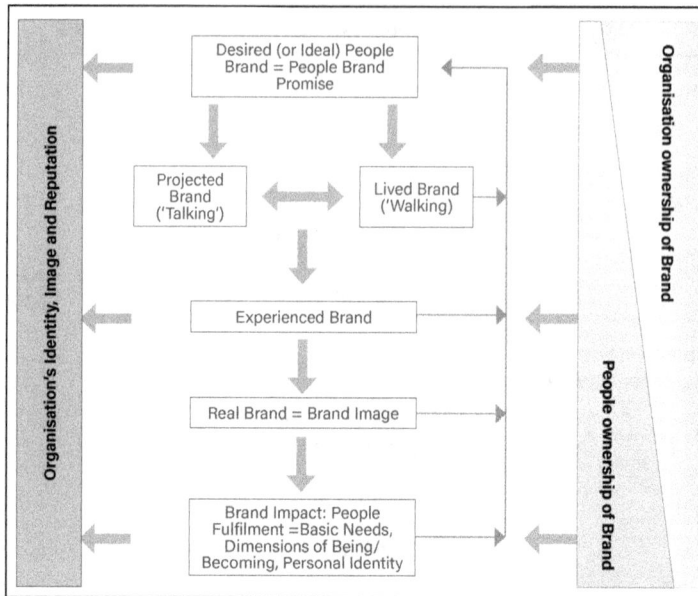

Figure 7.2: People Brand Promise journey

According to Figure 7.2, the People Brand journey consists of the crafting, explicitly or implicitly, of a Desired People Brand containing the People Brand Promise (Excellence Question 5: Differentiation) by the organisation. Next is the everyday operationalisation of the Desired Brand through Talking (=Projected Brand) and Walking (=Lived Brand) in the organisation, in particular by its leadership. Talking and Walking is the difference between what is espoused and enacted in the organisation, such as the espoused vs. enacted design; awarded vs. exercised autonomy; and stated vs. perceived People Practices.[5]

Jointly, the Projected and Lived Brands generate the Experienced Brand – the delivered Promise – as concretely experienced by organisational members – prospective and current. This Experienced Brand gives rise to the Real Brand: 'This is what this organisation truly is known and stand for; is actually experiencing in terms of its people thinking, feeling, deciding, responding, and doing; and is genuinely delivering on its People Brand Promise.'

The Desired and Real Brands may differ significantly, however, in the eyes of the organisation's people. The Real People Brand is how the People Brand Promise is believed and experienced as being actually and truly delivered on. It is how the expectations contained in, and conveyed by, the Desired People Brand are realised through the totality of the successive, lived experiences of the Brand – from Desired, through Projected and Lived to Experienced – by people, individually and collectively – in their interactions with the organisation in real time.

The Real People Brand equates to the active People Brand Image. In turn, the Real People Brand has a certain People Brand Impact: to what degree do people genuinely feel fulfilled because they are thriving, given the actual delivery on the People Brand Promise? Successive Brands, constituting the unfurling Brand journey, feedback to earlier Brands. Ideally, the feedback must result in iterative adjustments and re-inventions in earlier Brands.

If kept, the People Brand Promise sets the organisation up for an upward spiralling, virtuous cycle of even higher levels of People Excellence going into the future because of the experienced fulfilment of its people, especially because of higher levels of committed ownership and engagement. Concurrently, the organisation is experienced as trustworthy and authentic. It delivers on what it promises/promised.[6] People-wise, the future likely viability of the organisation – performance- and success-wise – is more secure because of the ever-increasing positive cycle of truly delivering on the People Brand Promise, expressive of the organisation's PVP – and experienced as such by its people.

As can be seen in Figure 7.2, the Brand journey must be aligned to, and affect, the organisation's Identity, Image, and Reputation within its operating arena. On the right-hand side of the figure, the 'ownership' is depicted in terms of how the People Brand ownership varies over the unfolding, emerging Brand journey. The organisation – and particularly its leadership – has greater ownership of the experience over the earlier part of the journey: the Desired, Projected, and Lived People Brands. In contrast, organisational members have more dominant ownership of the experience over the latter part of the Brand journey: the Experienced and Real People Brands with the consequential People Brand Impact. I.e., their actual experience of the Brand of the organisation through a feeling of being fulfilled or not.

Hearing and listening to the People's Voice

An organisation must monitor and track the degree of its people's voice to meet the People Brand Promise in real time, all of the time.[7] Do people believe and experience that they flourish, thrive and are fulfilled as whole persons in the organisation? Actions must be taken in real time, all the time, dependent on the answers to this question. If the voice is positive, to build on and strengthen the organisation's People Brand Promise. If negative, to identify and deal with the sources of negativity.

The **affirmative answer** to the People Excellence Question 17: Fulfilment, is: *the people of the organisation feel genuinely fulfilled as whole persons because they believe and experience unambiguously that their organisation is truly delivering on its People Brand Promise in real time, all the time.*

You can now do a Reflective Assessment: Fulfilment (Work Sheet 22 in the Work Book), if you wish to do so.

PEOPLE EXCELLENCE QUESTION 18: SUCCESS

Does the organisation have real time, in time, intelligent insight regarding the contribution of its people towards its success and ultimate viability?

As was stated above, Excellence Question 18: Fulfilment deals with a *people-centric* Outcome view: how fulfilled people believe and experience they are relative to the organisation's Real People Brand. This Excellence Question takes an *organisation-centric* Outcome view. It refers to the real time, in time, interrogative intelligence available in the organisation regarding the contribution of its people towards its continued viability according to the actual organisational outcomes achieved, in particular value unlocking and wealth creation.[8] The organisation is applying intelligence-based insights instead of personal opinion, conventional wisdom, positional power, or the popular fads of the moment.

Achievement People Balanced Scorecard

This requires, *firstly,* an Achievement People Balanced Scorecard (or Dashboard) that shows, monitors, and tracks in real-time in an integrated, systemic, multi-dimensional way the contributions of the organisation's people in relation to the intended/desired organisational outcomes.[9][10] Figure 7.3 gives an example of what such an Achievement People Balanced Scorecard could look like.[11] Inter alia, the suggested metrics included in the Scorecard must be derived from the Organisation's Identity, specifically its Strategic Intent.[12] The type and number of metrics included in the Scorecard must be chosen, following a number of principles: (i) 'Less is more'; (ii) the Pareto principle of 'The 20% that will tell the 80%' story'; (iii) an 'Outside-In', 'Outcome-based' analytical perspective[13]; and (iv) be at the requisite Level of Work (LOW), in this case LOW4: Strategic Translation and Implementation.[14]

WEALTH CREATION WITH PEOPLE	EMPLOYER OF CHOICE OF EMPLOYEES OF CHOICE
• Benefit generated *Profit-driven organisation* – Profit/Full Time Equivalent Employees (FTEs) – Market Capitalisation/FTEs *Public sector organisation* – Citizen satisfaction: % Citizens believing they are living better lives because of better service delivery – People Service Excellence: % people recognised/ rewarded • Growth in market share, expressed financially/FTEs • Monetary value of new products/services introduced in last 4 years/ FTEs • Social Responsibility Expenditure/ FTEs	• People Representivity: Demographic distribution across organisational levels & Departments/ Functions • Institutional Memory: Average Tenure in mission-critical roles • People Retention: Resignation rates, especially for mission-critical roles & designated persons • People Well-Being: % Sick leave utilisation; Health Levels; Absenteeism • Leadership Image: Reputation and credibility • Organisational Reputation/Image: Acceptance rate of offers, especially within Core Organisational Capabilities, by scarce talent and/or by designated groups; % roles filled within 90 days • Employer net promoter score[15]
• Talent Abundance: Successors available as percentage of key talent group; Percentage vacancies filled from internal applications • Talent Availability: Percentage of key roles filled (or % vacancy in mission-critical roles for period) • Percentage of FTEs adjudged competent for mission-critical roles • People Investment: Training and Development Return on Investment • People Growth: Percentage of people fulfilling their Personal Development Plans	• Frequency and distribution of Desired Expected People Conduct • People Performance: Percentage of people fulfilling performance contracts; Percentage of outstanding performers • People Productivity: People Productivity per level & key work process; • Number of clients served/FTEs • Distribution of People Energised Immersion • People issues: % people issues resolved within prescribed time frames • Quality of employee relationships • Quality of work setting: safety, health & physical attractiveness • Extent to which people are knowledgeable on key organisational issues
PEOPLE GROWTH	INTERNAL PEOPLE STATE

Figure 7.3: Example of an Achievement People Balanced Scorecard

The Achievement People Balanced Scorecard is owned by, and must be used for, strategic insight and action by the organisation's Board, leadership, people, and even external stakeholders like investors. At most the role of the organisation's People Professionals is to prepare and report on the Scorecard. All organisational members must be kept informed at all times on how the organisation is doing on an ongoing basis, such that they can take insightful, corrective action in their areas of accountability. Additionally, the Scorecard must be used in real time to access, report, recognise, and celebrate organisational achievements and successes. In this way, it is building and nurturing committed ownership and engagement amongst organisational members.[16]

The most advanced evolutionary stage regarding the Achievement People Balanced Scorecard is when a sophisticated statistical measurement model – either a linkage model or a decision-making algorithm – has been empirically validated for its portfolio of metrics in order to establish an *Intelligent* Balanced Scorecard.[17] Such a model or algorithm will show the interdependency between the variables contained in the organisation's Achievement People Balanced Scorecard, allowing for the exploration of bold predictions and scenarios in a forward-looking, strategic manner, and not remaining locked in a historical, backward-looking picture.[18]

In this way, intelligent prognoses can be made regarding the expected future people contributions as the result of possible People Excellence interventions, which focus on different dimensions of the People Balanced Scorecard. Proactive, predictive actions can also be taken. This means opportunities can be capitalised on; risks can be mitigated; and organisational resilience can be bolstered.

Interrogative People Balanced Scorecard

Secondly, the Achievement People Balanced Scorecard given in Figure 7.3 can be mirrored by an Interrogative People Balanced Scorecard, addressing 'Why', 'Whereto', 'Who', 'What' and 'Where' questions. In this way, the Achievement and Interrogative Balanced Scorecards become two sides of the same coin. An example of an Interrogative Scorecard is given in Figure 7.4 with example questions.[19]

WEALTH CREATION WITH PEOPLE	EMPLOYER OF CHOICE OF EMPLOYEES OF CHOICE
• What are the people drivers of the profit-generated/ wealth-created for stakeholders in our organisation? • What turns people into true value unlockers and wealth creators in our organisation? • Will we have the right people at the right time in the right place to drive disruptive innovation in our organisation in the future? • Are we a good social citizen with which our people can identify with, and be committed to unconditionally? • How much goodwill do we have with our stakeholders, and why? • Is our organisation leaving behind a lasting, worthy legacy, and why?	• Does our organisation have a clearly defined, distinct, and strongly entrenched Identity? • Have we made the right Strategic People Choice and Position, and are we living it? • What is driving the delivering of our People Brand Promise? • Where are we drawing our critical talent from, and why? • How well are we delivering on our Brand Promise, and why? • What is the likelihood that strategically critical talent may leave our organisation, and why? • What affects the demographic representativity of our organisation? • What are the drivers of our leadership's legitimacy and credibility? • What is our organisation's reputation and image in general, and as an employer specifically in the market, and why, amongst our stakeholders?
• What will ensure that we have the right talent in the right place at the right time? • How effective are our talent strategies to close the gap between our talent demand and supply over our strategic horizon? • Are we maintaining our organisational memory at the right level? • How ready are our people for the future world of work? What is required to get them ready in time? • Are our people learning and growing faster than the rate of change? • Who is likely to resign over the next 18-24 months, and why? What will be the impact?	• Do we have the right organisational culture, and why? • What is the organisational climate in our organisation, and why? • Is our organisational and people resilience at the right level? • What drives the performance of our people? • What effects interpersonal relationships and collaboration in our organisation? • Do we have the right level of engagement in our organisation? • What drives the engagement of our people, and why? • What affects the well-being of our people, and how well are we protecting it? • How fairly and equitably are our recognition and rewards distributed across the diverse groupings in our organisation?
PEOPLE GROWTH	INTERNAL PEOPLE STATE

Figure 7.4: Example of an Interrogative People Balanced Scorecard

All-in-all, between the two complementary Balanced Scorecards, a sequence of interventions can be established through the linkage model/decision-making algorithm and interrogative questions, triggering a multiplier effect. This is akin to a strategic map that can be crafted for intelligently sequenced interventions. The organisation has thus capacitated itself with future-driven, predictive, people intelligence.[20] It can now become an architect of its future, and not a victim.

The **affirmative answer** to the People Excellence Question 18: Success, is: *the organisation has real time, in time, predictive, interrogative People Intelligence in place to monitor, track, and affect in real time the people contribution to organisational success and viability, used by all stakeholders.*

You can now do a Reflective Assessment: Success (Work Sheet 23 in the Work Book), if you wish to do so.

SYNERGISTIC FUSION WITHIN PEOPLE EXCELLENCE DOMAIN 4: OUTCOMES

Synergistically, *Wealth Created* regarding Excellence Domain 4: Outcomes entails the organisation's people believing and experiencing that the organisation is truly delivering on its People Brand Promise, as expressed in its People Value Proposition. They feel genuinely fulfilled because they are flourishing and thriving. People's contributions to the organisational performance and success are related, monitored, tracked, predicted, interrogated, and acted upon using real time, in time, proactive people intelligence.

Figure 7.5 depicts the above Excellence synergy graphically in the form of the fourth building block towards a complete People Excellence Value Chain, highlighted in the coloured circle. Again, it is important to note the reciprocal interdependencies of recursive, iterative matching between the Excellence elements making up this Excellence Domain. Of note are the feedback relationships of this Excellence Domain with the preceding Excellence Domains: Identity, Capacity, and Delivery. Over time, these relationships will 'pour fuel' on the upward-spiralling virtuous or downward-spiralling vicious cycles of People Excellence in these Domains, further strengthening or eroding People Excellence within them. The essence of the synergistic fusion in this Domain lies in *Wisdom*. Wisdom entails understanding when, how, and with whom to do what. Put differently, Wisdom refers to Intelligent Insight.

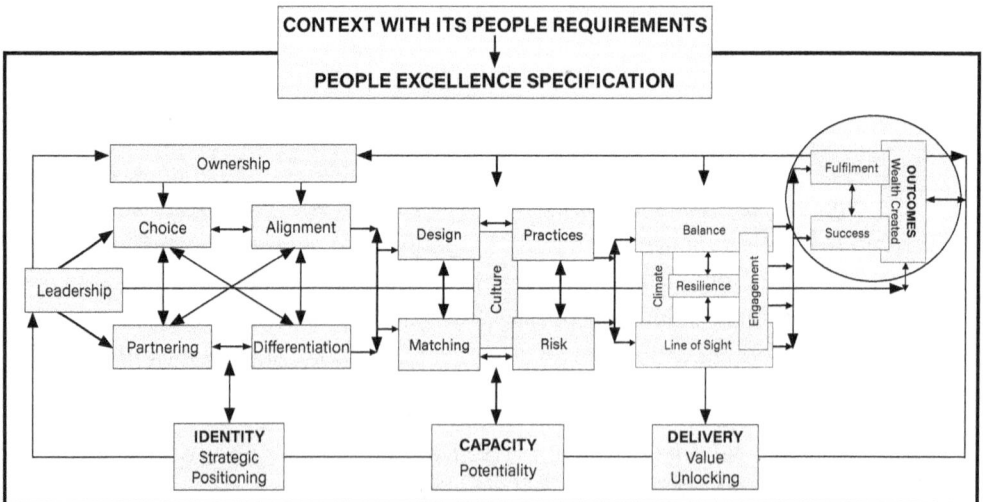

Figure 7.5: Synergistic fusion of Wisdom within the Excellence Dimension 4: Outcomes

The desired synergy to be generated by People Excellence Domain 4, as explicated above in terms of leading thinking and practices with regard to its two Excellence Elements: Fulfilment and Success – as referenced against the People Excellence Specification of the emerging new order – is given in the shaded box below.

PEOPLE EXCELLENCE SPECIFICATION

Highly enabled, empowered and resilient people, who strongly identify with and feel valued by the organisation, and are productively and innovatively engaging collaboratively through personally purposeful and meaningful ways, to viably and sustainably create inimitable, delightful experiences for stakeholders.

PEOPLE EXCELLENCE DIMENSION 4: OUTCOMES

Wealth Created

People in our organisation believe and experience that it is truly delivering on the promise contained in our People Value Proposition – our People Brand Promise. They are flourishing and thriving, and hence feel fulfilled as whole persons in terms of their Needs, Being/ Becoming Dimensions, and Personal Identity. Delivery on our Promise also resonates directly with us in living our organisation's Strategic People Choice of people being central to the success of our organisation as value unlockers and wealth creators with its commensurate Psychosocial Contract of Partnering/Identification. It also re-affirms our Strategic People Choice, made up of our People Charter, Desired People Profile, and People Value Proposition within the strategic configuration of the World of Work in our organisation.

At any given point in time, we know in real time what the contribution of our people is to the performance and success of our organisation, and can even proactively predict their contribution going into the future. This interrogative intelligence is expressed in a systemic, multi-dimensional People Balanced Scorecard. The 'two-sided' predictive and interrogative Scorecard is used on an ongoing basis by our Board, leadership, people, and other stakeholders to monitor, track, and affect in real time our people contribution and outcomes, and to take wise decisions accordingly. I.e., decisions based on intelligent insight, in the present and going into the future.

You can now do a Summative Reflective Assessment: Synergistic fusion – Wisdom of Excellence Dimension 4: Outcomes (Work Sheet 24 in the Work Book), if you wish to do so.

PEOPLE EXCELLENCE STAR

RELATIONSHIPS: REPUTATION

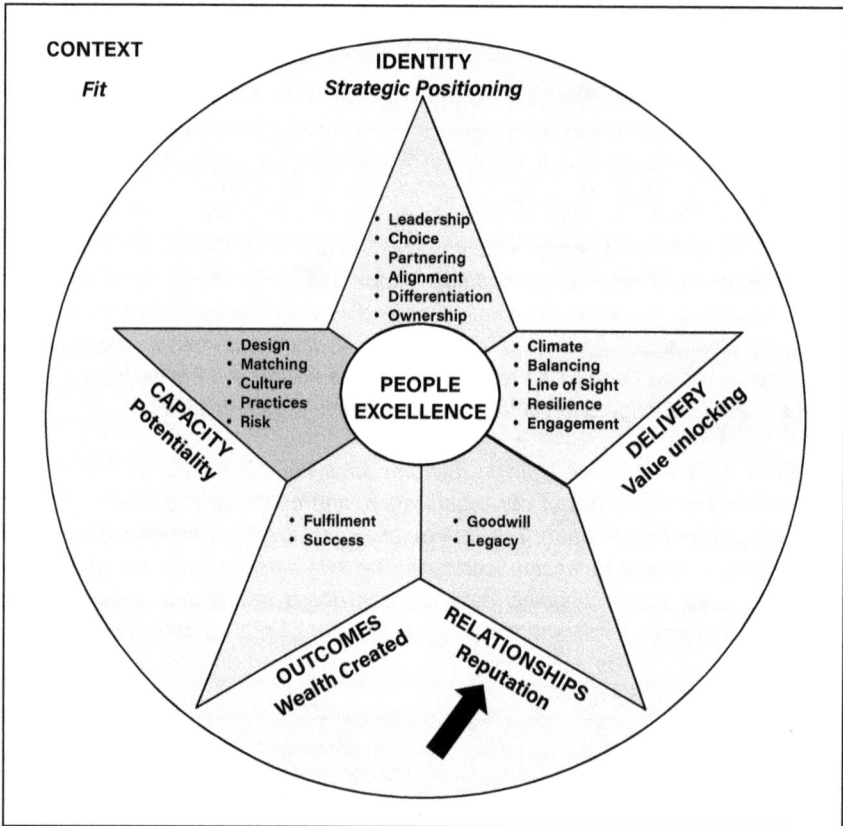

PEOPLE EXCELLENCE DOMAIN 5 – RELATIONSHIPS: REPUTATION

"Wealth does not bring about excellence, but excellence makes wealth and everything else good for men, both individually and collectively." (Socrates)

"The extent of your impact on the world depends on the size of your devotion to excellence." (Robin Sharma)

"Excellence encourages one about life generally; it shows the spiritual wealth of the world." (George Eliot)

Excellence Domains 1: Identity – Strategic Positioning; 2: Capacity – Potentiality; 3: Delivery – Value Unlocking; and 4: Outcomes – Wealth Created have been stress-tested. At this point we know our organisation's People Creditworthiness, and possible interventions, regarding *firstly*, the strategic positioning of our people in the future viability of our organisation; *secondly*, whether we have made the required people investment to capacitate our organisation for success; *thirdly*, whether our organisation is unlocking value with its people; and *fourthly*: if wealth has been created by the organisation's people for its stakeholders.

Finally, the *People Excellence Domain 5: Relationships* has to be stress-tested. This Excellence Domain centres around the reputation the organisation has amongst its key stakeholders within its operating arena in terms of the difference it is making. This Excellence Dimension provides the ultimate stress test of the goodness-of-fit of the organisation within its context, and hence its long term viability. This goodness-of-fit provides the organisation with its 'licence to operate' in its operating arena – economically, socially, morally, and spiritually – by its stakeholders.

As illustrated in the People Excellence Star on the opposite page, *Excellence Domain 5: Relationships* embraces the *Excellence Elements* of Goodwill and Legacy. Each is discussed in turn in the order listed.

PEOPLE EXCELLENCE QUESTION 19: GOODWILL

How much goodwill does the organisation have in the bank with its stakeholders?

Value unlocking and wealth creation by an organisation and its people are ultimately about meeting the diverse needs/interests of multiple stakeholders in a balanced, fair, and equitable manner.[1] It is the way in which the organisation connects the

Purpose of its Organisational Identity – its 'Why' – with its multiple stakeholders.[2] A stakeholder can be described as anyone – an individual, individuals, groups and/ or institutions – that can affect and/or is affected by the actions of the organisation and its people, intended or unintended. These actions consequently impact on the reputation, legitimacy, and continued viability of the organisation within its operating arena, embedded in the broader context. It is about setting up and maintaining mutually beneficial relationships with all of the organisation's stakeholders.[3]

Multiple stakeholders in the emerging new order

A wide range of diverse stakeholders with multiple needs/interests are the heartbeat of the emerging new order.[4] In this order not only has the range of stakeholders expanded, but their needs/interests have become manifold, and they have become more publicly activistic about them. Empowered by social media, they can mobilise globally, literally in seconds, around an issue. (See also the Force of Change: The Rise of diverse, activist Stakeholders in Chapter 3.)

Figure 8.1 depicts a possible set of stakeholders with multiple diverse needs/ interests. The dynamic tensions between these multiple needs/interests for a given stakeholder and across stakeholders have intensified significantly in the new order. Not 'Either-Or', but 'Both/And' resolutions of these dynamic tensions are required by the organisation's leadership.[5]

Figure 8.1: A possible set of stakeholders with multiple diverse needs/interests

According to Figure 8.1, each and every stakeholder (given in the outer circle of the figure) has a range of diverse needs/interests (given in the inner circle of the figure) which must be fused in a Both/And manner dynamically. Not only for the specific stakeholder concerned, but also simultaneously across all stakeholders. For example, for shareowners' compliance (=sound corporate governance); return on investment (=an attractive, recurring dividend pay-out); and sustainability (=assuring the organisation is a future going concern) must be balanced. However, these very same needs/interests for organisational members (i.e., employees) take on different form. In their case, compliance pertains to the meeting of an agreed-upon employment contract(s); a return on investment in the form of a favourable effort/performance to reward ratio; and sustainability expressed as job security and employability. Needs/interests are thus not only in dynamic tension for a given stakeholder, but also across stakeholders, with differing interpretations for the same need/interest.

The organisation as a complex web of relationships, nurturing social capital

By giving stakeholders a key place in People Excellence, relationships become the fulcrum of wealth creation by the organisation and its people. Organisations unlock value in order to create wealth for stakeholders. From this perspective, the organisation equates in its very essence to a complex web (or connectivity) of relationships – internally and externally – which must be formed, nourished, grown, and terminated relative to critical stakeholders. Put differently, the organisation exists by virtue of an ecosystem of value-adding and wealth-creating relationships.[6] In many quarters it is argued that social (or relationship) capital[7] – the goodwill earned and nurtured by the organisation – has become the most important asset of an organisation.[8] High goodwill with stakeholders provides the organisation with continued access to opportunities, resources, expertise, and capacity because the organisation is seen as reputable, legitimate, credible, and trustworthy.[9][10]

It has been found that there are increasingly significant disparities in the way organisations are setting themselves up for success. Successful organisations are re-inventing themselves to become more relationship-driven. Organisations that focus on 'relationship-centric' activities while emphasising growth opportunities and adapting to the changing market place are more likely to be top performers than organisations focusing on decreasing working capital; increasing supply chain efficiency; and spinning off non-core businesses in order to gain a competitive edge.[11]

The wider and more constructive the network of relationships, the more social capital exists because parties can work together in trust. People and social capital are intimately linked in a threefold way: the people of the organisation use networking to get work done; external stakeholders give the organisation a 'licence to operate'; and in turn, the social stability in society – to which the organisation contributes – allows the organisation to operate more effectively and efficiently.[12] Social capital also bolsters organisational resilience because the organisation can draw on a wider network of resources and support when dealing with a crisis.[13]

By meeting the diverse needs/interests of multiple stakeholders in a balanced, fair, equitable, and purpose-linked manner, the organisation puts goodwill in the bank through the good reputation the organisation has built/is building. Its deep and dense relationships with its stakeholders allow the organisation and its leadership to pursue a longer term, and/or more risky, Vision and/or Strategic Intent. Organisational leadership is trusted and empowered to take bigger, calculated risks. They are given the leeway to take on greater opportunities as they journey into the future in pursuit of even more daring dreams and legacies.[12]

At stake here in terms of People Excellence is:

- whether the organisation recognises the full range of all of its stakeholders and deals with the complete range of their needs/interests in a balanced, fair, and equitable fashion; and

- the amount of goodwill – i.e., social capital – the organisation has in the bank with each stakeholder because of the degree of mutual benefit grown through relationships.

The **affirmative answer** to the People Excellence Question 19: Goodwill, is: *the organisation has a high amount of goodwill in the bank with all of its stakeholders because it meets their diverse needs/interests in a balanced, fair, and equitable manner, deeply connecting them with the organisation's Purpose (='Why'), which positively enhances its legitimacy, reputation, trustworthiness, and ultimately, its viability.*

You can now do a Reflective Assessment: Goodwill (Work Sheet 25 in the Work Book), if you wish to do so.

PEOPLE EXCELLENCE QUESTION 20: LEGACY

Is the organisation building a lasting, worthy legacy?

Every organisation leaves behind an intended/unintended, tangible/intangible, and positive/negative legacy of some kind for current and upcoming generations. A legacy is the ultimate way the organisation realises the 'Why" (=Purpose) of its Identity. It hence forms the ultimate rationale for its existence, its 'Wherefore'[15] This People Excellence Question deals with the worthiness and durability of the organisation's legacy: is the organisation creating a better/good tomorrow for all by leaving a lasting, worthy legacy?

Sustainability as a core value orientation in the emerging new order

In Chapter 3, the ever-widening adoption of the core value orientation of sustainability through *stewardship* was elucidated. I.e., using the assets entrusted to the organisation by society in such a way as to leave the world a better place for future generations. Put in a different way: Is the organisation a good social citizen?[16] The make-up of a lasting, worthy legacy of the organisation from a People Excellence vantage point in terms of sustainability was also elucidated as the five-fold legacy of Productivity, Prosperity, People, Peace, and Planet (see Force of Change: Drive for Sustainability in Chapter 3 for the description of each P).

Responsible Leadership

The quest to leave a lasting, worthy legacy necessitates Responsible Leadership. It refers to leadership that seeks to realise virtuously – i.e., in an ethical manner as directed by an inner moral compass – the common good in a balanced, fair, and equitable way for all the organisation's stakeholders and society at large. It is about leaving the world a better place for upcoming generations by doing good and avoiding harm.[17] This leadership reaches beyond the confines of their own organisational boundaries into the context in which their organisation is embedded.[18] Responsible Leadership gives practical substance to the organisation's role as a genuine social citizen, expressed in terms of its corporate social responsibility (=CSR).[19]

Responsible Leadership aligns the organisation's Identity with its context. It complements the people-centric, servant leadership which forms the departure point for People Excellence in the organisation (see Excellence Question 1: Leadership). Whereas Responsible Leadership connects the organisation with its context, Servant Leadership focuses internally on making the organisation's people flourish and thrive. Responsible Leadership permeates – from the 'outside-in' – the organisation's inner context with its external duty as an active social citizen. A foundational loop has now been closed for People Excellence. It starts and ends with leadership which in the final instance must provide a 'Why' to the existence of the organisation – its Purpose – and Legacy – its 'Whereto' – which now becomes societally shared, endorsed, and legitimatised.[20]

To the degree that good social citizenship forms part of the organisation's Identity – as manifested in the exercise of genuine corporate social responsibility – people with the same moral identity are more affectively committed to the organisation, see their work as more meaningful, and are more highly engaged.[21] All of these are People Excellence Elements discussed before.

People Excellence necessitates that the organisation monitors and tracks its unfolding legacy through real time, integrated sustainability reporting, which it discloses publicly. It takes corrective action accordingly in order to be, remain, and be seen as a good social citizen. The organisation publicly shows that it is doing good *and* avoiding harm.

The **affirmative answer** to the People Excellence Question 20: Legacy, is: *the organisation is leaving behind a lasting, worthy legacy. It is creating a better/good tomorrow for all to the benefit of all through the exercise of Responsible Leadership by doing good and avoiding harm.*

You can now do a Reflective Assessment: Legacy (Work Sheet 26 in the Work Book), if you wish to do so.

SYNERGISTIC FUSION WITHIN PEOPLE EXCELLENCE DOMAIN 5: RELATIONSHIPS

Synergistically, *Reputation* with regard to Excellence Domain 5 encompasses the organisation having a high amount of goodwill in the bank with all of its stakeholders; positively enhancing its legitimacy, reputation, and trustworthiness amongst its stakeholders; enabling the actualisation of the organisation's Identity, specifically its Purpose as Why; and leaving behind a lasting, worthy legacy, its Whereto.

Figure 8.2 depicts, highlighted in the coloured circle, the above Excellence synergy graphically in the form of the fifth, and final, building block in a now complete People Excellence Value Chain. Again, it is important to note the reciprocal independencies of recursive, iterative matching between the Excellence elements making up this Excellence Domain – Goodwill and Legacy – and also between the Excellence Domains: Outcomes and Relationships. Furthermore, the feedback relationship of this Excellence Domain to the preceding Excellence Domains.

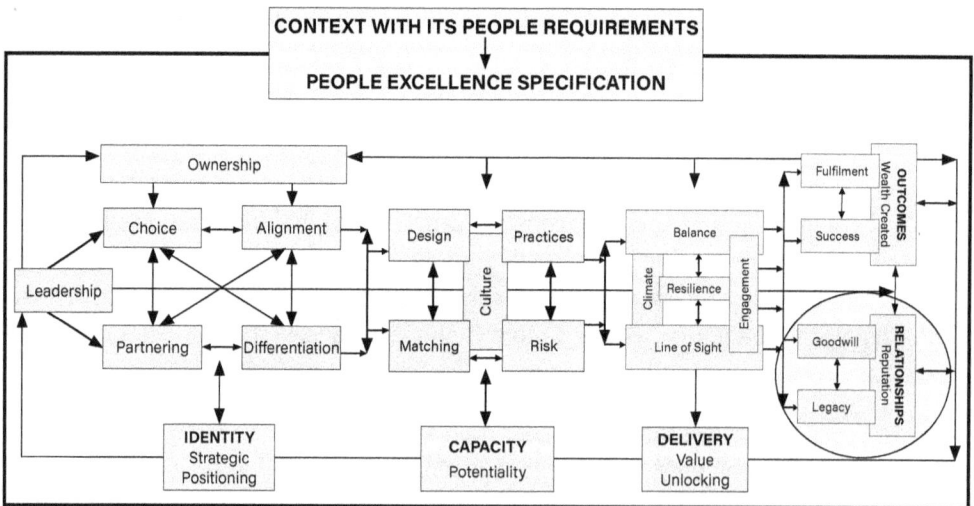

Figure 8.2: Synergistic fusion of Legitimacy within the Excellence Dimension 5: Relationships

The state of this Excellence Domain as an ultimate stress test of the goodness-of-fit of the organisation with its context will over time strengthen or erode People Excellence in the preceding Domains by accelerating either the upward spiralling, virtuous or a downward spiralling, vicious cycles of People Excellence within those Domains. The essence of the synergistic fusion in the dimension lies in *Legitimacy*. This is expressed in the organisation being awarded 'a licence to exist and operate' by the communities and society in which it is embedded, and publicly is showing how it is doing good and avoiding harm.

The desired synergy to be generated by the People Excellence Domain 5: Relationships, as explicated above in terms of leading thinking and practices with regard to its two Excellence Elements: Goodwill and Legacy – as referenced against the People Excellence Specification of the emerging new order – is given in the shaded box below.

PEOPLE EXCELLENCE SPECIFICATION

Highly enabled, empowered and resilient people, who strongly identify with and feel valued by the organisation, and are productively and innovatively engaging collaboratively through personally purposeful and meaningful ways, to viably and sustainably create inimitable, delightful experiences for stakeholders.

PEOPLE EXCELLENCE DOMAIN 5: RELATIONSHIPS

Reputation

We see relationship capital as an inherent element of our organisation's competitive edge. We live by the mantra that unlocking value and creating wealth are ultimately about meeting the diverse needs/interests of our multiple stakeholders in a balanced, fair, and equitable manner. We are truly living our organisation's Purpose (='Why') with respect to them.

Because we put relationships first, our organisation has a high amount of goodwill in the bank with all of our stakeholders. This goodwill positively enhances the legitimacy, reputation, trustworthiness, and ultimately the viability, of our organisation. This provides us with the required legitimacy through which we can actualise the Identity we are pursuing as an organisation.

By stewarding the assets entrusted by society to us, and exercising Responsible Leadership, we are passionate about bringing about a lasting, worthy legacy of sustainability, and leaving behind a better world for current and upcoming generations. This aspiration is core to the 'Whereto' of our organisation's Identity – the ultimate reason for our organisation's existence. We have translated and operationalised sustainability into a five-fold legacy, expressed in the five interdependent Ps: Productivity, Prosperity, People, Peace, and Planet.

We monitor and track our unfolding legacy through real time, integrated sustainability reporting, which we disclose publicly. We publicly show how we are doing good and avoiding harm, and take corrective action in order to be, and remain, a responsible, good social citizen through the unfolding lasting, worthy legacy we are leaving behind. In this way, we are also growing the committed ownership of our people to our organisation.

You can now do a Summative Reflective Assessment: Synergistic fusion – Legitimacy of the Excellence Dimension 5: Relationships (Work Sheet 27 in the Work Book), if you wish to do so.

PEOPLE EXCELLENCE STAR

OVERALL SYNERGISTIC FUSION

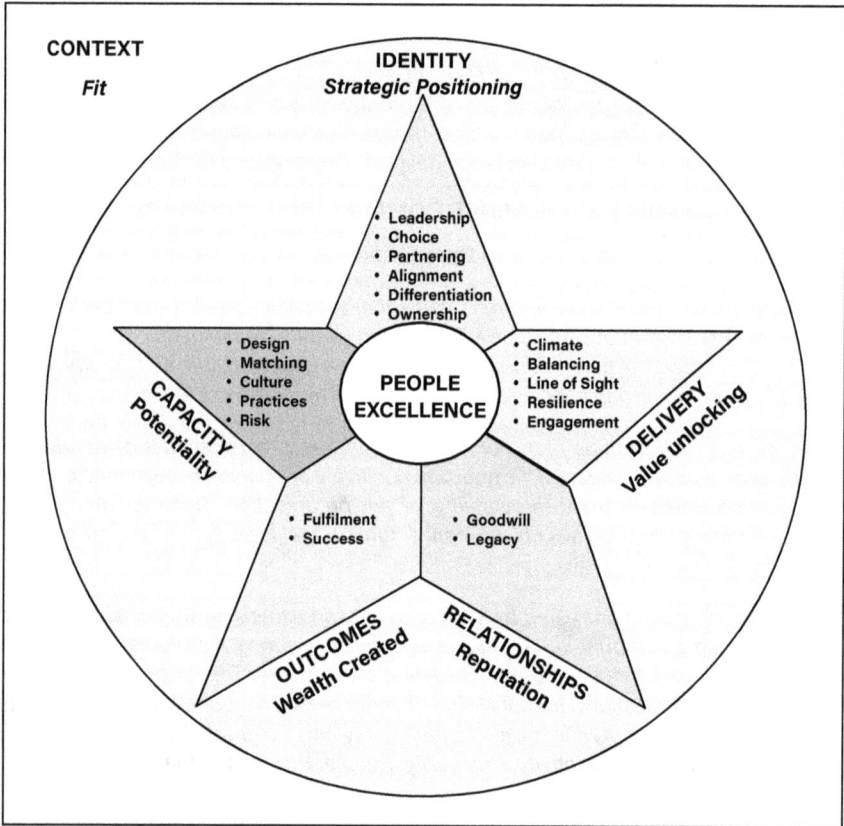

CHAPTER 9

PEOPLE EXCELLENCE AS THE SYNERGISTIC FUSION ENERGISING THE ORGANISATION

"Perfection has to do with the end product, but excellence has to do with the process." (Jerry Moran)

"It is not in the stars to hold our destiny but in ourselves." (Unknown)

"Excellence is not a skill. It is an attitude." (Ralph Marston)

Analogous to the continuous nuclear fusion of hydrogen and helium in the core of a star, creating ongoing light and energy, People Excellence is the continuous outcome of the powerful, virtuous fusion between *all* of the Excellence Domains and their constituent Elements. They act in synergistic concert through an upward virtuous cycle of increasing People Excellence. (Or, inversely, a downward vicious cycle of decreasing People Excellence.) This allows the organisation to achieve exceedingly well with its people. Indeed, being a shining 'Star' with respect to its people.

The overall synergy finds its concrete expression in the complete infusion of the total organisation with a coherent People Excellence story regarding the answers given to the 20 Excellence Questions, contained in the five Excellence Domains making up the People Excellence Star. In this way, People Excellence becomes encrypted into the very genetic code of the organisation's being and becoming.

WHY TELL AN ORGANISATION'S PEOPLE EXCELLENCE STORY?

Based on the overall People Excellence Star, a story can be told about the People Creditworthiness of an organisation, drawing on the explication in the previous chapters of the five Excellence Domains and their associated 20 Excellence Questions. The purpose of the People Excellence story is to weave an integrated, systemic and dynamic picture of People Excellence in the organisation to unleash overall synergistic fusion.

Three People Excellence stories can and need to be told by, and in, an organisation:

- An aspirational, 'To Be' story regarding what People Excellence should look like in the organisation.
- What People Excellence currently looks like in the organisation – the 'As Is' story.
- What must and will be done – the required interventions – to close the gap between the 'To Be' and 'As Is' People Excellence states. I.e., the change navigation journey story. The quantum of the gap indicates the degree of People Creditworthiness of the organisation.

The *purpose* of this chapter is to enable one to tell the above three stories:

- A coherent, aspirational People Excellence story – a 'To Be' story – as elucidated in the previous chapters, based on the best thought leadership, research evidence, and leading practices. This story will be told from a first person, organisational perspective in order to give it a personal flavour.

- This story will allow you as a reader to integrate your organisation's 'As Is' People Excellence story into an overall, single story by consolidating the piecemeal assessments you did of your organisation's People Creditworthiness whilst working through the book.

- Concurrently, in telling the integrated 'As Is' People Excellence story of your organisation, developing an integrated view of the People Excellence interventions required to enhance your organisation's People Creditworthiness. These interventions could also have been identified piecemeal by you whilst working through the book.

Before elucidating the overall People Excellence story, the ingredients to the overall synergistic fusion of the People Excellence Star will first be explicated.

INGREDIENTS TRIGGERING THE OVERALL SYNERGISTIC FUSION WITHIN THE PEOPLE EXCELLENCE STAR

Figure 9.1 illustrates the ingredients making up and triggering the overall synergistic fusion in the People Excellence Star. They were progressively unpacked in the form of a People Excellence Value Chain through Chapters 3 to 8.

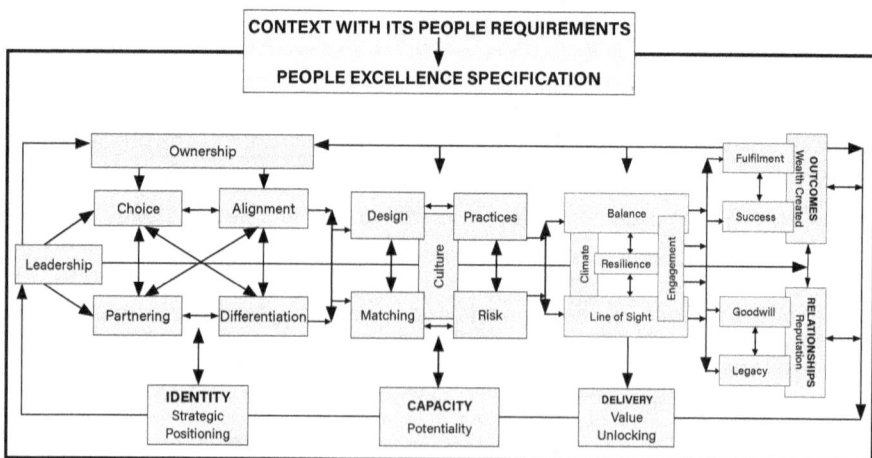

Figure 9.1: Ingredients triggering the overall synergistic fusion within the People Excellence Star: The People Excellence Value Chain

With reference to Figure 9.1, Table 9.1 provides a dynamic overview of the ingredients of the overall synergistic fusion of the Star by People Excellence Domains with their respective Excellence Elements.

Table 9.1: A dynamic overview of the ingredients of the overall synergistic fusion within the People Excellence Star by Domains and Elements

PEOPLE EXCELLENCE DOMAIN	SYNERGISTIC FUSION BY DOMAINS WITH THEIR COMMENSURATE ELEMENTS
PEOPLE CONTEXT *Fit* Fit between the People Excellence Requirements and the emerging new order faced by the organisation	***Context*** Fit Synergy embraces: • leveraging from a selected, *Strategic Contextual Posture and Engagement Attitude*, formulating an overarching *People Excellence Specification*, befitting the operating arena of the organisation. This Specification directs and guides the organisation in terms of the content it must award to its People Excellence Domains with their respective Elements relative to the organisation's Identity.
1: IDENTIFICATION ***Strategic Positioning*** Leadership, Choice, Partnering, Alignment, Differentiation, Ownership	*Identity: Strategic Positioning* Congruence Synergy encompasses: • putting the appropriate *leadership* in place as a departure point to direct, guide and grow People Excellence in the organisation; • making a clear, deliberate *strategic choice* with regard to the strategic, value-adding role people must play in the organisation's performance and success, and consequently in its competitive edge and continued viability; • awarding the right role to *People Professionals* in the organisation, given the adopted strategic people choice; • ensuring *strategic alignment* between the organisation's Identity and Key People Imperatives to generate strategic synergy between the Organisation's Identity and Strategic People Intent; • formulating an inimitable, distinct, and coherent *Strategic People Position* made up of a clear, explicit, and shared People Charter, Desired People Profile, and a compelling (segmented) People Value Proposition, framed by a strategically configured World of Work for the organisation; and lastly, • building and nurturing a progressively deepening *committed ownership* by all organisational members to all of the above Excellence Elements, and the Excellence Elements still to be put in place.

PEOPLE EXCELLENCE DOMAIN	SYNERGISTIC FUSION BY DOMAINS WITH THEIR COMMENSURATE ELEMENTS
2: CAPACITY *Potentiality* Design, Matching, Culture, Practices, Risk	*Capacity: Potentiality* Reinforcement synergy entails: • conceiving a fit-for-purpose *organisational design*, architected around meaningful work for everyone; • dynamically matching the *Core Organisational and People Capabilities* required by the organisation within its progressively unfolding strategic horizon; • congruently knitting the organisation together through a distinct, strong, but flexible *Organisational Culture*; • crafting a coherent, strategically aligned bundle of High Commitment/High Involvement *People Practices* – able to solicit the Expected Desired People Conduct and reinforce the Design and Culture – and effectively translating the Practices into a commensurate people management tool set for daily use in the organisation; and • formulating a people risk mitigation strategy and plan, proactively addressing the organisation's *people risks* relative to its risk appetite.
3: DELIVERY *Value unlocking* Climate, Balance, Line of Sight, Resilience, Engagement	*Delivery: Value Unlocking* Multiplication Synergy entails: • permeating the organisation with an invigorating *Organisational Climate* – a uplifting, positive vibe – nurturing a high stock of psychosocial capital and virtue-ality in the organisation; • ensuring in real time the achievement of an *optimal balance between work demands and required resources* through the appropriate autonomy being awarded and taken up across the organisation; • concurrently establishing a *clear line of sight* between Effort – Performance – Valued Recognition/Rewards in the organisation; • growing change-fit people with the right change navigation mindset and attitude, demonstrating confident *resilience; and* • culminating in highly *engaged people*, performing outstandingly above the normal call of duty in 'Within Self' and 'Beyond Self' collaborative ways.

PEOPLE EXCELLENCE DOMAIN	SYNERGISTIC FUSION BY DOMAINS WITH THEIR COMMENSURATE ELEMENTS
4: OUTCOMES *Achievement* Fulfilment, Success	*Outcomes: Wealth Created* Wisdom Synergy encompasses: • the organisation's *people believing and experiencing that the organisation is truly delivering on its People Brand Promise* as expressed in its People Value Proposition, and hence feeling genuinely fulfilled because they are flourishing and thriving; and • knowing at all times *people's contribution to the organisation's performance, success, and viability* through monitoring, tracking, predicting, and acting by using real time, in time, predictive and interrogative people intelligence.
5: RELATIONSHIPS *Wealth Creation* Goodwill, Legacy	*Relationships: Reputation* Legitimacy Synergy encompasses: • the organisation having a high amount of *goodwill* in the bank with all its stakeholders, which positively enhances its legitimacy, reputation, and trustworthiness, enabling the actualisation of the organisation's Identity, specifically its Purpose as its 'Why'; and • simultaneously, the organisation leaving behind a lasting, worthy *Legacy* as its 'Wherefore' – a better/good tomorrow for all to the benefit of all through the exercise of Responsible Leadership by doing good and avoiding harm.

Within the basic foundation of ingredients making up the overall People Excellence synergistic fusion as reflected in Table 9.1, the full 'To Be' People Story can be told next. The story will move from the People Excellence Context through the respective People Excellence Domains: Identity, Capacity, Delivery, Outcomes, and Relationships.

THE 'TO BE' PEOPLE EXCELLENCE STORY

The People Excellence Context

Befitting People Requirements and Specification

We accept that every organisation is embedded in a chosen context – our organisation's operating arena. Within the operating arena, we have chosen as a vantage point the Strategic Contextual Posture and Engagement Attitude of a Proactive Instigator of change.

The emerging new order faced by our organisation – rapidly accelerating, constant oscillation between Divergence and Convergence, and Order and Chaos – is infused by five interdependent Forces of Change, namely:

- the growth of the VICCAS World;

- exponentially accelerating DIVAS technological innovation;

- shifts in the profile of the future worker in different employment relationships with organisations, against the backdrop of the increasing dominance of Intangible Assets resident in especially people's creativity, innovation, expertise, knowledge, skills, and experience;

- the morally-referenced, sometimes regulatory-enforced, drive towards sustainability, demanding a socially responsible organisation, accountable in transparent ways to society; and

- the rise of diverse, activist stakeholders, whose voices are amplified in unfettered ways by the social media.

These Forces are infused by the 'Maths' of the emerging new world order: 'Intelligently respond twice as fast, deliver twice as much, at twice the speed, at half the cost, within half the accepted product/service life span, and doing all of the aforesaid on a continuous, sustainable basis – everywhere, anytime, anyone, anyhow, anything.' In turn, this 'Maths' is fuelled by the Competitive Equation of this order: the continuous delivery of innovative, customised, high quality products/services, simultaneously bringing costs down and getting products/services more quickly to markets, from conception to commercialisation. This Maths and Competitive Equation invokes the consequential, merciless imperative of relentless, ongoing, disruptive innovation, requiring continuous deep relearning, learning, and unlearning for our organisation.

The emerging new order sets the People Requirements that are necessary for a good context-organisation-person fit to be attained. Regarding the emerging new order we face, we have formulated the following overarching People Excellence Specification, which directs and guides us in terms of the content we aspire to award to our People Excellence Domains with their respective Elements:

> Highly enabled, empowered and resilient people, who strongly identify with and feel valued by the organisation, and are productively and innovatively engaging collaboratively through personally purposeful and meaningful ways, to viably and sustainably create inimitable, delightful experiences for stakeholders.

Our People Excellence Specification – befitting our context – provides a fixed reference point of what People Excellence as desired end-state in the final instance must look like when our organisation is achieving exceedingly well, with our people unlocking real, differentiating value and creating worthy, lasting wealth – consistently and continuously – to the amazed delight of our organisation's stakeholders.

People Excellence Dimension 1: Identity

The appropriate Strategic Positioning of people in the future, sustainable success and viability of our organisation: Leadership, Choice, Partnering, Alignment, Differentiation, Ownership

Our organisation has adopted an appropriate mix of shared How (=Transactional), Whereto (=Transformational) and Why (=Transcendental) leadership, with a predominant weighting of a Transformational/Transcendental Leadership Stance. Whilst visibly demonstrating the leadership qualities of legitimacy, inspiration, humility, integrity, ethical, and authenticity, our shared leadership enables and empowers participatively our organisation's people through a productive, healthy Leadership Process to actualise a desired, inspiring future for the organisation for all. Our Leadership Stance, as translated into a Leadership Philosophy, directs and guides the overall People Excellence journey of our organisation.

The Strategic People Choice of our people being the only true value unlockers and wealth creators in our organisation is seen as critical to the success and viability of our organisation. Our Choice is reinforced by a commensurate High Commitment/ High Involvement Psychosocial Contract of Partnering/Identification with our people. As true partners, our people take co-responsibility for our organisation's success, and strongly identify with who and what we are as an organisation, what we stand for, and what we aspire to. In an uncompromising and consistent manner, we talk and walk our People Choice and Psychosocial Contract in all our thinking, decisions and actions affecting our people.

Given the Strategic People Choice of our people as value unlockers and wealth creators, the People Professionals in our organisation are seen as true strategic partners whose value-adding and innovative contributions are eagerly sought out and truly cherished in attaining viable organisational success. Our People Professionals co-enable and co-ensure a high likelihood that our people will thrive as boundary-busting value unlockers and wealth creators through productive, satisfying, individualised experiences. In their role as Credible Activists, our People Professionals actively partner as People Experts with the leadership of our organisation to take co-responsibility to bring about and maintain the enabling and empowering conditions under which our organisation's people can, want to, and do contribute to achieve our organisation's Purpose and the realisation of our envisioned Legacy.

Our People Professionals ensure that our organisation's People Strategic Aspiration is operationalised in our organisation, which is capacitated to act excellently, people-wise. We know we have a secure, competitive advantage, making us through our people a viable organisation because of the strategic contribution made by our People Professionals.

We achieve *strategic alignment* by optimising the multiplicative relationships between the constituent pairs of our Organisational Identity and People Imperatives, creating ongoing strategic synergy. This alignment finds its expression in our Organisational Effectiveness Equation:

Organisational Effectiveness = f(People Capabilities/Organisational Purpose x People Energy/Organisational Vision x People Legitimacy/Organisational Core Values x People Autonomy/Strategic intent x People Fulfilment/Legacy)

At all times, all our people actions are directed and guided by our *inimitable, distinct and coherent Strategic People Position,* embedded in our organisation's *strategic configuration* of a humane *World of Work*:

- *People Charter*: Our organisation's basic beliefs regarding our people – the operationalisation of our Partnering/Identification Psychosocial Contract – which directs and guides the day-to-day, people-organisation relationship within our organisation.
- Our *Desired People Profile*: a comprehensive, integrated picture of the ideal person we want to strategically attract, engage, and retain, who will capacitate us to navigate towards our shared, chosen, desired future.
- Our all-pervasive, compelling *People Value Proposition,* equating to our People Brand Promise. I.e., the compelling reasons why the desired people our organisation wishes to employ will join, engage, and stay with our organisation. Our PVP contains the promise of providing conditions under which people can flourish, thrive, and be fulfilled.

Our Strategic People Position is re-affirmed on an ongoing basis by our people's beliefs about, and daily experiences of, our organisation. Our Position is also translated into subsequent Excellence Elements.

Everyone in our organisation, regardless of level or status, has taken committed *ownership* of our organisation's *Identity,* as well as our *Strategic People Choice* and *Position.* This committed ownership is both personalised, internalised and externalised, localised into everyone's role and work space. This committed ownership by our people is all-embracing: physically, cognitively, emotionally, spiritually, and morally. Everyone understands, engages with, and is committed to who and what our organisation is; what it stands for; where it is going; what it wants to achieve; and what lasting difference it wants to make, organisationally and people-wise.

In the final instance, our organisation's Identity finds its concrete manifestation in our espoused and experienced Organisational Image and Reputation within our organisation's operating arena.

People Excellence Domain 2: Capacity

The necessary people investment has been made to set up the potentiality in our organisation to perform excellently with our people: Design, Matching, Culture, Practices, Risk

Our organisation has a fit-for-purpose design that ensures that the right things get done in the right places at the right times by the right people, teams, and units, governed by the necessary checks and balances. Everyone within his/her area of accountability/responsibility can deliver effectively (=Doing the right things) and efficiently (=Doing things right). Our design is architected around meaningful work: people experience their work – and its resultant outcome – as being of real, lasting significance and worth to themselves and our stakeholders.

Because we have moved from a Command-and-Control Organisational Shape to a High Network/High Engagement/High Responsibility Organisational Shape, our design enables and empowers everyone to contribute continuously to create inimitable, memorable experiences for our customers/clients and employees, who for this very reason choose us and stay with us. We are indeed competing with our organisational design through the amazing value we unlock and the abundance of wealth we create – consistently and predictably – in innovative ways.

In our organisation a dynamic match exists at any given time between our strategically required Core Organisational and People Core Capacities, which are closely synchronised within our progressively unfolding strategic horizon. We have a clear understanding of the strategic talent mix we require going into the future in accordance with the different categories of our overall talent profile, as guided by our organisation's Strategic Intent. At all times we have the right people in the right numbers at the right time in the right place, who are able, willing, allowed, and want to perform, and are driven by a personalised sense of purpose and meaning. All in all, we have a strong, strategic people pipeline with respect to our different Talent Pools.

Our organisation is glued together by a distinct, strong, but flexible Achievement/Caring Organisational Culture – our shared ways of seeing, interpreting, and acting upon the world, i.e., the personality of our organisation – aligned to our Organisational Identity. Our Culture has been translated seamlessly into our organisation's hard- and software. I.e., our design, mode of working, and interpersonal interactions.

Our Culture enables and empowers our people to perform outstandingly in mutually supportive and caring ways. Though strong, our Culture is flexible enough to adapt easily in response to organisational Identity changes, disruptive innovations, and/or contextual challenges, demands and requirement shifts.

Specific to our organisation – and reinforcing our distinct, differentiating People Value Proposition – we have crafted a coherent, strategically aligned bundle of High Commitment/High Involvement People Practices, which is able to direct, shape, and support Agile, Creative, People Conduct. This bundle has been converted into a powerful people management tool set, enabling, energising, and empowering people to be the very best they can and want to be, and hence thrive.

We are prepared – proactively and reactively – for the people risks our organisation may have to deal with at any time. In this way we have enhanced our organisation's capacity to deal excellently with unexpected, adverse people events. Through learning from such events, we become better prepared to address future people risks even more effectively.

People Excellence Dimension 3: Delivery

Real time, amazing value-unlocking by people, with resultant outstanding organisational performance and success, contributing to a viable organisation: Climate, Balancing, Line of Sight, Resilience, Engagement

Our organisation is infused at all times by an invigorating *Organisational Climate* – a shared, positive and healthy vibe about events, actions, decisions, and experiences in our organisation. Our climate nurtures a high stock of psychosocial capital – a high sense of self-efficacy, optimism, hope, perseverance and resilience. It also engenders a strong virtue-ality amongst leadership – a high presence of humaneness, courage, open-mindedness, creativity, curiosity, and prudence. Our high 'stock' of psychosocial capital and virtue-ality is recursively engendering an even more Invigorating Climate.

Within the delivery space of our fit-for-purpose design – across all organisational levels and areas – our people ensure through exercising real, moment-by-moment autonomy and work crafting, that a *dynamic optimal balance* exists in real time *between their work demands and the resources they require to meet these demands*. In this way we are not only creating multiple self-management opportunities for our people in which they feel that they are always personally in control of their work settings, but are also engendering high levels of commitment, engagement, performance and well-being.

In our organisation a clear link exists between *Effort – Performance – Valued Recognition/Rewards*. Our people believe and experience – individually and collectively – that a high likelihood exists that a certain Effort by them will result in a certain Performance. Consequently, that there is a high chance that they will receive the fair, equitable Recognition/Rewards that they value.

We accept that people are unique in what they need and want – from the need for Meaning/Purpose through to Security. For this reason, we have different permutations of Recognition/Rewards to fit the different needs and wants of our people. Our people thrive because their specific permutation of basic needs across all of their Being/ Becoming Dimensions – embedded in their Personal Identity – are fulfilled through the valued Recognition/Rewards they receive for their Effort and Performance.

The types and permutations of Recognition/Rewards in our organisation are not only aligned to the needs and wants of organisational members, but also resonate with and reinforce the distinct, differentiating, and congruent Strategic People Position of our organisation.

Our organisation has change-fit people. We thus have a high presence of resilient people with the right change navigation mindset and attitude, who face with robust, quiet confidence the intended change journey of our organisation as the surest way of securing a viable future for our organisation and themselves. We regard resilience as a Core Organisational and People Capability. For us, resilience refers to the ability of our organisation and people to respond proactively and reactively to expected and unexpected events and changes – whether constructive or destructive – in our operating arena to establish a better fit. In this way, we strengthen and retain our organisation's continued viability. Our organisation is infused by the minimum prevalence of Bad Stress, Burnout and Derailment because our people are change-fit.

Increasingly our organisation is realising its people potential as manifested in the positive, more-than-expected, upward spiralling of value unlocking and wealth creation by our highly engaged people. This is demonstrated in their vigour, dedication, absorption, and collaboration. Our organisation is able to completely harness and utilise the full capability contained in our people through the deployment of their available capabilities (hard and soft), expertise, experience, energy, enthusiasm, creativity, and diversity, and the effective use of the resources at their disposal.

Through their enhanced engagement, our people become even more masterful at greater value unlocking and wealth creation, leveraged by continuous, disruptive innovation and re-invention. We are therefore obtaining – consistently and predictably – a high *return on the people investment* of our organisation through the upward spiralling, actual, innovative value that people unlock, and the real wealth they create for our stakeholders through the never-ending re-invention of our Client Value Proposition(s).

People Excellence Dimension 4: Outcomes

Within its chosen operating arena, ongoing wealth creation for the organisation's key stakeholders is par for the course: Fulfilment, Success

People in our organisation believe and experience that our organisation is truly delivering on the promise contained in our People Value Proposition, as translated into our People Brand Promise. They are flourishing, and therefore, thriving, resulting in them feeling fulfilled as whole persons in terms of their Needs (=satisfied), Being/ Becoming Dimensions (=maturity and well-being), and Personal Identity (=unique, integrated, robust, continuous). Delivery on our Promise also resonates directly with us living our Strategic People Choice of people being central to the success of our organisation as value unlockers and wealth creators, with our commensurate Psychosocial Contract of Partnering/Identification. Our Experienced People Brand – the Real People Brand – equates fully to our Projected (=Talking) and Lived (=Walking) People Brands, which are all congruent.

At any given point in time, we know in real time what our people's contribution is to the performance and success of our organisation, and can even proactively predict their contribution going into the future. This interrogative intelligence is expressed in a systemic, multi-dimensional People Balanced Scorecard. The 'two-sided' predictive and interrogative Scorecard is used on an ongoing basis by our Board, leadership, people, and other stakeholders to monitor, track, and affect in real time our people contribution and outcomes, and to make wise decisions based on intelligent insight.

People Excellence Domain 5: Relationships

An enviable Reputation, setting the golden standard: Goodwill, Legacy

We live by the mantra that value unlocking and wealth creation by our organisation and people is, in the final instance, about meeting the diverse needs/interests of our multiple stakeholders in a balanced, fair, and equitable manner. In this way, we are connecting the Purpose – our Why – of our organisation with our stakeholders. We have set up and maintain mutually beneficial relationships with all of our stakeholders. We see *social (or relationship) capital* – the goodwill earned by our organisation – as the pre-eminent asset in ensuring our organisation's continued viability.

Because we put relationships first, our organisation has a high amount of *goodwill* in the bank with all our stakeholders. This goodwill positively enhances our organisation's legitimacy, reputation, and trustworthiness. This provides us with the required enabling space in which we can actualise our vision – a component of our Identity. Our high amount of goodwill also allows us to pursue longer term, more daring and/or riskier visions. We are trusted and empowered by stakeholders to take greater calculated risks as we journey into the future in pursuit of even bigger dreams and legacies.

Being the steward of the assets entrusted by society to us, and by exercising Responsible Leadership, we are passionate about bringing about a *lasting, worthy legacy* of sustainability: leaving behind a better world for current and future generations. This aspiration is core to the 'Whereto' of our organisation's legacy – the ultimate reason for our organisation's existence.

We have translated and operationalised sustainability into a five-fold legacy, expressed in five interdependent Ps: Productivity, Prosperity, People, Peace, and Planet. We monitor and track our unfolding legacy real time, in time, through integrated sustainability reporting, which we disclose openly and truthfully. We demonstrate publicly how we are doing good and preventing harm.

We take corrective action in order to be, and remain, a good, responsible social citizen through the unfolding, lasting and worthy legacy we are establishing. In this way we also grow the committed ownership by our people to our organisation. They can identify with what we stand for, aspire to, and want to leave behind.

THE 'AS IS' PEOPLE EXCELLENCE STORY IN YOUR OWN ORGANISATION: THE TO-BE-CLOSED GAP BETWEEN THE 'TO BE' AND 'AS IS' STATES

An organisation's 'As Is' People Excellence story has to be compared to the above 'To Be' People Excellence story to determine the People Creditworthiness of the organisation. The reader has had the choice in working through the book to assess the 'As Is' People Excellence story of his/her organisation for the respective Excellence Domains and Elements.

The summative assessments for each Domain done along the way can now be transferred to Work Sheet 28 in the Work Book to arrive at the integrated 'As Is' People Excellence story of the reader's own organisation compared to the desired 'To be' People Excellence (elucidated in the previous section), reflecting its People Creditworthiness. Concurrently, the gap between the 'As Is' and 'To Be' People Excellence States can also be determined. Accordingly People Excellence interventions can be identified.

JOURNEY TO PEOPLE EXCELLENCE

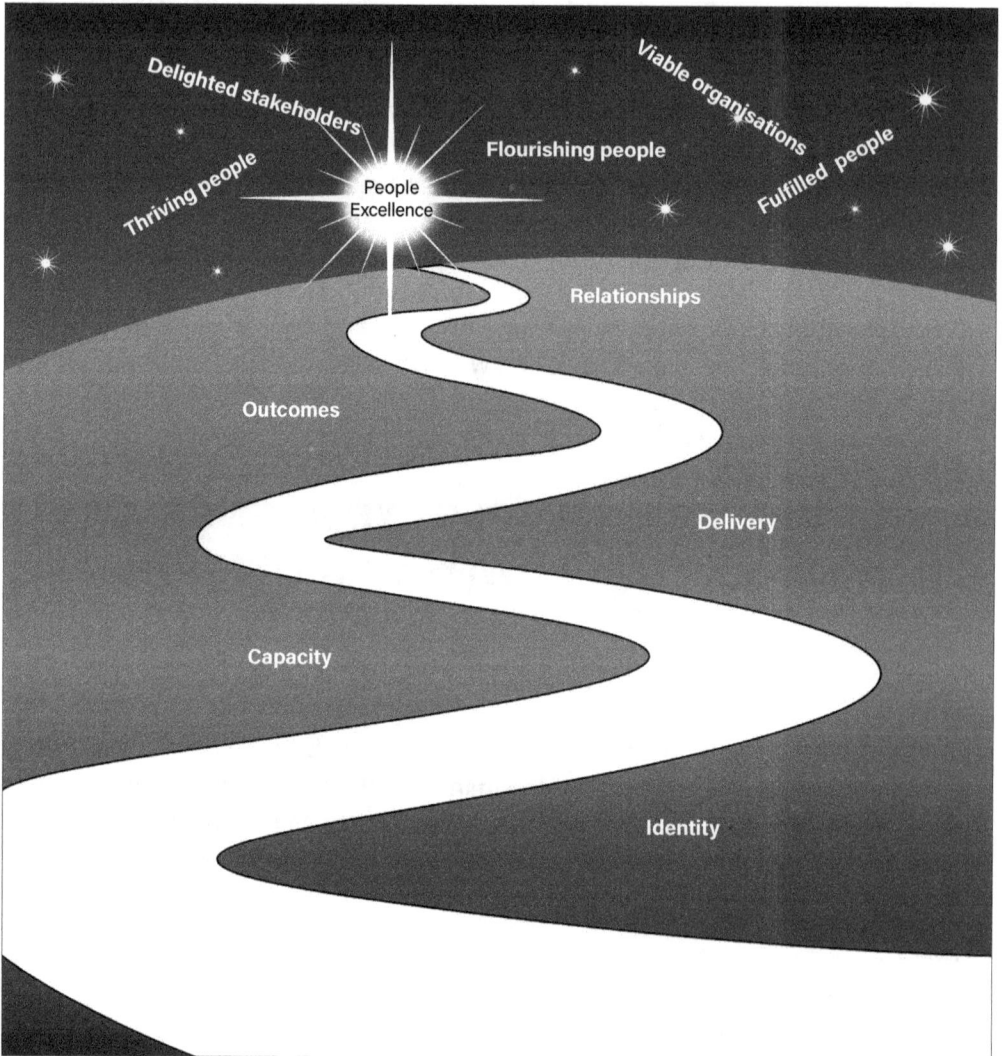

CHAPTER 10

THE JOURNEY TOWARDS PEOPLE EXCELLENCE – UNLEASHING OVERALL ONGOING SYNERGISTIC FUSION WITHIN THE ORGANISATION

"I would not give a fig for the simplicity this side of complexity, but I would give my life for the simplicity on the other side of complexity." (Justice Oliver Wendell Holmes)

"Excellence is the gradual result of always striving to do better." (Pat Riley)

"The road to excellence is always under construction." (Unknown)

Chapter 9 gave an elucidation of an integrated 'To Be' People Excellence story as progressively explicated in the preceding chapters – based on the latest thought leadership, research evidence, and leading practices – in the process applying the People Excellence Star as an integrated Strategic Stress Test of an organisation's People Creditworthiness. Next, the reader could compare her/his organisation's integrated 'As Is' People Excellence story to the 'To Be' People Excellence story to determine the People Creditworthiness of her/his own organisation. Concurrently, the gap between the 'As Is' and 'To Be' Excellence states could be determined. People Excellence interventions to close the gap could have been identified accordingly.

An organisation is now ready to embark on the journey towards People Excellence. But are we sure we are truly ready? Have we adopted the right strategic People Excellence meta-thinking framework at the requisite complexity level to infuse People Excellence into the very DNA of the organisation to unleash overall synergistic fusion? In the preceding chapters, the progressively unfolding story of People Excellence was explicated: from an Intra-Domain Perspective through to a dynamic, reciprocally interdepent Inter-Domain Perspective – the People Excellence Value Chain. The challenge we now face is to put the case for the adoption of a Systemic, Dynamic, Holistic Perspective of People Excellence, a full blown Complexity view (see Figure 2.2).

Are we still not thinking about People Excellence perhaps in a mechanistic, linear, siloed, the-sum-total-of-separate-parts way? Yes, we have accepted interdependencies and feedback loops (refer Figure 9.1), but is our overall mapping of the People Excellence Landscape at the requisite level of synergistic complexity? That is to say, if we have a framework to begin with! I have some serious doubts which I wish to explore in this chapter, and then offer a solution for consideration. The *purpose* of this chapter is thus to propose a systemic, dynamic, holistic Strategic People Excellence Meta-thinking

Framework at the requisite complexity level, which is able to direct and guide the journey towards fully unleashing ongoing, genuine, synergistic People Excellence fusion in an organisation in a sustainable manner.

The discussion in the chapter proceeds as follows: *Firstly,* by posing the daunting challenge of unleashing ongoing, genuine, overall synergic fusion within the People Excellence Star to the full benefit of the organisation; *secondly,* by offering a solution to this challenge in the form of a holistic, systemic and dynamic Strategic People Excellence Meta-thinking Framework, able to unleash ongoing, genuine, overall synergistic fusion in the organisation; *thirdly,* by making a practical recommendation on how to make this type of thinking an everyday reality in the organisation; *fourthly,* locating the People Excellence Star as Stress Test in the Strategic People Landscape; and *fifthly,* suggesting some high level guidelines for the journey towards People Excellence in the organisation.

THE DAUNTING CHALLENGE OF UNLEASHING ONGOING, GENUINE, OVERALL SYNERGIC FUSION WITHIN THE PEOPLE EXCELLENCE STAR

Stepping back for a moment to the integrated elucidation in story-form of the People Excellence Star expressed in the People Excellence Value Chain (see Figure 9.1) in the previous chapter, the following critical, reflective question can be posed: Does this integrated 'To Be' People Excellence story genuinely reflect true, overall synergistic fusion within the People Excellence Star, pivotal in unleashing the continuous, full, self-renewing, 'atomic' power of People Excellence in the organisation through the ongoing synergistic fusion of the Excellence Domains/Elements? Is the story told in Chapter 9 still not too strongly linear in its exposition?

Despite the progressive addition of one ingredient after the other – the Excellence Domains with their Elements – highlighting reciprocal and recursive relationships in the exposition, one has a lingering doubt that the story still does not elucidate the genuine, ongoing, overall synergistic fusion within the People Excellence Star in its full force.

The baseline complexity challenge

In the first instance, the People Excellence Star is made up of five Excellence Domains and 20 Excellence Elements, giving in its simplest form between 25 (for Domains) and 400 (for Elements) first-order, basic, straight line relationships. These 25 and 400 relationships exclude any possible feedback or feedforward relationships, or the different effects that Excellence Elements can have (to be discussed below).

Furthermore, it is also not a case of Either-Or relationships. One relationship between two Elements does not excludes other possible relationships with other Elements. It is rather a case of And/Both relationships. I.e., many possible relationships between all of the Elements. To use the analogy of interpersonal relationships: Excellence Elements do not have life-long, single monogamous relationships but ever-varying polyamorous relationships with each other. This also implies multiple meta-relationships on top of relationships between individual Elements, ad infinitum. Additionally, different contexts affect the types of relationships existing between Elements, and hence their effects.[1]

Jointly, all these bewildering number of relationship permutations form the dynamic, integrated whole of the People Excellence Star. Genuine People Excellence in the organisation is the total outcome of the overall, ongoing, powerful, virtuous fusion between *all possible* relationships between and amongst all of the Excellence Domains and their constituent Elements – concurrently and simultaneously. Everything affects everything because of the dense, multiple, interdependent, and reciprocally and recursively, influencing relationships.[2]

In an overwhelmingly complex way, the Domains/Elements function as an integrated, dynamic whole in a systemic, organic, and emergent way, producing overall People Excellence synergy like the continuous powerful nuclear fusion in a star. This dynamic perspective on the People Excellence Star resonates with the underlying foundational view of the organisation as a living, emergent, self-organising, social ecosystem, framed by a Complexity world view (explicated in Chapter 2).

Does the People Excellence story as told in Chapter 9, do full justice to the dynamic of this potential, powerful synergistic fusion? Figure 9.1 graphically endeavoured to represent this dynamic, synergistic 'wholeness' of the People Excellence Star through two-way arrows, as well as feedforward and feedback loops. At the risk of being repetitive: although tied together by multi-directional relationships, Figure 9.1 of the People Excellence Value Chain still conveys a strong sense of the linear progression of the sum total of parts.

Moving the complexity challenge to the next level

Further proof for the bewildering array of relationship permutations is to be found in the research evidence used to explicate the People Excellence Star. *Firstly,* in support of the above argument, the research-informed discussion of the five Excellence Domains and 20 Excellence Elements in Chapters 4 to 8 uncovered wide-ranging evidence for dense, multi-directional relationships between all of the Excellence Elements making up the People Excellence Star.

Secondly, the elucidation of the People Excellence Star furthermore also gave strong evidence that a given Excellence Element, hypothetically called Element A in the exposition below, can vary in its effect in bringing People Excellence about, dependent on its relative location in the People Excellence Star (see Figure 9.1), and the ever-varying polyamorous relationships of Excellence Elements referred to above.

Element A can be[3]:

- a *cause* (=antecedent): the state of an 'earlier' Element A directly affects the state of a subsequent Element(s) as outcome;

- an *outcome* (=consequence): the state of Element A is the direct result of the state of an immediately preceding Element(s) as cause;

- a *precondition:* Element A affects the state of another Element as a cause, which in turn affects a subsequent Element(s) as an outcome;[4]

- a *recursor:* the state of a 'later' Element A as a cause affects the state of an 'earlier', preconditioning Element(s);

- a *mediator:* the state of Element A affects the nature of the relationship between a cause and outcome(s) of two other Elements;

- an *amplifier:* the presence of Element A augments (=strengthens/weakens) the effect of the relationships between a precondition(s), a cause, and an outcome(s); and/or

- a *moderator* (or contingency): Element A sets the boundary conditions for when, where, and by how much, the effects of Element(s) on each other will be present.

Based on the above discussion, Figure 10.1 depicts the seven different effects that the very same Excellent Element, called Element A, can have.

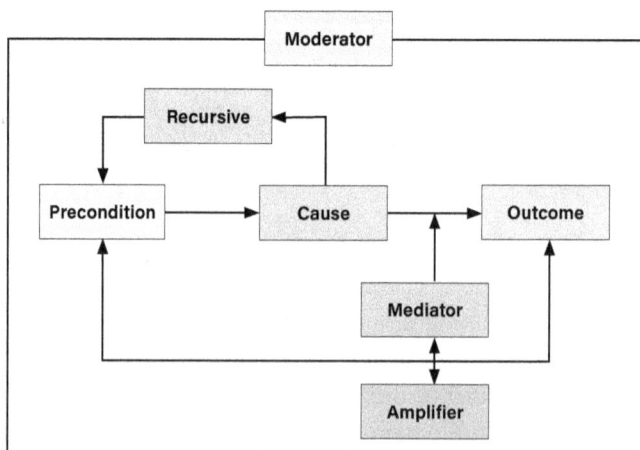

Figure 10.1: The possible different effects of the same Excellent Element[5]

Using Figure 10.1 as the basis, a research-sourced illustration will be given to demonstrate the different effects that the same Excellent Element can have in the People Excellence Star, depending on its location in the People Excellence Value Chain (refer Figure 9.1). The Excellence Element 'Engagement' will be used as an example, given the vast amount of research on this Element:[6]

- Engagement is a direct *cause* of outcomes related to the self (e.g., less stress, less absenteeism, an intention to stay, well-being, basic need satisfaction); the quality of work done (performance, creativity, innovation, productivity, job satisfaction); and the organisation (safety, customer service/satisfaction, organisational performance, financial performance, competitiveness).[7]
- Transformational/Transcendental (or Engaging) Leadership[8] and (High Commitment/High Involvement) People Practices[9] are *preconditions* for High/ Low Engagement as an outcome.
- Engagement as a cause has a *recursive* (=feedback) effect on how positively (read 'Engaging') Leadership[10] and People Practices as preconditions are perceived.[11]
- Engagement *mediates* the effect of an individual's organisational identification on his/her organisational commitment. Higher Engagement will heighten the positive impact that her/his organisational identification has on her/his organisational commitment.[12]
- Engagement *amplifies* (=strengthens or weakens) the three-way relationship between People Practices (=Precondition), Organisational Climate (=Mediator), and Personal/Organisational Outcomes (=Outcome).[13]

The above effects of Engagement are well established in the available research, but it can further be hypothesised that Engagement could also have the following effect, not reported in the current research literature to the best of my knowledge:

- Engagement *moderates* the types and states of the relationships that can exist between People Practices (=Precondition), Organisational Climate (=Mediator), Committed Ownership (=Amplifier), and Personal/Organisational Outcomes (=Outcome) by setting certain boundaries. I.e., a minimum level of Engagement must be present for the relationships between the abovementioned Excellence Elements to hold.

Based on the above discussion, the daunting challenge of People Excellence complexity can be taken to the next level. In total, an Excellence Element can have seven potential effects in terms of Figure 10.1. Assuming that all 20 Excellence Elements can have all seven effects, it implies that there are potentially 20^7 relationship permutations. This equates to 1.28 billion possible relationships between the 20 Excellence Elements. This is even without the moderating effect of different contexts and types of people!

The need for a Strategic People Excellence Meta-thinking Framework

All in all, I would submit that the above exposition unequivocally demonstrates the dense, multi-directional, ever-varying polyamorous relationships between the Excellence Dimensions and Elements. The unleashing of the full and continuous energy of the synergistic fusion within the People Excellence Star in an organisation demands crafting a Strategic People Excellence Meta-thinking Framework based on a complexity (also called a chaos) view of reality (i.e., a world view). In this view, the world forms wholes of reciprocally interacting variables – with probabilistic effects and counter-effects – configuring into patterns which form virtuous or vicious cycles, and moving between order (=patterns) and chaos (=no patterns). A pattern is the manifestation of a few underlying rules. Within this view, the organisation is a living, social ecosystem, having all of the above features (see Chapter 2).

In the next section, a suggested Strategic People Excellence Meta-thinking Framework – framed by a complexity view of reality – is elucidated, aimed at capacitating organisations to unleash ongoing, genuine, overall People Excellence synergistic fusion in their organisations.

TOWARDS UNLEASHING ONGOING, GENUINE, OVERALL PEOPLE EXCELLENCE SYNERGETIC FUSION IN THE ORGANISATION: THE PEOPLE EXCELLENCE INTERDEPENDENCY MATRIX

The People Excellence Interdependency Matrix is proposed as a systemic whole, complexity-framed, Strategic Meta-thinking Framework of People Excellence. In this Framework, People Excellence – represented by the People Excellence Star – is seen as an integrated, dynamic, systemic, complex whole, made up of multiple variables in dense, multi-directional, ever-varying polygamous relationships, configuring into constructive (=order) or destructive patterns (=chaos), acting in accordance with a few underlying rules. A pattern represents a specific synergistic fusion that is active in an organisation at a given time.

The aim of the proposed Matrix is to provide the means through which the organisation can unleash ongoing, genuine, full-blown, overall People Excellence synergistic fusion by conceiving and crafting desired configurations of People Excellence Dimensions and Elements. I.e., virtuous People Excellence patterns. This Matrix would enable the organisation to take account of the multiple, ever-varying, polyamorous effects of the

Excellence Elements as discussed above (see Figure 10.1). In this way, the organisation can map its journey at the requisite complexity level towards unleashing ongoing, genuine, overall synergistic fusion regarding its People Excellence.

In its configuration, the proposed People Excellence Interdependency Matrix is strongly influenced by Cross-Impact Analysis (CIA), a well-accepted and widely-applied methodology in futuristic/strategic thinking/planning and in the intelligence community, such as the Central Intelligence Agency.[14] The premise on which CIA rests is that events are probabilistically interdependence. The occurrence of one event will make the occurrence of other event(s) more or less likely. The intent of CIA is to provide the means to predict the probabilities of interdependent events occurring with the accompanying likely cross-impacts on each other.

Apart from mathematical probabilities, more qualitative estimates can also be used to assess the likely occurrence of events and their cross-impacts, such as 'enhancing', 'inhibiting', or 'unrelated'. The analysis is presented in the form of a Cross-impact Matrix. Based on the estimated, probable cross-impacts, different scenarios can be built about likely future events. I.e., stories about probable futures. Suitable responses to the generated probable scenarios can then be formulated proactively.

The following topics are addressed: *firstly,* an explication is given of the proposed People Excellence Interdependency Matrix; and *secondly,* the practical application of the Matrix is demonstrated.

The proposed People Excellence Interdependency Matrix

Figure 10.2 depicts the proposed People Excellence Interdependency Matrix as the operationalisation of a complexity-framed, Strategic People Excellence Meta-thinking Framework.

PEOPLE EXCELLENCE CONTEXT: PEOPLE EXCELLENCE SPECIFICATION		RELATIONSHIPS		OUTCOMES		DELIVERY					CAPACITY					IDENTITY					
		LEGACY	GOOD-WILL	SUCCESS	FULFIL-MENT	ENGAGE-MENT	RESILIENCE	LINE OF SIGHT	BALANCING	CLIMATE	RISK	PRACTICES	CULTURE	MATCH-ING	DESIGN	OWNER-SHIP	DIFFEREN-TIATION	ALIGN-MENT	PART-NERING	CHOICE	LEADER-SHIP
RELATION-SHIPS	LEGACY																				
	GOODWILL																				
OUTCOMES	SUCCESS																				
	FULFILMENT																				
DELIVERY	ENGAGEMENT																				
	RESILIENCE																				
	LINE OF SIGHT																				
	BALANCING																				
	CLIMATE																				
CAPACITY	RISK																				
	PRACTICES																				
	CULTURE																				
	MATCHING																				
	DESIGN																				
IDENTITY	OWNERSHIP																				
	DIFFEREN-TIATION																				
	ALIGNMENT																				
	PARTNERING																				
	CHOICE																				
	LEADERSHIP																				

Figure 10.2: The proposed People Excellence Interdependency Matrix

According to Figure 10.2 the proposed People Excellence Interdependency Matrix is constructed as follows: *firstly,* to accommodate the People Excellence complexity challenge posed in the previous section; and *secondly,* to provide the means of achieving overall synergistic fusion in the People Excellence Star. The Matrix is constructed as follows:

- A *20 x 20 cell Matrix*, mapping the People Excellence Territory, made up of the five Excellence Domains with their commensurate Excellence Elements (similarly colour coded). The Excellence Elements/Domains with their relative order and relationships are drawn from the People Excellence Value Chain (see Figure 9.1). This construction of the Matrix aims to reflect the dense, multiple, first-order (or baseline), interdependent and reciprocally influencing relationships making up the People Excellence Star, in which everything affects everything else. Not depicted are meta-relationships, i.e., relationships of relationships. An attempt at this will be explicated later.

- The *order in which the Domains and Elements* are placed along the Matrix represents the typical order in which an organisation will normally proceed with its People Excellence journey though the Excellence Domains/Elements – 'Outside-In-Outside'. From Identity (bottom-left and top-right), through Capacity and Delivery, to Outcomes and Relationships (top-left/right).

  (As an aside, in Chapter 7, the consideration was raised that one can work 'backwards' by using the actual People Excellence achieved in respectively Domains 4: Outcomes and 5: Relationships to provide clues to prioritise the needed People Excellence Elements with interventions in the other three preceding Excellence Domains: Identity, Capacity, and Delivery. Practically, this means that one could, firstly, specify the 'To Be' Domains 4: Outcomes and 5: Relationships desired (the top left corner of the Matrix), and then work 'backwards', i.e., horizontally right and vertically left in the Matrix, into Domains 1: Identity, Domains 2: Capacity, and 3: Delivery to specify the desired 'To Be' Excellence in those Domains.)

- The cells on the *diagonal* (or *lateral) axis* – shaded in the figure in the same shades as their associated Domains – represent the desired 'To Be' states of the respective Excellence Elements, as formulated by the organisation relative to the set People Excellence Specification (top left cell). These are the thought leadership, research-sourced, and leading practices answers given to the Excellence Questions in Chapters 4 to 8, combined into a coherent People Excellence story in Chapter 9, and graphically depicted in Figure 9.1.

  These 'To Be' states all have to be aligned, *firstly,* to the People Excellence Specification (top left cell), representing the required Context-Organisation-People Fit, and then, *secondly,* must run as a golden thread diagonally through all of the 20 People Excellence Elements on the diagonal axis of the Matrix to form an aligned, normative 'To Be' People Excellence story line: 'This is what our

185

organisation should look like as a shining star when we are achieving People Excellence.'

Next, the lateral axis cells can be split into the desired 'To Be' states (as described above) and the current 'As Is' states in the organisation with respect to the Excellence Element concerned. These states are the outcome of having stress-tested the People Creditworthiness of the organisation as manifested in its present People Excellence. In this way, the excellence gap with respect to Excellence Elements can be established through a comparison of the two states on the diagonal axis.

- The *off-diagonal cells* in the Matrix depict the spaces in which the nature and the status of the reciprocal interaction between two Excellence Elements can be mapped, also in terms of the desired 'To Be' states – derived from research evidence and leading practices – and the current 'As Is' state in the organisation. In these cells, the two interacting Elements can have any of the effects explicated in Figure 10.1, such as being a cause, precondition, or outcome. The multiplicity of the off-diagonal cells is reflective of the dense, multi-directional, ever-varying polyamorous relationships between the Excellence Dimensions and Elements. Each Element has at least 30 basic relationships.

Two examples:

- Design and Culture (Excellence Domain 2: Capacity): Is the Design of the organisation fully translated into the Culture? Inversely, does the Culture reinforce the Design?

- Leadership (Excellence Domain 1: Identity) and Engagement (Excellence Domain 3: Delivery): What is the reciprocal relationship between Leadership and Engagement? Does Leadership set up favourable preconditions for high Engagement as an outcome to occur? Recursively, how does the level of Engagement affect the experience of Leadership in the organisation?

The ever-varying polyamorous effects that an Excellence Element can have across the total Matrix (see Figure 10.1 again) will be dealt with in the practical illustration of an organisation embarking on the Excellence journey (explicated in the next section). All in all, the People Excellence Interdependency Matrix unequivocally illustrates the complexity of attaining and maintaining People Excellence in an organisation, but provides an handy means to deal with the simplicity on the other side of the complexity.

The practical application of the People Excellence Interdependency Matrix

The previous section has explicated the proposed People Excellence Interdependency Matrix as a Strategic People Excellence Meta-thinking Framework, given in Figure

10.2. The purpose of this section is to answer the question: How can the Matrix be used in practice within a specific organisation embarking on a People Excellence journey, aimed at enhancing the People Creditworthiness of the organisation?

Firstly, the practical application of the Matrix as a journey towards People Excellence in the organisation will be explicated. *Secondly*, a hypothetical example of this journey will be discussed.

Mapping the journey towards People Excellence in an organisation

The journey towards People Excellence in applying the People Excellence Interdependency Matrix as a Strategic Meta-thinking Framework consists of the following Phases:

- **Phase 1: Set the People Excellence Specification demanded by the organisation's operating arena** (Matrix: Top left/right cell)

  Aligned to the organisation's strategic horizon, a future-referenced People Excellence Specification must be set for its operating arena (cf. Chapter 3). The People Excellence Specification, befitting the People Requirements imposed by the organisation's context, spells out what People Excellence will look like when the organisation is achieving exceedingly well with its people in that context, as and when a goodness of context-organisation-people fit has been achieved. It provides the baseline ingredients of the People Vision of the organisation. The People Excellence Specification establishes the parameters within which the 'To Be' Excellence Elements of the organisation must be formulated.

- **Phase 2: Define the desired 'To Be' states for the organisation's People Excellence Dimensions/Elements** (Matrix: Cells on diagonal axis)

  Moving diagonally across the Matrix – from Excellence Dimension 1: Identity to the Excellence Dimension 5: Relationships – the laterally aligned 'To Be' state for each Excellence Element must be generated, as referenced against the set People Excellence Specification. These 'To Be' states define the desired People Creditworthiness of the organisation. The diagonal axis alignment will serve as the comparative, normative benchmark for the organisation's Excellence journey.

  Next, split each diagonal axis Excellence cell into two, and include alongside the 'To Be' state, the assessed current 'As Is' state of that Excellence Element in the organisation. This assessment reflects the stress testing of the organisation's People Creditworthiness. Based on the comparisons of the desired 'To Be' and 'As Is' states on the diagonal axis cells, Excellence gaps can be determined for the respective Excellence Elements. The gaps can be summated by Excellence Domain. Gaps (also those discussed below) can be coloured according to their strategic significance – red: critical; yellow: important; and green: unimportant.

During the unfolding Excellence journey, one also may depict in the diagonal axis cells how the 'As Is' state of an Excellence Element/Domain is progressively approaching the 'To Be' state as the gap closes through interventions.

- **Phase 3: Identify and prioritised successive Strategic People Excellence Thrusts** (Matrix: Selected diagonal axis cell)

  Relative to the organisation's Purpose, Vision and Strategic Intent within its strategic horizon, the People Excellence gaps – reflected in the cells on the diagonal axis – must be prioritised strategically to determine the order in which they have to be addressed. With which Excellence Domain/Elements and gaps does one want to start? And, in which order does one want to move across the Matrix with respect to Excellence Elements/Domains gaps in terms of the organisation's strategic time horizon? The prioritised Excellence gaps can be called 'Strategic People Excellence Thrusts'.

  Given the multi-dimensional and multi-relationship complexity of People Excellence, Strategic Intervention Waves may be constructed per prioritised Strategic People Excellence Thrust to make the journey to People Excellence manageable, and increase the likelihood of success: Time Period 1, Time Period 2, Time Period 3...., each with its own sub-thrust as a core theme. It would be a high-risk strategy to tackle all of the People Excellence gaps on the diagonal axis simultaneously.

- **Phase 4: Generate an integrated, systemic, and coherent portfolio of People Excellence Interventions to realise a chosen Strategic People Excellence Thrust** (Matrix: Related off-diagonal axis cells)

  The relevant Excellence Element(s) by Domains – with their associated interventions – must be identified, which would enable the realisation of the chosen Strategic People Excellence Thrust within a certain strategic horizon period. Put differently: which interventions must be undertaken to close the Excellence gap represented by the Trust?

  The relationships and interactions between relevant Excellence Elements and a Strategic People Excellence Thrust are represented by the off-diagonal cells in the Matrix. The goodness-of-fit of an Element/Domain with a chosen Strategic People Excellence Thrust is an important consideration here. Determining the relevance of an Excellence Element to a Thrust is in the final instance a judgement call. However, it would be more than wise to draw on thought leadership, research evidence, and leading practices such as those reported in Chapters 4 to 8 to identify relevant Elements.

  The 'To Be' and 'As Is' states are defined in the off-diagonal cells for each of the relevant Excellence Elements/Domains relative to the Strategic People Excellence Thrust. Next, interventions must be identified/designed to close the gap between the two states to affect the Strategic People Excellence Thrust. In turn, all of these Excellence Elements/Domains ('To Be' and 'As Is') – with their accompanying interventions – must be moulded into an integrated, systemic, and coherent portfolio of Strategic People Excellence Elements/Domains Interventions.

Overall, this portfolio represents the Strategic People Excellence Intervention Plan of the organisation – the what, why, when, who, how and whereto with respect to a prioritised Strategic People Excellence Thrust. The People Excellence Interdependency Matrix – incorporating and in combination with the People Excellence Value Chain (refer Figure 9.1) – can be used to construct such a needed portfolio. Jointly applied, the Matrix and the People Excellence Value Chain as incorporated into the Matrix, enable the portfolio to meet the requirements of being integrated, systemic, and coherent.

The identification of the relevant Excellence Element(s) by Domains – with their associated interventions – can proceed as follows:

- Sub-Phase 4.1: Relative to the specific Strategic People Excellence Thrust, specify the desired impact (=results), as reflected in Excellence Domains 4: Outcomes and 5: Relationships when a positive shift(s) has occurred in the Thrust.

- Sub-Phase 4.2: Identify on the 'input side' of the Strategic People Excellence Thrust – the horizontal axis of the Matrix – the relevant Excellence Elements/ Domains in terms of their reciprocal relationships with the Thrust, as well as the associated interventions, to be leveraged as Excellence Drivers to bring about the desired People Excellence impact, attributable to shifts in the Strategic People Excellence Thrust.

- Sub-Phase 4.3: Identify on the 'output side' of the Strategic People Excellence Thrust – the vertical axis of the Matrix – the affected Excellence Elements/ Domains' reciprocal relationships which are expected to be enhanced recursively as a consequence of the 'input' Excellence Drivers bringing about the desired People Excellence impact. These are the positive 'knock-on' effects of the Excellence Drivers. The affected 'output' Excellence Elements/Domains' relationships may be the same or different to the 'input' Excellence Drivers.

Relative to the Strategic People Excellence Thrust, the relevant/affected Excellence Elements/ Domains' reciprocal relationships can be classified as follows:

- *Immediate (or intra-Domain)*: Excellence Element relationships belonging to the same Excellence Domain as the Strategic People Excellence Thrust.

- *Intermediate*: Excellence Element relationships belonging to Excellence Domains bordering on the Excellence Domain in which the Strategic People Excellence Thrust is resident.

- *Removed*: Excellence Element relationships belonging to Excellence Domains beyond the bordering Excellence Domains.

Additionally, the intended types of effect of the implicated Excellence Driver Elements in bringing about the desired change with respect to the Strategic People Excellence Thrust may be indicated. With respect to a Strategic People Excellence Thrust, what likely effect will an Excellence Driver have? Is the Driver a precondition, outcome, recursor, mediator, amplifier, or moderator (see Figure 10.1). The types of effect give strong clues as to what role an Element as Excellence Driver will play in the change journey and/or the order in which Elements must be addressed. A precondition must be addressed before an amplifier, for example, to make a cause effective.

Figure 10.3 gives a graphic illustration of the above discussion. Typical effects are given for Immediate, Intermediate and Removed locations. Examples of Element/Domain-specific Excellence interventions are excluded.

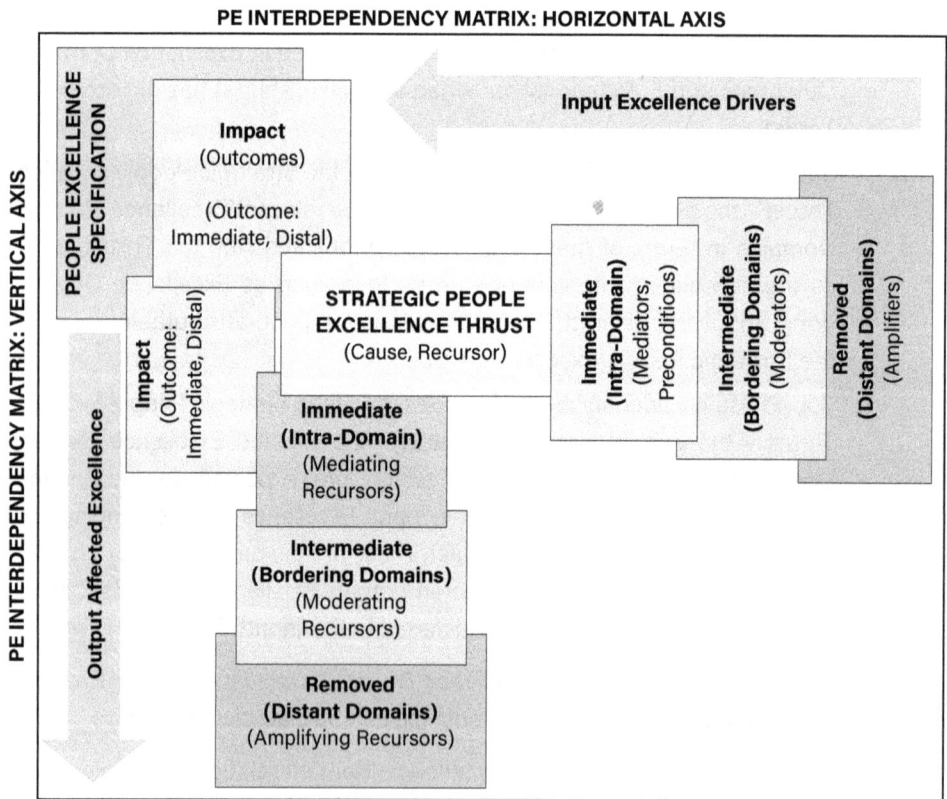

Figure 10.3: The structure of the People Excellence Elements/Domains Portfolio relative to a Strategic People Excellence Thrust

According to Figure 10.3, the structure of the People Excellence Elements/ Domains Portfolio, based on the People Excellence Interdependency Matrix, is made up of:

- the set *People Excellence Specification* (Matrix: Top, left/right cell), acting as normative reference point for the 'To Be' state of the Strategic People Excellence Thrust;
- the *Strategic People Excellence Thrust* (Matrix: diagonal axis cell), which forms the strategic Excellence focus of the intervention portfolio;
- the *Horizontal Axis of the Matrix* (Matrix: Off-diagonal cells) on the 'input' side of the Strategic People Excellence Thrust, the selected Excellence Drivers (=Excellence Elements/Domains' relationships, with associated interventions) (not shown in the figure), and their desired impact, categorised in terms of expected effects;
- the *Vertical Dimension of the Matrix* (Matrix: Off-diagonal cells), the 'output' side of the Strategic People Excellence Thrust, reflecting the affected impact and Excellence Elements/Domains' relationships (no specifics shown in the figure) which are expected to be enhanced recursively as knock-on effects by the 'input' Excellence Drivers.

In the building of its detailed People Excellence Elements/Domains Portfolio with associated interventions – i.e., populating the above portfolio structure given in Figure 10.3 – equating to the organisation's Strategic People Excellence Intervention Plan, an organisation is, so-to-speak, generating its own People Excellence theory-in-practice. The most sophisticated approach to this theory-in-practice would be if an organisation's journey to People Excellence is done from an action research and learning perspective. In this way, the organisation is, *firstly*, crafting an organisation-specific, real time People Excellence theory; and, *secondly*, generating its own research evidence to inform its People Excellence decisions. The organisation is thus intervening with intelligent insight.

- **Phase 5: Roll out the Strategic People Excellence Intervention Plan, and monitor and track its impact in realising the selected Strategic People Excellence Thrust**

   This is the usual implementation, monitoring, tracking and corrective intervention action process. The only difference is that these actions happen in real time as the roll out proceeds, and are guided by real time, intelligent insight.

Phases 3 to 5 must be repeated as many times as there are Strategic Excellence Thrusts (reflecting Strategic Excellence Gaps), each with their respective intervention Waves operationalised into Strategic People Excellence Intervention Plans. This must be repeated until all of the strategically prioritised Excellence gaps on the diagonal Excellence axis of the Matrix have been closed, and dynamic stability has been attained. Alternatively, newly initiated as different Excellence gaps open because of the need to re-imagine and re-invent the organisation's People Excellence because of shifts in the organisation's operating arena and/or its internal context.

A hypothetical example of the People Excellence journey

Applying the above explicated Phases making up People Excellence practically to a hypothetical example – using a first person, organisational vantage point – would be as follows:

- **Phase 1: Set the People Excellence Specification demanded by our organisation's operating arena** (Matrix: Top left/right cell)

  Based on a thorough People Excellence Context assessment (see Chapter 3), the derived People Excellence Specification for our organisation's operating arena could be:

  > *Highly enabled, empowered and resilient people, who strongly identify with and feel valued by the organisation, and are productively and innovatively engaging collaboratively in personally purposeful and meaningful ways, to viably and sustainably create inimitable, delightful experiences for stakeholders.*

  Our People Excellence Specification establishes the normative reference point for the 'To Be' Excellence Elements/Domains of our organisation by setting up their strategic parameters.

- **Phase 2: Define the desired 'To Be' states for our organisation's People Excellence Dimensions/Elements** (Matrix: Diagonal axis cells)

  For our organisation, define the 'To Be' Excellence states for each Excellence Element, and by implication for the Excellence Domains, in the diagonal axis cells of the Matrix. Do a strategic stress test to assess our organisation's People Creditworthiness regarding each Excellence Element/Domain to establish the current Excellence gaps.

  In the case of this hypothetical example, Engagement is chosen. Based on the discussion of this Excellence Element in Chapter 6, the 'To Be' Engagement state for our organisation is defined as:

  > *The majority of our people (> 75%) demonstrate high levels of vigour, dedication, absorption, and collaboration, unlocking more value and creating greater wealth for our stakeholders than what can be expected normally. They are creating amazing Client Value Propositions that are delighting clients, on which they deliver consistently and predictably.*

Similarly, 'To Be' states will be defined for the other 19 Excellence Elements for our organisation, and their 'As Is' states assessed to determine our Excellence gaps. In the case of Engagement, the 'As Is' state shown by the stress test could be:

Only 25% to 30% of our people are highly engaged,
with a particular gap around collaboration.

- **Phase 3: Identify the top priority Strategic People Excellence Thrust for the coming strategic period** (Matrix: Diagonal axis cell)

Given the strategic focus of our organisation on disruptive innovation to ensure our competitive edge and long term viability over our coming strategic planning horizon, Engagement is set as our highest Excellence priority. It will thus be our Strategic People Excellence Thrust for the next strategic period.

- **Phase 4: Generate an integrated, systemic, and coherent portfolio of People Excellence Interventions, enabling the realisation of our prioritised Strategic People Excellence Thrust** (Matrix: Off-diagonal cells)

Using the People Excellence Interdependency Matrix – and drawing on thought leadership, research evidence and leading practice – identify, map, and specify the relevant/related Excellence Elements/Domains – in the off-diagonal cells of the Matrix – with their desired impact to enhance Engagement in our organisation. Define the 'To Be' and 'As Is' states for our organisation regarding each relationship with our Strategic People Excellence Thrust: Engagement.

Generate an integrated, systemic and coherent portfolio of People Excellence Element/Domain Interventions to close the gap in our organisation, and compile them into a Strategic Intervention Plan. This Phase requires intense, iterative thinking and debate over a prolonged time before a fit-for-purpose, portfolio – translated into a well-crafted plan – can be produced for our organisation.

Figure 10.4 gives the structure of such an Intervention Portfolio (following Figure 10.3) for Engagement as our prioritised Strategic People Excellence Thrust.

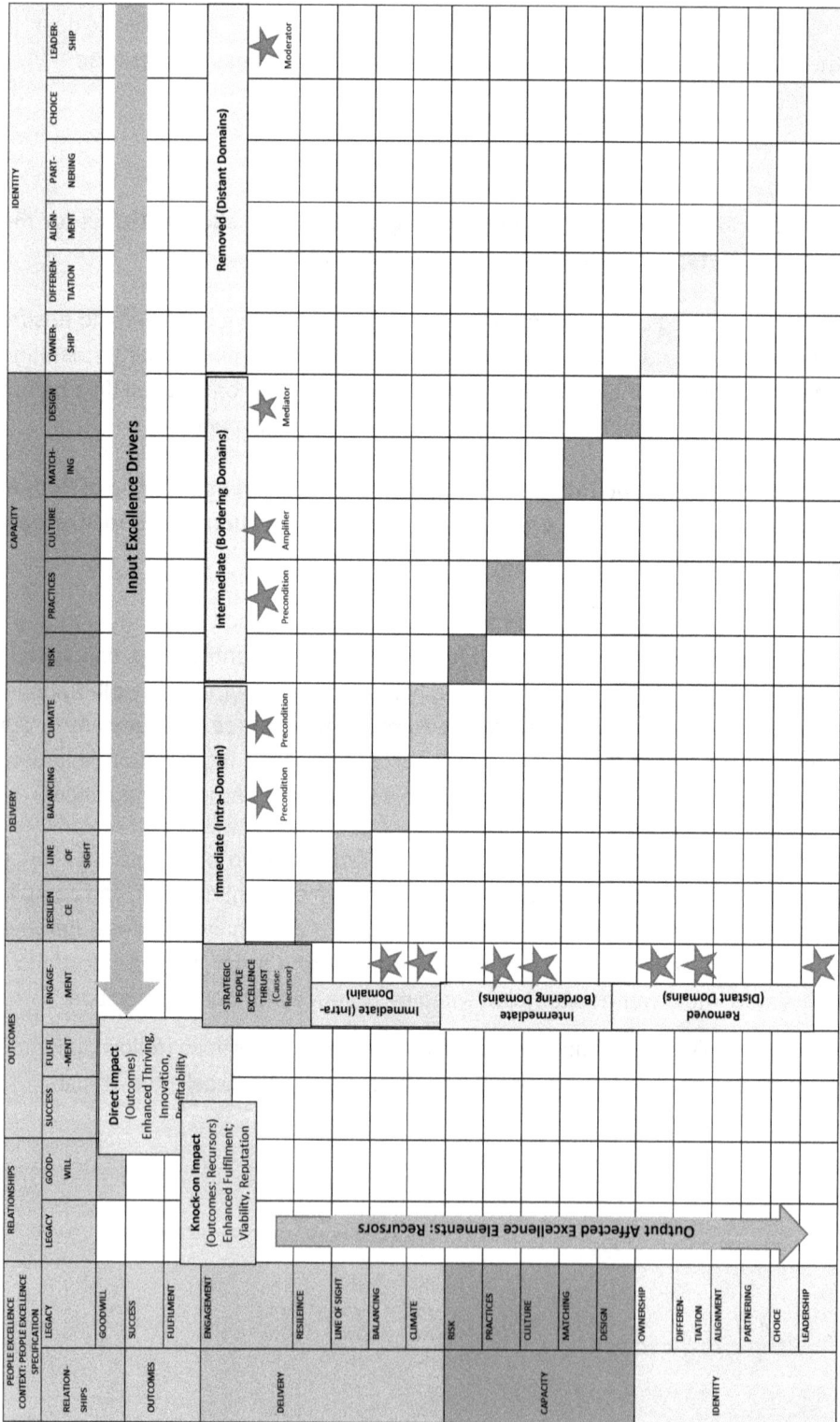

Figure 10.4: A hypothetical example of the structure of an integrated, systemic, and coherent Intervention Portfolio for Engagement as prioritised Strategic People Excellence Thrust in our organisation

According to Figure 10.4, our Engagement Intervention Portfolio for our chosen Strategic People Excellence Thrust: Engagement, consists of:

- *Expected Direct Impact (Outcomes)*
  - Enhanced Thriving; Innovation, Profitability (Excellence Domain 4: Outcomes)
- *Knock-on Impact (Outcomes, Recursors)*
  - Enhanced Fulfilment, Viability (Excellence Domain 4: Outcomes); Reputation (Excellence Domain 5: Relationships)
- *Input Excellence Drivers* with respect to Engagement (indicated by stars in the Matrix)
  - *Immediate (Intra-Domain):* Balancing (Precondition); Climate (Precondition) (Excellence Domain 3: Delivery)
  - *Intermediate:* Practices (Precondition); Culture (Amplifier); Design (Mediator) (Excellence Domain 2: Capacity)
  - *Removed:* Leadership (Moderator) (Excellence Domain 1: Identity)
- *Output Affected Excellence Elements* with respect to Engagement (Recursors) (indicated by stars in the Matrix)
  - *Immediate (Intra-Domain):* Balancing; Climate (Excellence Domain 3: Delivery)
  - *Intermediate:* Practices; Culture; Design (Excellence Domain 2: Capacity)
  - *Removed:* Differentiation (especially our PVP); Ownership, Leadership (Excellence Domain 1: Identity)

Next, our integrated 'To Be' People Excellence story must be told about the desired overall synergistic fusion we want to establish and maintain in our organisation regarding Engagement as our Strategic People Excellence Thrust. In parallel, our 'As Is' story must be told, followed by the interventions we have chosen to close the gap between the two states in our organisation. The template given in Table 10.1 can be used to tell this overall story.

Table 10.1: The 'To Be' and 'As Is' People Excellence story with respect to Engagement as Strategic People Excellence Thrust

OUR PEOPLE EXCELLENCE SPECIFICATION		
Highly enabled, empowered and resilient people, who strongly identify with and feel valued by the organisation, and are productively and innovatively engaging collaboratively in personally purposeful and meaningful ways, to viably and sustainably create inimitable, delightful experiences for stakeholders.		
OUR CHOSEN STRATEGIC PEOPLE EXCELLENCE THRUST: ENGAGEMENT		
The majority of our people (> 75%) demonstrate high levels of vigour, dedication, absorption, and collaboration, unlocking more value and creating greater wealth for our stakeholders than what is to be expected. They are creating amazing Client Value Propositions that are delighting clients, on which they deliver consistently and predictably.		
Our 'To Be' State	**Our 'As Is' State**	**Closing our Gap: Our Required Interventions**
We endeavour to have a high percentage of highly engaged people in our organisation who thrive in what they do. The intention is to be a highly disruptively innovative and profitable organisation. In this way our people will feel fulfilled, and our organisation will be viable and reputable in our operating arena. *We endeavour to enhance the engagement of our people by them having the confidence to take up the autonomy awarded to them to balance optimally - through ongoing work crafting – their work demands and the resources required to get the work done. All of this is engendered by an invigorating Organisational Climate. In this way we wish to nurture a high stock of psychosocial capital in our people and virtue-ality in our leadership.*	*Currently, only 25% to 30% of our people are highly engaged, with a particular gap around collaboration. The desired rate of innovation in our organisation is unacceptable, placing the future viability of our organisation of risk. More than 70% of our annual revenue is generated by products/services older than five years.* *Although our people experience their work to be meaningful and purposeful, they feel psychologically unsafe. For this reason, they do not fully take up the autonomy awarded to them to craft an optimal daily balance between their work demands and the resources required by them to get the work done in their work setting.*	*The key intervention in our organisation would be to affect a significant shift to enabling and empowering people-centric leadership.* *This leadership must bring about an Achievement/ Caring Culture and invigorating Climate, building positive psychosocial capital, in which our people would feel psychologically safe to innovate.* *All of the above must be reinforced by a coherent bundle of People Practices that solicit Agile, Creative People Conduct, engendering High Commitment/ High Involvement.* *To this end, we will recraft our leadership competency model to be aligned to our 'To Be' Excellence state. All our leadership*

Our 'To Be' State	Our 'As Is' State	Closing our Gap: Our Required Interventions
Establishing High Commitment/High Involvement People Practices to engender Agile, Creative People Conduct; an Achievement/Caring Organisational Culture; and meaningful work, will create favourable conditions for high engagement. Overall, our people-centric, purpose-driven leadership will enable and empower our people to be the very best they can, and want to, be. They will be energised to take up the autonomy awarded to them.

All of the above will recursively further enhance and strengthen our people's engagement, with the added benefit of deepening the affective commitment of our people to our organisation, providing us with a differentiating, compelling PVP and People Brand in our operating arena as a genuinely high engagement organisation. | Our people experience our Organisational Climate as suffocating, leading to a pervasive sense of pessimism, inefficacy and despair, which adds to them feeling psychologically unsafe. These negative experiences undermine the willingness of our people to take risks, and have the courage to innovate.

We have a Power Culture that demands unquestionable obedience and compliance. The source of this Culture is our leadership, which is highly autocratic-transactional, demanding non-negotiable, short-term results. So our people play it safe by bowing to all leadership requests, even if they are unreasonable. This leadership stance is reflected in our current Low Commitment/Low Involvement People Practices that do not solicit Agile, Creative People Conduct.

Overall, the underlying affective commitment of our people to our organisation is being eroded at a rapid rate. | will be assessed and developed against this model. Leaders who are incapable of meeting the requirements set by this model will be phased out of our organisation.

We will also craft and implement a bundle of High Commitment/ High Involvement People Practices to reinforce our people-centric leadership. Concurrently, we aim to bring about an Achievement/Caring Culture and an invigorating Climate, invoking a sense of efficacy, hope, and optimism for all as we phase in our new leadership.

All in all, we want to aggressively restore our people's affective commitment to our organisation's Identity.

Additionally, we want to restore aggressively our differentiating People Brand in the market as a truly high engagement organisation. |

The People Excellence Story told in Table 10.1 must next be translated into a Strategic Intervention Plan, indicating the what, why, when, who, how and whereto of affecting the desired change in Engagement as prioritised Strategic People Excellence Thrust.

- **Phase 5: Roll out our Strategic People Excellence Intervention Plan, and monitor and track its impact in realising the selected Strategic People Excellence Thrust**

   Monitor, track and take corrective action, informed by intelligent insight, with respect to increased engagement levels in our organisation as the Intervention Plan is rolled out, affecting the Engagement Excellence Drivers.

This concludes the hypothetical example of the People Excellence journey, demonstrating the application of the People Excellence Interdependency Matrix as a means to unleash ongoing, genuine, overall People Excellence synergetic fusion in the organisation. Similar, hypothetical examples can be generated for any of the 20 Excellence Domains as Strategic People Excellence Thrusts.

As a first attempt, you can take an example drawn from your 'To Be'/'As is' assessment (see Work Sheet 28) from your organisation, and complete the People Excellence Interdependency Matrix following the process outlined above (see Work Sheet 29).

MAKING STRATEGIC PEOPLE EXCELLENCE META-THINKING AN EVERYDAY REALITY IN THE ORGANISATION

All-in-all, the People Interdependency Matrix as a Strategic People Excellence Meta-thinking Framework can direct and guide an ongoing, integrated, systemic, and strategic dialogue at the requisite complexity level in the organisation, in its endeavour to unleash overall synergistic fusion regarding People Excellence. But how does one do it practically? How does one bring this dialogue to the everyday frontline in one's organisation, using the Matrix?

I would suggest that an organisation sets up a People Excellence "Operating Room". On one wall, visually display the total Matrix with all the cells filled with the desired 'To Be' and 'As Is' states of the organisation as they are known, reflecting where the organisation stands right now in real time. As discussed before, gaps can be colour coded as red, yellow, and green, giving an immediate, visual overall picture of the organisation's People Creditworthiness. (Displayed on the other walls could respectively be the current Strategic People Excellence Intervention Plan around the selected Strategic Excellence Thrust; the organisation's Strategic People Intent with strategic people initiatives; and the organisation's Identity with its constituent elements of Purpose, Vision, Strategic Intent, Core Values, and Legacy).

The organisation's Executive and People Leadership Group could hold regular meetings in the Room, organised around selected People Excellence Themes, and work systematically across the displayed Matrix, updating the current state of People Excellence in the organisation as they understand it in real time. For example, they could take the desired 'To Be' vs. 'As Is' Leadership Element, and work across each cell in the Matrix to assess its relationship to, and impact on, all of the 19 other Excellence Elements.[15]

This critical strategic dialogue could move in two directions: (i) horizontally, seeing Leadership as an Excellence Driver affecting subsequent Excellence Elements; and (ii) vertically, seeing which Excellence Elements recursively affect the effectiveness of Leadership (see Figure 10.4 as an example regarding Engagement). This assessment becomes a real time, in time, People Creditworthiness Test of the organisation regarding Leadership. At the next meeting, for example, Culture can be taken as the theme, and so on.

Of course, the visual Matrix can be technologically-enabled into an highly interactive, digitised display, linking a cell to, for example, a video clip reflecting 'a day-in-the-life-of-the-organisation' in that cell; hearing people's voices regarding what is happening in the cell; providing the available intelligence regarding the cell; and/or giving the relevant interrogative questions one should ask to direct the dialogue with respect to the cell. Over time, even predictive People Excellence decision-making algorithms can generated. Only one's imagination limits what could be linked digitally to the Matrix to broaden and deepen the dialogue.

The People Function of the organisation – in particular its Organisational/People Effectiveness Unit – would set and maintain the People Excellence Interdependency Matrix, as well as the People Excellence Operating Room. The organisation's Executive and People Leadership Group would own and engage with the Matrix and dialogue around the Matrix, and the resultant decisions and actions.

LOCATION OF THE PEOPLE EXCELLENCE STRESS TEST – THE PEOPLE EXCELLENCE STAR – IN THE STRATEGIC PEOPLE LANDSCAPE

The critical question is where the People Excellence Star is located as Strategic Stress Test in the Strategic People Landscape. Figure 10.5 depicts the Strategic People Landscape, indicating the location of the People Excellence Star therein.

Operating Arena

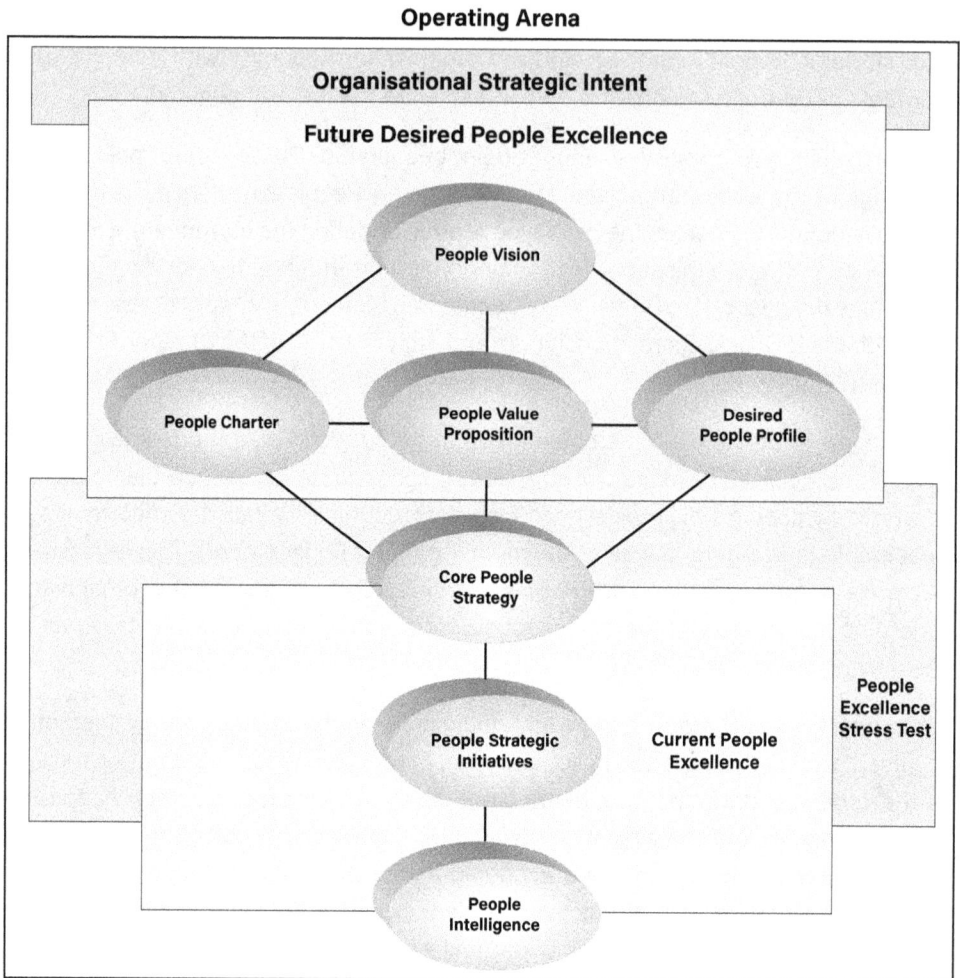

Figure 10.5: The Strategic People Landscape

All the building blocks of the Strategic Landscape contained in Figure 10.5 have already been defined and discussed in previous chapters. The only building block that may require clarity is *Core People Strategy*, i.e., the broad thrust (or intent) of the strategic journey to be undertaken by the organisation to realise its Desired Future State regarding People Excellence by converting its Current State into its Desired Future State.

According to Figure 10.5, the People Excellence Stress Test, i.e., the People Excellence Star, forms the foundation of the Strategic People Landscape. The outcome of applying this Stress Test 'enters' the Landscape through the chosen People Strategic Initiatives, identified through the application of the People Excellence Interdependency Matrix, explicated in the previous section.

In our earlier discussion, Engagement as a People Excellence Element was used as an example. I.e., Engagement would form the Core People Strategy for a given strategic period. The needed People Strategic Initiatives (=People Excellence Interventions) would be determined by means of the People Excellence Interdependency Matrix in terms of the relevant Excellence Elements affecting Engagement. These interventions will be moulded into an Excellence Intervention Plan.

HIGH LEVEL GUIDELINES FOR THE JOURNEY TOWARDS PEOPLE EXCELLENCE IN AN ORGANISATION

At least the following interdependent guidelines must inform the People Excellence journey:

- **Guideline 1: Adopt a Complexity World View, inter alia, treating the organisation as living, social ecosystem.**[16] This view was discussed in this chapter and Chapter 2.

- **Guideline 2: Engage with the People Excellence journey at the requisite level of complexity.** This chapter has argued this point extensively and in detail. The proposed People Excellence Interdependency Matrix as Strategic Meta-thinking Framework provides such an enabling tool.

- **Guideline 3: Take a long term perspective of People Excellence.** It will take at least three to five years to make People Excellence an inherent part of the organisation's DNA – its innate way of seeing, interpreting, understanding, thinking and doing. One must thus have patience, show perseverance, and have staying power in making People Excellence the ingrained way of thinking and doing in the organisation.

- **Guideline 4: People Excellence is a never-ending process of re-imagination and re-invention.** For viable organisational success, there needs to be an aspirational attitude of 'Good is never good enough' with respect to People Excellence pervading the total organisation into its very essence. It is a never-ending process of re-imagining and re-inventing People Excellence to attain increasingly higher levels of People Creditworthiness. This takes courage and daring.

- **Guideline 5: Institutionalise a learning attitude and culture towards People Excellence.** Remain up-to-date with the latest thought leadership, research findings, and leading practices regarding People Excellence. In addition, follow an action research and learning process with respect to the journey to People Excellence in one's own organisation in order to become smarter over time regarding People Excellence. In this way, build an organisation-unique theory-in-action of People Excellence befitting one's own context in order to enhance the context-organisation-people goodness-of-fit.

SUMMARY

We have reached the end of our challenging, extensive, and deep-dive journey. The endeavour of *The People Excellence Star. A Strategic Organisational Stress Test* was to propose and elucidate an integrated Strategic Stress Test of the overall People Creditworthiness of organisations within the frame of reference of the emerging new order. In the process, a praxeology of People Excellence was crafted – the 'science' dealing with the practice of People Excellence in organisations.

The basic premise of my book is that if people are central to the continued future viability of organisations, then knowing the state of an organisation's People Excellence, as well as becoming smarter at People Excellence, has a mission-critical imperative for every organisation. Is the organisation consistently achieving exceedingly well with its people? Are they unlocking real, amazing value and creating worthy, lasting wealth continuously, to the amazed delight of the organisation's stakeholders? In the process, is the organisation great at making its people thrive? Are people the best they can, and want to, be? Are they experiencing genuine, deep fulfilment, and hence flourishing?

The promised unique value-add of *The People Excellence Star. A Strategic Organisational Stress Test* was to offer an integrated Strategic Stress Test of the organisation's People Creditworthiness, entitled the People Excellence Star. The make-up of the People Excellence Star was explicated from an integrated, strategic vantage point in terms of five Excellence Dimensions – Identity, Capacity, Delivery, Outcomes and Relationships – with their 20 Excellence Elements.

The Star endeavours to balance in equal measures the organisational and people perspectives of the People Excellence Equation. It also seeks to seamlessly integrate the best thought leadership, latest research, and cutting-edge practice with a bias towards practical application, all within the emerging new order as it impacts on the new World of Work. Hopefully the promises of integration, balance, robustness, and relevance were fulfilled for the reader.

It can be contended that the ultimate, overarching value-add of *The People Excellence Star. A Strategic Organisational Stress Test* was the evolutionary increase in the requisite complexity level as the story unfolded regarding People Excellence, as depicted in the People Excellence Star: from the individual Excellence Domains/Elements (an Intra-Domain Perspective), through the People Excellence Value Chain (an Inter-Domain Perspective), to finally the People Excellence Interdependency Matrix as

Strategic People Excellence Meta-thinking Framework (a Systemic, Dynamic, Holistic Perspective, a Complexity view). In the final instance, the drive behind this evolution of increasing complexity was to capacitate organisations to unleash the genuine, ongoing, synergistic fusion of People Excellence in their organisations.

All that remains is to wish the reader a difference-making, People Excellence journey with the organisations they are involved with. May your engagements – purposed at bringing about an organisation in which people can flourish and thrive, and thus feel fulfilled – leave our world a better place for future generations.

ENDNOTES

Chapter 1: Endnotes

(1)   Lev (2001); (2004). Cf. also Volini et al (2020)

(2)   Veldsman (2016a)

(3)   Kjaer & Associates (2020); Nel & Beudeker (2009); Shanker, Bhanugopan, Van der Heijden & Farrell (2017); Veldsman (2019a); Volini et al (2020)

(4)   Habraken, Bondarouk & Hoffman (2019); Mayer (2019); Volini et al (2020)

(5)   Jee (2019); Volini et al (2020)

(6)   The 'Create' economy needs a Blue Ocean strategic perspective (Kim & Mauborgne, 2020a; 2020b). This strategic perspective embraces the seeking/creation of untapped market spaces through demand creation – new value for customers – in which organisations gain a strategic edge through differentiation and low cost. In this way, competition is made irrelevant. In contrast, a Red Ocean strategic perspective is where organisations are competing in a given market with existing customers by taking market share away from competitors.

(7)   Bakker (2017); Boon, Eckardt, Lepak & Boselie (2018); Bronkhorst (2012); Bussin (2018); Castellano (2013); Covin (2015); Fenton & Pettigrew (2000); Friedman (2016); Forman (2017); Fitz-Enz (1997); Garrett-Cox (2016); Gill (2018); Ghosal & Bartlett (1997); Graham & Cascio (2018); Hamel (2015); Johennesse & Chou (2017); Lawler (2017); Laloux (2014); Martens (2019); Motyka (2018); Pfeffer (1998); Rød & Fridjhon (2016); Roux (2021); Shanker, Bhanugopan, Van der Heijden & Farrell (2017); Silzer & Dowell (2010); Thoren (2017); Ulrich & Ulrich (2017); Ungerer, Pretorius & Herholdt (2002); Veldsman (2011); (2014a); (2019a)

(8)   Gallup (2016) (quoted by Schiemann, 2017)

(9)   Pine and Gilmore (2011) (quoted by Castellano, 2013; Gruber, De Leon, George & Thompson, 2015) argue that the "experience economy" is the next economy succeeding the agrarian, industrial, and service economies. In an experience economy, organisations must orchestrate inimitable, memorable events for their customers and employees such that memory itself becomes the product. I.e., the experience invoked by the product/service.

(10)   The well accepted definition by the United Nations (1987, p. 1) of sustainability is: "Sustainable development is development that meets the needs of the present without compromising the ability of future generations to meet their own needs."

(11)   Angus & Westbrook (2021); Agarwal, Bersin, Lahiri, Schwartz & Volini (2018); Ashton (2017); Bersin, O'Reilly, Magoulas & Loukides (2019); Brown (2019); Castellano (2013); Hawken (2010); Kjaer & Associates (2020); Lankoski & Smith (2017); Lawler (2017); Lawler & Worley (2012); Lawler & Conger (2015); Nijhof, Schaveling & Zalesky (2019); Santos, Pache & Birkholz (2015); Veldsman (2015); Volini et al (2020); Yeoman & O'Hara (2017)

(12)   Joyce (2005); Nohria, Joyce & Robertson (2003)

(13)   Avedon & Scoles (2010); Bussin (2018); Castellano (2013); Gallardo-Gallardo, Thunnissen & Scullion (2020); Joyce (2005); McLean & Company (2020); Nohria, Joyce & Robertson (2003); Roodt (2018); SA Board of People Practices (2018); Silzer & Dowell (2010); Veldsman (2018); Veldsman & Pauw (2018)

(14)   In the 2017 PWC Global CEO survey, more than 75% of CEOs highlighted the scarcity of essential skills and capabilities as the key threat to the growth prospects of their

organisations (quoted in Gallardo-Gallardo, Thunnissen & Scullion, 2020). In the 2019 23rd Annual PWC Global CEO survey, the availability of key skills was regarded as the third most important threat (34%) after the top threat of overregulation (35%). The 2019 four key forces driving upskilling were increasing job automation; decreasing talent availability; decreasing talent mobility; and aging talent (PWC, 2019).

(15) Bersin & Enderes (2021); Claus (2019); Montet et al (2020); Parker, Rabolele & Joubert (2020); Rahmadani, Schaufeli, Ivanova & Osin (2019); Roux (2021); Schwartz, Hatfield, Jones & Anderson (2019); Volini et al (2020); World Economic Forum (2019); Whysall, Owtram & Brittain (2019)

(16) According to the Mercer Global Talent Trends 2020 Survey, organisations that exceed their performance goals are three times more likely to have employee experience as a core part of their people strategy, compared to organisations failing to achieve their goals. However, only 4% of responding People Teams believed that they were delivering an exemplary employee experience (Bravery et al, 2020).

According to research conducted by Willis Towers Watson (2019a), organisations with a high-performing employee experience outperformed the sector average return on assets by 2%; return on equity by 3%; and gross profit margin by 12%. Over the mid-term they outperformed the sector average three-year revenue growth by 4%, and the three-year change in gross profit margin by 4%. In short, a high-performing employee experience is a predictor for financial performance in the short- and mid-term (quoted in the World Economic Forum, 2019)

(17) Bersin & Enderes (2021)

(18) Coetzee (2019c). See also the references listed under (15)

(19) My intention is to locate my exposition of People Excellence squarely within the space of Positive Psychology. Positive Psychology is a study of the circumstance and processes necessary for the optimal functioning of human beings and organisations to make life worth living because they are thriving and flourishing. It is about wellness, well-being, and happiness (cf. Cameron, Dutton & Quinn, 2003; Coetzee, 2019c; Seligman & Csikszentmihayi, 2000).

Three waves of Positive Psychology can be distinguished (Lomas, Waters, Williams, Oades & Kern, 2020). In *Wave 1: Positivity*, the exclusive focus is on enhancing and promoting positive, individual functioning. It is about the thriving, flourishing, fulfilled person in contrast to the malfunctioning, to-be-fixed, person. What positive individual features make life worth living? In *Wave 2: Polarity*, the focus shifts to an understanding of the fundamentally dialectical nature of well-being. Flourishing entails both the positive and negative aspects of living; the positives and negatives must be harmonised dynamically through the balancing of opposites within a whole. An emerging *Wave 3: Complexity* goes, inter alia, beyond the individual person as the primary focus. In this wave, people's well-being is contextually embedded. Individual well-being must be considered within the context of the groups, organisations, and broader systems to which they belong or interact with. Multiple socio-cultural factors and processes that impact upon personal well-being (from politics to economics) must also be taken into account. My exposition in *The People Excellence Star. A Strategic Organisational Stress Test* is firmly placed within Wave 3.

(20) Petriglieri (2020)

(21) See the references listed under (11)

(22) Bersin & Enderes (2021); Kjaer & Associates (2020)

(23) Ghosal & Bartlett (1997); Hock (1999); Jee (2019); Montet et al (2020); Murray (2019); The

British Academy, 2019; Volini et al (2020)

(24)   Reported by Raj Sisodia, author of the book entitled *Firms of Endearment* (quoted in EY, 2018)

(25)   EY (2018)

(26)   Beer (2009); EY (2018); Kjaer & Associates (2020); Lawler (2017); Ulrich & Ulrich (2017)

(27)   Crous (2020)

(28)   Volini et al (2020)

(29)   Veldsman (2007a); (2007b)

(30)   Veldsman (2019c)

Chapter 2: Endnotes

(1)   The People Excellence Star is a stress test of an organisation's People Creditworthiness. Ever since November 2013, INSEAD (2020), the French Business School, has published a Global Talent Competitiveness Index (GTCI), which is a 'stress test' of countries' People Creditworthiness. INSEAD argues that given the vital importance of talent for the prosperity of a nation, the ambition of GTCI is to be an action tool for continuous improvement in linking talent to economic development in a country. GTCI intends to be an instrument to stimulate dialogue between governments, businesses, academia, professionals and their associations, and citizens.

The GTCI is a composite index, relying on a simple but robust Input-Output model. The Index has: (i) four pillars on the Input side — Enable, Attract, Grow, and Retain – which focus on actions for policymakers and business leaders; and (iii) two Output pillars that benchmark national performances in Technical/Vocational and Global Knowledge Skills, respectively.

The *Input side* of the Index consists of:

- Enable: Regulatory Landscape, Market Landscape, Business and Labour Landscape
- Attract: External Openness, Internal Openness
- Grow: Formal Education, Lifelong Learning, Access to Growth Opportunities

The *Output side* of the Index is made up of:

- Vocational Skills: Mid-Level Skills, Employability
- Global Knowledge Skills: High-Level Skills, Talent Impact

The top five countries in the 2020 report focusing on Artificial Intelligence (AI) and talent competitiveness were: Switzerland, USA, Singapore, Sweden, and Denmark.

(2)   Coetzee (2019); De Geus (1997); Gallardo-Gallardo, Thunnissen & Scullion (2020); Jee (2019); Johns (2006); Seligman & Csikszentmihayi (2000); Ungerer, Ungerer & Herholdt (2016); Veldsman, Benade & Rossouw (2019); Van der Walt & Lezar (2019)

(3)   Coetzee (2019b); De Cooman, Mol, Billsberry, Boon & Den Hartog (2019); Gallardo-Gallardo, Thunnissen & Scullion (2020); Jianga & Messersmith (2018)

(4)   Veldsman (2019a)

(5)   Wikipedia (2020)

(6)   Bronkhorst (2012)

(7)   Beer (2009); Collins & Porras (1994) (quoted by Kirby 2005); Fitz-Enz (1997); Gallardo-Gallardo, Thunnissen & Scullion (2020); Whysall, Owtram & Brittain (2019)

(8)   The other term used to describe this view of the organisation as a "social ecosystem" is the organisation as a "complex adaptive system" (CAS) (e.g., Barasa, Mbau & Gilson, 2018; Morales, Martınez, Gomez, Romero & Torres-Argűelles, 2019; Cantoni, Graziano, Maiocchi & Rizzi, 2019).

I believe that organisations are more than merely adaptive systems. Frequently, they re-invent themselves in a fit-for-purpose way, and/or re-constitute the context to better fit them, given their chosen purpose as a function of their adopted Strategic Contextual Posture and Attitude (see Chapter 3).

(9)   Boulton, Allen & Bowman (2015); Veldsman (2019a); Veldsman, Benade & Rossouw (2019); Tower (2013); Wheatley (2013)

(10)   Cf. Christie (2009); Denning (2011)

(11)   Jiang, Takeuchi & Lepak (2013); Kuenzi & Schminke (2009); Van Beurden, Van De Voorde & Van Veldhoven (2021)

(12)   For example, Joubert and Roodt (2019) found that employee engagement is a multi-level construct based on the multiple roles that people occupy in organisations – individual, team, management – with different push and pull factors for each role.

(13)   Jiang, Takeuchi & Lepak (2013)

(14)   Jiang, Takeuchi & Lepak (2013)

(15)   Boxall & Macky (2009); Jiang, Takeuchi & Lepak (2013)

Chapter 3: Endnotes

(1)   Coetzee (2019); De Geus (1997); Gallardo-Gallardo, Thunnissen & Scullion (2020); Jee (2019); Jianga & Messersmith (2018); Johns (2006); Veldsman, Benade & Rossouw (2019); Van der Walt & Lezar (2019)

(2)   Coetzee (2019b); De Cooman, Mol, Billsberry, Boon & Den Hartog (2019); Gallardo-Gallardo, Thunnissen & Scullion (2020); Seligman & Csikszentmihayi (2000)

(3)   The discussion in this chapter is based on a central theoretical concept in the field of Work Psychology, namely Person-Environment fit (or as I prefer, 'Context', because Environment conveys a physical environment bias) (De Cooman, Mol, Billsberry Boon & Den Hartog, 2019; Follmer, 2019; Hicklenton, Hine & Loi, 2019; Morley, 2007). For the purpose of the discussion in the chapter, Environment represents the organisation-in-its-context. Thus, this chapter is all about the Organisation-in-its-context-People fit.

In the ensuing discussion, this fit is conceived to run from the shallow, visible fit of people conduct and abilities/capabilities to the deep, invisible fit of people's world views, values and needs. A meta-analysis by Kristof-Brown et al. (2005) found that Person-Organisation (PO) (read 'context') fit correlates strongly and positively with job satisfaction, organisational commitment and organisation satisfaction. A negative correlation exists with the intention to quit (quoted by Hicklenton, Hine & Loi, 2019).

(4)   Veldsman (2016c)

(5)   Hock (1999)

(6)   Fitz-Enz (1997); Hamel & Zanini (2020); Volini et al (2016)

(7)   Miller (1992)

(8)   Crous (2020)

(9)   Kurtz & Snowden (2003); Snowden & Boone (2007). See also Blignaut (2020)

(10)   Hawryszkiewycz (2017). According to him, wicked problems carry the following features: each is unique; each is owned by many diverse stakeholders with conflicting interests/needs; an unclear problem formulation exists; a range of possible solutions is possible; solutions are better or worse, not true or false; no clear test exists whether a solution will work; every solution is unique to a specific situation; and there is no clear termination point as and when the desired impact has been attained by a solution.

(11)   Section based on Veldsman (Chapter 11, 2019a; 2013a), except where otherwise noted. See also the following authors on the following topics: Veldsman & Pauw (2018) and Veldsman, Benade & Rossouw (2019): the VUCA World of Work; Gallardo-Gallardo, Thunnissen & Scullion (2020): the 4th Industrial Revolution; Coetzee (2019); Kohl & Swartz (2019) and Ludike (2018): the future digital workplace and working digitally; Castellano (2013): the changing world in general; and Santana & Cobo (2020) and Veldsman & Van Aarde (2021): expected trends with respect to the future of work.

(12)   Seamlessness (i.e., boundarylessness) is manifested concretely in globalisation. At present there appears to be a slow-down or even reversal of globalisation, called 'slowbalisation' (*The Economist*). This slowdown is attributed to the rise of nationalism, populism, inter-nation tensions, and geo-security concerns.

(13)   Baran & Woznyj (2021)

(14)   Ungerer, Ungerer & Herholdt (2016)

(15)   Veldsman (2019a). See also Jedynak, Czakon, Kuzniarska & Mania (2021)

(16)   Angus & Westbrook (2021)

(17)   Based primarily on Veldsman (2019a). Cf. also Cascio & Montealegre (2016); Montealegre & Cascio (2017); Kjaer & Associates (2020) and Malhotra (2021); Schwartz, Hatfield, Jones & Anderson (2019); Volini et al (2020); World Economic Forum (2019). See Schwab (2018) for an in-depth discussion of the 4th Industrial Revolution with its associated technologies.

(18)   Coetzee and Deas (2021) present a collection of research studies that address the impact of the digital era (read DIVAS) on the psychological contract (to be discussed in the next chapter), using many of the examples of DIVAS' ways of working depicted in Table 3.1.

(19)   Whysall, Owtram & Brittain (2019); World Economic Forum (2019)

(20)   Quoted by Van Dam (2017)

(21)   Since 2004, every new robot installed displaced an average of 1.6 factory, blue collar workers (Montet et al, 2020)

(22)   Claus (2019)

(23)   In the 2020 Deloitte Global Human Capital Trends survey, 53% of respondents said that between half and all of their workforce will need to change their skills and capabilities in the next three years (Volini et al, 2020).

(24)   Business Roundtable (quoted in World Economic Forum, 2019)

(25)   Volini et al (2020)

(26)   Walter (2020)

(27)   Lawler (2017); Schwab (2018); Veldsman (2019a)

(28)   Cf. e.g., Boon, Eckardt, Lepak & Boselie (2018); Bravery, Baldwin, Ketenci, Cernigol, Cline, De Malo, Gutowski, Hudson, Ladd, Roberts & Silva, 2020; Jee (2019); Kohl & Swartz

(2019); Ludike (2018); Mayer (2019); Montet et al (2020); Parker, Rabolele & Joubert (2020); Roux (2021); Van Dam (2017); Veldsman, Benade & Rossouw (2019); Volini et al (2020); Walter (2020); Whysall, Owtram & Brittain (2019); World Economic Forum (2016)

(29) Veldsman (2019a). See also Kjaer & Associates (2020); Kohl & Swartz (2019); Lawler (2017); Ludike (2018); Schwartz, Hatfield, Jones & Anderson (2019)

(30) Angus & Westbrook (2021); EY (2018)

(31) Veldsman (2019a). See also Korten (2019)

(32) Hawken (2010); Korten (2019)

(33) Kakutani (2018)

(34) An 'Outside-In' vantage point is reflective of Design Thinking. This thinking is about transforming existing conditions into the preferred conditions by starting Outside-In with the experiences of prospective beneficiaries – current or desired. Because of its open-enddedness and –mindedness, there is no upfront and/or imposed solution. Design Thinking is imminently suited to craft plausible solutions, not correct solutions, under conditions of uncertainty, ambiguity, and instability (see Claus, 2019; Elsbach & Stigliani, 2018; Kolko, 2015).

(35) See Figure 2.2 in Veldsman (2019a)

(36) See Figure 2.2 in Veldsman (2019a)

(37) Christensen & Overdorf (2000); Covin (2015); Friedman (2016); Silva & Guerrini (2018). Clayton M. Christensen and his colleagues introduced the term "Disruptive innovation" in 1995, although the Austrian economist Joseph Schumpeter already coined the term "Creative destruction" in 1942.

(38) Castellano (2013); Coetzee (2019); Fitz-Enz (1997); Foster & Kaplan (2001) (quoted in Kirby 2005); Hamel & Zanini (2020); Joyce (2005); Nohria, Joyce & Robertson (2003); Kjaer & Associates (2020); Kohl & Swartz (2019); Ludike (2018); Parker & Veldsman (2010); Shanker, Bhanugopan, Van der Heijden & Farrell (2017); Veldsman (Chapter 11, 2019); Veldsman & Pauw (2018); Veldsman, Benade & Rossouw (2019)

(39) Ahmetoglu, Akhtar, Tsivrikos & Chamorro-Premuzic (2018); Katzenburg (2000) (quoted in Kirby, 2005)

(40) Surprise competitors, such as Uber, Amazon and Airbnb, are re-inventing the competitive landscape with new products, services, and ways of acquiring them, leaving 50% of today's Fortune 500 at risk of extinction within a decade (Berman, Dorrier, & Hill, 2016; Mochari (2016) (quoted by Pulakos, Schneider & Kantrowitz, 2019).

(41) Arets (2019); Beer (2009); Birkinshaw & Ridderstråle (2017); Edmondson (2012); Fitz-Enz (1997); Friedman (2016); Ghosal & Bartlett (1997); Hamel (2015); Kjaer & Associates (2020); Kohl & Swartz (2019); Laloux (2014); Martens (2019); McChrystal (2015); Petković, Mirić & Čudanov (2014); Silva & Guerrini (2018)

(42) Cf. Kohl & Swartz (2019); Ludike (2018); Mayer (2019); Ungerer, Ungerer & Herholdt (2016); Veldsman, Benade & Rossouw (2019)

(43) See Note (34)

Chapter 4: Endnotes

(1) Ghosal & Bartlett (1997); Katzenbach (2000) (quoted in Kirby, 2005); Nel & Beudeker (2009); Roux (2021); Ungerer, Ungerer & Herholdt (2016)

(2)   Veldsman, Benade & Rossouw (2019)

(3)   2020 McKinsey Global Survey on External Relations (Geddes, Nuttall & Parekh, 2020)

(4)   Top Employers Institute (2021)

(5)   The theoretical approach informing Organisational Identity is Social Identity Theory. This theory seeks to understand the process by which people form an 'oneness with' or 'belonging to' an organisation (Mostafa et al, 2019; Veldsman & Veldsman, 2020a).

(6)   Veldsman & Veldsman (2020a); (2020b)

(7)   EY (2018); Veldsman & Veldsman (2020a)

(8)   Veldsman (2019a). See also Hock (1999)

(9)   With reference to the constituent elements of Organisational Identity, a few comments:

- *Purpose.* At present this element is centre stage – a burning platform: (i) in the intense discussion of the organisation's – especially business organisation's – relationship as a social enterprise with society (see Chapter 1); (ii) amongst the workers of the future – in particular millennials, who are seeking to make a meaningful difference through work, asking penetrating questions regarding an organisation's purpose in serving humanity (see Chapter 3) (see also Angus & Westbrook, 2021; Bersin & Enderes (2021); EY, 2018); and (iii) the requirement for Transcendental ('Why') leadership for the organisation (see this chapter).

- *Vision and Core Values.* The need for Principle-based Transformational ('Whereto') leadership relates to these elements (see this chapter).

- *Strategic Intent.* The criticality of an exceptional commitment to a focused, inspiring, future-centric Strategic Intent, well executed, as a key characteristic of high performance/high engagement organisations, is stressed by Fitz-Enz (1997), Joyce (2005) and Nohria, Joyce & Robertson (2003).

- *Legacy.* The core value orientation of sustainability through stewardship has brought this element strongly to the fore (see Chapter 3).

(10)   Hseih, Meyer, Rodin and Van 'T Klooster (2018) draw a distinction between organisations having respectively social and corporate goals. The former refers to the contribution that an organisation makes to realising societal ends, deliberately or by default. The latter refers to the goals the corporation actively pursues. In terms of the elements of Organisational Identity, given in Figure 4.1, a social goal refers to Purpose while a corporate goal refers to Vision and Strategic Intent.

(11)   Ungerer, Pretorius & Herholdt (2002); Ungerer, Ungerer & Herholdt (2016)

(12)   Joyce (2005); Nohria, Joyce & Robertson (2003); Veldsman & Roodt (2002)

(13)   Collins (2001)

(14)   Bronkhorst (2012); Beer (2009); Kotter & Heskett (1992)

(15)   Quoted by Bussin (2018)

(16)   E.g., Joyce (2005); Nohria, Joyce & Robertson (2003); Wasserman, Anand & Nohria (2010)

(17)   Research by DDI, a global leadership consulting firm, found that half of the organisations surveyed believed that their leaders were not skilled to lead effectively at present. A further 71% indicated that their leaders were not ready to lead their organisations into the future (Morgan, 2020).

(18)   World Economic Forum (2019)

(19)   Called 'engaging leaders' by Nikolova, Schaufeli & Notelaers (2019) and Rahmadani, Schaufeli, Ivanova & Osin (2019). These leaders are able to nurture engaging employees. A recent meta-analysis found that various leadership styles are all positively related to work engagement: ethical, transformational, servant, authentic, and empowering leadership (DeCuypere & Schaufeli, 2018) (quoted by Rahmadani, Schaufeli, Ivanova & Osin, 2019); Li et al, 2021). All of these manifestations of leadership are discussed below.

A strong, positive relationship between transformational leadership and employee engagement was also reported on by Alfesa, Shantz, Truss & Soane (2013); Bedarkar & Pandit (2014); Borah & Barua (2018); Chin, Lok & Kong (2019); Lee, Shin, Park, Kim & Cho (2017); Nikolova, Schaufeli & Notelaers (2019) and Saks (2017). Li et al (2021) found that the leadership–employee engagement relationship in some cases depends on national cultural characteristics (e.g., gender egalitarianism, human orientation, performance orientation, future orientation, power distance, uncertainty avoidance), especifically transactional leadership, ethical leadership, and servant leadership. The relationship between ethical, servant, transactional leadership and engagement is not mediated by national cultural characteristics.

(20)   Veldsman (2016d). Also Nel & Beudeker (2009)

(21)   This section draws heavily on Veldsman (2016). See also Ludike (2018) in this regard.

(22)   Cf. Kempster, Jackson & Conroy (2011)

(23)   Veldsman (2016a)

(24)   Transcendental leadership can also be equated to conscious leadership. I.e., a leader who demonstrates a servant-orientation, stewarding, and a safeguarding of the organisation for future generations (Jee, 2019).

(25)   Bakker (2017); Borah & Barua (2018); Castellano (2013); Chin, Lok & Kong (2019); Hai, Wu, Park, Li, Chang, & Tang (2020); Jee (2019); Mayer (2019); Nel & Beudeker (2009); Parker & Veldsman (2010)

(26)   Adapted and expanded from Kouzes & Posner (2012). See also Veldsman (2016a).

(27)   Beer (2009)

(28)   Veldsman (2016a)

(29)   Borah & Barua (2018); Chin, Lok & Kong (2019); Rahmadani, Schaufeli, Ivanova & Osin (2019); Veldsman (2020)

(30)   Van Dierendonck & Nuijten (2011)

(31)   Collins (2001) sees humility as THE key quality of a great leader.

(32)   Melé (2016); Veldsman (2011). See also Park & Kim (2019), who talk of leadership's vision of talent for their organisation.

(33)   Cf. Canning, Murphy, Emerson, Chatman Dweck & Kray (2020). These authors found that these respective mindsets – fixed or growth – shape the Organisational Culture. Employees who perceive their organisation to endorse a fixed mindset indicated that their organisation's culture was characterised by less collaboration, innovation, and integrity, with employees experiencing lower organisational trust, and commitment. In organisations with a growth mindset, employees saw their Organisational Culture as characterised by greater collaboration, innovation, integrity, organisational trust and commitment. Ishak and Williams (2018) made a similar point regarding organisational resilience: organisations with a growth mindset demonstrated more resilience than

those with a fixed mindset (see Excellence 15: Resilience). See Dweck (2008) for the original exposition on fixed and growth mindsets.

(34) This Strategic People Choice is embedded in the Strategic Resource-based View of the organisation in the strategic management literature. Strategic Resources as an investment are valuable, rare, and inimitable, resulting in superior organisational/financial performance, giving the organisation a competitive edge.

Human Capital (HC) as strategic resource of the organisation has the potential to be a source of competitive advantage because: (i) it can be a key determinant of the quality of outputs and/or efficiency of operations (=HC resources are valuable); (ii) HC resources are differentially distributed amongst organisations (=HC resources can be rare); and (iii) factors such as specificity, social complexity, and causal ambiguity can hinder the flow and replication of human capital resources amongst organisations (=HC resources can be difficult to imitate).

Different from other types of resources, human capital is owned by employees and can be transferred to other organisations when employees leave. Therefore it is critical for organisations to use HRM systems to enhance existing levels of human capital (e.g., attracting and training employees) and prevent the loss of their human capital investments to other organisations (e.g., by motivating and retaining employees).

The Strategic Human Capital approach focuses on human capital by, in and of itself, apart from the people themselves. The Strategic HRM approach focuses on the individual owning the human capital in the form of their attitudes, motivations, and effort. Cf. Beer (2009); Boon, Eckardt, Lepak & Boselie (2018); Collings, Mellahi & Cascio, (2019); Jianga & Messersmith (2018); Jiang, Takeuchi & Lepak (2013) and Shin & Konrad (2014).

(35) It is ironic in this Choice that whilst people are seen as an asset of the organisation, even the most important asset, they are not reflected as an asset on the organisation's Balance Sheet. At most people are included only as a liability, e.g., the monetary value of the outstanding leave commitment. At a minimum people can be included as an asset in terms of their replacement value – how much it will cost to replace the current people in the organisation if they are to leave; or an estimated people value-add = the average tenure x expected value-add of people by Level of Work (see Figure 5.2).

(36) Within self-determination theory, Ryan and Deci (2000) distinguished three needs for thriving: autonomy (=the freedom to self-organise one's life, concordant with one's own self), competence (=proficiency) and relatedness (=social connectivity) (quoted by Hicklenton, Hine & Loi, 2019; Jee, 2019; Nikolova, Schaufeli & Notelaers, 2019; Veldsman, Benade & Rossouw, 2019; Coetzee, 2019). (See also Brown et al, 2017; Knight, Patterson & Dawson, 2017; Meyer, 2017; Seligman & Csikszentmihayi, 2000; Veldsman, Benade & Rossouw, 2019, in this regard.) The fulfilment of all of these needs is necessary for healthy human functioning and development (Ryan & Deci, 2000). Relatedness (=belonging) has also been found to be a critical need for people in the new of World of Work (Volini et al, 2020).

The need for meaning was proposed by Frankl (1959). This need can be translated into current language as the need for purpose. Robertson and Cooper (2010) also distinguished a sense of purpose as being central to people's motivational make-up (quoted by Albrecht, Bakker, Gruman, Macey & Saks, 2015). This need currently stands central amongst people in the new World of Work (Volini et al, 2020).

(37) This concentric arrangement is contrary to Maslow's hierarchically arranged needs, in which a 'lower' need has to be satisfied before a next 'higher' one becomes active. Self-actualisation is at the top of the hierarchy. The proposed concentric arrangement in Figure 4.6 implies that any need can be active at any given time to a lesser or greater extent.

(38) Rahmadani, Schaufeli, Ivanova & Osin (2019); Ryan & Deci (2000)

(39) 2020 Deloitte Global Human Capital Report (Volini et al, 2020)

(40) Bankins, Griep & Hansen (2020); Beer (2009); Castellano (2013); Deas (2019); Guest (2004); Jee (2019); Lee, Chiang, van Esch & Cai (2018); Ludike (2018); Rousseau (1995); Veldsman (2011); Van Beurden, Van De Voorde & Van Veldhoven (2021); Veldsman & Pauw (2018); Zupan, Mihelič & Aleksić (2018)

(41) The dominant term in the literature is 'Psychological Contract'. I prefer the term 'Psychosocial Contract' because the contract is in its very essence between social parties.

(42) The Psychosocial Contract view of the relationship between the organisation and its people is based on social exchange theory: individuals who receive positive benefits from another party tend to respond reciprocally in kind. For example, the HRM practices of the organisation – which are intended to benefit employees – may be perceived as an investment in its people for its people. People may then reciprocate with positive attitudes and conduct toward the organisation, in this way engendering a positive exchange relationship (cf. e.g., Afsar, Al-Ghazali & Umrani, 2020; Alfesa, Shantz, Truss & Soane, 2013; Bankins, Griep & Hansen, 2020; Coetzee & Deas, 2021; Chooi, Ramayah & Doris, 2018; Coyle-Shapiro, Costa, Doden & Chang, 2019; Eldor & Vigoda-Gadot, 2017; Jiang, Takeuchi & Lepak, 2013; Jianga & Messersmith, 2018; Lee, Chiang, van Esch & Cai, 2018; Meng, Luo, Huang, Wen Ma & Xi, 2019; Mostafa, Bottomley, Gould-Williams, Abouarghoub & Lythreatis, 2019).

(43) See the references under Note (42). Refer also Bersin & Enderes (2021).

(44) Coyle-Shapiro, Costa, Doden & Chang (2019)

(45) Bankins, Griep & Hansen (2020)

(46) Bankins, Griep & Hansen (2020); Castellano (2013); Coyle-Shapiro, Costa, Doden & Chang (2019); Zupan, Mihelič & Aleksić (2018)

(47) After Baruch (2006), but expanded and adapted from Bankins, Griep & Hansen (2020), Coetzee (2021), and Veldsman & Van Aarde (2021). See also Note (40).

(48) Coetzee (2021); Coyle-Shapiro, Costa, Doden & Chang (2019); Rouseau (2000) (quoted by Zupan, Mihelič & Aleksić, 2018); Deas (2019); Veldsman (2011)

(49) Deas (2019); Zupan, Mihelič & Aleksić (2018)

(50) Beer (2009)

(51) Strategic Choices 1: People as a cost, and 2: People as an asset are based primarily on respectively Coercive and Bargaining Contracts.

(52) A High Commitment/High Performance Contract is fully grounded in personal, intrinsic motivation as explicated in self-determination theory (cf. Ryan & Deci, 2000). See Note (36) above.

(53) Based on, adapted and expanded from Beer (2009).

(54)   Albrecht, Bakker, Gruman, Macey, & Saks (2015); Bedarkar & Pandit (2014); Castellano (2013); Claus (2019); Forman (2017); Lawler (2017); Losey, Meisinger & Ulrich (2005); Ludike (2018); Roux (2021); Top Employers Institute (2021); Ulrich (1997); Ulrich & Brockbank (2005); Ulrich, Brockbank, Younger & Ulrich (2012); (2013); Silzer & Dowell (2010); Veldsman (2011; 2013a; 2018); World Economic Forum (2019)

(55)   In terms of Stratified Systems Theory, this is a People Function operating at a Requisite Complexity Level of Work 4: Strategy Translation and Implementation (Veldsman, 2014b; 2019a).

(56)   Lawler (2017); Park & Kim (2019); Veldsman (2013)

(57)   Veldsman (2014a)

(58)   Ulrich, Brockbank, Younger & Ulrich (2012); (2013); Veldsman (2014a)

(59)   Veldsman (2014a)

(60)   Top Employers Institute (2021)

(61)   Adapted from Veldsman (2013a), with some updates from Roux (2021) and Volini et al (2020)

(62)   Avedon & Scoles (2010); Lawler (2017); Nohria, Joyce & Robertson (2003); Roux (2021); Veldsman (2019a); World Economic Forum (2019)

(63)   PricewaterHouseCoopers (2002)

(64)   Veldsman (2014a). Roux (2021) makes the same point, but applies a different conceptual framework (see Figure 3.3).

(65)   The five Key People Imperatives (KPIs) are closely aligned to the Abilities-Motivation-Opportunity (AMO) Framework widely used within Strategic HRM, which is a variant on the Behavioural Perspective within Strategic HRM – how does an organisation invoke the desired conduct from employees? The AMO Framework states that employees' performance is a function of their abilities (A); motivation (M); and the opportunity (O) to perform. Abilities refer to employees' expertise, skills and experience (=KPI: People Capabilities – Can do); Motivation to exert effort at work (=KPI: People Energy – Will do); and Opportunities for employees to be involved in organisational decision-making, problem-solving, and information-sharing activities, as well as in teaming and collaboration with others (=KPI: People Autonomy – Allowed to do) (e.g., Albrecht, Bakker, Gruman, Macey, & Saks, 2015; Boon, Eckardt, Lepak & Boselie, 2018; Jiang, Takeuchi & Lepak, 2013; Jianga & Messersmith, 2018). The KPIs: People Legitimacy – Should do; and People Fulfilment – Want to do, are not covered in the AMO Framework, which I would submit it should.

(66)   The ethical challenges faced by organisations were stressed as a major focus area in the 2020 Deloitte Global Human Capital Survey. It is the shift from "Could we?" to "How should we?" The current predominant risk is around the people-technology interface in the context of 4IR. But there was also the question of ethical issues such as fair access to health care, rising inequality, and climate change (Volini et al, 2020). (Refer also to Excellence Question 11: Risk).

(67)   Veldsman (2014a)

(68)   Contained in the Organisational Effectiveness Equation is the People Effectiveness Equation: *People Effectiveness = f(People Capabilities x People Energy x People Legitimacy x People Autonomy x People Fulfilment).*

(69) The discussion of the Strategic People Triangle draws heavily on Veldsman (2014a), except where otherwise mentioned.

(70) Up to the present, most of the times organisations have not deliberately and systemically strategically considered the configuration of the World of Work for and in their organisations. The typical approach in the past has been ad hoc, piecemeal, and tactical-operational in response to contextual, competitive and delivery demands. E.g., the government imposed, working-from-home, response to the COVID-19 lock-downs worldwide. Or, in reactive response to the demands and opportunities offered by the Fourth Industrial Revolution.

(71) Drawing inter alia on Angus & Westbrook (2021); Bankins, Griep & Hansen (2020); Coetzee (2019); Dyer, C. (2021); Gratton, 2021; Kohl & Swartz (2019); Henry, Le Roux & Parry (2021); Ludike (2018); Malhotra (2021); Roux (2021); Spreitzer, Cameron & Garrett (2017); Top Employers Institute (2021); World Economic Forum (2019)

(72) A report by McKinsey (2021) demonstrates how COVID-19 has – perhaps for the first time – elevated the critical importance of work's physical dimension. They developed a novel way to quantify the proximity required in more than 800 occupations by grouping them into ten work arenas according to their proximity to co-workers and customers; the number of interpersonal interactions involved; and their on-site and indoor nature.

They found that jobs in work arenas with higher levels of physical proximity are likely to see greater transformation after the pandemic, triggering knock-on responses in other work areas such as business models. About 20% to 25% of the workforces in advanced economies could work from home between three and five days a week. This represents four to five times more remote work than before the pandemic. This could prompt a large change in the geography of work, as individuals and organisations shift out of large cities into suburbs and small cities.

(73) Called 'hybrid' work: the mixing of onsite and off site working by the same persons. From executives' point of view (Alexander et al, 2021a), the future of work will be more hybrid. Prior to the COVID-19 crisis, the majority of organisations required employees to spend most of their time on-site. But as the pandemic eases, the surveyed executives say that the hybrid model will become far more common. Going into the future, the majority of executives expect that – for all roles that are not essential to perform on-site – employees will be on-site between 21% to 80% of the time. Or, one to four days per week. Most C-suite executives report improvements in their organszations' productivity, customer satisfaction, employee engagement, and diversity/inclusion because of hybrid work.

Although nine out of ten of the organisations reported on envisioning a hybrid model going forward, most have at best a high-level plan for how to carry it out. Nearly a third of them say that their organisations lack alignment on a high-level vision among the top team. Although another third of organisations have a more detailed vision in place, only one in ten organisations have begun communicating and piloting that vision.

From an employee's perspective (Alexander et al, 2021b), more than half of employees surveyed would like their organisations to adopt more flexible hybrid virtual-working models. More than a quarter of those surveyed reported that they would consider switching employers if their organisation returned to full on-site work. However, 40% indicated that they have yet to hear about any hybrid working vision from their organisations, with another 28% saying that what they have heard remains vague. At organisations that are communicating vaguely, or not at all, about the future of post-pandemic work, nearly half of employees say it is causing them concern or anxiety which contributes to them feeling burnout. Nearly half of employees surveyed say they are feeling some symptoms of being burned out at work.

The Work Trend Index survey (Microsoft, 2021) – conducted amongst 31,092 full-time employed or self-employed workers across 31 markets between January 12, 2021 and January 25, 2021 – reported that 66% of leaders stated that their organisations are considering redesigning office work space for hybrid work. Seventy three percent of the surveyed employees want flexible work remote options to stay.

(74) Ghosal and Bartlett (1997) also stress the criticality of establishing a moral-values foundation to the organisation-people relationship.

(75) Veldsman (2019b). (Cf. also the Constitution of the Republic of South Africa (Act no. 108) (Chapter 2) (1996); Küng (2009); Mele (2016); Nkoma (2021); the United Nations Universal Declaration of Human Rights (2020))

(76) Theories X and Y – given below – as proposed by Douglas McGregor many years ago, resonate with the People Charter given in Table 4.6, although at a deeper, people beliefs level.

THEORY X	THEORY Y
• The average person has an inherent dislike of work, and will avoid it if at all possible. • Most people must be coerced, controlled, directed, or threatened with punishment to get them to put forth adequate effort towards the achievement of organisational objectives. • The average person prefers to be directed, wishes to avoid responsibility, has little ambition, and wants security above all.	• Work is as natural as play or rest. • People will exercise self-direction and self-control in pursuit of objectives they are committed to. • Commitment to objectives is a function of the recognition and rewards associated with their achievement. • The average person learns and seeks responsibility. • Imagination, creativity, and ingenuity are widely distributed among all people.

(77) Generating an upfront, intended, desired people experience as the normative reference point in architecting a fit-for-purpose organisational design, and formulating a corresponding People Value Proposition with corresponding personas for their organisation, was the approach used in a case study of their organisation, reported on by Veldsman and Van Aarde (2021). Given the moving beauty of the desired people experience – crafted participatively by the people of their organisation: their intended, desired people experience – reading like a free-rhyme poem, an ode to fulfilling work – is given here in full:

"This is it...

This is the space where I can bring my best

I am the master of my own fate
I show up, dressed in confidence and armed with skills
I know that I can't succeed without my tribe

It's not about what I can do, it's about what we can achieve
Together, we step out of our boxes and work towards a common goal
We use our collective talents and creativity to make a difference
We are open-minded, proud, and committed
To achieve our goals, we communicate, apply discipline, consistency, and swag
We share our successes and failures
And when we win, we own our bragging rights
Our foundation is transparency, trust, and integrity
Through collaboration, we can achieve greater things
Though sometimes we may trip over ourselves, we always get up
How we get up determines our success
We are convicted, but can be flexible
We are diverse, but unified
We know when to follow the rules and when to disrupt
We actively listen, but we can also speak our minds
Our purpose is to create value by putting our clients first
Welcome to the future."

(78) Berger & Berger (2017); Kohl & Swartz (2019); Schiemann (2017); Sorenson & Pearce (2017)

(79) Veldsman (2011)

(80) Schuler & Jackson (1987)

(81) The discussion draws primarily on Veldsman (2011) but also on Bussin (2018); Berger & Berger (2017); Claus (2019); Schiemann (2017); Veldsman & Pauw (2018); Whysall, Owtram & Brittain (2019)

(82) Coetzee (2019a); McLean & Company (2020); Veldsman, Benade & Rossouw (2019); Veldsman & Van Aarde (2021); Van der Walt & Lezar (2019)

(83) Webcast by Willis Towers Watson (Kibbe, Sejen & Yates, 2010)

(84) Willis Towers Watson (2016)

(85) Aon (2018) (quoted by McLean & Company, 2020)

(86) Coetzee (2019a); Veldsman, Benade & Rossouw (2019); Van der Walt & Lezar (2019)

(87) Parker and Veldsman (2010) found powerful internal and external branding essential in building and supporting a strong Organisational Identity, one of seven criteria of world class organisations.

(88) Cascio & Graham (2016); Graham & Cascio (2018); Lawler (2017); Ludike (2018); Schiemann (2017); Veldsman & Pauw (2018)

(89) Cascio & Graham (2016)

(90) Whysall, Owtram & Brittain (2019)

(91) Draws on Veldsman (2011)

(92) The Corporate Leadership Council (CLC) (2002) (quoted in Veldsman & Pauw, 2018) distinguishes the following PVP elements (CCARLLO elements are given in brackets after the CLC elements):

- Work environment (e.g., physical environment) (=Context).
- Affiliations (e.g., values, culture and quality of colleagues, managers, and leaders) (=Colleagues, Leadership).

- Work content (e.g., challenging work, work-life balance) (=Work Role).

- Benefits (including development and career growth (e.g., indirect financial reward) (=Work Arrangements).

- Remuneration (e.g., direct financial reward) (=Rewards and Recognition).

CCARLLO includes the additional element, Organisation, and separates Colleagues and Leadership.

(93) According to the Mercer Global Talent Trends 2020 Survey, 50% of employees want to work for organisations that offer equitable rewards; 49% for organisations that protect their health and financial well-being (also endorsed by Roux, 2021); 37% for organisations with strong values, mission and purpose (=Organisational Identity); and 36% for organisations that focus on social equity and environmental protection. Thriving employees – who believe they have a valuable job, a compelling career, and a meaningful purpose – are twice as likely to work for an organisation that effectively balances Emotional Intelligence (EQ) and Intellectual Intelligence (IQ) in its decision-making. Currently less than half of responding organisations get this balance right (Bravery et al, 2020).

In the Top Employers Institute HR Trends Report 2020, being seen as a socially responsible organisation was the top PVP element (Montet et al, 2020). In 2021, 92% of top employers believed well-being is a strategic imperative for their businesses, up from 83% one year ago (Top Employers Institute, 2021). Key themes in employer branding for 2021 were demonstrating a sense of purpose (89%); consistent policies ensuring a consistent employee experience (86%); making employees' voice audible (75%); and showcasing a diverse and inclusive culture (Ibid).

(94) Eldor and Vigoda-Gadot (2017) found a strong, positive relationship between work engagement and work centrality.

(95) Currently a vigorous debate is raging regarding whether to segment, for the purpose of differentiated PVPs, an organisation's employees: (i) by generations or (ii) by the centrality work has in the life of the employee (e.g., Bussin, 2018; Castellano, 2013; Deas, 2019; Lawler, 2017; Zupan, Mihelič & Aleksić, 2018). This is because, firstly, the boundaries between generations are vague, and sometimes even arbitrary. A Baby Boomer can act workwise like a Millennial, and vice versa. Secondly, work centrality is a more enduring, substantive characteristic of a working person moving along his/her work life cycle. My own preference is for segmentation by work centrality. The shrinking preferred choice of generations as a basis for having differentiated PVP is also supported by Bravery et al (2020); Gratton & Scott (2016) (quoted by Volini et al, 2020); Pollak (2019); Roux (2021) and Volini et al (2020). They all argue that fundamental work needs are the same across generations. However, the expression of those needs with the accompanying expectations may differ across generations.

(96) Ghosal & Bartlett (1997); Jain (1998) (quoted in Kirby 2005); Nel & Beudeker (2009); Parker & Veldsman (2010); Veldsman (2018)

(97) Afsar, Al-Ghazali & Umrani (2020); Bedarkar & Pandit (2014); Gupta (2017); Kjaer & Associates (2020); Lin & Liu (2019); Volini et al (2020)

(98) In the 2020 Deloitte Global Human Capital Trends Report, 75% of respondents stated that fostering a sense of belonging in the workforce was important to their organisation's success in the next 12–18 months. Ninety-three percent agreed that a sense of belonging drives organisational performance. However, only 13% said they were highly ready to address this trend (Volini et al, 2020). A sense of belonging was also stressed in the

Mercer Global Talent Trends 2020 Survey (Bravery et al, 2020).

(99)   Beer (2009); De Geus (1997); Hamel & Zanini (2020). In turn, a strong Identity allows for the building of powerful internal and external brands (Parker & Veldsman (2010).

(100)   Meyer (2017) distinguished three types of commitment: (i) affective, relationship/cause-bound commitment – 'a want to'; (ii) normative (or obligation) commitment – 'an ought to'; and (iii) cost (or continuance) commitment – 'need to avoid' (negative) consequences, like loss of pay (see also Castellano, 2013; Chooi, Ramayah & Doris, 2018). Personally, I would suggest a fourth type: (iv) enforced commitment – 'forced to stay' through coercion. Committed ownership refers to affective-normative commitment.

(101)   Veldsman & Veldsman (2020b)

(102)   In the 2020 Deloitte Global Human Capital Trends Report, 44% of respondents reported that feeling aligned to the organisation's purpose, mission, and values (=Organisational Identity), AND being valued for their individual contributions, was the biggest driver of belonging at work (Volini et al, 2020). According to a Gallup survey, worldwide only 5% of organisational members understand their organisation's strategy, implying that they do not know why they work for their organisations (quoted in SA Board of People Practices, 2018).

(103)   Malhotra (2021)

(104)   Bedarkar & Pandit (2014); Meyer (2017); Wikipedia (2020c)

(105)   Reported by Watson Wyatt (quoted in Wikipedia, 2020c)

(106)   2019 BetterUp study (quoted by Volini et al, 2020)

Chapter 5: Endnotes

(1)   Beer (2009); Berger & Berger (2017)

(2)   This section draws heavily on Veldsman (2019a), except where otherwise quoted.

(3)   From 2016 to the present, 'organisation of the future' (read 'Organisational Design') has been the most important focus of Deloitte's annual Global Human Capital Trends survey amongst executives. The rated unreadiness of organisations to redesign themselves varied from 14% in 2016, making a quantum jump to 46% in 2018 (Agarwal et la, 2018; Bersin et al, 2016; Bersin et al, 2017).

(4)   Veldsman (2019a)

(5)   If People Professionals of an organisation are to fulfill their strategic partnership role, the People Function also needs a congruent, fit-for-purpose organisational design (including the People or Organisational Effectiveness Unit of the organisation). See in this regard Lawler (2017); Roux (2021) and Veldsman (2014b; 2019a: Chapter 9).

(6)   Nel & Beudeker (2009)

(7)   The virtuous (i.e., value-referenced) optimal integration of people and technology requires intensive design considerations, especially in the context of the Fourth Industrial Revolution. For such a discussion see Veldsman (2019a: Chapter 5, p. 94 onwards), as well as Bravery et al (2020), Vaiman et al (2021), Volini et al (2020) and World Economic Forum (2019). A greater use of (Fourth Industrial Revolution) technology is predicated given the rise of hybrid working because of the consequential, lasting impact of COVID-19 (McKinsey Global Institute, 2021).

(8)   The People Function must take a lead role in establishing a virtuous, optimal people-technology integration (World Economic Forum, 2019). However, in a recent study on

the future of the CHRO, it was found that only 36% of CHROs are prepared to consider how technology is changing work in the future. Furthermore, only 26% said they have the technical acumen to evaluate new technology (Willis Towers Watson, 2019) (quoted in the World Economic Forum, 2019).

(9)   I would argue that the virtuous, optimal integration of people and technology must be based on the basic people requirements of work, as illustrated in the diagram below (Veldsman, 2019a: Chapter 5, p. 94 onwards).

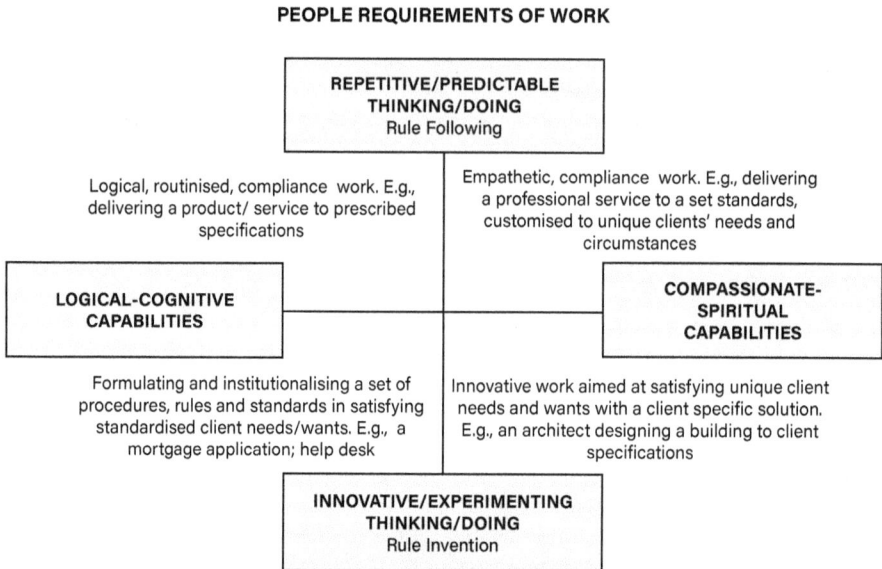

PEOPLE REQUIREMENTS OF WORK

REPETITIVE/PREDICTABLE
THINKING/DOING
Rule Following

Logical, routinised, compliance work. E.g., delivering a product/ service to prescribed specifications

Empathetic, compliance work. E.g., delivering a professional service to a set standards, customised to unique clients' needs and circumstances

LOGICAL-COGNITIVE
CAPABILITIES

COMPASSIONATE-
SPIRITUAL
CAPABILITIES

Formulating and institutionalising a set of procedures, rules and standards in satisfying standardised client needs/wants. E.g., a mortgage application; help desk

Innovative work aimed at satisfying unique client needs and wants with a client specific solution. E.g., an architect designing a building to client specifications

INNOVATIVE/EXPERIMENTING
THINKING/DOING
Rule Invention

Based on the above basic people requirements, a Technology Enablement Model can be crafted, aimed at guiding the virtuous, optimised People-Technology integration (Veldsman, Ibid).

TECHNOLOGY ENABLEMENT MODEL: OPTIMISED PEOPLE-TECHNOLOGY INTEGRATION

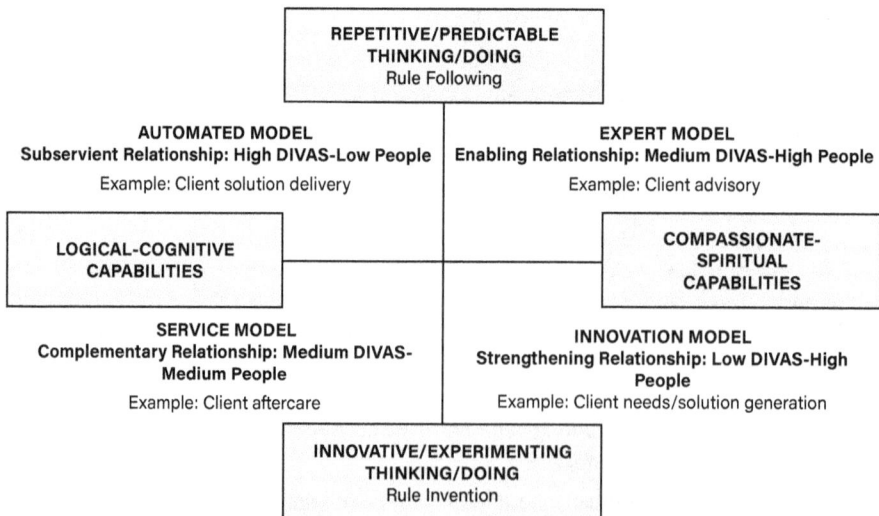

REPETITIVE/PREDICTABLE
THINKING/DOING
Rule Following

AUTOMATED MODEL
Subservient Relationship: High DIVAS-Low People
Example: Client solution delivery

EXPERT MODEL
Enabling Relationship: Medium DIVAS-High People
Example: Client advisory

LOGICAL-COGNITIVE
CAPABILITIES

COMPASSIONATE-
SPIRITUAL
CAPABILITIES

SERVICE MODEL
Complementary Relationship: Medium DIVAS-Medium People
Example: Client aftercare

INNOVATION MODEL
Strengthening Relationship: Low DIVAS-High People
Example: Client needs/solution generation

INNOVATIVE/EXPERIMENTING
THINKING/DOING
Rule Invention

(10) In a report entitled *Work 2035* (Citrix, 2020), alternative visions of the future of work in 2035, and how people and technology will work together to create value, are explored. The report is based on a two-part research study combining alternative futures scenario planning and robust opinion research amongst business leaders and employees across the US and Europe. Four 2035 scenarios are proposed, which are given in the table below.

Work in 2035: Four Scenarios

	DISTRIBUTED WORK (Organisations) *Work gets done in collaboration across a number of boutique-like organisations in tandem, connected digitally*		
AUGMENTED WORKER *Worker and Technology complement each other*	**FREELANCE FRONTIERS**[1] Organisations have few permanent employees, rather drawing on a large pool of on-demand workers enhanced with technology. Increasingly the highest value-adding work is performed by 'swarms' of specialist professionals. Sophisticated technology tools enable efficient and effective remote working and collaboration in the same setting, using virtual reality platforms.	**PLATFORM PLUGINS**[3] Technology has leveled the playing field for smaller organisations, giving them the reach and scale of much bigger rivals. AI, machine learning, and smart data tools have become so powerful and reliable that they have enabled organisations to drastically downsize their permanent human workforce. The people still needed are specialists who help to build, tweak, check and manage technology, usually working on a freelance basis.	**REPLACED WORKER** *Technology replaces workers*
	POWERED PRODUCTIVES[2] Organisations benefit from boosted productivity levels due to the successful integration of humans and technology. Through real time, in time data-turned-into-intelligence, leaders have an ongoing, ever-evolving picture of their workplace and workforce. Organisations with the most sophisticated human-technology integration, and the most adaptable workers perform best which can create monopolies in some sectors. Workers enjoy more meaningful work. Logically integrated technology improves their performance. However, workers must decide how they feel about being monitored and controlled continuously by their employer.	**AUTOMATED CORPORATIONS** The biggest organisations that control the entire work process have the greatest scope for finding new efficiencies and can adopt new technologies faster, which gives them an edge over their rivals. Permanent employment prevails. Human talent has become more important, even though human labor has become more replaceable. But as more and more roles are automated, roles shift quickly, and workers need to keep retraining to stay relevant.	
	CENTRALISED WORK (Organisations) *Work gets done in a single organisation*		

Notes: (1) COVID-19 impact (2) Leaders' preferred vision (3) Workers' preferred vision

In the report, it is postulated that the organisations that will thrive in the future will be those whose leaders align their positive future vision with the needs and expectations of workers, taking workers with them on the road into the future of work, and enabling a transformational human-technology partnership.

(11) Veldsman (2018)

(12) Adapted and expanded from Hinrichs (2013)

(13) Veldsman (2019a). See also Castellano (2013); Joyce (2005); Ghosal & Bartlett (1997); Nohria, Joyce & Robertson (2003); Kjaer & Associates (2020); Kohl & Swartz (2019); Ludike (2018); Roux (2021); Parker & Veldsman (2010); Pulakos, Schneider & Kantrowitz (2019); Volini et al (2020) and World Economic Forum (2019)

(14) Mayer (2019); Habraken, Bondarouk & Hoffman (2019); Hamel & Zanini (2020) and Veldsman (2019a) place collaboration central to 21st century workspaces and the organisation of the future.

(15) Pfeffer (2018); Roux (2021); World Economic Forum (2019)

(16) According to the Mercer Global Talent Trends 2020 Survey, 98% of executives plan to design their organisations into a more matrixed organisational shape (=read network organisation) (Bravery et al, 2020). In the 2019 Deloitte Global Human Capital Trends Report, 65% of responding organisations viewed the shift from functional hierarchies to team-centric and network-based organisational models as important or very important. Fifty-three percent of the organisations that were already operating in terms of teams indicated that the transition had resulted in a significant improvement in performance (Volini et al, 2020).

(17) The pressing need to move from a Command-and-Control Organisational Shape (=bureaucratic organisation) to a High Network/High Engagement/High Responsibility Organisational Shape, i.e., a people-centric organisation called a Humanocracy, and how to affect such a move, is the central, passionate plea and theme of Hamel and Zanini's (2020) recent book. Humanocracy is made up of many of the features listed for a High Network/High Engagement/ High Responsibility Organisational Shape in Figure 5.1.

(18) The specific challenges of global/globalising and/or virtual organisations which impose their own demands on a fit-for-purpose design, and consequently on People Excellence, are not discussed here. See Veldsman (2019a) in this regard.

(19) Also called "structural ambidexterity" (see Fiset & Dostaler, 2013). Galbraith (2014) talks about the re-configurable organisation.

(20) Birkinshaw & Ridderstråle (2017); Bustinzaa, Vendrell-Herrerob, Perez-Arosteguia & Parry (2019); Christos (2017); Fiset & Dostaler (2013); Galbraith (2014); Hamel & Zanini (2020); Keller & Meaney (2017); Liu, Wang & Chen (2019); Mullins (2018); Nonaka, Kodama, Hirose & Kohlbacker (2014); Silva & Guerrini (2018); Stokes, Smith, Wall, Moore, Rowland, Ward & Cronshaw (2019); Worley & Lawler (2010)

(21) Boynton & Victor (1991)

(22) Keller & Meaney (2017)

(23) In the Mercer Global Talent Trends 2020 Survey, 58% of responding organisations are redesigning themselves to become more people-centric (Bravery et al, 2020). See also Hamel & Zanini (2020); Roux (2021) and Note (17).

(24) Parker, Rabolele & Joubert (2020)

(25) Cf. Afsar, Al-Ghazali & Umrani (2020); Bailey, Madden Alfes, Shantz & Soane (2017); Berg, Dutton & Wrzesniewski (2013); Bersin & Enderes (2021); Castellano (2013); Champion,

Mumford, Morgeson & Nahrgang (2005); Dik, Byrne & Steger (2013); Hackman & Oldham (1976); (1980); Han, Sung & Suh, 2021; Hansen (2013); Hirschi (2018); Johns (2010); Kahn & Fellows (2013); Kjaer & Associates (2020) Lysova, Blake, Dik, Duff & Steger (2019); Malhotra (2021); Morgeson & Campion (2003); Morgeson & Humphrey (2008); Morgeson et al (2010); Morgeson & Humphrey (2006); Mullins (2018); Parker, Wall & Cordery (2001); Ryde & Sofianos (2014); Volini et al (2020); Yeoman & O'Hara (2017); Yeoman & O'Hara (2017)

(26) According to Achor, Reece, Rosen Kellerman & Robichaux (2018), nine out of ten people are willing to earn less money in doing more meaningful work (quoted by Petriglieri, 2020).

(27) Bailey, Madden Alfes, Shantz & Soane (2017); Lysova, Blake, Dik, Duff & Steger (2019)

(28) Afsar, Al-Ghazali & Umrani (2020); Beadle & Knight (2012); Lysova, Blake, Dik, Duff & Steger (2019); Ryde & Sofianos (2014)

(29) Michaelson (2021); Pratt, Pradies & Lepisto (2013)

(30) Pratt, Pradies & Lepisto (2013); Rahmadani, Schaufeli, Ivanova & Osin (2019)

(31) Afsar, Al-Ghazali & Umrani (2020); Han, Sung & Suh (2021)

(32) Bronkhorst (2012); Castellano (2013); Joyce (2005); Nohria, Joyce & Robertson (2003); Veldsman (2019a); Veldsman & Roodt (2002)

(33) Veldsman (2019a)

(34) Davis-Pecoud & Moolman (2015)

(35) Sheppard et al (2018)

(36) The discussion of Core Organisational and People Capabilities fits snugly in the Strategic Resource-Based View of the organisation in strategic management. As has been indicated before, Strategic Resources – representing core organisational capabilities – is an investment by an organisation that is valuable, rare, and inimitable, resulting in superior organisational/financial performance. They give the organisation a competitive edge (Bustinzaa, Vendrell-Herrerob, Perez-Arosteguia & Parry, 2019; Collings, Mellahi & Cascio, 2019; Crook, Todd, Combs, Woehr & Ketchen, 2011; Jiang, Takeuchi & Lepak, 2013; Ungerer, Pretorius & Herholdt, 2002). Dynamic Capability Theory refers to the organisation's capability to purposefully and strategically adapt and reconfigure the organisation's resource base such that it cannot easily be duplicated or substituted, in this way gaining an unassailable competitive edge (Arokodare, Asikhia & Makinde, 2019; Collings, Mellahi & Cascio, 2019; Crook, Todd, Combs, Woehr & Ketchen, 2011).

The equivalent views of the Strategic Resource-Based View regarding people are: (i) Strategic HRM with its emphasis on Human Capital Theory (Cf. Boon, Eckardt, Lepak & Boselie, 2018; Collings, Mellahi & Cascio, 2019; Collins, 2021; Crook, Todd, Combs, Woehr & Ketchen, 2011; Jianga & Messersmith, 2018; Jiang, Takeuchi & Lepak, 2013; Shin & Konrad, 2014; Whysall, Owtram & Brittain, 2019); and (ii) Strategic Talent Management (Cf. Anlesinya, Dartey-Baah & Amponsah-Tawiah, 2019; Berger & Berger, 2017; Gallardo-Gallardo, Thunnissen & Scullion, 2020; Nel & Beudeker, 2009; Veldsman, 2014).

Strategic HRM focuses on the potential value of the sum total of people capabilities as capital of the organisation, e.g., the sum total of the personal attributes, knowledge/expertise/skills, leadership, personal/interpersonal/organisational abilities, values and attitudes lodged in the people of the organisation. Strategic Talent Management deals with the effective management of the talent pipeline through the people value chain of attract-perform-grow-retain.

(37)   E.g., Veldsman & Roodt (2002); Veldsman & Van Aarde (2021)

(38)   Morley (2007)

(39)   Burke (2007)

(40)   Collins (2021)

(41)   Eisenhardt & Martin (2000); Prahalad & Hamel (1990); Zook with Allen (2001) (quoted in Kirby 2005)

(42)   Ulrich and Ulrich (2017) found that Organisational Capabilities are four times more important in predicting organisational performance than individual talent. Building winning Organisational Capabilities may therefore be more important than winning the talent war.

(43)   Roux (2021); Veldsman (2011); Veldsman & Van Aarde (2021); Vaiman et al (2021)

(44)   Crook, Todd, Combs, Woehr & Ketchen (2011)

(45)   See Veldsman (2011) for a detailed discussion on strategic talent management which deals with most of the elements contained in Figure 5.2.

(46)   In a global survey by Deloitte (2017), it was found that only 9% of companies believed that they had a good understanding of which talent dimensions drive performance in their organisations. It was anticipated that this situation is only likely to get worse, given the changing world (Volini et al, 2020). According to the Mercer Global Talent Trends 2020 Survey, two out of every five responding People Leaders did not know what skills they had in their workforce. Only one in three were quantifying the skills gap against organisational goals, which 50% said was a challenge (Bravery et al, 2020).

(47)   Bussin (n.d.)

(48)   Verwey (2018)

(49)   Cf. Avedon & Scoles (2010); Boon, Eckardt, Lepak & Boselie (2018); Bussin (2018); Becker & Huselid (2010); Collings, Mellahi & Cascio (2019); Lawler (2017); Schiemann (2017). In identifying strategically pivotal Roles in the organisation, they can be classified into three categories (not hierarchically based) (Becker & Huselid, 2010):

- *A Work Roles.* Disproportionate importance to success of organisation now and in future. High value-add. High variability in incumbent performance.

- *B Work Roles.* Direct support to A Work Roles. Maintenance of existing value-add. Potentially strategic. Medium variability in incumbent performance.

- *C Work Roles.* Ancillary Work Roles which are of little strategic importance. Low variability in incumbent performance.

Vaiman et al (2021) raise the caveat that roles that have been critical in the past may be overtaken by technology, forcing organisations to re-evaluate their talent strategies.

(50)   Montet et al (2020); Whysall, Owtram & Brittain (2019)

(51)   More than 75% of CEOs globally highlighted the lack of available people capabilities as a primary threat to their organisations' growth prospects (PwC, 2017). A recent study of CEOs in the United States identified their top three priorities as talent; operating in a global marketplace; and regulation/legislation (Groysberg & Connolly, 2015) (quoted by Collings, Mellahi & Cascio, 2019).

(52)   According to the Mercer Global Talent Trends 2020 Survey, 65% of responding People Leaders stated that even if they raised salaries, they would not be able to attract the

right talent due to talent shortages. Seventy-six percent of them aimed to build their own talent (Bravery et al, 2020).

(53)   Lawler (2017); Roux (2021); Veldsman (2011)

(54)   Berger & Berger (2017); Claus (2019); Collins (2001); Veldsman (2011)

(55)   Park and Kim (2019) referred to leadership's vision of talent, i.e., the ability to see the current situation of selecting, hiring, retaining, and developing talented people; caring for and respecting them; and then envisioning the right future talent. The leader's vision of talent plays a critical role in: (i) transforming the leader's ideal image of talent into reality; and (ii) identifying the people who will be committed over the long-term.

(56)   Collings, Mellahi & Cascio (2019)

(57)   Cascio and Aguinis' (2019) highly regarded text, now in its 8th edition, is an excellent example of the depth and breadth of the complexity – from an applied psychological perspective – that must be covered with respect to the building and maintenance of people capabilities. Intriguing to note, however, is that in the subject index of this comprehensive text, and hence in the content of the book itself, the terms 'people excellence/effectiveness' or 'organisational effectiveness' do not appear at all.

(58)   World Economic Forum (2019)

(59)   Going into the future, Kjaer and Associates (2020) see building a strong Organisational Culture as the top priority.

(60)   Arokodare, Asikhia & Makinde (2019); Cameron & Quinn (2006); Castellano (2013); Chapman Reeves & Chaplin (2018); Ehrhart, Schneider & Macey (2014); Elsbach & Stigliani (2018); Fitz-Enz (1997); Graham, Harvey, Popadak & Rajgopal (2017); Harrison & Bazzy (2017); Hicklenton, Hine & Loi (2019); Lee, Chiang, van Esch & Cai (2018); Ludike (2018); Schein (2013); Schneider, González-Romá, Ostroff & West (2017); Park & Kim (2019); Ulrich & Ulrich (2017); Veldsman (2002a); Volini et al (2020); Wikipedia (2020a)

(61)   Avedon & Scoles (2010); Chong, Shang Richards & Zhu (2018); Ehrhart, Schneider & Macey (2014); Fitz-Enz (1997); Gao (2017); Graham, Harvey, Popadak & Rajgopal (2017); Schein (1990); (2010)

(62)   Roux (2021); Schiemann (2017)

(63)   Ahmetoglu, Akhtar, Tsivrikos & Chamorro-Premuzic (2018); Castellano (2013); Chapman Reeves & Chaplin (2018); Ehrhart, Schneider & Macey (2014); Fitz-Enz (1997); Jain & D'lima (2017); Park & Kim (2019); Schein (1990); (2010); Veldsman & Pauw (2018); Wikipedia (2020a)

(64)   Arokodare, Asikhia & Makinde (2019); Bravery, Baldwin, Ketenci, Cernigol, Cline, De Malo, Gutowski, Hudson, Ladd, Roberts & Silva (2020); Schneider, González-Romá, Ostroff & West (2017)

(65)   Arokodare, Asikhia & Makinde (2019); Avedon & Scoles (2010); Byrne, Dwyer & Doyle (2018); Joyce (2005); Nohria, Joyce & Robertson (2003); Ritala, Vanhala, & Järveläinen (2020); Wikipedia (2020a)

(66)   Ulrich and Ulrich (2017) regarded Organisational Culture as a Core Organisational Capability.

(67)   Harrison & Bazzy (2017)

(68)   Veldsman (2019a)

(69)   E.g., Adisa, Mordi & Osabutey (2017) found that a non-caring, working-at-all-cost, Organisational Culture – demanded by supervisors and expected by peers – nullified

the formally espoused, people practice of work-life balance for medical doctors in six Nigerian medical facilities. The external socio-cultural context of the organisation also shaped the organisation's culture, which in turn determined what people practices could be/were adopted as acceptable by the organisations (Rodriguez & Stewart, 2017). Cf. also Park & Kim (2019).

(70)   Kotter & Heskett (1992)

(71)   A recent survey of nearly 1,900 CEOs and CFOs revealed that over half of senior executives place the company culture as one of the top-three predictors of firm value. Although more than 92% stated that improving Organisational Culture would increase their firm's value, only 16% of these executives believed that their firm's culture was where it needed to be (Graham, Harvey, Popadak, & Rajgopal, 2017).

(72)   Park & Kim (2019); Wikipedia (2020a); Schneider, González-Romá, Ostroff & West (2017); Wollard & Shuck (2011)

(73)   Corritore, Goldberg & Srivastava (2020); Kotter & Heskett (1992)

(74)   Ehrhart, Schneider & Macey (2014); Graham, Harvey, Popadak & Rajgopal (2017); Lee, Chiang, van Esch & Cai (2018); Veldsman (2002a); Wikipedia (2020a)

(75)   Nahar & Nigah (2018)

(76)   Canning, Murphy, Emerson, Chatman, Dweck & Kray (2020)

(77)   Denison's Organisational Culture model (Denison et al., 2004; Fey & Denison, 2003) (quoted by Lee, Chiang, van Esch & Cai, 2018) is based on the two culture dimensions of external adaption and internal integration originally proposed by Schein (1990); (2010).

(78)   Lee, Chiang, van Esch & Cai (2018)

(79)   Adapted from Schein (1990); (2010); (2017). See also Byrne, Dwyer & Doyle (2018).

(80)   Cf. Booysen (2016)

(81)   Cf. Fitz-Enz (1997); Schein (1990); (2010); (2017); Veldsman (2002a)

(82)   In a similar vein is the Cultural Web proposed by Sun (2008) (quoted by Morris, 2020). Within the Cultural Web, Organisational Culture is explicated as an organic, systemic, dynamic whole made up of the following reciprocally influencing elements: paradigms, routines, rituals, stories, symbols, control systems, power structures, and organisational structures.

(83)   Corritore, Goldberg and Srivastava (2020) propagated the linguistic diagnosis of organisations' e-mails and social media traffic, including on Twitter, WhatsApp and Instagram, to determine an organisation's actual, active Organisational Culture.

(84)   Cf. Schein (1990); (2010); (2017); Veldsman (2002a)

(85)   Corritore, Goldberg and Srivastava (2020) stress the importance of maintaining a balance between people-cultural fit and diversity. An overemphasis on the former to the detriment of the latter can stifle creativity and innovation.

(86)   Adapted and extended in terms of underlying core qualities from Harrison (1972). Handy (1976) made this Organisational Culture typology, as adapted by him, well known.

(87)   Another well accepted Organisational Culture typology is the Competing Values Framework (Cameron & Quinn, 2006). In this typology four types of cultures are distinguished: *Hierarchy* – Controlling (Stability/Control; Internal Focus/Integration); *Market* – Competing (Stability/Control; External Focus/Differentiation); *Clan* – Collaborative (Internal Focus/ Integration; Flexibility/Discretion); and *Adhocracy* – Creative (Flexibility/Discretion;

External Focus/Differentiation). Kleiner (2013) distinguishes the same types, except for Adhocracy which he calls Network.

(88) A Caring (or Empathic) Organisational Culture was found to be stressed by responding organisations in respectively the 2020 Deloitte Global Human Capital Survey (Volini et al, 2020), the Mercer Global Talent Trends 2020 Survey (Bravery et al, 2020), and the 2021 Top Employers Institute Survey (Top Employers Institute, 2021). Looking forward, Kjaer & Associates (2020), Roux (2021), Bersin & Enderes (2021), the World Economic Forum (2019) and Stallard (2021) also stress an inclusive/caring/connected Organisational Culture.

(89) Bourke (2016) (quoted in the 2020 Deloitte Global Human Capital Survey; Volini et al (2020); and World Economic Forum (2019)).

(90) Ritala, Vanhala & Järveläinen (2020)

(91) Bravery et al (2020); World Economic Forum (2019)

(92) A caring Organisational Culture is also propagated under different terms such as a learning culture (e.g., Beer, 2009; Kohl & Swartz, 2019; and World Economic Forum (2019)), emotional capital (Veldsman, Benade & Rossouw, 2019), and social support (Habraken, Bondarouk & Hoffman, 2019).

(93) Posthuma, Campion, Masimova and Campion (2013) propose a taxonomy of a high performance (HP) work practices, consisting of HR Principles, Policies, Practices and Competencies/Products:

- HR principles: the general philosophy that guides the design of the HR system (=People Charter within the People Excellence Star).

- Policy: statements that describe how the organisation will direct efforts toward enhancing organisational performance (=People Practices within the People Excellence Star).

- Practice: the specific methods and procedures that the organisation adopts to implement the organisation's Principles and Policies (=People Tools within the People Excellence Star).

- Product: the people competencies that the organisational and HR architectures create for the organisation (=Desired People Profile within the People Excellence Star).

Analoguous to Stratified Sytems Theory (=Level of Works (LOW)) (Jaques, 2006), the above authors stacked these elements hierarchically in parallel to the organisational architecture with which it must be aligned: HR Principles (=LOW5); Policy (=LOW4); Practice (=LOW3).

(94) People Practices are typically called HR Systems in the Strategic HRM literature. They are dealt with under the Behavioural Perspective of Strategic HRM: how does an organisation strategically invoke the desired attitudes and conduct from employees to attain outstanding organisational performance and success (cf. Schuler & Jackson, 1987)?

(95) Huselid & Becker (1997); Liao, Yi & Jiang (2021); Van Beurden, Van De Voorde & Van Veldhoven (2021)

(96) Albrecht, Bakker, Gruman, Macey & Saks (2015); Castellano (2013); Veldsman, Benade & Rossouw (2019). Veldsman, Benade and Rossouw (2019) refer to an enabling environment which forms part of the organisation's emotional capital.

(97) Bouaziz and Hachicha (2018) and Han, Kang, Oh, Kehoe and Lepak (2019) refer to the horizontal and vertical fit of a bundle of People Practices. Horizontal fit relates to the

internal coherence of a bundle of People Practices in mutually supporting each other. Vertical fit refers to the linking of People Practices to the Strategic People Intent of the organisation, and by implication its overall strategy. Vertical fit also applies to multi-national/global organisations in which People Practices must be aligned across different geographically dispersed, organisational unit levels (Collings, Mellahi & Cascio, 2019).

(98) Albrecht, Bakker, Gruman, Macey, & Saks (2015); Alfesa, Shantz, Truss & Soane (2013); Bardoel, Pettit, Cieri & McMillan (2014); Boon, Eckardt, Lepak & Boselie (2018); Boxall & Macky (2009); Bustinzaa, Vendrell-Herrerob, Perez-Arosteguia & Parry (2019); Ehrnrooth et al (2021); Gahlawat & Kundu (2019); Guthrie, Spell & Nyamori (2002); Han, Kang, Oh, Kehoe & Lepak (2019); Jiang, Takeuchi & Lepak (2013); Jianga & Messersmith (2018); Lin & Liu (2019); Messersmith, Patel, Lepak & Gould-Williams (2011); Posthuma, Campion, Masimova & Campion (2013); Woznyj, Heggestad, Kennerly & Yap (2019)

(99) E.g., Alfesa, Shantz, Truss & Soane (2013); Boon, Eckardt, Lepak & Boselie (2018); Bos-Nehles & Veenendaal (2019); Gahlawat & Kundu (2019); Hai, Wu, Park, Li, Chang, & Tang (2020); Jiang, Takeuchi & Lepak (2013); Jing, Avery & Bergsteiner (2020); Lin & Liu (2019); Makhathini & Van Dyk (2018); Posthuma, Campion, Masimova & Campion (2013); Raza & Nadeem (2018); Saks (2017); Schneider, González-Romá, Ostroff & West (2017); Sethibe (2018); Veldsman, Benade & Rossouw (2019); Wang, Kim, Rafferty & Sanders (2020); Wikipedia (2020c)

(100) Albrecht, Bakker, Gruman, Macey, & Saks (2015); Gahlawat & Kundu (2019)

(101) Castellano (2013); Guthrie, Spell & Nyamori (2002); Huselid & Becker (1997)

(102) Collings, Mellahi & Cascio (2019); Han, Kang, Oh, Kehoe & Lepak (2019); Huselid & Becker (1997). Collings, Mellahi and Cascio (2019) and Han, Kang, Oh, Kehoe and Lepak (2019) call this the vertical fit of a bundle of People Practices.

(103) Collings, Mellahi & Cascio (2019); Schuler & Jackson (1987). See also Posthuma, Campion, Masimova & Campion (2013)

(104) Boon, Eckardt, Lepak & Boselie (2018); Guthrie, Spell & Nyamori (2002); Huselid & Becker (1997); Wang, Kim, Rafferty & Sanders (2020)

(105) Boon, Eckardt, Lepak & Boselie (2018); Claus (2019)

(106) Boon, Eckardt, Lepak & Boselie (2018); Collings, Mellahi & Cascio (2019); Gahlawat & Kundu (2019); Jianga & Messersmith (2018); Lin & Liu (2019); Lucas, Ardichvili, de Castro Casa Nova, Bittencourt & Carpenedo (2018); Rodriguez & Stewart (2017); Wang, Kim, Rafferty & Sanders (2020)

(107) For example, in a study by Lucas, Ardichvili, de Castro Casa Nova, Bittencourt & Carpenedo (2018) of the Training and Development (TD) practices in a large Brazilian steel company, it was found that the implementation of a Western-based TD system based on meritocratic principles did not fully align with a nationally-derived, Organisational Culture characterised by high power distance, paternalism, collectivism, and an emphasis on personal relationships over merit.

(108) The terms 'Enable', 'Energise' and 'Empower' are adaptions of the Abilities-Motivation-Opportunity (AMO) Framework widely used in Strategic HRM which was discussed under Note (64), Chapter 4.

(109) Another well known typology of High Commitment/High Involvement People Practices is that of Lawler (1986), who differentiates Practices into those related to power (=awarding autonomy); information (=being informed); knowledge (=skills, expertise); and rewards (=recognition/rewards for effort and contribution). See also Konrad (2006)

(110) Hai, Wu, Park, Li, Chang, & Tang (2020)

(111) Ehrnrooth et al (2021) found that High Commitment/High Involvement People Practices moderate the positive relationship between Transformational leadership and people's attitudes regarding organisational identification, self-efficacy, engagement, and turnover intention. However, all these positive relationships of transformational leadership with these attitudes are significantly weakened when the effect of High Commitment/High Involvement People Practices is accounted for. Independent of High Commitment/High Involvement People Practices, Transformational leadership is directly related to only one of these attitudes, namely engagement. When High Commitment/High Involvement People Practices was accounted for, the independent relationship between leadership and engagement was still significant but reduced by about 50%. On the other hand, independent of Transformational leadership, High Commitment/High Involvement People Practices is strongly related to all four attitudes. These relationships are only marginally reduced when the effect of transformational leadership is accounted for.

(112) Various terms are used in the literature, such as high-commitment, high-performance, high-involvement work systems (HPWS), work practices, or HR practices (Cf. Ehrnrooth et al, 2021; Gahlawat & Kundu, 2019; Hai, Wu, Park, Li, Chang, & Tang, 2020; Jiang, Takeuchi & Lepak, 2013; Lin & Liu, 2019; Posthuma, Campion, Masimova & Campion, 2013; Shin & Konrad, 2014), as well as all of the references given under Note (33).

My own preference is for High Commitment/High Involvement. 'High Commitment', because People Practices must get organisational members to own Practices as total persons. 'High Involvement', because Practices must 'draw' (or 'pull') organisational members to be fully engaged with the organisation's identity and work.

(113) Al-Ayed (2019); Albrecht, Bakker, Gruman, Macey, & Saks (2015); Bersin & Enderes (2021); Boxall & Macky (2009); Bussin (2018); Bustinzaa, Vendrell-Herrerob, Perez-Arosteguia & Parry (2019); Cappelli & Tavis (2018); Castellano (2013); Collings, Mellahi & Cascio (2019); Gahlawat & Kundu (2019); Gill (2018); Konrad (2006); Laloux (2014); Lawler (1986); Lawler, Mohrman & Ledford (1995); Lee & Edmondson (2017); Lin & Liu (2019); Ludike (2018); Martens (2019); Montet et al (2020); Morley (2007); Mostafa, Bottomley, Gould-Williams, Abouarghoub & Lythreatis (2019); Parker & Veldsman (2010); Pfeffer (1998); Shin & Konrad (2014); Thoren (2017); Veldsman (2018); Walton & Hackman (1986); Wood & de Menezesb (2011); Worley & Lawler (2010)

(114) World Economic Forum (2019). See also Jedynak, Czakon, Kuzniarska & Mania (2021)

(115) Bersin & Enderes (2021); Garret-Cox (2016); Sutcliffe & Allgrove (2018); Top Employers Institute (2021)

(116) Gahlawat & Kundu (2019)

(117) Alfesa, Shantz, Truss & Soane (2013); Boxall & Macky (2009); Gahlawat & Kundu (2019); Hai, Wu, Park, Li, Chang, & Tang (2020); Jiang, Takeuchi & Lepak (2013); Seligman & Csikszentmihayi (2000); Van Beurden, Van De Voorde & Van Veldhoven (2021); Veld, Paauwe & Boselie (2010); Wang, Kim, Rafferty & Sanders (2020)

(118) SA Board of People Practices (2018)

(119) Kaur & Kaur (2021)

(120) Jianga & Messersmith (2018); Pfeffer (1998). See also Alrecht, Bakker, Gruman, Macey & Saks (2015); Posthuma, Campion, Masimova & Campion (2013)

(121) Huselid & Becker (1997)

(122) Fitz-Enz (1997)

(123) It is intriguing to note that in the World Economic Forum's 2020 Global Risk Report, infectious diseases/pandemics is not listed amongst the top 10 most likely 2020 risks and only number 10 in terms of a 2020 impact as a risk (Venter, 2020). The year 2020 and beyond have shown unequivocally the unimaginable severity of this misjudgement regarding COVID-19, which is a pre-eminent example of a Black Swan.

(124) 2009 Ernst and Young Business Risk Report; Meyer & Abbott (2017); Whysall, Owtram & Brittain (2019)

(125) IODSA (2012)

(126) Deloitte (2013) (quoted by Meyer & Abbott (2017)

(127) The 2020 Deloitte Global Human Capital report found that the ethical people risks were seen by respondents as critical, and were especially pronounced at the intersection between humans and emerging technologies arising from the Fourth Industrial Revolution: privacy and confidentiality of information; overcontrol; and knowledge, skills and abilities (KSA) obsolescence (Volini et al, 2020). See also Schwab (2018) in this regard.

(128) In the 2020 Report of the Institute of Risk Management of SA, 12 risks were identified, two of which were people-related: (i) sparseness of an unified ethical and visionary leadership; and (ii) the failure to develop, attract and/or retain talent. Disruptive technologies were also identified as a risk (Marais, 2020). Organisations cited competition from other employers as the number one reason why they have difficulty hiring the right talent (SHRM, 2019) (quoted by McLean & Company, 2020).

See also in this regard, the 7th Global Trends 2040 published by the Strategic Futures Group of the USA Office of National Intelligence (Strategic Futures Group, 2021). Major trends/risks discerned by them are COVID-19, climate change, technological disruptions, and societal fragmentation, disillusionment and conflict.

Chapter 6: Endnotes

(1) Fitz-Enz (1997)

(2) Coetzee (2019); Ehrhart, Schneider & Macey (2014); Kuenzi & Schminke (2009); Veldsman (2013b); Wikipedia (2020b)

(3) Bos-Nehles & Veenendaal (2019); Jing, Avery & Bergsteiner (2020); Kuenzi & Schminke (2009); Makhathini & Van Dyk (2018); Schneider, González-Romá, Ostroff & West (2017); Sethibe (2018)

(4) Ahmad, Jasimuddin & Kee (2018); Albrecht, Bakker, Gruman, Macey & Saks (2015); Chooi, Ramayah & Doris (2018); Hicklenton, Hine & Loi (2019); Jiang, Takeuchi & Lepak (2013); Kanga & Busser (2018); Kuenzi & Schminke (2009); Lin & Liu (2019); Schneider, González-Romá, Ostroff & West (2017) Sethibe (2018); Wikipedia (2020b); Willis, Reynolds & Lee (2019); Woznyj, Heggestad, Kennerly & Yap (2019)

(5) Cf. Bos-Nehles & Veenendaal (2019); Gahlawat & Kundu (2019); Lin & Liu (2019)

(6) Kuenzi & Schminke (2009)

(7) Kuenzi & Schminke (2009)

(8) Ahmad, Jasimuddin & Kee (2018); Ehrhart, Schneider & Macey (2014); Veldsman (2013b); Willis, Reynolds & Lee (2019)

(9)   Organisational Climate dimensions can also be distinguished in terms of typical organisational components such as individual autonomy (e.g., too much or too little); structure/standards (e.g., red tape, rules, prescribed procedures); recognition/reward orientation (i.e., who, when and what), people growth/development (i.e., when and what); and relationships (i.e., warmth and support) (cf. Ahmad, Jasimuddin & Kee, 2018; Willis, Reynolds & Lee, 2019).

(10)   Albrecht, Breidahl & Marty (2018); Bos-Nehles & Veenendaal (2019); Kuenzi & Schminke (2009); Lin & Liu (2019); Schneider, González-Romá, Ostroff & West (2017); Shanker, Bhanugopan, Van der Heijden & Farrell (2017); Woznyj, Heggestad, Kennerly & Yap (2019)

(11)   Organisational facet-specific climates which are currently receiving much attention are a climate for: innovation (e.g., Bos-Nehles & Veenendaal, 2019; Jing, Avery & Bergsteiner, 2020; Sethibe, 2018; Shanker, Bhanugopan, Van der Heijden & Farrell, 2017; Woznyj, Heggestad, Kennerly & Yap, 2019); service (e.g., Kanga & Busser, 2018; Woznyj, Heggestad, Kennerly & Yap, 2019); engagement (Albrecht, Breidahl & Marty, 2018; Joubert & Roodt, 2019); and safety (e.g., Schneider, González-Romá, Ostroff & West, 2017).

(12)   Veldsman (2013b)

(13)   Albrecht, Bakker, Gruman, Macey, & Saks (2015); Castellano (2013); Coetzee (2019); Edmondson, A.C. & Zhike, L. (2014); Frazier, Fainshmidt, Klinger, Pezeshkan & Vraceva (2017); Joo, Lim & Kim (2016); Kahn (1990); Seligman & Csikszentmihayi (2000)

(14)   Edmondson, A.C. & Zhike, L. (2014); Frazier, Fainshmidt, Klinger, Pezeshkan & Vraceva (2017)

(15)   Kanga & Busser (2018); Williams, Haarhoff & Fox (2015)

(16)   Kim & Beehr (2021); Luthans, Youssef & Avolio (2007); Roodt (2018); Seligman & Csikszentmihayi (2000). See also Bhattacharya & Banerjee (2018); Joo, Lim & Kim (2016); Williams, Haarhoff & Fox (2015)

(17)   Ungerer, Herholdt & Le Roux (2013). See also Volini et al (2020)

(18)   Coetzee (2019); Jiang, Takeuchi & Lepak (2013); Potgieter (2018); Veld, Paauwe & Boselie (2010)

(19)   Boon, Eckardt, Lepak & Boselie (2018); Jiang, Takeuchi & Lepak (2013); Veld, Paauwe & Boselie (2010)

(20)   Ahmad, Jasimuddin & Kee (2018); Bhattacharya & Banerjee (2018); Chooi, Ramayah & Doris (2018); Edmondson, A.C. & Zhike, L. (2014); Frazier, Fainshmidt, Klinger, Pezeshkan & Vraceva (2017); Gahlawat & Kundu (2019); Ghosal & Bartlett (1997); Hicklenton, Hine & Loi (2019); Jing, Avery & Bergsteiner (2020); Kanga & Busser (2018); Kim & Beehr (2021); Kuenzi & Schminke (2009); Lin & Liu (2019); Makhathini & Van Dyk (2018); Shanker, Bhanugopan, Van der Heijden & Farrell (2017); Wikipedia (2020b); Willis, Reynolds & Lee (2019); Wollard & Shuck (2011); Woznyj, Heggestad, Kennerly & Yap (2019)

(21)   Hicklenton, Hine & Loi (2019)

(22)   Kim & Beehr (2021)

(23)   The psychosocial value of autonomy is at the heart of, and forms the basis of, self-determination theory. This theory states that autonomy is the centrepiece of fulfilled and thriving people, and hence their well-being. Autonomy refers to the freedom of a person to make independent decisions, in this way taking charge and being in control of situations and one's own life (Ryan & Deci, 2000). See also Liu, Wang & Chen (2019).

(24) Ahmetoglu, Akhtar, Tsivrikos & Chamorro-Premuzic (2018); Demerouti & Bakker (2014); Castellano (2013); Coetzee, M. (2019); Ghosal & Bartlett (1997); Hamel & Zanini (2020); Kahn & Fellows (2013); Kjaer & Associates (2020); Knight, Patterson & Dawson (2017); Roodt (2018); Tims, Bakker, Derks & van Rhenen (2013); Veldsman (2018); Veldsman, Benade & Rossouw (2019); Wrzesniewski & Dutton (2001); Zhang & Parker (2019)

(25) The widely accepted, dominant theoretical perspective informing this view is the Job Demands–Resources Model (JD-R Model) propagated by A.B. Bakker and E. Demerouti (cf. Bakker, 2021; Demerouti & Bakker, 2014). The JD-R model also forms the predominant theoretical foundation of employee engagement. The JD-R assumes two distinct underlying psychological processes. The health impairment process focuses on *job demands* as a source of adverse psychological and organisational outcomes. The motivational process covers *job and personal resources* as a source of positive motivational and organisational outcomes. Job resources are physical, psychological, social, or organisational aspects of a job that facilitate achieving work goals, reducing job demands, and stimulating personal development (Cf. also Albrecht, Bakker, Gruman, Macey, & Saks, 2015; Albrecht, Breidahl & Marty, 2018).

(26) Malhotra (2021)

(27) See references under Note (22), as well as Van Beurden, Van De Voorde & Van Veldhoven (2021), Kim & Beehr (2021), Saira, Mansoor & Ali (2021) and Van Veldhoven, Van den Broeck, Daniels, Bakker, Tavares & Ogbonnaya (2020).

(28) Van Veldhoven, Van den Broeck, Daniels, Bakker, Tavares & Ogbonnaya (2020)

(29) Van Veldhoven, Van den Broeck, Daniels, Bakker, Tavares & Ogbonnaya (2020)

(30) Autonomy awarded is also called self-determination or self-regulation according to Ryan and Deci (2000). See also Roodt (2018).

(31) Eldor & Vigoda-Gadot (2017); Johennesse & Chou (2017); Malhotra (2021); Pfeffer (2018); Roodt (2018)

(32) Ungerer, Ungerer & Herholdt (2016)

(33) Organisations that delegated more power from their central headquarters to local plant managers prior to the 2008/9 Great Recession outperformed their centralised counterparts in sectors that were hardest hit by the subsequent crisis (measured by export growth and product durability). Measures of turbulence based on product churn and stock market volatility provided further support to the localised delegation view.

Large downturns have less dramatic consequences for decentralised firms where local managers are empowered to take decisions under conditions of uncertainty and ambiguity. Under such conditions, decisions must be made on the spur of the moment. They also have the most up-to-date and accurate information about local conditions (Aghion, Bloom, Lucking, Sadun & Van Reene, 2021).

(34) Liu, Wang & Chen (2019)

(35) Liu, Wang & Chen (2019); Saira, Mansoor & Ali (2021)

(36) For example, Berg, Dutton & Wrzesniewski (2013); Demerouti & Bakker (2014); Lysova, Blake, Dik, Duff & Steger (2019); Tims, Bakker & Derks (2015); Wrzesniewski & Dutton (2001); Wrzesniewski, Berg & Dutton (2010)

(37) Bailey, Madden Alfes, Shantz & Soane (2017); Berg, Dutton & Wrzesniewski (2013); Veldsman (2019a); Zhang & Parker, 2019)

(38) Zhang & Parker (2019)

(39)   Giving people the necessary autonomy to make the needed decisions, acknowledge that at a fundamental level human beings are self-organising, self-directed, adaptive entities. They are decision makers with choices and preferences, and have the potential of becoming masterful and efficacious (Seligman & Csikszentmihayi, 2000). See also Note (30).

(40)   Frazier, Fainshmidt, Klinger, Pezeshkan & Vraceva (2017)

(41)   Follmer (2019); Morley (2007)

(42)   Demerouti & Bakker (2014); Johennesse & Chou (2017); Knight, Patterson & Dawson (2017); Pfeffer (2018); Raza & Nadeem (2018); Roodt (2018); Saira, Mansoor & Ali (2021); Van Dierendonck & Nuijten (2011)

(43)   Coyle-Shapiro, Costa, Doden & Chang (2019); Kim & Beehr (2021); Saira, Mansoor & Ali (2021)

(44)   Albrecht, Bakker, Gruman, Macey & Saks (2015); Ahmetoglu, Akhtar, Tsivrikos & Chamorro-Premuzic (2018); Bronkhorst (2012); Castellano (2013); Katzenburg (2000) (quoted in Kirby 2005); Raza & Nadeem (2018); Roodt (2018)

(45)   Bussin (2018); Lawler (2017); Raza & Nadeem (2018); Roux (2021); Wilson (2017)

(46)   This linkage is derived from the Expectancy-Valence (Vroom, 1964) and Goal Setting motivation theories (Locke, 1975).

(47)   As much as 25% of the 'stay' decisions of organisational members are related to monetary remuneration (Schwabel, 2016, quoted by Bussin, 2018).

(48)   Seligman & Csikszentmihayi (2000)

(49)   World Economic Forum (2019)

(50)   Seligman & Csikszentmihayi (2000)

(51)   De Vries & Florent-Treacy (2002); Hock (1999)

(52)   Bussin (2018); Nel & Beudeker (2009)

(53)   Bakker (2017); Bussin (2018); Habraken, Bondarouk & Hoffman (2019) Johennesse & Chou (2017); Lawler (2017); Roux (2021); Veldsman (2018); Veldsman, Benade & Rossouw (2019)

(54)   The re-invention of performance management and rewards are also stressed in the 2020 Deloitte Global Human Capital report by respondents, as well as in the 2021 Top Employers Institute Report (2021). Organisations' People Practices in these areas have essentially remained stuck in the past (Volini et al, 2020). See also Schrage, Kiron, Hancock & Bresch (2019) who deal with performance management that befits a digital age.

(55)   Nel & Beudeker (2009); Top Employers Institute (2021)

(56)   In the 2020 global Deloitte Human Capital Survey, 90% of respondents said that the accelerating need for organisations to change at scale and speed was important to their success over the next 10 years. Yet only 55% felt that their organisations were ready for change at the scale and speed required. The survey also highlighted the need for re-invention: 53% of respondents stated that between half and all of their workforce will need to change their skills and capabilities in the next three years (Volini et al, 2020).

(57)   Roux (2021)

(58)   Beer (2009); De Geus (1997); Veldsman (2019a)

(59)   Bustinzaa, Vendrell-Herrerob, Perez-Arosteguia & Parry (2019)

(60)   Draws on SIOPSA (2020); Veldsman (2002b)

(61)   SIOPSA (2020); Veldsman (2002b)

(62)   The concept 'resilience' originated from the physical sciences, where it refers to a physical system's capacity to return to its original form after a disturbance (Barasa, Mbau & Gilson, 2018).

(63)   Kantur & Eri-Say (2012); Limnios, Mazzarol, Ghadouani & Scilizzi (2014); McChrystal (2015); Ungerer, Ungerer & Herholdt (2016); Veldsman (2019a)

(64)   Nel & Beudeker (2009)

(65)   Duchek (2020); Gover & Duxbury (2018)

(66)   Kjaer & Associates (2020); Montet et al (2020); Roux (2021); Walter (2020); World Economic Forum (2019)

(67)   According to the Mercer Global Talent Trends 2020 Survey, there is a race to reskill. Executives see this as the top people intervention most capable of delivering a good ROI (Bravery et al, 2020; Parker, Rabolele & Joubert, 2020). In the 2020 PWC Global Survey of CEOs, 75% are concerned whether they have the talent needed for the future. Only 18% believe they have made significant progress in establishing upskilling programmes, and one out of every 10 state they have not made any progress at all (quoted by Walter, 2020).

(68)   World Economic Forum (2019)

(69)   2020 Global Deloitte Global Human Capital Survey (Volini et al, 2020)

(70)   Angus & Westbrook (2021); Bardoel, Pettit, Cieri & McMillan (2014); Bustinzaa, Vendrell-Herrerob, Perez-Arosteguia & Parry (2019); Ishak & Williams (2018); Morales, Martınez, Gomez, Romero & Torres-Argűelles (2019); Pulakos, Schneider & Kantrowitz (2019); Rook, Smith, Johnstone, Rossato, Sánchez, Suárez & Roberts (2018)

(71)   Resilience can be conceived as a capability (=set of abilities to bounce back), a process (=stages of bouncing back), or an outcome (=the sources and results of bouncing back, positive or negative). All three of these perspectives are used in the elucidation to follow (Cf. Duchek, 2020; Fisher & Ragsdale, 2019; Fisher & Law, 2021).

(72)   Al-Ayed (2019); Barasa, Mbau & Gilson (2018); Bardoel, Pettit, Cieri & McMillan (2014); Beer (2009); Bouaziz & Hachicha (2018); Bustinzaa, Vendrell-Herrerob, Perez-Arosteguia & Parry (2019); Cantoni, Graziano, Maiocchi & Rizzi (2019); Darkow (2019); Degbey & Einola (2020); Duchek (2020); Fisher & Ragsdale (2019); Gover & Duxbury (2018); Hartmann, Weiss, Newman & Hoegl (2020); Ishak & Williams (2018); Lim, Hur, Ho, Yoo & Yoon (2019); Mitsakis (2020); Morales, Martınez, Gomez, Romero & Torres-Argűelles (2019); Pulakos, Schneider & Kantrowitz (2019); Rook, Smith, Johnstone, Rossato, Sánchez, Suárez & Roberts (2018); Stokes, Smith, Wall, Moore, Rowland, Ward & Cronshaw (2019); Vera, Samba, Kong, & Maldonado (2021)

(73)   Related terms to be distinguished from resilience are:
- Adaptability (=flexibility): the ability to meet contextual demands and requirements on an ongoing basis.
- Agility (=responsiveness): the ability at speed to recognise/capitalise on opportunities, change direction, reconfigure resources, or avoid collisions/disasters.
- Robustness: the ability of the organisation to maintain its functionality despite disruptions.

See Al-Ayed (2019); Arokodare, Asikhia & Makinde (2019); Duchek (2020); Pulakos, Schneider & Kantrowitz (2019); Rook, Smith, Johnstone, Rossato, Sánchez, Suárez & Roberts (2018).

(74) See the references given under Note (70).

(75) Based on and adapted from Duchek (2020); Fisher & Ragsdale (2019) and Vera, Samba, Kong, & Maldonado (2021).

(76) Bouaziz & Hachicha (2018); Duchek (2020); Fisher & Ragsdale (2019); Gover & Duxbury (2018)

(77) Gover & Duxbury (2018); Hartmann, Weiss, Newman & Hoegl (2020); Stokes, Smith, Wall, Moore, Rowland, Ward & Cronshaw (2019)

(78) Cf. Bardoel, Pettit, Cieri & McMillan (2014); Bartone & Stein (2020); Caniëls & Baaten (2019); De Beer, Rothmann & Scherrer (2016); Fisher & Ragsdale (2019); Gover & Duxbury (2018); Rook, Smith, Johnstone, Rossato, Sánchez, Suárez & Roberts (2018); Malik & Garg (2020)

(79) De Beer, Rothmann & Scherrer (2016); Castellano (2013)

(80) In the 2020 Global Deloitte Global Human Capital Survey, people's well-being had the largest gap between importance and readiness across that year's trends, with 80% of organisations saying that people's well-being was important or very important for their success over the next 12–18 months. However, only 12% stated they were most ready to address this issue (Volini et al, 2020). Similarly, according to the Mercer Global Talent Trends 2020 Survey, the most important people concern for executives (48%) was employee health and well-being (Bravery et al, 2020).

(81) See, e.g., Degbey & Einola (2020); Hartmann, Weiss, Newman & Hoegl (2020); Stoverink, Kirkman, Mistry & Rosen (2020).

(82) Veldsman (2019a)

(83) Kirkman & Stoverink (2021)

(84) Suarez & Montes (2020)

(85) Cf. Bouaziz & Hachicha (2018); Bustinzaa, Vendrell-Herrerob, Perez-Arosteguia & Parry (2019); Stokes, Smith, Wall, Moore, Rowland, Ward & Cronshaw (2019); Vera, Samba, Kong, & Maldonado (2021)

(86) Barasa, Mbau & Gilson (2018)

(87) Morales, Martınez, Gomez, Romero & Torres-Argűelles (2019); Stokes, Smith, Wall, Moore, Rowland, Ward & Cronshaw (2019)

(88) Barasa, Mbau & Gilson (2018); Morales, Martınez, Gomez, Romero & Torres-Argűelles (2019); Gover & Duxbury (2018); Vera, Samba, Kong, & Maldonado (2021)

(89) Bardoel, Pettit, Cieri & McMillan (2014); Mitsakis (2020); Bustinzaa, Vendrell-Herrerob, Perez-Arosteguia & Parry (2019)

(90) Morales, Martınez, Gomez, Romero & Torres-Argűelles (2019)

(91) Barasa, Mbau & Gilson (2018); Darkow (2019); Duchek (2020); Bustinzaa, Vendrell-Herrerob, Perez-Arosteguia & Parry (2019); Morales, Martınez, Gomez, Romero & Torres-Argűelles (2019); Pulakos, Schneider & Kantrowitz, 2019)

(92) Pulakos, Schneider & Kantrowitz (2019); Stokes, Smith, Wall, Moore, Rowland, Ward & Cronshaw (2019)

(93) Barasa, Mbau & Gilson (2018)

(94) Pulakos, Schneider & Kantrowitz (2019)

(95) Barasa, Mbau & Gilson (2018)

(96)   Barasa, Mbau & Gilson (2018); Morales, Martınez, Gomez, Romero & Torres-Argűelles (2019); Gover & Duxbury (2018); Vera, Samba, Kong, & Maldonado (2021)

(97)   Al-Ayed (2019); Bardoel, Pettit, Cieri & McMillan (2014); Bouaziz & Hachicha (2018); Bustinzaa, Vendrell-Herrerob, Perez-Arosteguia & Parry (2019); Mitsakis (2020)

(98)   Barasa, Mbau & Gilson (2018); Bardoel, Pettit, Cieri & McMillan (2014); Darkow (2019); Mitsakis (2020) Morales, Martınez, Gomez, Romero & Torres-Argűelles (2019)

(99)   Ishak & Williams (2018)

(100) Caniëls & Baaten (2019); Malik & Garg (2020); Morales, Martınez, Gomez, Romero & Torres-Argűelles (2019)

(101) Bardoel, Pettit, Cieri & McMillan (2014); Mitsakis (2020); Rook, Smith, Johnstone, Rossato, Sánchez, Suárez & Roberts (2018); Morales, Martınez, Gomez, Romero & Torres-Argűelles (2019)

(102) Barasa, Mbau & Gilson (2018); Duchek (2020); Hartmann, Weiss, Newman & Hoegl (2020); Malik & Garg (2020); Morales, Martınez, Gomez, Romero & Torres-Argűelles (2019)

(103) Barasa, Mbau & Gilson (2018)

(104) Bardoel, Pettit, Cieri & McMillan (2014); Bustinzaa, Vendrell-Herrerob, Perez-Arosteguia & Parry (2019); Caniëls & Baaten (2019); Fisher & Ragsdale (2019); Hartmann, Weiss, Newman & Hoegl (2020); Meng, Luo, Huang, Wen Ma & Xi (2019); Pulakos, Schneider & Kantrowitz (2019); Rook, Smith, Johnstone, Rossato, Sánchez, Suárez & Roberts (2018)

(105) The following terms are used in the literature – 'employee engagement', 'work engagement' and 'job engagement' – which are all related to performing a specific task/role; and 'organisation engagement', which is related to performing a role as an organisational member (cf. Bedarkar & Pandit 2014; Borah & Barua, 2018; Motyka, 2018; Schaufeli & Bakker, 2010; Shuck, Osam, Zigarmi & Nimon, 2017). The shorthand term 'engagement' will be used in the discussion, relating to the performance of a specific work role in the organisation.

       Additionally, the term 'employee engagement' is used in the literature as an outcome; an (innate) psychological state; or a process (cf. Borah & Barua, 2018; Kahn, 1990; Motyka, 2018; Schaufeli & Bakker, 2010; Shuck, Osam, Zigarmi & Nimon, 2017). In my elucidation, employee engagement refers to a psychological state.

(106) Albrecht, Bakker, Gruman, Macey & Saks (2015)

(107) A distinction can be drawn between: (i) strategic/top down approaches taken by leadership to engagement (called the preconditions for engagement by myself); and (ii) proactive, bottom-up approaches taken by the people themselves as active agents by becoming engaged through a direct, personal investment in their work, such as job crafting (Bakker, 2017; Shantz, 2017).

(108) The well-known Gallup Workplace audit of engagement (see Castellano, 2013; Schaufeli & Bakker, 2010) is made up of 12 Engagement Questions – antecedents of engagement which are cross-referenced with the Excellence Questions (EQ) – that have been found to be significant organisational indicators of profits, productivity, retention, customer loyalty and employee loyalty:

- My supervisor or someone at work cares about me as a person (EQ1: Leadership).
- At work my opinion seems to count (EQ1: Leadership).
- The mission/purpose of my company makes me feel my job is important (EQ2: Choice).

- I know what is expected of me at work (EQ7: Design).
- This last year I have had opportunities at work to learn and grow (EQ10: Practices).
- There is someone at work who encourages my development (EQ10: Practices).
- In the last six months someone at work has talked about my progress (EQ10: Practices).
- In the last seven days I have received recognition/praise for doing good work (EQ14: Line of Sight).
- My fellow employees are committed to doing quality work (EQ12: Climate).
- I have a best friend at work (EQ13: Climate).
- I have the materials and equipment I need to do my work right (EQ13: Balancing).
- At work I have the opportunity to do what I do best every day (EQ13: Balancing).

(109) In the Mercer Global Talent Trends 2020 Survey, the antecedents of energised people's work experiences are conceived to be work conditions that are empathic (=supportive and caring); enriching (=learning and growth); embracing (=a sense of belonging); and efficient (or empowered) (=a frictionless work setting) (Bravery et al, 2020).

(110) Messersmith, Patel, Lepak & Gould-Williams (2011); Motyka (2018)

(111) Albrecht, Bakker, Gruman, Macey & Saks (2015); Bedarkar & Pandit (2014); Borah & Barua (2018); Castellano (2013); Chin, Lok & Kong (2019); Chooi, Ramayah & Doris (2018); Costa, Passos & Bakker (2016); Eldor & Vigoda-Gadot (2017); Joubert & Roodt (2019); Kahn (1990); Kahn & Fellows (2013); Kanga & Busser (2018); Knight, Patterson & Dawson (2017); Konrad (2006); Lee, Shin, Park, Kim & Cho (2017); Meyer (2017); Motyka (2018); Saks (2017); Nienaber & Martins (2020); Saks (2017); Schaufeli & Bakker (2010); Shuck, Osam, Zigarmi & Nimon (2017); Veldsman (2018); Wikipedia (2020c); Wollard & Shuck (2011)

(112) Joubert & Roodt (2019)

(113) Cf. Afsar, Al-Ghazali & Umrani (2020); Chooi, Ramayah & Doris (2018); Holtom & Darabi (2018); Schaufeli & Bakker (2010)

(114) Ahmetoglu, Akhtar, Tsivrikos & Chamorro-Premuzic (2018); Albrecht, Breidahl & Marty (2018); Messersmith, Patel, Lepak & Gould-Williams (2011); Meyer (2017)

(115) Bedarkar & Pandit (2014); Castellano (2013); Fitz-Enz (1997); Habraken, Bondarouk & Hoffman (2019); Hicklenton, Hine & Loi (2019); Mayer (2019); Messersmith, Patel, Lepak & Gould-Williams (2011); Nel & Beudeker (2009); Parker & Veldsman (2010); Saks (2017); Veldsman (2019a)

(116) Volini et al (2020)

(117) Narayanan (2016)

(118) Castellano (2013); Jiang, Takeuchi & Lepak (2013)

(119) 2017 Gallup Institute (quoted Motyka, 2018). See also Albrecht, Bakker, Gruman, Macey, & Saks (2015); Bedarkar & Pandit (2014); Hamel & Zanini (2020); Li et al (2021); Nienaber & Martins (2020); Saks (2017).

(120) Adapted and expanded from the Utrecht Work Engagement Scale (Schaufeli, Salanova, González-Romá & Bakker, 2002; Schaufeli, Bakker & Salanova, 2006). See also Bakker (2017); Castellano (2013); Kahn & Fellows (2013); Meyer (2017); Pfeffer (2018); Schaufeli & Bakker (2010).

The first three dimensions, Vigour, Dedication and Absorption, make up the original scale, and are extensively quoted in the literature as the key indicators of work engagement (refer Note (105)). The fourth element – Collaboration – has been added by myself to reflect the movement towards the network, team-based organisation (see Excellence Question 7: Design), which requires engagement beyond self though collaborative work. Work has become shared in its execution.

(121)   A highly engaged person can be said to be in a 'state of flow' when manifesting this profile (Seligman & Csikszentmihayi, 2000).

(122)   Corporate Leadership Council (2004)

(123)   Afsar, Al-Ghazali & Umrani (2020); Albrecht, Bakker, Gruman, Macey, & Saks (2015); Albrecht, Breidahl & Marty (2018); Anthony-McMann, Ellinger, Astakhova & Halbesleben (2017); Bedarkar & Pandit (2014); Borah & Barua (2018); Chooi, Ramayah & Doris (2018); Eldor & Vigoda-Gadot (2017); Harter, Schmidt & Hayes (2002); Kanga & Busser (2018); Konrad (2006); Lee, Shin, Park, Kim & Cho (2017); Motyka (2018); Nienaber & Martins (2020); Saks (2017); Zhou, Chen, & Liu (2019)

(124)   30% (Gallup survey quoted by Schiemann, 2018); 87% (Hay Group, quoted in Wikipedia, 2020c).

(125)   According to the Mercer Global Talent Trends 2020 Survey (Bravery et al, 2020).

(126)   SA Board of People Practices (2018)

(127)   Based on a study of 360 000 employees across 41 companies (ISR, 2003).

Chapter 7: Endnotes

(1)   Ludike (2018); Schiemann (2017)

(2)   Brown et al (2017) (quoted in Coetzee, 2019a); Kjaer & Associates (2020); Van der Walt & Lezar (2019); Veldsman, Benade & Rossouw (2019)

(3)   Ghielen, De Cooman, & Sels (2021)

(4)   Veldsman (2017); Verwey & Verwey (2016)

(5)   Jiang, Takeuchi & Lepak (2013)

(6)   Veldsman & Pauw (2018)

(7)   In the HR Trends Report 2020 of the Top Employers Institute, 60% of respondents reported that they now complement their main engagement survey with more frequent pulse surveys to connect employee feedback to core strategic and business objectives, using the insights gained to plan goals and priorities (Montet et al, 2020). See also Bersin & Enderes (2021).

(8)   Castellano (2013); Nalbantian (2017); Roux (2021)

(9)   Castellano (2013); Kaplan & Norton (1992); Lawler (2017); Roux (2021); World Economic Forum (2019)

(10)   Deloitte found that although 75% of surveyed organisations believed that using people analytics is important for business performance, only 8% viewed their organisational capabilities in this area as "strong" (Bersin et al., 2015) (quoted by Boudreau & Cascio, 2017). According to the Mercer Global Talent Trends 2020 Survey, 66% of responding executives stated that the use of people analytics to inform decision-making is the number one people trend that has delivered an impact. However, only 26% of the organisations leverage talent intelligence for talent demand and supply planning (Bravery et al, 2020).

According to Boudreau and Cascio (2017), although people analytics has invoked keen interest in organisations, most are struggling to move from operational reporting to people analytics. Proposing the LAMP model, they identified four elements as potential reasons why people analytics are not sufficiently being 'pushed' toward their audience. Similarly, they named five conditions why the wider use of Human Capital Analytics is not 'pulled' in by the analytics user.

The LAMP model includes the following elements, which can act either as a push or pull factor:

- Logic: frameworks that articulate the connections between talent and strategic success, as well as the principles and conditions that predict individual and organisational behaviour.

- Analytics: tools and techniques to transform data into rigorous and relevant insights, e.g., statistical analysis and research design.

- Measures: the numbers and indices calculated from data systems.

- Process: communication and knowledge transfer mechanisms through which the information becomes accepted and acted upon by key organisation decision makers.

(11) A task force of the SA Board of People Practices (SABPP) under the leadership of Penny Abbott and the author developed a Human Capital Measurement Model, depicted in the figure below (Veldsman & Abbott, 2015).

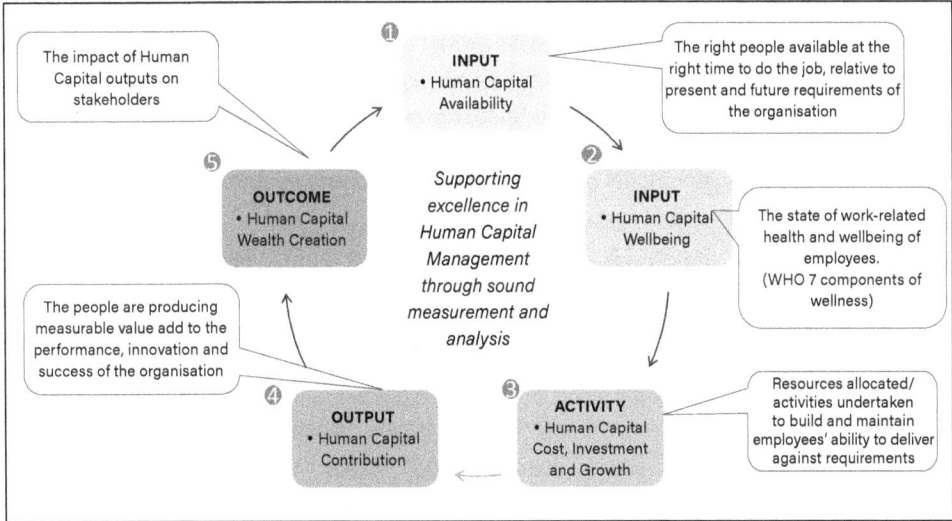

(12) Roux (2021)

(13) Claus (2019); Jianga & Messersmith (2018); Nel & Beudeker (2009)

(14) In accordance with Stratified Systems Theory (see Veldsman, 2019a).

(15) The Employee Net Promoter Score (eNPS) is a measure of how likely an organisation's people will recommend the organisation as a desirable place to work to other prospective employees and peers. This measure is derived from the NPS (Net Promotor Score) measure more typically used in many customer satisfaction surveys today.

eNPS asks an organisation's people how likely it is that they would 'promote' the organisation as a place to work on a scale from 0 to 10. In terms of their answers, respondents are grouped as 'Promoters', 'Neutrals' or 'Detractors'. An eNPS score is next calculated by taking the percentage of Detractors and subtracting it from the percentage of Promoters to give the organisation an eNPS score from 0 to 100 (Roux, 2021).

(16) Fitz-Enz (1997); Nel & Beudeker (2009); Shin & Konrad (2014)

(17) This represents Maturity Stage 3 of People Analytics (Bravery et al, 2020).

(18) 2020 Deloitte Global Human Capital Trends (Volini et al, 2020).

(19) Draws on the Mercer's Global Talent Trends 2020 Report (Bravery et al, 2020).

(20) Jianga & Messersmith (2018); Kaplan & Norton (1992); Kohl & Swartz (2019).

Chapter 8: Endnotes

(1) Discussion based predominantly on Freeman (2011) and Veldsman (2016). See also Volini et al (2020)

(2) EY (2018); Geddes, Nuttall & Parekh (2020)

(3) Freeman (2011); Jianga & Messersmith (2018); Nel & Beudeker (2009); Titus & Hoole (2021)

(4) The view of multiple stakeholders, and not only shareholders, is supported by Beer (2009); Freeman (2011); Parker, Rabolele & Joubert (2020); Veldsman (2016); and Volini et al (2020). Freeman is the originator of Stakeholder Theory. He proposed that shareholders are not the only stakeholders of the organisation. For him, the term 'Stakeholder' must include any party who is affected by/or affects the achievement of, the organisation's objectives.

(5) According to the Mercer Global Talent Trends 2020 Survey, one in three employees prefer to work for an organisation that shows responsibility towards all stakeholders. Fifty percent of responding executives intended to align their business practices to a multiple stakeholder model in the coming years (Bravery et al, 2020).

(6) Abbott (2014); Freeman (2011); Volini et al (2020)

(7) Titus & Hoole (2021); Veldsman, Benade & Rossouw (2019); Volini et al (2020)

(8) In the 2020 McKinsey Global Survey on External Relations (Geddes, Nuttall & Parekh, 2020), 58% of respondents said that their organisations' CEOs have the management of external engagement as either a top three or top priority on their agendas. That share has increased significantly since 2013. Thirty eight percent of respondents reported that their CEOs spend at least one-quarter of their time managing external engagement.

(9) Abbott (2014); Fitz-Enz (1997); Freeman (2011); Geddes, Nuttall & Parekh (2020)

(10) In the 2020 McKinsey Global Survey on External Relations, 24% of respondents at high performing organisations – twice the share of other respondents – predicted that the effective involvement in external issues would increase their organisations' operating income by 10% or more. Even as leaders have increasingly focused on external engagement, the findings suggested that organisations are no better at external engagement now than in 2015. Just 7% of respondents reported that their organisations frequently aligned the interests of stakeholders and those of their businesses (Geddes, Nuttall & Parekh, 2020).

(11) Booz Allen Hamilton & Kellogg School of Management, Northwestern University, USA (reference could not be traced)

(12) Angus & Westbrook (2021); Abbott (2014)

(13)   Duchek (2020)

(14)   Geddes, Nuttall & Parekh (2020)

(15)   Agarwal, Bersin, Lahiri, Schwartz & Volini (2018); Ashton (2017); Bersin, O'Reilly, Magoulas & Loukides (2019); Brown (2019); Hawken (2010); Lankoski & Smith (2017); Lawler & Worley (2012); Lawler & Conger (2015); Murray (2019); Nijhof, Schaveling & Zalesky (2019); Santos, Pache & Birkholz (2015); The British Academy (2019); Veldsman (2015); Yeoman & O'Hara (2017)

(16)   Montet et al, 2020; Volini et al (2020)

(17)   Angus & Westbrook (2021); Miska & Mendenhall (2018); Veldsman (2015)

(18)   Lalor (2020); Lawler and Conger (2015); Miska & Mendenhall (2018)

(19)   Lalor (2020); Lawler and Conger (2015); Miska & Mendenhall (2018); Veldsman (2015)

(20)   Lalor (2020); Miska & Mendenhall (2018)

(21)   Afsar, Al-Ghazali & Umrani (2020); Gupta (2017)

Chapter 10: Endnotes

(1)   Two examples to illustrate the effect of context. In a study by Lucas, Ardichvili, de Castro Casa Nova, Bittencourt and Carpenedo (2018) of the Training and Development (TD) practices in a large Brazilian steel company, it was found that the implementation of a Western-based TD system based on meritocratic principles did not fully align with a national-derived Organisational Culture characterised by high power distance, paternalism, collectivism, and an emphasis on personal relationships over merit.

Adisa, Mordi and Osabutey (2017) found that a non-caring, working-at-all-cost Organisational Culture – demanded by supervisors and expected by peers – nullified the formally espoused, People Practice of work-life balance for medical doctors in six Nigerian medical facilities. The external socio-cultural context of the organisation also shaped the organisation's culture, which in turn determined what People Practices could be/were adopted as acceptable by the organisation (Rodriguez & Stewart, 2017). Cf. also Park & Kim (2019).

(2)   Having proposed an Engagement Model consisting of 14 variable categories, which in many cases had multiple variables per category, Albrecht, Bakker, Gruman, Macey and Saks (2015) openly acknowledged the complexity challenge of having multiple variables in dense relationships. They admitted that their model, because of its complexity, cannot be tested as a whole. Their proposed solution was to use structural equation modelling to test more focused relationships contained in the model, and in this way build a progressively validated, overall model. Nikolova, Schaufeli and Notelaers (2019) also recognised the same complexity challenge.

(3)   The types of relationships (read 'effects') variables (read 'Excellence Elements') can have, are derived from discussions by Afsar, Al-Ghazali & Umrani (2020); Albrecht, Bakker, Gruman, Macey, & Saks (2015); Albrecht, Breidahl & Marty (2018); Anthony-McMann, Ellinger, Astakhova & Halbesleben (2017); Bedarkar & Pandit (2014); Borah & Barua (2018); Chooi, Ramayah & Doris (2018); Eldor & Vigoda-Gadot (2017); Hartmann, Weiss, Newman & Hoegl (2020); Harter, Schmidt & Hayes (2002); Kanga & Busser (2018); Konrad (2006); Kuenzi & Schminke (2009); Lee, Shin, Park, Kim & Cho (2017); Lin & Liu (2019); Motyka (2018); Nienaber & Martins (2020); Saks (2017); Van Beurden, Van De Voorde & Van Veldhoven (2021) and Zhou, Chen, & Liu (2019).

(4)   Called "upstream conditions" regarding engagement by Albrecht, Bakker, Gruman, Macey and Saks (2015) and Albrecht, Breidahl and Marty (2018).

(5)   The dominant research paradigm in Industrial-Organisational Psychological research, and reinforced by leading academic journals in the field as gate-keepers of what gets published or not, is the antecedent-moderator-outcome paradigm. Relating to Figure 10.1, an antecedent = a precondition; a moderator = a cause; and an outcome = a result. This research paradigm reflects a mechanistic (or Newtonian) view of reality. In this view, the world is regarded as the sum total of its parts; parts relate linearly in cause-effect relationships; and, in their linear interaction, parts strive for homeostasis (Bal, 2019; Veldsman, 2019).

(6)   A similar discussion regarding resilience with its different effects can be found in Hartmann, Weiss, Newman and Hoegl (2020).

(7)   Afsar, Al-Ghazali & Umrani (2020); Albrecht, Bakker, Gruman, Macey, & Saks (2015); Albrecht, Breidahl & Marty (2018); Anthony-McMann, Ellinger, Astakhova & Halbesleben (2017); Bedarkar & Pandit (2014); Borah & Barua (2018); Chooi, Ramayah & Doris (2018); Eldor & Vigoda-Gadot (2017); Harter, Schmidt & Hayes (2002); Kanga & Busser (2018); Konrad (2006); Lee, Shin, Park, Kim & Cho (2017); Motyka (2018); Nienaber & Martins (2020); Saks (2017); Zhou, Chen, & Liu (2019)

(8)   Bedarkar & Pandit (2014); Borah & Barua (2018); Chin, Lok & Kong (2019); Lee, Shin, Park, Kim & Cho (2017); Nikolova, Schaufeli & Notelaers (2019); Rahmadani, Schaufeli, Ivanova & Osin (2019)

(9)   Albrecht, Bakker, Gruman, Macey & Saks (2015); Albrecht, Breidal & Marty (2018); Borah & Barua (2018); Konrad (2006)

(10)   Nikolova, Schaufeli & Notelaers (2019)

(11)   Albrecht, Bakker, Gruman, Macey, & Saks (2015)

(12)   Gupta (2017); Hicklenton, Hine & Loi (2019)

(13)   Cf. Albrecht, Bakker, Gruman, Macey and Saks (2015), who posited engagement as a central integrating concept in explaining individual performance, organisational performance, and competitive advantage.

(14)   Cf. Pravinkumar, Sanket, Manish, Uttam & Singh (2018); Wikipedia (2020d).

(15)   See Beer (2020) on having on having difficult, honest, collective, and public conversations in the organisation regarding strategic fitness.

(16)   Volini et al (2020)

REFERENCES

Abbott, P. (2014). The role of social capital. In D. van Eden (Ed.). *The Chief Human Resource Officer.* Johannesburg: Knowledge Resources, 31-47.

Adisa, T.A., Mordi, C. & Osabutey, E.L.C. (2017). Exploring the implications of the influence of Organisational Culture on work-life balance practices. Evidence from Nigerian medical doctors. *Personnel Review,* 46(3), 454-473. DOI 10.1108/PR-05-2015-0138.

Afsar, B., Al-Ghazali, B. & Umrani, W. (2020). Corporate social responsibility, work meaningfulness, and employee engagement: The joint moderating effects of incremental moral belief and moral identity centrality. *Corporate Social Responsibility and Environmental Management,* 27, 1264–1278. DOI: 10.1002/csr.1882.

Agarwal, D., Bersin, J., Lahiri, G., Schwartz, J. & Volini, E. (2018). *The rise of the social enterprise. 2018 Deloitte Global Human Capital Trends Report.* Place of publication uncited: Deloitte Development LLC.

Aghion, P., Bloom, N., Lucking, B., Sadun, R. & Van Reene, J. (2021). Turbulence, firm decentralization, and growth in bad times. *American Economic Journal: Applied Economics,* 13(1), 133–169. https://doi.org/10.1257/app.20180752.

Ahmad, K.Z.B., Jasimuddin, S.M. & Kee, W.L. (2018). Organizational climate and job satisfaction: Do employees' personalities matter? *Management Decision,* 56(2), 421-440. DOI 10.1108/MD-10-2016-0713.

Ahmetoglu, G., Akhtar, R., Tsivrikos, D. & Chamorro-Premuzic, T. (2018). The entrepreneurial organization: The effects organizational culture on innovation output. *Consulting Psychology Journal: Practice and Research,* 70(4), 318–338. http://dx.doi.org/10.1037/cpb0000121.

Albrecht, S., Breidal, E. & Marty, A. (2018). Organisational resources, organisational engagement climate, and employee engagement. *The Career Development International*, 23(1), 67-85.

Al-Ayed, S.I. (2019). The impact of strategic human resource management on organizational resilience: An empirical study on hospitals. *Business: Theory and Practice,* 20, 179–186. https://doi.org/10.3846/btp.2019.17.

Albrecht, S.L., Bakker, A.B., Gruman, J.A., Macey, W.H. & Saks, A.M. (2015). Employee engagement, human resource management practices and competitive advantage. *Journal of Organisational Effectiveness,* 2(1), 7-35.

Alexander, A., Cracknell, R., De Smet, A., Langstaff, M., Mysore, M. & Ravid, D. (2021a). What are executives saying about the future of hybrid work, McKinsey Quarterly, 17 *May* 2021 (accessed on 15 June 2021).

Alexander, A., De Met, A., Langstaff, M. & Ravid, D. (2021B). What are employees are saying about the future of remote work. McKinsey Quarterly, 1 April 2021 (accessed on 15 June 2021).

Alfesa, K., Shantz, A.D, Truss, C. & Soane, E.C. (2013). The link between perceived human resource management practices, engagement and employee behaviour: a moderated mediation model. *The International Journal of Human Resource Management*, 24(2), 330–351.

Angus, A. & Westbrook, G. (2021). *Top 10 global consumer trends 2021.* London: Euromonitor International.

Anlesinya, A., Dartey-Baah, K. & Amponsah-Tawiah, K. (2019). A review of empirical research on global talent management. *FIIB Business Review,* 8(2), 147–160.

Anthony-McMann, P.E., Ellinger, A.D., Astakhova, M. & Halbesleben, J.R.B. (2017). Exploring different operationalizations of employee engagement and their relationships with workplace stress and burnout. *Human Resource Development Quarterly*, 28(2), 163-195. DOI: 10.1002/hrdq.21276.

Arets, J. (2019). *Improving organisational performance? Reinvent your L&D business model in changing times.* Paper presented at Organisational Development Conference 2019 on 27 February, Knowres, Sandton, South Africa.

Arokodare, M.A., Asikhia, O.U. & Makinde, G.O. (2019). Strategic agility and firm performance: The moderating role of Organisational Culture. *Business Management Dynamics*, 9(3), 1-12.

Bailey, C., Madden, A., Alfes, K., Shantz, A. & Soane, E. (2017). The mismanaged soul: Existential labour and the erosion of meaningful work. *Human Resource Management Review*, 27, 416–430.

Bal, P.M. (2019). *The future of work and organisational psychology – A working session. IOP 4.0,* 2019 SIOPSA Conference, 23 July 2019, Pretoria.

Bakker, A.B. (2017). Strategic and pro-active approaches to work engagement. *Organisational Dynamics*, 46, 67-75.

Bakker, A.B. (2021). New developments in Job Demands–Resources theory. 1st workshop on 21 May 2021 in Workplace Well-being Webinar. Johannesburg: University of Johannesburg: https://youtu.be/udv_8Zs1Bys 21 May 2021

Bankins, S., Griep, Y. & Hansen, S.D. (2020). Charting directions for a new research era: addressing gaps and advancing scholarship in the study of psychological contracts, *European Journal of Work and Organizational Psychology*, 29(2), 159-163. DOI: 10.1080/1359432X.2020.1737219.

Baran, B.E. & Woznyj, H.M. (2021). Managing VUCA: The human dynamics of agility. *Organisational Dynamics*, 50, 100787. https://doi.org/10.1016/j.orgdyn.2020.100787.

Barasa, E., Mbau, R. & Gilson, L. (2018). What is resilience and how can it be nurtured? A systematic review of empirical literature on organizational resilience. *International Journal of Health Policy Management*, 7(6), 491–503. doi 10.15171/ijhpm.2018.06.

Bardoel, E.A., Pettit, T.M., Cieri, H.D. & McMillan, L. (2014). Employee resilience: An emerging challenge for HRM. *Asia Pacific Journal of Human Resources*, 52, 279-297.

Bartone, P.T. & Stein, S.J. (2020). Build "Hardiness" into your organizational culture. *Harvard Business Review*, 9 March 2020, 2-4.

Baruch, Y. (2006). Career development in organisations and beyond: Balancing traditional and contemporary viewpoints. *Human Resource Management Review*, 16, 125-138.

Beadle, R. & Knight, K. (2012). Virtue and meaningful work. *Business Ethics Quarterly*, 22(2), 433-450.

Becker, B.E. & Huselid, M.A. (2010). Commentary. SHRM and job design: narrowing the divide. *Journal of Organisational Behaviour*, 31, 379-388.

Bedarkar, M. & Pandit, D. (2014). A study on the drivers of employee engagement impacting employee performance. *Procedia – Social and Behavioural Sciences*, 133, 106 – 115.

Beer M. (2020). *Fit to compete.* Boston: Harvard Business Press.

Berg, J.M., Dutton, J.E. & Wrzesniewski, A. (2013). Job crafting and meaningful work. In B.J. Dik, Z.S. Byrne & M.F. Steger (Eds.). *Purpose and meaning in the workplace.* Washington, DC: American Psychological Association, 81-104.

Berger, L.A. & Berger, D.R. (2017). (Eds.). *The Talent Management Handbook.* New York: McGraw-Hill.

Bersin, J. & Enderes, K. (2021). *The definitive guide: Employee experience.* Place of publication uncited. The Josh Bersin Company.

Bersin, J., Geller, J. Wakefield, N. & Walsh, B. (Eds.). (2016). *Global Human Capital Trends 2016. The new organisation: Different by design.* Place of publication uncited: Deloitte University Press.

Bersin, J., McDowell, T. Rahnema, A. & van Durme, Y. (2017). The organization of the future. In *Rewriting the rules of the digital age. 2017 Deloitte Global Human Capital Trends.* Place of publication uncited: Deloitte University Press, 18-27.

Bersin, J., O'Reilly, T., Magoulas, R. & Loukides, M. (2019). *Future of the firm.* Sebastopol, CA: O'Reilly Media, Inc.

Bhattacharya, S. & Banerjee, E. (2018). Employee engagement, perceived stress and psychological capital: An empirical study. *ASBM Journal of Management*, 11(2), 1-10.

Birkinshaw, J. & Ridderstråle, J. (2017*). Fast/ Forward. Make your company fit for the future.* Stanford, CA: Stanford Business Books.

Boon, C., Eckardt, R., Lepak, D.P. & Boselie, P. (2018). Integrating strategic human capital and strategic human resource management. *The International Journal of Human Resource Management*, 29(1), 34–67. https://doi.org/10.1080/09585192.2017.1380063.

Booysen, E. (2016). Leadership excellence across cultural settings. In T.H. Veldsman & A.J. Johnson (Eds.). *Leadership. Perspectives from the front line.* Johannesburg: KR Publishing, 361-381.

Borah, N. & Barua, M. (2018). Employee engagement: a critical review of literature. *Journal of Organisation & Human Behaviour,* 7(4), 22-30.

Bos-Nehles, A.C. & Veenendaal, A.A.R. (2019). Perceptions of HR practices and innovative work behavior: The moderating effect of an innovative climate. *The International Journal of Human Resource Management,* 30(18), 2661-2683. DOI: 10.1080/09585192.2017.1380680.

Bouaziz, F. & Hachicha, Z.S. (2018). Strategic human resource management practices and organizational resilience. *Journal of Management Development,* 37(7), 537-551. DOI 10.1108/JMD-11-2017-0358.

Boudreau, J. & Cascio, W.F. (2017). Human capital analytics: why are we not there? *Journal of Organizational Effectiveness: People and Performance*, 4(2), 119-126. DOI 10.1108/JOEPP-03-2017-0021.

Boulton, J.G., Allen, P.M. & Bowman, C. (2015). *Embarking complexity. Strategic perceptive for an age of turbulence.* Oxford: Oxford University Press.

Boynton, A.C. & Victor, B. (1991). Beyond flexibility: Building and managing the dynamically stable organisation. *California Management Review,* Fall, 53-66.

Boxall, P. & Macky, K. (2009). Research and theory on high-performance work systems: progressing the high involvement stream. *Human Resource Management Journal*, 19(1), 3–23.

Blignaut, S. (2020). Managing uncertainty, complexity and chaos in a crisis vortex. In W. Crous (Ed.). *Managing organisations during COVID-19 vortex.* Johannesburg: KnowRes, 17-22.

Bravery, K., Baldwin, S., Ketenci, I.C., Cernigol, A., Cline, M., De Malo, A., Gutowski, D., Hudson, T., Ladd, M., Roberts, J. & Silva, J. (2020). *Win with empathy. Global talent trends 2020.* Place of publication uncited: Mercer LLC.

Bronkhorst (2012). *The architecture of high-performance organisations. Building corporate capability.* Place of publication uncited: Evalex.

Brown, T. with Barry Katz (March 2019). The new blueprint. *Fortune*, 41-43.

Burke, E. (2007). Reference could not be traced.

Bussin, M. (Date unknown). Personal communication.

Bussin, M. (2018). Reward solutions to retention questions. In M. Coetzee, M., I.L. Potgieter & N. Ferreira (Eds.). *Psychology of retention. Theory, research and practice.* Switzerland: Nature Springer, 395-413.

Bustinzaa, O.F., Vendrell-Herrerob, F., Perez-Arosteguia, M. & Parry, G. (2019). Technological capabilities, resilience capabilities and organizational effectiveness. *The International Journal of Human Resource Management*, 30(8), 1370–1392. http://dx.doi.org/10.1080/09585192.2016.1216878.

Byrne, J., Dwyer, T. & Doyle, D. (2018). Understanding the layers of a market-oriented Organisational Culture. *Irish Journal of Management*, 37(1), 16-30. DOI: 10.2478/ijm-2018-0002

Cameron, K.S., Dutton, J.E. & Quinn, R.E. (Eds.). (2003). *Positive organisational scholarship; Foundations of a new discipline*. San Francisco: Berrett-Koehler Publishing.

Cameron, K.S. & Quinn, R.E. (2006). *Diagnosing and changing Organisational Culture. Based on the competing values framework.* San Francisco: Jossey-Bass.

Campion, M.A., Mumford, T.V., Morgeson, F.R. & Nahrgang, J.D. (2005). Work redesign: Eight obstacles and opportunities. *Human Resource Management*, 44(4), 367-390.

Caniëls, M.C.J. & Baaten, S.M.J. (2019). How a learning-oriented organizational climate is linked to different proactive behaviors: The role of employee resilience. *Social Indicators Research*, 143, 561–577. https://doi.org/10.1007/s11205-018-1996-y.

Canning, E.A., Murphy, M.C., Emerson, K.T.U., Chatman, J.A., Dweck, C.S. & Kray, L.J. (2020). Cultures of genius at work: Organizational mindsets predict cultural norms, trust, and commitment. *Personality and Social Psychology Bulletin*, 46(4), 626 –642. DOI: 10.1177/0146167219872473.

Cantoni, F., Graziano, P., Maiocchi, F. & Rizzi, P. (2019). A territorial and organizational approach to resilience. *Symphonya. Emerging Issues in Management*, 2, 109-118. http://dx.doi.org/10.4468/2019.2.10cantoni.graziano.maiocchi.rizzi 109.

Cappelli, P. & Tavis, A. (2018). HR goes agile. *Harvard Business Review*, 96(2), 46-52.

Cascio, W.F. & Graham, B.Z. (2016). New strategic role for HR: Leading the employer-branding process, *Organization Management Journal*, 13(4), 182-192. DOI: 10.1080/15416518.2016.1244640

Cascio, W.F. & Montealegre, R. (2016). How technology is changing work and organizations. *Annual Review of Organisational Psychology and Organisational Behaviour*, 3, 349–75. DOI: 10.1146/annurev-orgpsych-041015-062352.

Cascio, W.F. & Aguinis, H. (2019). *Applied psychology in talent management.* Los Angeles: Sage.

Castellano, W.G. (2013). *Practices for engaging the 21st century workforce. Challenges of talent management in a changing workplace.* Upper Saddle River: Pearson Education.

Chapman, D.S., Reeves, P. & Chaplin, M. (2018). A lexical approach to identifying dimensions of organizational culture. *Frontiers in Psychology*, No volume, issue number or pages cited. . https://doi.org/10.3389/fpsyg.2018.00876.

Chin, T.L., Lok, S.Y.P. & Kong, P.K.P. (2019). Does transformational leadership influence employee engagement. *Global Business and Management Research: An International Journal*, 11(2), 92-96.

Chong, M.P.M., Shang, Y., Richards, M. & Zhu, X. (2018). Two sides of the same coin? Leadership and organizational culture. *Leadership & Organization Development Journal*, 39(8), 975-994. DOI 10.1108/LODJ-05-2017-0122.

Chooi, A.M., Ramayah, T. & Doris, D. (2018). Psychological climate, employee engagement and affective organisational commitment: The oil and gas employees' perspective. *International Journal of Economics and Management*, 12(2), 621-639.

Christie, P. (2009). *Every leader a story teller.* Johannesburg: Knowres.

Christensen, C.M. & Overdorf, M. (2000). Meeting the challenge of disruptive change. *Harvard Business Review*, March–April, 3-12.

Christos, D. (2017). The future requires a new operating model – The virtual organization. In M. Bussin (Ed.). *Organisation design for Uber times. Structuring organisations in times of radical change.* Johannesburg: KR Publishing, 89-122.

Citrix (2020). *Work 2035. How people and technology will pioneer new ways of working.* Fort Lauderdale, FL: Citrix.

Claus, L. (2019). HR disruption – Time already to reinvent talent management. *Business Research Quarterly*, 22, 207-215.

Coetzee, M. (2019a). Thriving in digital workspaces: An introductory chapter. M. Coetzee (Ed.). *Thriving in digital workspaces.* Switzerland: Nature Springer, 1-11.

Coetzee, M. (2019b). Organisational Climate conditions of psychological safety as thriving mechanism in digital workspaces. In M. Coetzee (Ed.). *Thriving in digital workspaces.* Switzerland: Nature Springer, 311-327.

Coetzee, M. (Ed.). (2019c). *Thriving in digital workspaces.* Switzerland: Nature Springer.

Coetzee, M. (2021). When Protean Career Values Intertwine with Employee–Employer Obligations: Reviewing Digital Era Work Mindsets for Modern Psychological Contract Practices. In M. Coetzee & A. Deas (2021). (Eds.). *Redefining the psychological contract in the digital era. Issues for research and practice.* Switzerland: Nature Springer, 95-110.

Coetzee, M. & Deas, A. (Eds.). (2021). *Redefining the psychological contract in the digital era. Issues for research and practice.* Switzerland: Nature, Springer.

Collings, D.G., Mellahi, K. & Cascio, W.F. (2019). Global talent management and performance in multinational enterprises: A multilevel perspective. *Journal of Management,* 45(2), 540 –566. DOI: 10.1177/0149206318757018.

Collins, C.J. (2021). Expanding the resource based view model of strategic human resource management. *The International Journal of Human Resource Management*, 32(2) 331-358. DOI: 10.1080/09585192.2019.1711442.

Collins, J. (2001). *Good to great.* New York: HarperBusiness.

Constitution of the Republic of South Africa (Act no. 108). (1996). SA Government Gazette, 378(17678), 18 December 1996. Available at: https://www.gov.za/sites/default/files/gcis_document/201409/act108of1996s.pdf (accessed on 1 May 2020).

Corporate Leadership Council. (2004). *Driving performance and retention through employee engagement: A quantitative analysis of effective engagement strategies.* Washington, DC: Corporate Leadership Council.

Corritore, M., Goldberg, A. & Srivastava, S.B. (2020). The new analytics of culture. What email, Slack, and Glassdoor reveal about your organization. *Harvard Business Review,* January–February, 77-83.

Costa, P.L., Passos, A.M. & Bakker, A.B. (2016). The work engagement grid: predicting engagement from two core dimensions. *Journal of Managerial Psychology*, 31(4), 774-789. DOI 10.1108/JMP-11-2014-0336

Covin, G. (1 November 2015). The 21st century corporation. Every aspect of your business is about to change. *Fortune,* 39-47.

Coyle-Shapiro, J.A. M., Costa, S.P., Doden, W. & Chang, C. (2019). Psychological contracts: Past, present and future. *Annual Review of Organizational Psychology and Organizational Behavior*, 6(1), 145–169. https://doi.org/10.1146/annurev-orgpsych-012218-015212.

Crook, T., Todd, S.Y., Combs, J.G., Woehr, D.J. & Ketchen, D.J. (2011). Does human capital matter? A meta-analysis of the relationship between human capital and human performance. *Journal of Applied Psychology*, 96(3), 443-456.

Crous, W. (Ed.). (2020). *Managing during the Coronavirus Vortex.* Johannesburg: KnowRes.

Darkow, P.M. (2019). Beyond "bouncing back": Towards an integral, capability based understanding of organizational resilience. *Journal of Contingencies and Crisis Management, 27,* 145–156.

Davis-Peccoud, J. & Moolman, T. (18 March 2015). Invest smartly by redesigning your operating model, *Business Day.*

Deas, A. (2019). Mapping antecedents of the psychological contract for digital natives: A review and future research agenda. In M. Coetzee (Ed.). *Thriving in digital workspaces.* Cham, Switzerland: Springer, 237-252.

De Beer, J. Rothmann, I. & Scherrer, R. (2016). Stress, burnout, derailment and resilience in leadership. In T.H. Veldsman & A.J. Johnson (Eds.). *Leadership. Perspectives at from the Front Line.* Johannesburg: KnowRes, 725-744.

De Cooman, R., Mol, S.T., Billsberry, J. Boon, C. & Den Hartog, D.N. (2019). Epilogue: Frontiers in person–environment fit research, *European Journal of Work and Organizational Psychology,* 28(5), 646-652. DOI: 10.1080/1359432X.2019.1630480.

Degbey, W.Y. & Einola, K. (2020). Resilience in virtual teams: Developing the capacity to bounce back. *Applied Psychology: An International Review,* 69(4), 1301–1337. Doi: 10.1111/apps.12220.

De Geus, A. (1997). *The living company.* Boston: Harvard Business Press.

Deloitte. (2017). *Rewriting the rules for the digital age: 2017 Deloitte Global Human Capital Trends.* London: Deloitte University Press.

Demerouti, E. & Bakker, A.B. (2014). Job crafting. In M.C.W. Peeters, J. de Jonge and T.W. Taris (Eds.). *An Introduction to Contemporary Work Psychology.* London: John Wiley, 414-433.

Denning, S. (2011). *The leaders's guide to story telling.* San Francisco: Jossey-Bass.

De Vries, M.F.R. & Florent-Treacy, E. (2002). Global leadership from A to Z: Creating high commitment organisations. *Organisational Dynamics,* 30(4), 295-309.

Dik, B.J., Byrne, Z.S. & Steger, M.F. (2013). Introduction. Towards an integrative science and practice of meaningful work. In B.J. Dik, Z.S. Byrne & M.F. Steger (Eds.). *Purpose and meaning in the workplace.* Washington, DC: American Psychological Association, 3-14.

Duchek, S. (2020). Organizational resilience: a capability-based conceptualization. *Business Research,* 13, 215–246. https://doi.org/10.1007/s40685-019-0085-7.

Dweck, C.S. (2008). *Mindset. The new psychology of success.* New York: Ballantine Books.

Dyer, C. (2021). *Remote work: Design processes, practices and strategies to engage a remote workforce and boost business performance.* International key note address. Online 2021 Oganisational Development Conference on 24 and 25 February 2021, organised by Knowledge Resources. South Africa.

Edmondson, A.C. (2012). *Teaming. How organisations learn, innovate, and compete in the knowledge economy.* San Francisco: Jossey-Bass.

Edmondson, A.C. & Zhike, L. (2014). Psychological safety: The history, renaissance, and future of an interpersonal construct. *Annual Review of Organisational Psychology and Organisational Behaviour,* 1, 23–43.

Ehrhart, M.G., Schneider, B. & Macey, W.H. (2014). *Organisational culture and climate. An introduction to theory, research and practice.* New York: Routledge, Taylor & Francis.

Ehrnrooth, M., Barner-Rasmusse, W., Koveshnikov, A. & Törnroos, M. (2021). A new look at the relationships between transformational leadership and employee attitudes—Does a high-performance work system substitute and/or enhance these relationships? *Human Resource Management,* 60, 377-398.

Eisenhardt, K.M. & Martin, J.A. (2000). Dynamic capabilities: what are they? *Strategic Management Journal,* 21(10-11), 1105-1121.

Eldor, I. & Vigoda-Gadot, E. (2017). The nature of employee engagement: rethinking the employee–organization relationship. *The International Journal of Human Resource Management*, 28(3), 526–552. http://dx.doi.org/10.1080/09585192.2016.1180312.

Elsbach, K.D. & Stigliani, D.I. (2018). Design thinking and organizational culture: A review and framework for future research. *Journal of Management*, 44(6), 2274 –2306. DOI: 10.1177/0149206317744252.

EY. (2018). *Why business must harness the power of purpose.* Available at: https://www.ey.com/en_za/purpose/why-business-must-harness-the-power-of-purpose (Accessed on 14 January 2021).

Fenton, E.M. & Pettigrew, A.M. (2000). Theoretical perspectives on new forms of organizing. In A.M. Pettigrew & E.M. Fenton (Eds.). *The innovating organisation.* London: Sage, 1-46.

Fiset, J. & Dostaler, I. (2013). Combining old and new tricks: ambidexterity in aerospace design and integration teams. *Team Performance Management*, 19(7/8), 314-330. DOI 10.1108/TPM-10-2012-0031.

Fisher, D.M. & Law, R.D. (2021). How to choose a measure of resilience: An organizing framework for resilience measurement. *Applied Psychology,* 70 (2), 643–673. doi: 10.1111/apps.12243.

Fisher, D.M. & Ragsdale, J.M. (2019). The importance of definitional and temporal issues in the study of resilience. *Applied Psychology: An International Review*, 68(4), 583–620. doi: 10.1111/apps.12162.

Fitz-Enz, J. (1997). *The 8 practices of exceptional companies. How great organisations make most of their human assets.* New York: Amacon.

Follmer, E.H. (2019). Prologue: considering how fit changes. *European Journal of Work and Organisational Psychology,* 28(5), 567–571. https://doi.org/10.1080/1359432X.2019.1649716.

Forman, D.C. (2017). HR levers that drive business results. In L.A. Berger & D.R. (Eds.). *The Talent Management Handbook.* New York: McGraw-Hill, 646-662.

Frankl, V.E. (1959). *Man's search for meaning. An introduction to logotheraphy.* New York: Washington Square Press.

Frazier, M.L., Fainshmidt, S., Klinger, R.L., Pezeshkan, A. & Vraceva, V. (2017). Psychological safety: A meta-analytic review and extension. *Personnel Psychology*, 70, 113–165.

Freeman, R.E. (2011). Some thoughts on the development of stakeholder theory. In R.A. Phillips (Ed.). *Stakeholder theory. Impact and prospects.* Cheltenham: Edward Elgar, 212-233.

Friedman, T.L. (2016). *Thank you for being late. An optimist's guide to thriving in the age of accelerations.* Random House, Great Britain: Allen Lane.

Gahlawat, N. & Kundu, S.C. (2019). Participatory HRM and firm performance. Unlocking the box through organizational climate and employee outcomes *Employee Relations: The International Journal*, 41(5), 1098-1119.

Galbraith, J.R. (2014). *Designing organisations.* San Francisco: Jossey-Bass.

Gallardo-Gallardo, E., Thunnissen, M. & Scullion, H. (2020). Talent management: context matters. *The International Journal of Human Resource Management*, 31(4), 457–473. https://doi.org/10.1080/09585192.2019.1642645.

Gao, Y. (2017). Business leaders' personal values, Organisational Culture and market orientation. *Journal of Strategic Marketing*, 25(1), 49–64. http://dx.doi.org/10.1080/0965254X.2015.1076879

Garrett-Cox, K. (2016). (Chair). *Values and the Fourth Industrial Revolution. Connecting the dots between value, values, profit and purpose.* White Paper, Global Agenda Council on Values (2014-2016), September 2016. Cologne/Geneva: World Economic Forum.

Geddes, L., Nuttall, R. & Parekh, E-J (2020). *The pivotal factors for effective external engagement.* McKinsey Global Survey on External Relations. Boston: McKinsey & Company.

Ghielen, S.T.S., De Cooman, R. & Sels, L. (2021). The interacting content and process of the employer brand: person-organization fit and employer brand clarity. *European Journal of Work and Organizational Psychology*, 30(2), 292-30 DOI: 10.1080/1359432X.2020.1761445.

Ghosal, S. & Bartlett, C.A. (1997). *The individualized corporation.* New York: HarperBusiness Book.

Gill, L. (2018). 10 Components that successfully abolished hierarchy (in 70+ companies). *Blog Corporate Rebels*, 22 March 2018.

Gover, L. & Duxbury, L. (2018). Inside the onion: Understanding what enhances and inhibits organizational resilience. *The Journal of Applied Behavioral Science*, 54(4), 477-501. DOI: 10.1177/0021886318797597 journals.sagepub.com/home/jabs.

Graham, B.Z. & Cascio, W.F. (2018). The employer-branding journey. Its relationship with cross-cultural branding, brand reputation, and brand repair. *Management Research*, 6(4), 363-379. DOI 10.1108/MRJIAM-09-2017-0779

Graham, J.R., Harvey, C.R., Popadak, J.A. & Rajgopal, S. (2017). *Corporate culture: Evidence from the field* (SSRN Scholarly Paper No. ID 2805602). Rochester, NY: Social Science Research Network. Available at: https://papers.ssrn. com/abstract=2805602 (Accessed on 27 February 2021).

Gratton, L. (2021). How to do hybrid right. *Harvard Business Review*, May/June 2021, AA.

Gruber, M., De Leon, N., George, G. & Thompson, P. (2015). Managing by design. *Academy of Management Journal*, 58(1), 1–7. http://dx.doi.org/10.5465/amj.2015.4001.

Guest, D.E. (2004). The psychology of the employment relationship: an analysis based on the psychological contract. *Applied Psychology*, 53, 541-555.

Gupta. M. (2017). Corporate social responsibility, employee–company identification, and organizational commitment: Mediation by employee engagement. *Current Psychology*, 36, 101–109. DOI 10.1007/s12144-015-9389-8.

Guthrie, J.P., Spell, C.S. & Nyamori, R.O. (2002). Correlates and consequences of high involvement work practices: the role of competitive strategy. *International Journal of Human Resources Management*, 13(1), 183-197.

Habraken, M., Bondarouk, T. & Hoffman, D. (2019). Shaking up the status quo? An analysis of developments in the social context of work stemming from Industry 4.0. In M. Coetzee (Ed.). *Thriving in digital workspaces*. Switzerland: Nature Springer, 197-216.

Hackman, J.R. & Oldham, G.R. (1976). Motivation through the design of work: Test of a theory. *Organizational Behavior and Human Performance*, 16, 250–279.

Hackman, J.R. & Oldham, G.R. (1980). *Work redesign.* Reading, MA: Addison-Wesley.

Hai, S., Wu, K., Park, I-J., Li, Y., Chang, Q. & Tang, Y. (2020). The role of perceived high performance HR practices and transformational leadership on employee engagement and citizenship behaviors. *Journal of Managerial Psychology*, 35(6), 513-526. DOI 10.1108/JMP-03-2019-0139.

Hamel, G. (2015). What really matters now. *London Business School Review*, 1, 32-33.

Hamel, G. & Zanini, M. (2020). *Humanocracy: Creating organisations as amazing as the people inside them.* Boston: Harvard Business Press.

Han, J.H., Kang, S., Oh, I-S, Kehoe, R.R. & Lepak, D.P. (2019). The goldilocks effect of strategic human resource management? Optimising the benefits of a high-performance work system through the dual alignment of vertical and horizontal fit. *Academy of Management Journal*, 62(5), 1388–1412. https://doi.org/10.5465/amj.2016.1187.

Han, S-H, Sung, M & Suh, B. (2021). Linking meaningfulness to work outcomes through job characteristics and work engagement. *Human Resource Development International*, 24(1), 3-22. DOI: 10.1080/13678868.2020.1744999.

Handy, C.B. (1976). *Understanding organisations.* Oxford: Oxford University Press.

Hansen, J-I. (2013). A person-environment fit approach to cultivating meaning. In B.J. Dik, Z.S. Byrne & M.F. Steger (Eds.). *Purpose and meaning in the workplace.* Washington, DC: American Psychological Association, 37-55.

Harrison, R. (1972). Understanding your organisation's character. *Harvard Business Review*, May-June, 119-128.

Harrison, T. & Bazzy, J.D. (2017). Aligning organizational culture and strategic human resource management. *Journal of Management Development*, 36(10), 1260-1269. https://0-doi-org. ujlink.uj.ac.za/10.1108/JMD-12-2016-0335.

Harter, J.K., Schmidt, F.L. & Hayes, T.L. (2002). Business-unit-level relationship between employee satisfaction, employee engagement, and business outcomes: A meta-analysis. *Journal of Applied Psychology*, 87(2), 268–279.

Hartmann, S., Weiss, M., Newman, A. & Hoegl, M. (2020). Resilience in the workplace: A multilevel review and synthesis. *Applied Psychology: An International Review*, 69(3), 913–959. doi: 10.1111/apps.12191.

Hawken, P. (2010). *The ecology of commerce.* New Yorker: Harper Business.

Hawryszkiewycz, I. (2017). *Designing creative organisations. Tools, processes and practice.* United Kingdom: Emerald.

Henry, M.S., Le Roux, D.B., & Parry, D.A. (2021). Working in a post Covid-19 world: Towards a conceptual framework for distributed work. *South African Journal of Business Management*, 52(1), a2155. https://doi.org/10.4102/ sajbm.v52i1.2155.

Hicklenton, C., Hine, D.W. & Loi, N.M. (2019). Does Green-Person Organization fit predict intrinsic need satisfaction and workplace engagement? *Frontiers in Psychology*, 10, 2285. doi: 10.3389/fpsyg.2019.02285.

Hinrichs, G. (2013). Organic organisational (Org²) design. In J. Vogelsang, M. Townsend, M. Minahan, D. Jamieson, J. Vogel, A. Viets, C. Royal & L. Valek (Eds.). *Handbook for strategic HR.* New York: Amacon, 281-293.

Hirschi, A. (2018). The Fourth Industrial Revolution: Issues and implications for career research and practice. *The Career Development Quarterly*, 66, 192-204. DOI: 10.1002/CDQ.12142.

Hock, D.E.E. (1999). *Birth of the chaordic age.* San Francisco: Berrett-Koehler.

Holtom, B.C. & Darabi, T. (2018). Job embeddedness theory as a tool for improving employee retention. In M. Coetzee, M., I.L. Potgieter & N. Ferreira (Eds.). *Psychology of retention. Theory, research and practice.* Switzerland: Nature Springer, 95-117.

Hseih, N-E., Meyer, M., Rodin, D. & Van 'T Klooster J. (2018). The social purpose of corporations. *Journal of British Academy*, 6(1), 49-73.

Huselid, M.A. (1995). The impact of human resources practices on turnover, productivity, corporate financial performance. *Academy of Management Journal* 38(3), 635-672.

Huselid, M.A. & Becker, B. (1997). The impact of high performance work systems, implementation effectiveness, and alignment with strategy on shareholder wealth. *Academy of Management Best Papers Proceedings*, 144–148.

INSEAD. (2020). *The Global Talent Competitiveness Index. Global talent in the age of Artificial Intelligence. 2020 Highlights.* Fontainebleau: INSEAD.

ISR. (2003). Reference could not be traced.

IODSA. (2012). *King III Report and Code on Governance for South Africa.* Sandton: Institute of Directors.

Ishak, A.W. & Williams, E.A. (2018). A dynamic model of organizational resilience: adaptive and anchored approaches. *Corporate Communications: An International Journal*, 23(2), 180-196. DOI 10.1108/CCIJ-04-2017-0037.

Jain, N. & D'lima, C. (2017). Organisational culture preference for gen Y's prospective job aspirants: a personality-culture fit perspective. *International Journal of Process Management and Benchmarking,* 7(2), 262–275.

Jaques, E. (2006). *Requisite Organisation: A Total System for Effective Managerial Organisation and Managerial Leadership for the 21st Century.* Baltimore: Cason Hall & Co. Publishers.

Jedynak, M., Czakon, W., Kuzniarska, A. & Mania, K. (2021). Digital transformation of organizations: what do we know and where to go next? *Journal of Organizational Change Management,* 34(3), 629-652. DOI 10.1108/JOCM-10-2020-0336.

Jee, G. (2019). Thriving in digital workspaces: From compete to create – exploring new tools. In M. Coetzee (Ed.). *Thriving in digital workspaces.* Switzerland: Nature Springer, 61-81.

Jiang, K., Lepak, D.P., Hu, J. & Baer, J.C. (2012). How does human resource management influence organizational outcomes? A meta-analytic investigation of mediating mechanisms. *Academy of Management Journal,* 55, 1264–1294.

Jiang, K., Takeuchi, R. & Lepak, D.P. (2013). Where do we go from here? New perspectives on the black box in strategic human resource management research. *Journal of Management Studies,* 50, 1448–1480.

Jianga, K. & Messersmith, J. (2018). On the shoulders of giants: a meta-review of strategic human resource management. *The International Journal of Human Resource Management,* 29(1), 6–33. https://doi.org/10.1080/09585192.2017.1384930.

Jing, F.F., Avery, G.C. & Bergsteiner, H. (2020). Leadership variables and business performance: Mediating and interaction effects. *Journal of Leadership & Organizational Studies,* 27(1), 80 –97.

Johennesse, L-A.C. & Chou, T-K. (2017). Employee perceptions of talent management effectiveness on retention. *Global Business and Management Research: An International Journal,* 9(3), 46-58.

Johns, G. (2006). The essential impact of context on organisational behaviour. *Academy of Management Review,* 31(2), 386-408.

Johns, G. (2010). Commentary. Some unintended consequences of job design. *Journal of Organisational Behaviour,* 31, 361-369.

Joo, B-K., Lim, D.H. & Kim, S. (2016). Enhancing work engagement. The roles of psychological capital, authentic leadership, and work empowerment. *Leadership & Organization Development Journal,* 37(8), 1117-1134. DOI 10.1108/LODJ-01-2015-0005.

Joubert, M. & Roodt, G. (2019). Conceptualising and measuring employee engagement as a role-related, multi-level construct. *Acta Commercii,* 19(1), a605. https://doi. org/10.4102/ac.v19i1.605.

Joyce, W.F. (2005). What really works. Building the 4 + 2 organisation. *Organisational Dynamics,* 34(2), 118-129.

Kahn, W.A. (1990). Psychological conditions of personal engagement and disengagement at work. *Academy of Management Journal,* 33(4), 692-724.

Kahn, W.A. & Fellows, S. (2013). Employee engagement and meaningful work. In B.J. Dik, Z.S. Byrne & M.F. Steger (Eds.). *Purpose and meaning in the workplace.* Washington, DC: American Psychological Association, 105-126.

Kakutani, M. (2018). *The death of truth.* London: William Collins.

Kanga, H.J. & Busser, J.A. (2018). Impact of service climate and psychological capital on employee engagement: The role of organizational hierarchy. *International Journal of Hospitality Management,* 75, 1-9.

Kantur, D. & Eri-Say, A. (2012). Organizational resilience: A conceptual integrative framework. *Journal of Management & Organization,* 18(6), 762–773.

Kaplan, R.S. & Norton, D.P. (1992). The balanced scorecard – measures that drive performance. *Harvard Business Review*, January-February, 71-79.

Kaur, S., & Kaur, G. (2021). A meta-analytical study on the association of human resource management practices with financial, market and operational performance. *South African Journal of Busines Management*, 52(1), a2070. https://doi.org/10.4102/ sajbm.v52i1.2070.

Keller, S. & Meaney, M. (2017). *Leading organisations: Ten timeless truths*. London: Bloomsbury.

Kempster, S., Jackson, B. & Conroy, M. (2011). Leadership as purpose: Exploring the role of purpose in leadership practice. *Leadership*, 7(3), 317-334. DOI: 10.1177/1742715011407384.

Kibbe, K., Sejen, L. & Yates, K. (2010). *Why an Employee Value Proposition (EVP) matters: Creating alignment, engagement and stronger business results*. Towers Watson Webcast on 13 October 2010. Available at: https://www.slideshare.net/TowersWatson/towers-watson-employee-value-proposition-webcast-presentation-1013. (Accessed on 15 April 2021)

Kim, M. & Beehr, T.A. (2021). The power of empowering leadership: allowing and encouraging followers to take charge of their own jobs. *The International Journal of Human Resource Management*, 32(9), 1865-1898. DOI: 10.1080/09585192.2019.1657166.

Kim, W.C. & Mauborgne, R. (2020a). Blue ocean strategy: The primer. *INSEAD Knowledge*. Available at: http://knowledge.insead.edu (Accessed on 25 July 2020).

Kim, W.C. & Mauborgne, R. (2020b). How to be a blue ocean strategist in the post-pandemic world. *INSEAD Knowledge*, 25 November 2020. Available at: http://knowledge.insead.edu (Accessed on 30 November 2020).

Kirby, J. (2005). Towards a theory of high performance. *Harvard Business Review*, July-August, 30-39.

Kirkman, B.L. & Stoverink, A.C. (2021). Building resilient virtual teams. *Organisational Dynamics*, 50, 1-13.

Kjaer, A.L. & Associates (2020*). Future of the workplace 2030+*. Guilford, Surrey: Unily.

Kleiner, A. (2013). Organisational circulatory systems. An inquiry. In J. Vogelsang, M. Townsend, M. Minahan, D. Jamieson, J. Vogel, A. Viets, C. Royal & L. Valek (Eds.). *Handbook for Strategic HR*. New York: Amacon, 275-280.

Knight, C., Patterson, M. & Dawson, J. (2017). Building work engagement: A systematic review and meta-analysis investigating the effectiveness of work engagement interventions. *Journal of Organizational Behavior*, 38, 792–812. DOI: 10.1002/job.2167.

Kohl, K. & Swartz, J. (2019). Building Industry 4.0 talent. In M. Coetzee (Ed.). *Thriving in digital workspaces*. Switzerland: Nature Springer, 15-39.

Kolko, J. (2015). Design thinking comes of age. *Harvard Business Review*, September, 66-71.

Konrad, A.M. (2006). Engaging employees through high-involvement work practices. *Ivey Business Journal*, March/April, 1-6.

Korten, D. (2019). A 21st century economics for the people of a living earth. Available at: https://davidkorten.org/a-21st-century-economics-for-the-people-of-a-living-earth-2nd-revision/ (Accessed on 25 June 2020).

Kotter, J.P. & Heskett, J.L. (1992*). Corporate culture and performance*. New York: Free Press.

Kouzes, J. & Posner, B. (2012). *The leadership challenge*. San Francisco, Jossey-Bass.

Kuenzi, M. & Schminke, M. (2009). Assembling fragments into a lens: A review, critique, and proposed research agenda for the organizational work climate literature. *Journal of Management*, 35(3), 634-717. DOI: 10.1177/0149206308330559.

Küng, H. (2009). *Manifesto for a global economic ethic. Consequences for global businesses*. New York: United Nations. Available at: http://www.globaleconomicethic.org/main/pdf/ENG/we-manifest-ENG.pdf. (Accessed on 25 January 2020)

Kurtz, C. & Snowden, D.J. (2003). The new dynamics of strategy: sense-making in a complex and complicated world. *IBM Systems Journal*, 42, 462-483.

Lalor, C.A. (2020). *Responsible Leadership: Developing the concept of leader character from a virtue ethics perspective.* Unpublished Doctoral Thesis. Pretoria: University of Pretoria.

Laloux, F. (2014). *Reinventing organisations. A guide to creating organisations inspired by the next stage of human consciousness.* Brussels: Nelson Parker.

Lankoski, L. & Smith, N.G. (2017). Alternative objective functions for firms. *Organization & Environment*, 31(3), 1–21. DOI: 10.1177/1086026617722883.

Lawler, E.E. (1986). *High-involvement management.* San Francisco: Jossey-Bass.

Lawler, E.E. (2017). *Reinventing talent management: Principles and practices for the new world of work.* San Francisco: Berrett-Koehler.

Lawler, E.E., Mohrman, S.A. & Ledford, G.E. (1995). *Creating high performance organisations.* San Francisco: Jossey-Bass.

Lawler, E.E. & Worley, C.G. (2012). Designing organizations for sustainable effectiveness. *Organizational Dynamics*, 41, 265-270.

Lawler, E.E. & Conger, J.A. (2015). The sustainable effectiveness model: Moving corporations beyond the philanthropy paradigm. *Organizational Dynamics*, 44, 97-103.

Lee, M.Y. & Edmondson, A.C. (2017). Self-managing organisations: Exploring the limits of less-hierarchical organizing. *Research in Organizational Behavior*, January, 37, 35-58.

Lee, Y., Shin, H.Y., Park. J., Kim, W. & Cho, D. (2017). An integrative literature review on employee engagement in the field of human resource development: Exploring where we are and where we should go. *Asia Pacific Education Review*, 18, 541–557. https://doi.org/10.1007/s12564-017-9508-3.

Lee, J., Chiang, F.F.T., van Esch, E. & Cai, Z. (2018). Why and when organizational culture fosters affective commitment among knowledge workers: the mediating role of perceived psychological contract fulfilment and moderating role of organizational tenure. *The International Journal of Human Resource Management*, 29(6), 1178–1207. https://doi.org/10.1080/09585192.2016.1194870.

Lev, B. (2001). *Intangible Assets: Values, Measures and Risks.* Oxford: Oxford University Press.

Lev, B. (2004). Sharpening the Intangibles Edge. *Harvard Business Review*, June, 109-116.

Li, P., Sun, J-M., Taris, T.W., Xing, L. & Peeters, M.C.W. (2021). Country differences in the relationship between leadership and employee engagement: A meta-analysis. *The Leadership Quarterly*, 32, 101458.

Liao, Y-C., Yi, X. & Jiang, X. (2021). Unlocking the full potential of absorptive capacity: the systematic effects of high commitment work systems. *The International Journal of Human Resource Management*, 32(5), 1171-1199. DOI: 10.1080/09585192.2018.1522655.

Lim, D.H., Hur, H. Ho, Y., Yoo, S. & Yoon, S.W. (2019). Workforce resilience: Integrative review for human resource development. *Performance Improvement Quarterly*, 33(1), 77–101. DOI: 10.1002/piq.21318.

Limnios, E.A.M., Mazzarol, T., Ghadouani, A. & Scilizzi, G.M. (2014). The resilience architecture framework: Four organisational archetypes. *European Management Journal*, 32, 104-116.

Lin, Y-T. & Liu, N-C. (2019). Corporate citizenship and employee outcomes: Does a high commitment work system matter? *Journal of Business Ethics*, 156, 1079–1097. DOI 10.1007/s10551-017-3632-1.

Liu, Y., Wang, W. & Chen, D. (2019). Linking ambidextrous organizational culture to innovative behavior: A moderated mediation model of psychological empowerment and transformational leadership. *Frontiers of Psychology*, 10 (2192), 1-12. doi: 10.3389/fpsyg.2019.02192.

Locke, E.A. (1975). Personnel attitudes and motivation. *Annual Review of Psychology*, 26, 457-480.

Lomas, T., Waters, L., Williams, P., Oades, L.G. &. Kern, M.L. (2020). Third wave positive psychology: broadening towards complexity. *The Journal of Positive Psychology*, Published online on 10 August 2020. DOI: 10.1080/17439760.2020.1805501.

Losey, M. Meisinger, S. & Ulrich, D. (Eds.). (2005). *The future of human resource management.* New Jersey: John Wiley.

Lucas, A.C., Ardichvil, A., de Castro Casa Nova, S.P., Bittencourt, J.P. & Carpenedo, C. (2018). Challenges of implementing Western talent development models in a collectivist organizational culture. *Advances in Developing Human Resources*, 20(4), 517–532. DOI: 10.1177/1523422318803356.

Ludike, J. (2018). Digital employee experience engagement paradox: futureproofing retention practice. In M. Coetzee, M., I.L. Potgieter & N. Ferreira (Eds.). *Psychology of retention. Theory, research and practice.* Switzerland: Nature Springer, 55-73.

Luthans, F., Youssef, C.M. & Avolio, B.J. (2007). *Psychological capital. Developing the human competitive edge.* Oxford: Oxford University Press.

Lysova, E.I., Blake, B.A., Dik, B.J., Duff, R.D. & Steger, M.F. (2019). Fostering meaningful work in organizations: A multi-level review and integration. *Journal of Vocational Behavior*, 110, 374-389.

Makhathini, T.N. & Van Dyk, G.A .J. (2018). Organisational Climate, job satisfaction, and leadership style influences on organisational commitment among South African soldiers. *Journal of Psychology in Africa*, 28(1), 21–25. https://doi.org/10.1080/14330237.2018.1438834.

Malhotra, A. (2021). The postpandemic future of work. *Journal of Management*, 47(5), 1091–1102. DOI: 10.1177/01492063211000435.

Malik, P. & Garg, P. (2020). Learning organization and work engagement: the mediating role of employee resilience. *The International Journal of Human Resource Management*, 31(8), 1071-1094. DOI: 10.1080/09585192.2017.1396549.

Marais, C. (Chair). (2020). *IRMSA Report South Africa Risks 2020.* Sandton: Institute of Risk Management.

Martens, V. (2019). *Agile organisational development – the new kid on the block.* Paper presented at Organisational Development Conference 2019 on 27 February, Knowres, Sandton, South Africa.

Mayer, C-H. (2019). Key factors of creativity and the art of collaboration in twenty-first-century workspaces. In M. Coetzee (Ed.). *Thriving in digital workspaces.* Switzerland: Nature Springer, 147-166.

McChrystal, S. (with T. Collins, D. Silverman & C. Fussell). (2015). *Team of teams. New rules of engagement for a complex world.* Place of publication uncited: Portfolio Penguin.

McKinsey Global Institute (2021). *The future of work after COVID-19 (Report)*, 18 February 2021. Place of publication uncited: McKinsey Global Institute (Accessed on 25 June 2021).

McLean & Company (2020). *Uncover an Impactful Employee Value Proposition. Report.* Toronto: McLean & Company.

Melé, D. (2016). Understanding humanistic management. *Humanist Management Journal*, 1, 33–55. DOI 10.1007/s41463-016-0011-5.

Meng, H., Luo, Y., Huang, L., Wen, J., Ma, J. & Xi, J. (2019). On the relationships of resilience with organizational commitment and burnout: a social exchange perspective. *The International Journal of Human Resource Management*, 30(15), 2231-2250. DOI: 10.1080/09585192.2017.1381136.

Messersmith, J.G., Patel, P.C., Lepak, D.P. & Gould-Williams, J.S. (2011). Unlocking the black box: Exploring the link between high-performance work systems and performance. *Journal of Applied Psychology*, 96, 1105–1118.

Meyer, J.P. (2017). Has engagement had its day? What's next and does it matter? *Organisational Dynamics*, 46, 87-95.

Meyer, M. & Abbott, P.M. (2017). *HR risk management: Managing people risks and leveraging opportunities.* Johannesburg: SA Board for People Practices.

Michaelson, C. (2021). A normative meaning of meaningful work. *Journal of Business Ethics*, 170, 413–428. https://doi.org/10.1007/s10551-019-04389-0.

Microsoft (2021). *2021 Work Trend Index: Annual Report. The next great disruption Is hybrid work* – Are we ready?, 22 March 2021. Place of publication uncited: Microsoft (Accessed on 31 May 2021).

Miller, D. (1992). The Icarus Paradox: How exceptional companies bring about their own downfall. *Business Horizon*, January-February, 24-34.

Miska, C. & Mendenhall, M.E. (2018). Responsible leadership: A mapping of extant research and future directions. *Journal of Business Ethics*, 148, 117–134. https://doi.org/10.1007/s10551-015-2999-0.

Mitsakis, F.V. (2020). Human resource development (HRD) resilience: a new 'success element' of organizational resilience? *Human Resource Development International*, 23(3), 321-328. DOI: 10.1080/13678868.2019.1669385.

Montealegre, R. & Cascio, W.F. (2017). Technology driven changes in work and employment. *Communications of the ACM*. 60(12), 60-67.

Montet, B., Lo-Gesret, C., Naeem, A., Roelofs, J., De Mori, L., Martinez, I., Sanglier, C. & Wang, I. (2020). *HR Trends Report 2020.* Amsterdam: Top Employers Institute.

Morales, S.N., Martinez, R.L., Gomez, J.A.H., Romero, R.R. & Torres-Argüelles, V. (2019). Predictors of organizational resilience by factorial analysis. *International Journal of Engineering Business Management*, 11, 1–13. DOI: 10.1177/1847979019837046.

Morgan, J. (2020). *The future of work.* Newsletter on LinkedIn, 10 August 2020.

Morgeson, F.P. & Campion, M.A. (2003). Work design. In W.C. Borman, D.R. Ilgen, & R.J. Klimoski (Eds.). *Handbook of psychology: Industrial and organizational psychology.* Hoboken, NJ: Wiley, 423–452.

Morgeson, F.P. & Humphrey, S.E. (2008). Job and team design: Toward a more integrative conceptualization of work design. In J. Martocchio (Ed.). *Research in personnel and human resource management*, 27, 39–91. London: Emerald Group Publishing. http://dx.doi.org/10.1016/S0742-7301(08)27002-7.

Morgeson, F.P., Dierdorff, E.C. & Murovic, J.L. (2010). Commentary: Work design in situ: Understanding the role of occupational and organizational context. *Journal of Organisational Behavior*, (31), 351–360.

Morley, M.J. (2007). Person-organization fit, *Journal of Managerial Psychology*, 22(2), 109-117. https://doi.org/10.1108/02683940710726375.

Morris, J.P. (2020). Is this the culture of academies? Utilising the cultural web to investigate the Organisational Culture of an academy case study. *Educational Management Administration & Leadership*, 48(1), 164–185. DOI: 10.1177/1741143218788580.

Mostafa, A.M.S., Bottomley, P., Gould-Williams, J., Abouarghoub, W. & Lythreatis, S. (2019). High-commitment human resource practices and employee outcomes: The contingent role of organisational identification. *Human Resources Management Journal*, 29, 620–636.

Motyka, B. (2018). Employee engagement and performance: a systematic literature review. *International Journal of Management and Economics*, 54(3), 227–244.

Mullins, N. (2018). *Mercer Global talent trends 2018. Unlocking growth in the human age.* Presentation at SA Board of People Management, 21 June 2018, Midrand.

Murray, A. (2019). A new purpose for the corporation. *Fortune.* September, 42-48.

Nahar, A. & Nigah, R.K. (2018). Ethical organizational culture – a way to employee engagement. *Global Journal of Enterprise Information System,* 10(4), 18-29. DOI: 10.18311/gjeis/2018.

Nalbantian, H.R. (2017). The internal labour market paradigm: A model for using analytics to evaluate and interpret workforce and business performance data. In L.A. Berger & D.R. (Eds.). *The Talent Management Handbook.* New York: McGraw-Hill, 542-555.

Narayanan, A. (2016). Talent management and employee retention: implications of job embeddedness: a research agenda. *Journal of Strategic Human Resource Management,* 5(2), 34-40.

Nel, C. & Beudeker, N. (2009). *(R)evolution. How to create a high performance organization.* Cape Town: Village of Leaders Products.

Nienaber, H. & Martins, N. (2020). Exploratory study: Determine which dimensions enhance the levels of employee engagement to improve organisational effectiveness. *The TQM Journal,* 32(3), 475-495.

Nijhof, A., Schaveling, J. & Zalesky, N. (2019). Business, society, and the need for stewardship orientation. *Journal of Organizational Change Management,* 32(1), 145-163. https://doi.org/10.1108/JOCM-09-2017-0348.

Nikolova, I., Schaufeli, W. & Notelaers, G. (2019). Engaging leaders – Engaged employees? A cross-lagged study on employee engagement. *European Management Journal,* 37, 772-783.

Nkomo, S. (2021). *Keynote address: Imperatives for re-humanising work.* 23rd Annual SIOPSA Conference, 21-23 July 2021.

Nohria, N., Joyce, W.F. & Robertson, B. (2003). What really works. *Harvard Business Review,* July, 1-13.

Nonaka, I., Kodamaa, M., Hirose, A. & Kohlbacker, F. (2014). Dynamic fractal organisations for promoting knowledge-based transformation – A new paradigm for organisational theory. *European Management Journal,* 32, 137-146.

Park, S. & Kim, E-J. (2019). Organizational culture, leaders' vision of talent, and HR functions on career changers' commitment: the moderating effect of training in South Korea. *Asia Pacific Journal of Human Resources,* 57, 345–368. doi:10.1111/1744-7941.12192.

Parker, A.J. & Veldsman, T.H. (2010). The validity of world class business criteria across developed and developing countries. *SA Journal of Human Resource Management,* 8(1), 1-17. DOI: 10.4102/sajhrm.v8i1.255.

Parker, S.K., Wall, T.D. & Cordery, J.L. (2001). Future work design research and practice: Towards an elaborated model of work design. *Journal of Occupational and Organizational Psychology,* 74, 413–440.

Parker, T., Rabolele, Q. & Joubert, D. (2020). *Win with empathy 2020 Global Talent Trends.* Online Mercer HR Conference, 12 May 2020.

Petković, M., Mirić, A.A. & Čudanov, M. (2014). Designing a learning network organization. *Management,* 73, 17-24.

Petriglieri, G. (2020). F**k Science!? An invitation to humanize organization theory. *Organization Theory,* 1, 1–18. DOI: 10.1177/2631787719897663.

Pfeffer, J. (1998). *The human equation. Building profits by putting people first.* Boston: Harvard Business School Press.

Pfeffer, J. (2018). The overlooked essentials of employee well-being. *McKinsey Quarterly,* September, 1-7.

Posthuma, R.A., Campion, M.C., Masimova, M. & Campion, M.A. (2013). A high performance work practices taxonomy: Integrating the literature and directing future research. *Journal of Management*, 39(5), 1184-1220. DOI: 10.1177/0149206313478184.

Potgieter, I.L. (2018). Personal attributes framework for talent retention. In M. Coetzee, M., I.L. Potgieter & N. Ferreira (Eds.). *Psychology of retention. Theory, research and practice.* Switzerland: Nature Springer, 183-201.

Prahalad, C.K. & Hamel, G. (1990). The core competence of the corporation. *Harvard Business Review,* 68(3), 79–91.

Pratt, M.G., Pradies, C. & Lepisto, D.A. (2013). Doing well, Doing good, and Doing with. Organisational practices for effectively cultivating meaningful work. In B.J. Dik, Z.S. Byrne & M.F. Steger (Eds.). *Purpose and meaning in the workplace.* Washington, DC: American Psychological Association, 173-196.

Pravinkumar, J., Sanket, S., Manish, T., Uttam, U. & Singh, B.S. (2018). *Cross impact analysis (Concept and practices).* (PowerPoint presentation on 25 February 2018). Mumbai: Thakur Institute of Management. Available at: https://www.slideshare.net/ManishTripathi88/cross-impactanalysis (Accessed on 17 September 2020).

PricewaterhouseCoopers. (2019). *23rd Annual Global Human Capital Survey. Executive Briefing: Effective People Management and Profitability.* London: Global Centre of Excellence, PriceWaterhouseCoopers.

Pulakos, E.D., Schneider, B. & Kantrowitz, T. (2019). What leads to organizational agility: It's not what you think. *Consulting Psychology Journal: Practice and Research,* 71(4), 305–320. http://dx.doi.org/10.1037/cpb0000150.

Rahmadani, V.G., Schaufeli, W.B., Ivanova, T.Y. & Osin, E.N. (2019). Basic psychological need satisfaction mediates the relationship between engaging leadership and work engagement: A cross-national study. *Human Resource Development Quarterly,* 30, 453–471.

Raza, M. & Nadeem, S. (2018). Drivers of employee engagement and their impact on job satisfaction and turnover intentions. *Journal of Managerial Sciences,* 12(2), 171-191.

Ritala, P., Vanhala, M. & Järveläinen, K. (2020). The role of employee incentives and motivation on organizational innovativeness in different organizational cultures. *International Journal of Innovation Management,* 24(4), 2050075-1 to 2050075-32. DOI: 10.1142/S1363919620500759.

Rød, A. & Fridjhon, M. (2016). *Creating intelligent teams.* Johannesburg: KR Publishing.

Rodriguez, J.K. & Stewart, P. (2017). HRM and work practices in Chile: the regulatory power of Organisational Culture. *Employee Relations,* 39(3), 378-390 DOI 10.1108/ER-02-2017-0034.

Rook, C., Smith, L., Johnstone, J., Rossato, C., Sánchez, G.F.L., Suárez, A.D. & Roberts, J. (2018). Reconceptualising workplace resilience – A cross-disciplinary perspective. *Anales de Psicología,* 34(2), 332-339. http://dx.doi.O rg/10.6018/analesps.34.2.299371.

Roodt, G. (2018). A job demands-resources framework for explaining turnover intentions. In M. Coetzee, M., I.L. Potgieter & N. Ferreira (Eds.). *Psychology of retention. Theory, research and practice.* Switzerland: Nature Springer, 5-33.

Rousseau, D.M. (1995). *Psychological contracts in organisations. Understanding written and unwritten agreements.* Thousand Oaks, CA: Sage.

Roux, M. (2021). *Adaptive HR. Impactful HR for the new and virtual world of work.* Johannesburg: KR Publishing.

Ryan, R.M. & Deci, E.L. (2000). Self-Determination theory and the facilitation of intrinsic motivation, social development, and well-being. *American Psychologist,* 55(1), 68-78. DOI: 10.1037110003-066X.55.1.68.

Ryde, R. & Sofianos, L. (2014). *Creating authentic organisations. Bringing meaning and engagement back to work.* London: Kogan Page.

SA Board of People Practices. (2018). *Position paper on HR governance and guidelines for HR Directors* (Issue 1), September 2018. Johannesburg: SA Board of People Practices.

Saira, S., Mansoor, S. & Ali, M. (2021). Transformational leadership and employee outcomes: the mediating role of psychological empowerment. *Leadership & Organization Development Journal*, 42(1), 130-143. DOI 10.1108/LODJ-05-2020-0189.

Saks, A.M. (2017). Translating empoyee engagement research into practice. *Organisational Dynamics*, 46, 76-86.

Santana, M. & Cobo, M.J. (2020). What is the future of work? A science mapping analysis. *European Management Journal*, 38, 846-862.

Santos, F., Pache, A. & Birkholz, C. (2015). Making hybrids Work: Aligning business models and organizational design for social enterprises. *California Management Review*, 57(3), Spring, 36-58. DOI: 10.1525/cmr.2015.57.3.36.

Schaufeli, W.B., Bakker, A.B. & Salanova, M. (2006). The measurement of work engagement with a short questionnaire. *Educational and Psychological Measurement*, 66(4), 701-716. 10.1177/0013164405282471.

Schaufeli, W.B. & Bakker, A.B. (2010). Defining and measuring work engagement: Bringing clarity to the concept. In A.B. Bakker & M.P. Leiter. *Work engagement: A handbook of essential theory and research.* Hove: Psychology Press, 10–24.

Schein, E.H. (1990). *Organisational culture.* American Psychologist, 45, 109-119.

Schein, E.H. (2010). *Organisational culture and leadership* (4th ed.). San Francisco: Jossey-Bass.

Schein, E.H. (2013). Corporate culture. In J. Vogelsang, M. Townsend, M. Minahan, D. Jamieson, J. Vogel, A. Viets, C. Royal & L. Valek (Eds.). *Handbook for Strategic HR.* New York: Amacon, 253-258.

Schiemann, W.A. (2017). Creating an employer brand that attracts, grows, and retains the right people. In L.A. Berger & D.R. (Eds.). *The Talent Management Handbook.* New York: McGraw-Hill, 26-44.

Schneider, B., González-Romá, V., Ostroff, C. & West, M.A. (2017). Organizational climate and culture: Reflections on the history of the constructs in the Journal of Applied Psychology. *Journal of Applied Psychology*, 102(3), 468–482.

Schrage, M., Kiron, D, Hancock, B. & Bresch, R (2019). *Performance management's digital shift.* MITSloan Management Review Research Report (in conjunction with McKinsey and Company) (Reprint No 60321), February 2019.

Schuler, R.S. & Jackson, S.E. (1987). Linking competitive strategies with human resource management practices. *Academy of Management Executive*, 1, 207–219.

Schwab, K. with N. Davis (2018). *Shaping the future of the Fourth Industrial Revolution. A guide to building a better world.* Place of publication uncited: Portfolio Penguin.

Schwartz, J., Hatfield, S., Jones, R. & Anderson, S. (2019). *What is the future of work? Redefining work, workforces, and workplace. Deloittes Insights.* (Accessed on 7 August 2020).

Seligman, M.E.P. & Csikszentmihayi, M. (2000). Positive Psychology: An introduction. *American Psychologist*, 55, 1-14.

Sethibe, T.G. (2018). Towards a comprehensive model on the relationship between leadership styles, Organisational Climate, innovation and organisational performance. *International Journal of Innovation Management*, 22(2), 1850021-1-1850021-1. DOI: 10.1142/S1363919618500214.

Shanker, R., Bhanugopan, R., Van der Heijden, B.I.J.M. & Farrell, M. (2017). Organisational Climate for innovation and organisational performance: The mediating effect of innovative behaviour. *Journal of Vocational Behaviour*, 100, 67–77.

Shantz, A. (2017). Coming full circle: Putting engagement into practice. *Organisational Dynamics*, 46, 65-66.

Schaufeli, W.B., Salanova, M., González-Romá, V. & Bakker, A.B. (2002). The measurement of engagement and burnout: A confirmatory factor analytic approach. *Journal of Happiness Studies*, 3(1), 71-92.

Shuck, B., Osam, K., Zigarmi, D. & Nimon, K. (2017). Definitional and conceptual muddling: Identifying the positionality of employee engagement and defining the construct. *Human Resource Development Review*, 16(3), 263–293. DOI: 10.1177/1534484317720622.

Sheppard, B., Hugo Sarrazin, H., Kouyoumjian, G. & Dore, F. (2018). The business value of design. *McKinsey Quarterly*, 25 October 2018 (Accessed on 1 July 2021).

Shin, D. & Konrad, A.M. (2014). Causality between high-performance work systems and organizational performance. *Journal of Management*, 20, 1–25.

Silva, A.L. & Guerrini, F.M. (2018). Self-organized innovation networks from the perspective of complex systems: A comprehensive conceptual review. *Journal of Organizational Change Management*, 31(5), 962-983. https://doi.org/10.1108/JOCM-10-2016-0210.

SIOPSA. (2020). Online Panel Discussion: *Navigating forced, unplanned change processes in a sustainable way*. Panelists N. Winkler-Titus (Chair), R. Chia, D. Veldsman & F. Marupen, 30 June 2020.

Snowden, D.J. & Boone, M.E. (2007). A leaders' framework for decision making. *Harvard Business Review*, November, pp. 1-8.

Sorenson, A. & Pearce, A. (2017). Novel ways to win the battle for great talent. In L.A. Berger & D.R. (Eds.). *The Talent Management Handbook*. New York: McGraw-Hill, 255-268.

Spreitzer, G.M., Cameron, L. & Garrett, L. (2017). Alternative work arrangements: Two images of the new world of work. *The Annual Review of Organizational Psychology and Organizational Behavior*, 4, 473–99. https://doi.org/10.1146/annurev-orgpsych032516-113332.

Stallard, M.L. (2021). *Connection culture: The competitive advantage of shared identity, empathy and understanding at work*. International key note address. Online 2021 Oganisational Development Conference on 24 and 25 February 2021, organised by Knowledge Resources. South Africa.

Stokes, P., Smith, S., Wall, T.M, Moore, N., Rowland, C., Ward, T. & Cronshaw, S. (2019). Resilience and the (micro-) dynamics of organizational ambidexterity: implications for strategic HRM. *The International Journal of Human Resource Management*, 30(8), 1287-1322. DOI: 10.1080/09585192.2018.1474939.

Stoverink, A.C., Kirkman, B.L, Mistry, S. & Rosen, B. (2020). Bouncing back together: Towards a theoretical model of work team resilience. *Academy of Management Review*, 45(2), 395–422. https://doi.org/10.5465/amr.2017.0005.

Strategic Futures Group. (2021). *7ᵗʰ Report on Global Trends 2040. A more contested world.* Place of publication uncited: US Office of the Director of National Intelligence, March 2021 (Accessed on 20 June 2021).

Suarez, F.F. & Montes, J.S. (2020). Building organizational resilience. To cope—and thrive—in uncertain times, develop scripted routines, simple rules, and the ability to improvise. *Harvard Business Review*, November–December, 47-52.

The British Academy. (2019). *Principles for Purposeful Business. How to deliver the framework for the Future of the Corporation. An agenda for business in the 2020s and beyond*. London: The British Academy.

Tims, M., Bakker, A.B., Derks, D. & van Rhenen, W. (2013). Job crafting at the team and individual level: Implications for work engagement and performance. *Group & Organization Management*, 38(4), 427–454. DOI: 10.1177/1059601113492421.

Tims, M., Bakker, A.B. & Derks, D. (2015). Examining job crafting from an interpersonal perspective: Is employee job crafting related to the well-being of colleagues? *Applied Psychology: An International Review*, 64(4), 727–753. doi: 10.1111/apps.12043.

Titus, S., & Hoole, C. (2021). The development of an organisational effectiveness model. *SA Journal of Human Resource Management*. 19(0). a1509. https://doi. org/10.4102/sajhrm. v19i0.1509.

Thoren, P-M. (2017). *Agile people: A radical approval for HR Managers*. Sweden: Lioncrest & Johannesburg: Knowledge Resources.

Top Employers Institute (2021). *HR Trends Report 2021*. Amsterdam: Top Employers Institute.

Tower, D. (2013). Creating the complex adaptive organization. In J. Vogelsang, M. Townsend, M. Minahan, D. Jamieson, J. Vogel, A. Viets, C. Royal & L. Valek (Eds.). *Handbook for strategic HR*. New York: Amacon, 302-309.

Ulrich, D. (1997). *Human Resource Champions*. Boston: Harvard Business School Press.

Ulrich, D. & Brockbank, W. (2005). *The HR Value Proposition*. Boston: Harvard Publishing Company.

Ulrich, D., Brockbank, W., Younger, J. & Ulrich, M. (2012). *HR from the outside in. Six competencies for the future for human resources*. New York: McGrawHill.

Ulrich, D., Brockbank, W., Younger, J. & Ulrich, M. (2013). *Global HR competencies*. New York: McGrawHill.

Ulrich, D. & Ulrich, M. (2017). Balancing talent and organisation culture: A winning combination. In L.A. Berger & D.R. (Eds.). *The Talent Management Handbook*. New York: McGraw-Hill, 635-645.

United Nations Universal Declaration of Human Rights. (2020). Available at: https://www. un.org/en/udhrbook/pdf/udhr_booklet_en_web.pdf (Accessed on 1 May 2020).

United Nations. (1987). *Report of the World Commission on Environment and Development: Our Common Future*. Available at: http://www.un-documents.net/ocf-02.htm (Accessed on 1 May 2020).

Ungerer, M., Pretorius, M. & Herholdt, J. (2002). *Viable business strategies*. Johannesburg: KnowRes.

Ungerer, M., Herholdt, J. & Le Roux, J. (2013). *Leadership for all. Virtue practices to flourish*. Johannesburg: KnowRes.

Ungerer, M., Ungerer, G. & Herholdt, J. (2016). *Navigating strategic possibilities. Strategy formulation and execution practices to flourish*. Johannesburg: KnowRes.

Vaiman, Vlad, V., Cascio, W.F., Collings, D.G. & Swider, B.W. (2021). The shifting boundaries of talent management. *Human Resource Management*, 60, 253-257. DOI: https://doi. org/10.1002/HRM.22050.

Van Beurden, J., Van De Voorde, K. & Van Veldhoven, M. (2021). The employee perspective on HR practices: A systematic literature review, integration and outlook, *The International Journal of Human Resource Management*, 32(2), 359-393. DOI: 10.1080/09585192.2020.1759671.

Van Dam, N.H.M. (2017). *The 4th Industrial Revolution and the future of jobs*. Place of publication uncited: Bookboon.com.

Van der Walt, F. & Lezar, L.W.P. (2019). Flourishing and thriving for well-being. In M. Coetzee (Ed.). *Thriving in digital workspaces*. Switzerland: Nature Springer, 85-107.

Van Dierendonck, D. & Nuijten, I. (2011). The servant leadership survey: Development and validation of a multidimensional measure. *Journal of Business Psychology*, 26, 249–267. DOI 10.1007/s10869-010-9194-1.

Van Veldhoven, M., Van den Broeck, A., Daniels, K., Bakker, A.B., Tavares, S.M. & Ogbonnaya, C. (2020). Challenging the universality of job resources: Why, when, and for whom are they beneficial? *Applied Psychology: An International Review*, 69(1), 5–29 doi: 10.1111/apps.12211.

Veld, M., Paauwe, J. & Boselie, P. (2010). HRM and strategic climates in hospitals: Does the message come across at the ward level? *Human Resource Management Journal*, 20, 339–356.

Veldsman, D. (2018a). The Flow@Work model as a talent retention framework for the knowledge economy. In M. Coetzee, I.L. Potgieter & N. Ferreira (Eds.). *Psychology of retention. Theory, research and practice.* Switzerland: Nature Springer, 35-52.

Veldsman, D. & Pauw, D. (2018). The relevance of the employee value proposition for retention in the VUCA world of work. In M. Coetzee, M., I.L. Potgieter & N. Ferreira (Eds.). *Psychology of retention. Theory, research and practice.* Switzerland: Nature Springer, 75-89.

Veldsman, D., Benade, C. & Rossouw, P. (2019). Thriving and flourishing into the future: An ecosystems approach to building sustainable organisations. In M. Coetzee (Ed.). *Thriving in digital workspaces.* Switzerland: Nature Springer, 41-60.

Veldsman, D. & Van Aarde, N. (2021). The future of work: Implications for organisational design and the psychological contract. In M. Coetzee & A. Deas (2021). (Eds.). *Redefining the psychological contract in the digital era. Issues for research and practice.* Nature, Switzerland: Springer, 73-93.

Veldsman, T.H. (2002a). Knitting the organisation together. In T.H. Veldsman. *Into the people effectiveness arena. Navigating between chaos and order.* Johannesburg: Knowledge Resources, 214-239.

Veldsman, T.H. (2002b). Forging excellence through and from change: The art of thriving under hyperturbulence. In T.H. Veldsman. *Into the people effectiveness arena. Navigating between chaos and order.* Johannesburg: Knowledge Resources, 46-71.

Veldsman, T.H. (2007a). The people effectiveness compass: holding a steady course in worsening weather conditions (Part 1). *Management Today*, 23(8), 58-60.

Veldsman, T.H. (2007b). The people effectiveness compass: holding a steady course in worsening weather conditions (Part 2). *Management Today*, 23(9), 58-61.

Veldsman, T.H. (2011). Crafting and implementing strategic talent management in pursuit of sustainable talent excellence. In I. Boninelli & T. Meyer (Eds.). *Human Capital Trends.* Johannesburg: Knowres, 359-389.

Veldsman, T.H. (2013a). People professionals fit for emerging economies. In S. Bluen (Ed.). *Talent management in emerging markets.* Johannesburg: Knowres, 179-202.

Veldsman, T.H. (2013b). *Leadership culture and climate – Enhancing or destroying leadership excellence within the leadership community? Towards typology of different leadership cultures and climates infusing leadership communities, with consequential effect on leadership building blocks and excellence.* Paper presented at 16th Congress of 2013 European Association Work and Organisational Psychology, 22-25 May 2013, Münster, Germany.

Veldsman, T.H. (2014a). Leading HR. In D. van Eden (Ed.). *The Chief Human Resource Officer.* Johannesburg: Knowledge Resources, 357-378.

Veldsman, T.H. (2014b). Designing HR. In D. van Eden (Ed.). *The Chief Human Resource Officer.* Johannesburg: Knowledge Resources, 313-342.

Veldsman, T.H. (2015). The power of the fish is in the water. *African Journal of Business Ethics*, 9(1), 63-83.

Veldsman, T.H. (2016a). The Leadership Landscape as a meta-framework. In T.H. Veldsman and A.J. Johnson. (Eds). *Leadership. Perspectives from the Front Line.* Johannesburg: Knowres, 13-30.

Veldsman, T.H. (2016b). Leadership engagement with the context. In T.H. Veldsman & A.J. Johnson (Eds.). *Leadership: Perspectives from the front line.* Johannesburg: KR Publishing, 325–340.

Veldsman, T.H. (2016c). The world of tomorrow: Leadership challenges, demands and requirements. In T.H. Veldsman & A.J. Johnson (Eds.). *Leadership: Perspectives from the front line.* Johannesburg: KR Publishing, 169-188.

Veldsman, T.H. (2016d). A flourishing and thriving leadership community. In T.H. Veldsman & A.J. Johnson (Eds.). *Leadership: Perspectives from the front line.* Johannesburg: KR Publishing, 667-682.

Veldsman, T.H. (2017). Blog entitled 'Leadership Brand'. Available at: https://www.theohveldsman. com/post/157026091452/master-of-the-leadership-universe-travel-guide. (Accessed on 20 March 2020).

Veldsman, T.H. (2019a). *Designing fit-for-purpose organisations. A comprehensive, integrated route map.* Johannesburg: Knowres.

Veldsman, T.H. (2019b). Becoming a purpose-driven, values-based profession making a worthy, lasting difference: A call to action. *The HR Voice,* May, 29-33.

Veldsman, T.H. (2019c). *Next generation OD: How must OD adapt to the tsunamis of workplace change.* Presentation at the 2019 Organisational Development Conference, 24-25 October 2019, Knowres, Stellenbosch, South Africa.

Veldsman, T.H. (March 2020). Leadership Excellence Stress Test. *Human Capital Review.* Available at: http://www.humancapitalreview.org/content/default.asp?Article_ID=1648. (Accessed on 30 March 2021).

Veldsman, T.H. & Roodt, G. (2002). *Organisational success within the South African business context: a benchmarking study.* Johannesburg: Centre for Work Performance, RAU.

Veldsman, T.H. & Abbott, P. (2015). *A Human capital measurement model – the basis for intelligence about people.* Presentation at SA Board for People Practices, Leaderex Conference, 17 September 2015, Sandton.

Veldsman, T.H. (2019). Examining the strings of our violins whilst Rome is burning: A rebuttal. *SA Journal of Industrial Psychology,* 45(0), a1725. https://doi. org/10.4102/sajip.v45i0.1725.

Veldsman, T.H. & Veldsman, D. (2020a). Critically problematizing existing organisational identity theory against practice: Part 1 – The thinking framework of organisational identity. *SA Journal of Industrial Psychology,* 46(0), a1799. https://doi. org/10.4102/sajip.v46i0.1799.

Veldsman, T.H. & Veldsman, D. (2020b). Critically problematising existing organisational identity theory against practice: Part 2 – Organisational identity-inaction. *SA Journal of Industrial Psychology,* 46(0), a1800. https://doi. org/10.4102/sajip.v46i0.1800.

Venter, T. (23 January 2020). Protect your data in '20 (Translated from Afrikaans: Pas jou data op in '20). *Beeld.* 17.

Vera, D., Samba, C., Kong, D.T. & Maldonado, T. (2021). Resilience as thriving: The role of positive leadership practices, *Organisational Dynamics,* 50, 100784. https://doi.org/10.1016/j. orgdyn.2020.100784.

Verwey, A.M. (June 2018). Personal communication.

Verwey, A.M. & Verwey, S. (2016). Leadership brand modelling. In T.H. Veldsman & A.J. Johnson (Eds.). *Leadership. Perspectives at from the Front Line.* Johannesburg: KnowRes, 385-390.

Volini, E., Schwartz, J., Denny, B., Mallon, D., Van Durme, Y., Hauptmann, M., Yan, R. & Poynton, S. (2020). *The social enterprise at work: Paradox as a path forward.* 2020 Deloitte Global Human Capital Trends. Deloitte University Press.

Vroom, V.H. (1964). *Work and motivation.* New York: Wiley.

Walter, R. (2020). *The future of work. Futureproofing careers and workforces.* London: Robert Walters Group.

Walton, R.E. & Hackman, J.R. (1986). Groups under contrasting management strategies. In P.S. Goodman & Associates. *Designing effective work groups.* San Francisco: Jossey-Bass, 168-201.

Wang, Y., Kim, S., Rafferty, A. & Sanders, K. (2020). Employee perceptions of HR practices: A critical review and future directions. *The International Journal of Human Resource Management,* 31(1), 128–173. https://doi.org/10.1080/09585192.2019.1674360.

Wasserman, N., Anand, B. & Nohria, N. (2010). When does leadership matter? A contingent opportunities view of CEO leadership. In N. Nohria & R. Khurana (Eds.). *Handbook of Leadership Theory and Practice.* Boston: Harvard Business Press.

Wheatley, M. (2013). Chaos and complexity. What can science teach us? In J. Vogelsang, M. Townsend, M. Minahan, D. Jamieson, J. Vogel, A. Viets, C. Royal & L. Valek (Eds.). *Handbook for strategic HR.* New York: Amacon, 241-249.

Whysall, Z., Owtram, M. & Brittain, S. (2019). The new talent management challenges of Industry 4.0. *Journal of Management Development,* 38(2), 118-129. DOI 10.1108/JMD-06-2018-0181.

Wikipedia. (2020a). *Organisational culture* (Accessed on 26 May 2020).

Wikipedia. (2020b). *Organisational Climate* (Accessed on 26 May 2020).

Wikipedia. (2020c). *Employee engagement* (Accessed on 26 May 2020).

Wikipedia. (2020d). *Cross-impact analysis* (Accessed on 17 September 2020).

Wikipedia. (2020e). *Nuclear fusion* (Accessed on 25 October 2020).

Willis, L., Reynolds, K.J. & Lee, E. (2019). Being well at work: the impact of organizational climate and social identity on employee stress and self-esteem over time. *European Journal of Work and Organizational Psychology,* 28(3), 399-413. DOI: 10.1080/1359432X.2019.1587409.

Wilson, T.B. (2017). Aligning total compensation programs with organisation values, strategy, and talent management processes. In L.A. Berger & D.R. Berger (Eds.). *The Talent Management Handbook.* New York: McGraw-Hill, 358-374.

Wollard, K.K. & Shuck, B. (2011). Antecedents to employee engagement: A structured review of the literature. *Advances in Developing Human Resources,* 13(4), 429 –446. DOI:10.1177/1523422311431220.

Wood, S. & de Menezesb, L.M. (2011). High involvement management, high-performance work systems and well-being. *The International Journal of Human Resource Management,* 22(7), 1586–1610.

World Economic Forum. (2016). *The future of jobs: Employment, skills and workforce strategy in the Fourth Industrial Revolution.* Geneva: World Economic Forum.

World Economic Forum. (2019). *White Paper: HR4.0: Shaping People Strategies in the Fourth Industrial Revolution.* Cologny/Geneva: World Economic Forum.

Worley, C.G. & Lawler, E.E. (2010). Agility and organizational design: A diagnostic framework. *Organisational Dynamics,* 39(2), 194-204.

Woznyj, H.M., Heggestad, E.D., Kennerly, S. & Yap, T.L. (2019). Climate and organizational performance in long-term care facilities: The role of affective commitment. *Journal of Occupational and Organizational Psychology,* 92, 122–143.

Wrzesniewski, A. & Dutton, J.E. (2001). Crafting a job: Revisioning employees as active crafters of their work. *Academy of Management Review,* 26, 179-2017.

Wrzesniewski, A., Berg, J.M. & Dutton, J.E. (2010). Turn the job you have into the job you want. *Harvard Business Review,* 88, 114-117.

Yeoman, R. & O'Hara, J. (2017). *Meaningfulness and mutuality: Principles for organizational design.* Available at: http://www.hrmagazine.co.uk/article-details/meaningfulness-and-mutuality-principles-for- organizational-design, 29 November 2017 (Accessed on 5 June 2018).

Zhang, F. & Parker, S.K. (2019). Reorienting job crafting research: a hierarchical structure of job crafting concepts and integrative review. *Journal of Organisational Behaviour,* 40, 126-146.

Zhou, Q., Chen, G. & Liu, W. (2019). Impact of perceived organizational culture on job involvement and subjective well-being: A moderated mediation model. *Social Behavior and Personality,* 47(1), 1-13. https://doi.org/10.2224/sbp.7478.

Zupan, N., Mihelič, K.K. & Aleksić, D. (2018). Knowing me is the key: Implications of anticipatory psychological contract for millennials' retention. In M. Coetzee, M., I.L. Potgieter & N. Ferreira (Eds.). *Psychology of retention. Theory, research and practice.* Switzerland: Nature Springer, 307-330.

INDEX

www.ingramcontent.com/pod-product-compliance
Lightning Source LLC
Chambersburg PA
CBHW080606270326
41928CB00016B/2951